THE WORLD WAR I BOOK

THE
WORLD
WAR I
BOOK

DK LONDON

SENIOR ART EDITOR
Nicola Rodway

SENIOR EDITOR
Victoria Heyworth-Dunne

EDITORS
John Andrews, Rob Dimery,
Alethea Doran, Tim Harris,
Abigail Mitchell, Dorothy Stannard,
Rachel Warren Chadd, Ed Wilson

ILLUSTRATOR
James Graham

JACKET DESIGN DEVELOPMENT
MANAGER
Sophia MTT

SENIOR PRODUCTION EDITOR
Andy Hilliard

SENIOR PRODUCTION CONTROLLER
Rachel Ng

SENIOR MANAGING ART EDITOR
Lee Griffiths

MANAGING EDITOR
Gareth Jones

ASSOCIATE PUBLISHING DIRECTOR
Liz Wheeler

ART DIRECTOR
Karen Self

DESIGN DIRECTOR
Philip Ormerod

PUBLISHING DIRECTOR
Jonathan Metcalf

DK DELHI

DEPUTY MANAGING ART EDITOR
Vaibhav Rastogi

ART EDITOR
Debjyoti Mukherjee

DEPUTY MANAGING EDITOR
Dharini Ganesh

ASSISTANT EDITOR
Sarah Mathew

SENIOR PICTURE RESEARCHER
Sumedha Chopra

ASSISTANT PICTURE RESEARCHER
Shubhdeep Kaur

PICTURE RESEARCH MANAGER
Taiyaba Khatoon

SENIOR JACKETS COORDINATOR
Priyanka Sharma-Saddi

JACKET DESIGNER
Vidushi Chaudhry

JACKET DTP DESIGNER
Rakesh Kumar

DTP DESIGNERS
Jaypal Singh Chauhan, Vikram Singh

DTP COORDINATORS
Vishal Bhatia, Jagtar Singh

PRE-PRODUCTION MANAGER
Balwant Singh

PRODUCTION MANAGER
Pankaj Sharma

CREATIVE HEAD
Malavika Talukder

SANDS PUBLISHING SOLUTIONS

EDITORIAL PARTNERS
David and Silvia Tombesi-Walton

DESIGN PARTNER
Simon Murrell

original styling by
STUDIO 8

First published in Great Britain in 2024 by
Dorling Kindersley Limited
DK, One Embassy Gardens, 8 Viaduct Gardens,
London, SW11 7BW

The authorised representative in the EEA is
Dorling Kindersley Verlag GmbH. Arnulfstr. 124,
80636 Munich, Germany

A CIP catalogue record for this book
is available from the British Library.
ISBN: 978-0-2416-3509-4

Printed and bound in India

www.dk.com

This book was made with Forest Stewardship Council™
certified paper – one small step in DK's commitment
to a sustainable future.
**For more information go to
www.dk.com/our-green-pledge**

CONTRIBUTORS

DR LAWRENCE SONDHAUS — CONSULTANT

Lawrence Sondhaus is Gerald and Marjorie Morgan Professor of European History at the University of Indianapolis, US, and author of 13 books, several on World War I.

DAVID L. ANDERSON

David Anderson is a writer and Professor of History Emeritus at California State University, Monterey Bay, US.

JOANNE BOURNE

Joanne Bourne is a history writer and archaeologist.

TIM COOKE

Tim Cooke is a specialist history writer and has written extensively about wars and warfare.

HELEN DOUGLAS-COOPER

Helen Douglas-Cooper is an editor and writer, who has contributed to many books on history and other subjects.

JACOB F. FIELD

Jacob Field has worked as a research associate at the University of Cambridge, UK, and is a writer and historian.

ADRIAN GILBERT

Adrian Gilbert has written extensively about 20th-century wars. He was consultant for *The World War II Book* (DK, 2022).

MARK COLLINS JENKINS

Mark Collins Jenkins has written about US naval history and contributed to two DK books on America's early wars.

ANDREW KERR-JARRETT

Andrew Kerr-Jarrett is an editor and writer, who has written and contributed to a number of historical titles.

MICHAEL KERRIGAN

Michael Kerrigan has written many books on history and contributed to *The Second World War* (DK, 2009).

DR JENNY MACLEOD

Jenny Macleod is a senior lecturer in 20th-century history at the University of Hull, UK, and author of *Gallipoli* (2015).

DR SUSAN PATTIE

Susan Pattie is a cultural anthropologist, and author and expert on the Armenian diaspora.

DONALD SOMMERVILLE

Donald Sommerville has degrees in history and war studies from Oxford University and King's College London.

JOE YOGERST

Joe Yogerst is an American writer with a long-held interest in global affairs and military history.

CONTENTS

DEADLOCK
1915

TOTAL WAR
1916

REVOLUTION AND EXHAUSTION
1917

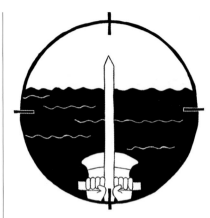

VICTORY AND DEFEAT
1918

A WAR TO END ALL WARS?
1919–23 AND BEYOND

INTRODU

CTION

World War I was a major watershed in history. It led to the collapse of four great imperial dynasties in Germany, Austria-Hungary, Russia, and Ottoman Turkey. The war was also a catalyst for the Bolshevik revolution in Russia, and created a series of new states in Europe and the Middle East. This huge political transformation came at immense material and human cost, with millions slaughtered in a collision of mass armies equipped with highly destructive weapons.

Battle lines are drawn

The war was triggered by a single death – the assassination of an Austrian archduke in the small Balkan city of Sarajevo. The mutual distrust that existed among the major European states, however, created the conditions for a wider conflict, dragging in allied nations on both sides and then other countries as the war progressed.

Germany and Austria-Hungary, known as the Central Powers because of their geographical position in Europe, were joined by the Ottoman Empire and Bulgaria. The Allied nations of France and Russia were immediately reinforced by Britain and its empire. Japan and Italy also joined the Allies and were followed by more than 20 other countries, of which the US was the most significant.

By the end of 1914, the war's great opening battles had resolved into two separate fronts to the west and east of Germany. The Western Front consisted of a line of trenches stretching northwards through France and Belgium from the Swiss border to the North Sea. The Eastern Front was more fluid and, as the war progressed, spanned an even greater distance between the Black and Baltic seas, with fighting in many of the surrounding nations.

A voice cried: 'Here come the cuirassiers!' In campaign kit, gigantic in their long cloaks, they filled the roadway. A formidable clamour rose from every lip: 'Vive la France! Vive l'armée!'

Raymond Recouly
Journalist reporting on French troops going to war, 1914

The Western Front would become emblematic of the war – a narrative of wretched conditions in trenches, alongside repeated offensives against well-defended positions that produced little gain but heavy casualties. While the generals were blamed for their lack of military imagination, it was the immense advances in military technology – especially in the development of powerful artillery – that quickly turned the fighting on the Western Front into a bitter war of attrition, as the firepower of one side attempted to grind down the strength and will of the other.

A worldwide conflict

Despite the primacy of the Western Front, World War I became a global conflict. Turkey's entry into the war – a result of hostile relations with its neighbour Russia and unrest in its empire – opened up new battlegrounds in the Middle East, at Gallipoli, and in Palestine and Mesopotamia. Britain and France could call on the immense reserves of manpower provided by their overseas empires. During the course of the war, millions of people in Africa and Asia, as well as the British Dominions, were co-opted to fight in the many theatres of war from Europe to the Pacific.

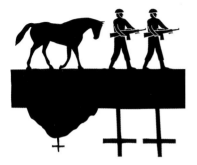  

The Allies had another great advantage – Britain's powerful Royal Navy. Against the constant threat of German U-boats, its Grand Fleet blockaded the North Sea and, with other Allied support, the Adriatic Sea, inflicting immense economic hardship on the Central Powers. With the help of Japan, the Royal Navy also isolated Germany's colonial possessions in the Pacific and Far East regions.

Advances in weaponry

World War I was a testing ground for innovation. Great strides were made in military technology, and in some areas, such as aviation, they were transformative. New lethal weapons emerged, including longer-range and rapid-firing guns, flame throwers, tanks and – more controversially – noxious gases. Developments in communications technology and manufacturing were influential, too, as were medical advances in the care of the wounded, including better prosthetics and plastic surgery and, gradually, a more enlightened understanding of the war trauma that was dubbed "shell shock".

The ability to mass-produce weapons of war proved vital to success. Industrial production greatly expanded in all countries, with the Allies benefiting from American economic assistance. Labour shortages opened up opportunities for the employment of women in a wide range of occupations normally reserved for men – just one of many social changes that would persist after the war came to an end in 1918.

Peace doomed to fail

When the combined might of the Allies finally secured victory on the Western Front, Allied leaders were keen to make Germany pay for the suffering and expense of the war,

At 11am there came a great cheering from the German lines … . But on our side there were only a few shouts. … The match was over; it had been a damned bad game.
Colonel W.N. Nicholson
Suffolk Regiment, on hearing news of the Armistice, 1918

and to weaken it enough to prevent a repetition. At the Paris Peace Conference in 1919, they determined to impose the severest terms on the defeated Central Powers. A clause in the Treaty of Versailles, drawn up at the peace talks, made Germany "responsible" for the war. Faced by overwhelming Allied military superiority – and the continuing economic blockade – the German deputation reluctantly signed the treaty.

World War I began as a battle for dominance in Europe, but the uncertain peace that ensued failed to settle the issue. Political and economic instability in Germany laid the ground for Adolf Hitler's rise to power. His determination to redress defeat and the humiliating terms imposed led to further conflict in 1939. World War II would continue the struggle, but its real victors would be the two superpowers – the US and the USSR.

The World War I Book examines how the war started and developed into a global conflict. It profiles the leading figures of the period, and analyses the strategies they employed and their consequences – some of which affect us to this day. Above all, the book reveals the big ideas that made World War I such a momentous event in world history. ∎

PRELUDE TO CONFL

1870–1914

CT

The **French army** is virtually **destroyed** by the Prussian army at the Battle of Sedan. Napoleon III is exiled and **France is declared a republic**.

At the Congress of Berlin, the major **European powers redraw the boundaries** of the **Balkan states** after the Russo-Turkish War.

European powers meet in Berlin to organize what becomes known as the **"Scramble for Africa"** – the colonization of much of that continent.

The **US** inflicts a decisive **defeat on Spain** in the Spanish-American War, gaining **control of Cuba, Puerto Rico, Guam, and the Philippines**.

1870 **1878** **1884–85** **1898**

1871 **1882** **1894–95** **1902**

In the Palace of Versailles, near Paris, the Prussian **King Wilhelm I is crowned emperor** of a new German Empire.

Germany, Austria-Hungary, and Italy form the **Triple Alliance**, a system of mutual defence that lasts until the outbreak of World War I.

In the First Sino-Japanese War, **Japan defeats China** and asserts its dominance throughout East Asia.

The **Second Boer War comes to an end**. Britain triumphs over the Boer republics, but the conflict reveals many **shortcomings in the British Army**.

O n 28 June 1914, the young Serb nationalist Gavrilo Princip fired his revolver at Archduke Franz Ferdinand in the Bosnian city of Sarajevo, killing the heir to the Austro-Hungarian throne. Few then could have foreseen that this particular Balkan "outrage" would lead to mass global conflict.

Imperial competition

The reason for war breaking out two months later lay in the fierce rivalry between the major European states. The rapid economic growth of 19th-century Europe relied on establishing new overseas markets and the expansion and safeguarding of sources of raw materials. This encouraged the conquest of overseas territories, which in turn led to disputes between European states over the ownership of these colonies.

The increase in colonial rivalry was aggravated by Germany's rise. The nation had only been unified in 1871, arriving late to the race for empire. Britain and France had benefited the most from colonialism, and Germany felt acute frustration at its lack of overseas possessions. The same was also true of Italy – a united nation from 1861 and keen to make its mark as a colonial power.

Beyond Europe, the world's newest industrial powerhouse, Japan, also embraced imperial ambitions. By 1914, it had defeated and taken territory from both China and Russia, becoming the most dominant state in East Asia.

Political instability

Although Germany was in the vanguard of military, economic, and scientific progress, it retained an authoritarian system of government. The Reichstag (parliament) was not as free to act as its French and British equivalents, with real power in Germany residing in an aristocratic military elite who dominated state legislation and bureaucracy.

Germany's closest ally, Austria-Hungary, was racked by a different kind of instability. While Germany was a single, ethnically cohesive nation state, the Austro-Hungarian Empire was a loose collection of largely Slavic nations, ruled over by a Germanic Austria and a Magyar Hungary. As an era of fierce nationalism came to the boil, the empire was facing imminent destruction from within, as its many and diverse ethnic minorities began to demand national self-determination.

Britain and France sign the **Entente Cordiale**, a treaty that rectifies colonial disagreements and encourages more **friendly relations** between the countries.

A wave of **protests and strikes in Russia** leads to some **limited political reform** and the establishment of a legislative assembly called the **State Duma**.

A group of officers, known as the **Young Turks, overthrow the regime of Sultan Abdul Hamid II** in an attempt to modernize the Ottoman Empire.

In the First Balkan War, the **Balkan states fight** for **territorial gain** against the Ottoman Empire, which loses most of its European lands.

 1904

 1905

 1909

 1912–13

1904–05

1908

1911–12

1913

Japan defeats Russia in the Russo-Japanese War, becoming the first Asian power to defeat a European state in the modern era.

Austria-Hungary unilaterally annexes Bosnia-Herzegovina, causing tensions with Russia and with Serbia and other Balkan states.

In the **Italo-Turkish War, Tripolitana and Cyrenaica** (today's Libya) fall to Italy. This reveals Ottoman weakness and Italy's colonial ambitions.

During the Second Balkan War, **Bulgaria** is involved in conflict with Serbia, Greece, and Romania, **losing territory** gained in the First Balkan War.

The slow decline of the other great Balkan empire – the Ottomans – enabled the emergence of the independent states of Serbia, Bulgaria, Romania, and Albania. Their ongoing belligerence towards Austria-Hungary and the Ottoman Empire (and each other) only added to the volatility of the region. Furthermore, Austria-Hungary had a rival in Russia for influence and control over much of Eastern Europe.

The animosity between Austria-Hungary and its Slavic neighbours was most lethally expressed in the deteriorating relationship between Austria-Hungary and Serbia. With some justification, Austria-Hungary accused Serbia of supporting terrorism within its empire. To the Austrian-Hungarian government, the assassination of Franz Ferdinand was a final provocation in a series of perceived humiliations by Serbia. It set on exacting revenge in the form of a punitive military expedition.

Europe's alliance system

The seeming illogicality of a local Balkan dispute leading rapidly to world war was rooted in the network of alliances that both tied and divided Europe into two armed camps. In the aftermath of the Franco-Prussian War (1870–71), the German chancellor, Otto von Bismarck, had followed up military victory with a series of treaties designed to maintain Germany's ascendancy in Central Europe. However, after German emperor Wilhelm II removed Bismarck in 1890 the system began to fall apart.

Russia, previously bound by a treaty of friendship with Germany, moved towards a diplomatic and military relationship with France, especially when Germany aligned itself with Austria-Hungary. Russia, like Austria-Hungary, was keen to exploit the decline of the Ottoman Empire in Europe, and also made clear its support for fellow Slav states in the Balkans, especially Serbia.

With the European powers ranged in two rival blocs, each drew up war plans to cover the growing threat of outright conflict. The strategic situation was determined geographically: Germany and Austria-Hungary held the centre, "surrounded" by France and Russia; Britain remained on the periphery, although a new naval rivalry with Germany was pushing it towards more friendly relations with France.

The assassination in Sarajevo was just the spark that lit the tinder box of national rivalry in Europe. ∎

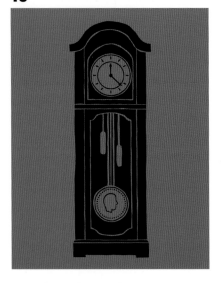

A SECURE AND PROSPEROUS AGE
THE SITUATION IN EUROPE (1870–1914)

IN CONTEXT

FOCUS
European politics

BEFORE
1814–15 At the Congress of Vienna, following the Napoleonic Wars, a series of diplomatic meetings establishes the national boundaries of Europe.

1848 A chain of revolutions – all attempts to overthrow established monarchies – breaks out across Europe.

1853–56 The Crimean War is fought between Russia and an alliance of Britain, France, the Ottoman Empire, and Sardinia-Piedmont.

AFTER
1919–20 At the Paris Peace Conference, the Treaty of Versailles strips Germany of its colonial territories and 10 per cent of its homeland.

1945 After World War II, Germany is divided into four zones, occupied by the Allies.

O n 28 January 1871, Paris surrendered to besieging German forces, ending the Franco-Prussian War. Germany's victory led to the completion of its unification and a new empire ruled by the king of Prussia, who became Kaiser Wilhelm I. With the exception of the Russo-Turkish War (1877–78), it also heralded four decades of peace between the major European powers, known as *La Belle Époque* and later perceived as a "golden age" before the carnage of the Great War.

The period's political stability encouraged economic growth and imperial expansion. New technology

I look on myself as an instrument of the Almighty and go on my way regardless of transient opinions and views.
Kaiser Wilhelm II

flourished. Electric power became increasingly common, lighting cities and powering factories, while the telegraph and the expansion of the railway system transformed communication and travel. Europe's dominant powers, particularly Britain and France, exploited their colonial empires, enjoying privileged access to raw materials such as rubber, oil, and gold, and a captive market for their products.

Fault lines amid the peace
During this era of peace, Europe's domestic politics were also largely stable, although fault lines existed. Britain, a democratic constitutional monarchy, remained an industrial powerhouse and ruled over the world's largest empire. When Edward VII succeeded his long-reigning mother Victoria in 1901, however, there was growing social unrest – notably among Irish nationalists and supporters of female suffrage.

Internal tensions also existed in France, a parliamentary republic since 1870. In Paris, resentment brewed over the loss of French territory in the Franco-Prussian War, while the Dreyfus affair – the notorious, society-dividing case of

See also: The rise of Germany 20–23 ▪ Crisis in Russia 24 ▪ The Balkans 25 ▪ The Ottoman Empire in decline 26–27 ▪ A lasting peace? 312–17

A political cartoon map of 1900, entitled "John Bull and his friends", caricatures the competing European nations. Russia is portrayed as an octopus, its tentacles reaching into Europe and Asia.

a French-Jewish army officer falsely imprisoned for treason – showed that antisemitism was still rife.

The emerging power was Germany, which combined military might and a burgeoning industrial sector poised to overtake that of Britain. The kaiser (emperor) had significant authority, although the elected German Reichstag (parliament) had legislative powers, and working-class activism led to the left-wing Social Democrats becoming the largest party in 1912. Austria-Hungary, a dual monarchy formed in 1867 under the rule of the Habsburg dynasty, was a major producer of manufactured goods, but its multiethnic nature created significant strains. Nationalists demanded autonomy, if not independence. Austria-Hungary's southern neighbour was Italy, another constitutional monarchy. Although it had been unified in 1861 under Victor Emanuel II, king of Sardinia, the nation was divided economically between north and south, and politically between radicals and conservatives.

Latent unrest in Russia

The House of Romanov had enjoyed autocratic power over Russia, the largest contiguous empire in the world. However, the 1905 Revolution, a social uprising against imperial rule, forced Tsar Nicholas II, to share some of his power with the elected Duma. Russia lagged behind its rivals but was modernizing, and its growth had eclipsed that of the Ottoman Empire, its once-mighty neighbour. After its territorial losses in the Balkans and North Africa, the Ottoman Empire now struggled to find a path between imperial rule, constitutional monarchy, and military dictatorship. ▪

Interrelated royals

Queen Victoria's nine children married into royal families across Europe. By 1914, the British, German, and Russian monarchs were all closely related (as were most of the continent's other crowned leaders). Kaiser Frederick III of Germany had married the queen's eldest daughter, also named Victoria, while the wife of Victoria's son and heir, Edward VII, was Alexandra of Denmark, whose sister Dagmar later married Tsar Alexander III of Russia.

The British king, George V, was thus first cousin to both Kaiser Wilhelm II and Tsar Nicholas II. Nicholas II's wife, Alix of Hesse, was also directly descended from Victoria through her mother, Princess Alice. The Russian and German monarchs were related, too, as both were descendants of King Frederick William III of Prussia and Tsar Paul I of Russia, making them simultaneously third cousins and second cousins once removed. Such family ties, however, would not prove strong enough to stop a war.

Cousins Tsar Nicholas II of Russia (left) and Kaiser Wilhelm II of Germany share a carriage in 1910 but would soon be adversaries.

WE DEMAND A PLACE FOR OURSELVES IN THE SUN

THE RISE OF GERMANY (1871–1914)

IN CONTEXT

FOCUS
Empire building

BEFORE
1834 The *Zollverein* (customs union) comes into force, an economic first step towards German unification.

1848–49 Uprisings sweep across Germany: liberal hopes are thwarted but a common national identity emerges.

1862 Amid a constitutional crisis in Prussia, Otto von Bismarck becomes minister president and foreign minister.

AFTER
1914 In August, Britain and its allies attack all of Germany's overseas colonies.

1919 Under the Treaty of Versailles, Germany's colonies become League of Nations mandates, and Alsace-Lorraine is returned to France.

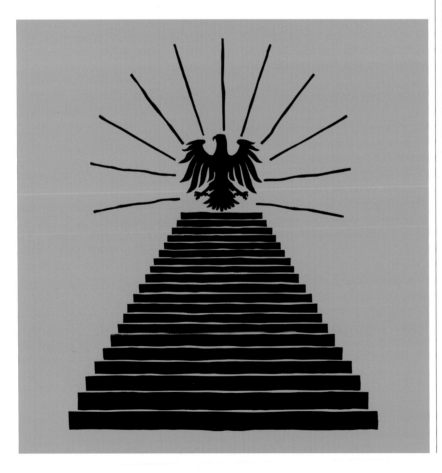

The Prussian king Wilhelm I was proclaimed kaiser (emperor) of a new, unified Germany in the palace of Versailles outside Paris on 18 January 1871. Before the coronation, the nation had been divided into 39 separate states, each with its own ruler, internal economic workings, customs barriers, and armed forces.

The driving force behind unification was Prussia's chief minister, Otto von Bismarck, soon to assume the position of German chancellor. Bismarck achieved his objectives by the shrewd application of military force, beginning with a war against Denmark for the provinces of Schleswig and Holstein

See also: The situation in Europe 18–19 ▪ Europe's colonies and empires 28–29 ▪ The Alliance System 30–31 ▪ The naval arms race 32–33 ▪ Planning for war 34–39 ▪ War is declared 42–43 ▪ The war at sea begins 88–93

Otto von Bismarck dictates peace terms to French ministers Jules Favre (centre) and Adolphe Thiers (right) at Versailles in February 1871, following the Prussian defeat of France.

> **Prussia is victorious** over **Austria** (1866) and **France** (1871).

> **The German general staff**, which plans and coordinates the armed forces, is a **powerful institution**.

> There is emphasis on **meticulous planning** and **attention to detail**.

> The **German** army dominates the **political sphere**.

> **Conditions are right for empire building.**

in 1864 and followed by war against Austria in 1866. Prussia's great victory at Königgrätz (Sadowa) forced Austria to acknowledge Prussian hegemony over Germany. As a result, Austria gave up its traditional role in German affairs and in 1867 reinvented itself as the Dual Monarchy of Austria-Hungary.

Bismarck's wars culminated in a carefully orchestrated conflict against France in 1870. Prussian success was absolute, culminating in the destruction of the French army at the Battle of Sedan in northeastern France. Germany was now Europe's leading military power. Vanquished and humiliated, France was made to pay large financial reparations and cede territory in Alsace and Lorraine.

Disputed borderland
Helmuth von Moltke, head of the Prussian army, had demanded the annexation of Alsace–Lorraine to provide a buffer zone in any subsequent conflict with France.

The incorporation of the region, with its valuable iron-ore deposits and thriving iron-and-steel industry, was also welcomed by German industrialists. Although most inhabitants of the two provinces spoke a Germanic dialect (especially in Alsace), many resented what was effectively a German military occupation.

Events came to a head in the Zabern Affair of 1913. Provocative comments made by a German officer against the population in the Alsatian town of Zabern prompted demonstrations and rioting. This led to heavy-handed repression by the German army garrison. Liberal and left-wing parties in the German Reichstag (parliament) condemned the garrison, subsequently drawing both the kaiser and chancellor into

a constitutional debate over the role of the army. The affair was widely reported abroad as a reflection of the undue influence of the military in German public life.

Industry and politics
One key driver of Germany's growth was its rapid industrialization in the second half of the 19th century. Benefiting from abundant natural resources and a skilled workforce, the nation soon became a major producer of coal, steel, and other »

After the defeat of the Habsburg Empire in 1866, other states were pressurized into joining a German federal unit. War against France in 1870–71 persuaded Bavaria and Baden to join. The seizure from France of most of Alsace and some of Lorraine (creating the territory Alsace–Lorraine) completed the development of the new Germany.

Key:

▪ Kingdom of Prussia

▪ Annexed by Prussia in 1866

▪ Joined the North German Confederation, 1867

▪ Joined the German Empire, 1871

▪ Annexed by Germany, 1871

— Full extent of the German Empire in 1914

goods. This growth provided economic support for Germany's territorial ambitions, but also caused social and economic disruption.

Politically, Germany was dominated by conservative elites who were wary of democratic reform. The government was led by the chancellor, who was not elected but appointed by the kaiser. Bismarck (the "Iron Chancellor") implemented

> The Prussian lieutenant stalked through the land like a young god.
> **Friedrich Meinecke**
> **German historian,**
> **on Prussian militarism**

policies that aimed to strengthen the new empire and consolidate power. Crucially, he created a formidable army, helping to ensure Germany's dominance in Europe.

The Reichstag represented a wide range of class interests but had limited powers and was often bullied by the autocratic government. Dissatisfaction with the status quo, centring on working-class unrest and middle-class aspirations for a meaningful say in the running of the country, was never properly addressed. Instead, it encouraged the German government to divert attention away from troubles in the domestic sphere towards an expansionist foreign policy, something supported by both the middle and working classes.

In 1888, Wilhelm II became kaiser after the death of his father, Frederick III. The new emperor soon clashed with Bismarck, who was forced to resign as chancellor in 1890. Wilhelm and his government pursued an ever more belligerent foreign policy, but, unlike Bismarck, the new kaiser had little ability in handling diplomatic complexities.

Wilhelm II's reign was marked by a series of aggressive statements and policy decisions that upset the diplomatic balance in Europe. This was evidenced in the militarization of the idea of *Mitteleuropa* (Central Europe), a concept of shared cultural values that had existed for centuries and covered the region ruled over by Germany and Austria-Hungary. However, by the late 19th century, German thinkers and politicians were broadening the term to include economic and political union under German control. It would later be used to justify German military action in Central and Eastern Europe after the outbreak of war in 1914.

An overseas empire

The new *Mitteleuropa* idea was mirrored by another expansionist policy, the seizure of overseas

Wilhelm I, king of Prussia, is proclaimed as the first German emperor in 1871, at the Palace of Versailles in newly conquered France.

territories. Although Bismarck had initially opposed the idea, he had a change of heart in the late 1870s and initiated a formal policy of territorial acquisition.

Having arrived late to the European colonization of Africa, Germany had to make do with limited possessions: Togoland (present day Togo), Cameroon, German Southwest Africa (Namibia), and German East Africa (Tanzania, Rwanda, and Burundi). Even by the brutal standards of European colonization, German policy in Africa was inhumane. Its administration relied heavily on forced labour, viciously suppressed any resistance, and it instigated military campaigns to expand territory and control its subjects.

In the Pacific, Germany acquired a scattering of islands, mainly in the Mariana, Caroline, Marshall, and Solomon groups. Much of northern New Guinea came under its control, as did territory around the port of Tsingtao in mainland China.

Wilhelm was aggrieved, however, by the failure to secure vast overseas empires like those of Britain and France. His ire became apparent in antagonistic pronouncements that alarmed the other great powers.

Alienation and isolation

Britain became a target of Wilhelm's anger. In January 1896, he sent a congratulatory telegram to President Kruger of the Transvaal, then in conflict with Britain, and in a 1908 newspaper interview he repeatedly criticized British foreign policy. He also intervened in the French

extension of control over Morocco, resulting in the Moroccan crises of 1905–06 and 1911, which ended in a French diplomatic victory. While Franco-British relations grew closer, Germany's isolation increased.

In hindsight, Germany's overseas empire was a resounding failure. Its colonies were a drain on economic resources and had no strategic advantage. After war was declared, they became a military liability and, aside from German East Africa, were captured by the Allies. Kaiser Wilhelm's dream of "a place in the sun" proved a costly mirage. ■

Kaiser Wilhelm II

Born in 1859, in Berlin, Wilhelm was the eldest child of Crown Prince Frederick and Princess Victoria, daughter of the British monarch, Queen Victoria. He was born with a withered left arm, a fact that he tried to hide throughout his life. He grew up in a strict, militaristic household, with his father (who subsequently became Frederick III) preparing him for his future role as kaiser.

In 1888, Wilhelm ascended to the throne after the death of his father, who had only reigned for 99 days. Wilhelm was known for his erratic and tactless behaviour,

and appetite for interfering in the affairs of foreign states. This did much to distance him from his fellow world leaders. After dismissing Otto von Bismarck as chancellor, he set Germany on a more forcefully imperialistic path.

Wilhelm personally backed Austria-Hungary in its conflict with Serbia in 1914, a factor that helped lead to the outbreak of war in Europe. With Germany's defeat in 1918, he was forced to abdicate and fled to the Netherlands, where he lived in exile until his death in 1941.

THERE IS NO GOD ANY LONGER! THERE IS NO TSAR!

CRISIS IN RUSSIA (1881–1905)

When Alexander III came to the Russian throne in 1881, he rolled back the liberal reforms supported by his father, Alexander II, and enacted antisemitic laws that led to a wave of persecutions against Russian Jews. Nicholas II, who succeeded Alexander III in 1894, also refused to consider reforms, particularly those that would introduce any measure of democracy, and harshly clamped down on opponents.

War and revolution

From the start, Nicholas II's reign was marked by unrest. Four days after his coronation, in 1896, a crush at a public celebration in Moscow killed more than 1,300 people, seriously undermining the tsar's authority. Military failure followed in February 1904, when Russia was attacked by Japan, its main rival in Asia. A series of defeats, including the destruction of the Russian Baltic Fleet in May 1905 at the Battle of Tsushima, forced Nicholas II to make peace in September 1905.

Meanwhile, the tsar's domestic control was unravelling. In January 1905, a massacre of demonstrating workers prompted a wave of strikes and revolts, compelling Nicholas II to accept reform, including the enactment of a constitution and an elected parliament, the Duma. Nicholas II had retained the crown, but his rule was on shaky ground. ∎

Police in St Petersburg fire on peaceful demonstrators, led by priest Georgy Gapon, on 22 January 1905. The killing of around 200 people became known as Bloody Sunday.

See also: The situation in Europe 18–19 ▪ The February Revolution 192–93 ▪ The October Revolution 240–41 ▪ German victory in Eastern Europe 258–59

THE POWDER KEG OF EUROPE
THE BALKANS (1903–14)

IN CONTEXT

FOCUS
Balkan politics

BEFORE
1830 Serbia is recognized as an autonomous principality inside the Ottoman Empire.

1859 The Romanian principalities of Moldavia and Wallachia gain autonomy within the Ottoman Empire.

1878 The Treaty of Berlin formally recognizes the full independence of Romania, Serbia, and Montenegro.

AFTER
1918 The Kingdom of the Serbs, Croats, and Slovenes is proclaimed in Belgrade.

1920 Under the Treaty of Trianon, Romania gains the region of Transylvania from Hungary.

1922 The Greco-Turkish War concludes with the Turks driving the Greeks out of Turkey's Anatolian mainland.

During the 19th century, a clutch of independent states – Greece, Serbia, Montenegro, Romania, and Bulgaria – emerged from the decaying Ottoman Empire's territories in southeastern Europe, known as the Balkans. Regional instability became inevitable. There were rivalries among the new states, and Austria-Hungary and Russia each regarded the Balkans as a special sphere of influence.

Upsetting the old order

A coup in 1903 brought a more hawkish regime to power in Serbia, the strategic centre of the Balkan region. At stake were the territories of Bosnia and Herzegovina, still nominally Ottoman but occupied by Austria-Hungary since 1878, and with large Serbian populations. Austria-Hungary annexed Bosnia and Herzegovina in 1908, but Serbia, undeterred, continued to stoke nationalist feelings there. Meanwhile, Russia urged Serbia, Montenegro, Bulgaria, and Greece to form a league against the Ottomans.

The Balkan War will obviously result in an Austrian cataclysm.
King Peter I of Serbia

In 1908, Bulgaria proclaimed its independence from the Ottoman Empire, as did Albania in 1912. This was followed by the First Balkan War (October 1912–May 1913), in which Serbia, Montenegro, Bulgaria, and Greece drove the Ottomans almost completely out of Europe. In the Second Balkan War (1913), Bulgaria, dissatisfied with its pickings from the first conflict, invaded Serbia and Greece, only to be defeated after Romania joined the conflict. By 1914, the Balkans remained a powder keg. ■

See also: The Ottoman Empire in decline 26–27 ■ The assassination of Franz Ferdinand 40–41 ■ Austro-Hungarian failures 82

WE HAVE ON OUR HANDS A SICK MAN

THE OTTOMAN EMPIRE IN DECLINE (1876–1914)

IN CONTEXT

FOCUS
Ottoman politics

BEFORE
1839 Sultan Abdulmejid I's Edict of Gülhane launches the Tanzimat – reforms aimed at reorganizing and modernizing the Ottoman Empire.

1856 The Ottoman Empire is part of a victorious alliance against Russia in the Crimean War but is left with large debts and no major territorial gains.

AFTER
2 August 1914 The Ottoman Empire secretly agrees to enter World War I on Germany's side at some point in the future.

29 October 1914 Launching a surprise raid on Russian ports in the Black Sea, the Ottoman Empire enters the war.

1923 After overturning a humiliating peace treaty imposed by the Allies, Mustafa Kemal becomes first president of the new Republic of Turkey.

Members of the Young Turks movement take to the streets in July 1908. Their uprising restored constitutional government to the empire, with the reopening of parliament five months later.

It sought to modernize the political system, and briefly introduced a two-chamber parliament.

At war with its neighbours
Montenegro, Romania, and Serbia were officially part of the Ottoman Empire, but all had a degree of independence. In spring 1877, they joined Russia in declaring war on the Ottomans. Even Constantinople (now Istanbul), the capital of the Ottoman Empire, was threatened.

In March 1878, the Ottomans signed a peace treaty that ceded territory to Russia in the Caucasus, recognized the full independence of Montenegro, Romania, and Serbia, and granted autonomy to Bulgaria and Bosnia-Herzegovina. Two weeks later, Abdul Hamid suspended parliament and the Ottoman constitution in a bid to regain absolute power. His personal rule could not repair the cracks in the empire; control of Egypt was lost to Britain in 1882, nationalist

Founded by Osman I as a small principality in 1299, the Ottoman Empire reached its greatest extent at the end of the 17th century. At that time, it stretched deep into Europe, the Middle East, and North Africa. However, from the mid-18th century it began to decline and was known as the "sick man of Europe" by the 1850s.

On 23 December 1876, in a bid to reduce social unrest throughout his multinational empire, Sultan Abdul Hamid II proclaimed the first-ever Ottoman constitution.

See also: The Balkans 25 ▪ Ottoman Turkey enters the war 84–85 ▪ The Gallipoli Campaign 122–29 ▪ The war in the Caucasus 130 ▪ The Armenian Genocide 132–33 ▪ The Arab Revolt 170–71 ▪ The Battle of Megiddo 286–87

groups were becoming increasingly influential, and the Ottoman economy was in sharp decline.

Rise of the Young Turks

In the early 20th century, a reformist movement known as the Young Turks emerged. It included the influential Committee of Union and Progress (CUP), which had supporters in the government and the military. In July 1908, CUP members revolted against Abdul Hamid, and forced him to restore the constitution and hold elections. When the sultan staged a counter-coup in April 1909, the CUP deposed him and, as a figurehead, set his half-brother Mehmed on the throne.

Defeat in the Italo-Turkish War (1911–12) cost the Ottoman Empire its last foothold in North Africa – the coastal region of what is now Libya. Just before the end of that war, an alliance of Balkan states attacked the Ottoman armies in the First Balkan War, defeating them in May 1913. At the same time, Albania also revolted against the empire and secured its autonomy.

Ottoman politics were equally violent and unstable at home, and a faction of CUP members seized power in January 1913. In the Second Balkan War (June–August 1913), the Ottomans regained some of the territory ceded in the First Balkan War but lost most of their remaining territory in Europe.

The "Three Pashas"

In 1913, three CUP members became leading figures in the Ottoman Empire and were dubbed the "Three Pashas" (*pasha* was an

Ottoman forces fight Italian troops outside the city of Tripoli in North Africa, in October 1911. Italy's victory in the Italo–Turkish War marked the end of Ottoman power in North Africa.

honorific Ottoman title). Cemal Pasha became minister of the navy, Enver Pasha was minister of war, and Talaat Pasha controlled the civilian government. Together, the three would lead the Ottoman Empire into a closer alliance with Germany and entry into World War I in October 1914. ▪

Sultan Abdul Hamid II

Born in Constantinople (Istanbul) in 1842, Abdul Hamid II was the final Ottoman sultan to enjoy sweeping personal powers. A son of Abdulmejid I (r. 1839–61), he became sultan in August 1876 after his sick half-brother Murad V was deposed.

Abdul Hamid approved the first Ottoman constitution but suspended it after quarrelling with the parliament. He oversaw reforms in education, reorganized the justice system, improved the nation's infrastructure, and built military schools, but incurred high debts in doing so. His reign

also saw atrocities committed against Armenians and Assyrians, and he used his secret police to clamp down on dissent, which prompted assassination attempts.

In 1909, after his failed bid to wrest back the absolute power he had lost a year earlier, when the constitution was restored, Abdul Hamid was imprisoned outside Salonika (Thessaloniki). In 1912, when Greece captured Salonika, he was sent back to Constantinople and remained there in custody at Beylerbeyi Palace until his death in 1918.

MY MAP OF AFRICA LIES IN EUROPE

EUROPE'S COLONIES AND EMPIRES (1884–1914)

By the 1880s, having already colonized much of the globe, the European powers set about carving up Africa, where colonies up until then had been mostly small and coastal. Alongside veteran imperialists Britain, France, Portugal, and Spain, new major European powers Germany and Italy were also set on acquiring African territory and resources. This competitive empire building was at the root of World War I.

The "Scramble for Africa"

To avoid armed confrontation, the Berlin Conference of 1884–85 pounded out an agreement to divide Africa between interested parties, without consulting those most affected by the decision – the Africans themselves. A racist perception of European intellectual and moral supremacy over the indigenous populations prevailed; the conference did not include a single African representative.

One of the provisions of the Berlin agreement was that a power had to occupy or control at least some of an intended conquest to claim rights over it. This led to a frantic "scramble", during which around 80 per cent of Africa was colonized within four decades.

Inevitably, competing claims generated conflict between the empires. During the Fashoda Incident of 1898, Britain and France almost came to blows over conflicting demands for the Upper Nile region, before the French eventually conceded. During the First Moroccan Crisis of 1905–06, Germany challenged French

A French cartoon depicts Otto von Bismarck, chancellor of Germany, slicing up a cake representing Africa at the Berlin Conference. During the congress, the continent was parcelled out among European powers.

See also: The rise of Germany 20–23 ▪ The Alliance System 30–31 ▪ The war in Africa 86–87 ▪ The war in Asia and Oceania 94–95 ▪ The war in Mesopotamia 131 ▪ The war in East Africa 244–45 ▪ Post-war conflicts 320–21

Ottoman and North African soldiers scatter as a Taube aircraft swoops towards them in the Italo-Turkish war of 1911–12.

Aerial bombardment in Libya

In September 1911, Italy claimed sovereignty over Cyrenaica and Tripolitania (most of present-day Libya) and declared war on the Ottoman Empire, rulers of the two regions. The conflict lasted just over a year and included the world's first-ever air raid.

On 1 November 1911, Second Lieutenant Giulio Gavotti, flying a German-made Taube monoplane (one of an Italian force of nine aircraft), dropped three grenades on the Tagiura oasis and one on Ottoman troops at Ain Zara just outside Tripoli. They did little damage, but the raid proved that attacks from the air could be a destructive force in warfare.

The Italians also made the first aerial reconnaissance missions, using photography to map enemy positions. Only eight years after aviation pioneers Orville and Wilbur Wright made the first heavier-than-air flight, Italian pilots had shown that aircraft were reliable and robust enough to potentially play a key part in future wars.

supremacy in North Africa. The resulting Treaty of Algeciras in 1906 limited France's ambitions, but Germany found its interests in the negotiations were supported only by Austria-Hungary. Other European powers, and the US, aligned with France – an early indication of future alliances.

France and Germany faced off again over Morocco during the Agadir Crisis of 1911. Open conflict was averted by Germany agreeing to accept unequivocal French domination of Morocco in exchange for Germany expanding its colony of Kamerun (now Cameroon) with land from the French Congo. Again, these disputes were settled with no input from the African populations.

Lingering legacy
The Scramble for Africa drew artificial boundaries that reflected neither precolonial tribal nor religious domains. In many cases, ethnic groups were split between competing colonial territories. Most of those artificial borders have persisted to the present day.

Wherever they settled, Europeans imposed their culture on indigenous peoples. The language of each colonial power became the lingua franca of its African dominions, which also had to accept European religion and even face recruitment into colonial armies, most notably those of the French. Imperial rule also had a lasting effect on the administration, economy, and infrastructure of African and other states, which is still observable in their governments, education, trading partners, military defence arrangements, and airline links. ▪

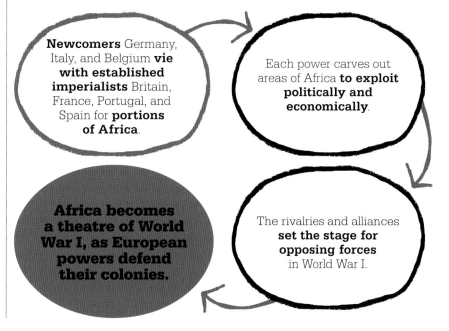

Newcomers Germany, Italy, and Belgium **vie with established imperialists** Britain, France, Portugal, and Spain for **portions of Africa**.

Each power carves out areas of Africa **to exploit politically and economically**.

The rivalries and alliances **set the stage for opposing forces** in World War I.

Africa becomes a theatre of World War I, as European powers defend their colonies.

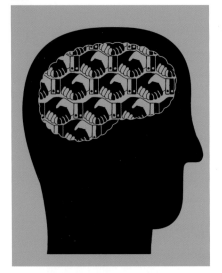

A NIGHTMARE OF COALITIONS
THE ALLIANCE SYSTEM (1879–1914)

IN CONTEXT

FOCUS
Diplomatic alliances

BEFORE
1815 Austria, Russia, and Prussia conclude the Holy Alliance, aiming to preserve Europe's monarchical rule.

1839 The Treaty of London pledges Europe's major powers to recognize and guarantee the independence and neutrality of Belgium.

1873 The League of Three Emperors, an alliance between Germany, Russia, and Austria-Hungary, is established.

AFTER
26 April 1915 Italy signs the Treaty of London, a secret agreement with the Triple Entente countries to enter World War I on their side.

3 March 1918 The Treaty of Brest-Litovsk is signed. Soviet Russia exits the war and ends its obligations to the other Allied powers.

During the late 19th and early 20th centuries, Europe's major powers made a series of alliances to promote their own interests and to protect themselves from the ambitions of other countries. This created a web of agreements and obligations that would eventually help drag the continent into war.

Dual to Triple Alliance

World War I's alliance system began to emerge in 1879, when Germany and Austria-Hungary, later known as the Central Powers on account of

their geographical location, pledged mutual support if either empire was attacked by Russia, whose rising power concerned both nations. This Dual Alliance became the Triple Alliance three years later when Italy joined, angered that France had won the contest to colonize Tunisia. The three countries promised to back each other if attacked by France, and Italy pledged neutrality in any war between Russia and Austria-Hungary. Although the alliance was renewed regularly, it did not resolve the long-standing territorial rivalries between Italy and Austria-Hungary.

Russia, France, and Britain

The Triple Alliance left Russia potentially isolated, and in 1887 it secretly signed the Reinsurance Treaty with Germany, under which both countries agreed to remain neutral if either one was attacked. When Germany allowed the treaty to lapse in 1890, Russia looked to France, which was seeking support against Germany. Diplomatic

A 1914 Russian poster depicts the Triple Entente. Mother Russia is flanked by Marianne (left), the national symbol of the French Republic, and Britannia (right), holding an anchor.

See also: The situation in Europe 18–19 ▪ Europe's colonies and empires 28–29 ▪ Planning for war 34–39 ▪ War is declared 42–43 ▪ The invasion of Belgium 50–51 ▪ Italy enters the war 120–21 ▪ A lasting peace? 312–17

The patterns of alliance

On the eve of World War I Europe's major powers were divided into two triple agreements, both tied to the Balkans, as was the Ottoman Empire. Britain and Japan also sought to protect their interests in China and Korea.

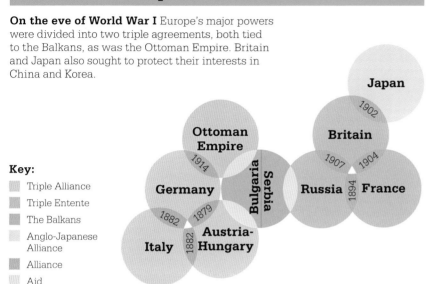

Key:
- Triple Alliance
- Triple Entente
- The Balkans
- Anglo-Japanese Alliance
- Alliance
- Aid

discussions began in 1891, leading to the Franco-Russian Alliance of 1894. Both nations pledged military support if either was attacked by the Triple Alliance. Emboldened by their agreement, Russia and France pursued more aggressive imperial policies in Africa and Asia.

In 1902, Britain abandoned its policy of "splendid isolation" by signing a defence agreement with Japan. Two years later, the French and British governments settled their colonial disputes through a series of agreements – the Entente Cordiale – that recognized each other's imperial claims. Although not a military alliance, it represented a significant improvement in Anglo-French relations, and left Germany feeling increasingly vulnerable.

Two power blocks emerge

The Russo-Japanese War (1904–05) threatened to drag Britain and Russia, long-term imperial rivals

in Asia, into conflict. On the night of 21–22 October 1904, Russian ships fired on British fishing trawlers in the Dogger Bank area of the North Sea, believing they were Japanese vessels. War appeared to be a possibility, but the two sides settled the issue by submitting it to a neutral international commission. Russia and Britain eventually resolved their Asian disputes in Persia, Afghanistan, and Tibet through the 1907 Anglo-Russian Convention. France's existing links with Russia and Britain now brought all three countries into a new alliance – the Triple Entente.

On 2 August 1914, the Ottoman Empire signed a secret treaty with Germany, with which it had deep economic ties. The Ottoman government agreed to ally with the Central Powers after Germany declared war on Russia. With that, Europe's major powers were split into two coalitions. ▪

Concessions in Asia

By the early 19th century, China was the last great market to exploit for the West. Chinese goods such as tea and silk were sought-after, while China's vast population represented millions of new consumers for industrial goods and potential converts for Christian missionaries. However, the ruling Qing Dynasty had little interest in Western products and imposed limitations on foreign traders.

Over the second half of the 19th century, under military and diplomatic pressure, China granted Western powers (and Japan) territorial concessions, where they could station troops and ships, and their citizens could live, trade, and carry out missionary work. By 1914, there were dozens of concessions along the Chinese coast and some inland, including one in Peking (Beijing), the capital city.

These forces shall engage to the full with such speed that Germany will have to fight simultaneously on the East and on the West.
Franco-Russian Alliance Military Convention 18 August 1892

ENGLAND INDISPUTABLY RULES THE SEA

THE NAVAL ARMS RACE (1896–1914)

IN CONTEXT

FOCUS
Naval supremacy

BEFORE
1805 Britain's victory over French and Spanish fleets at the Battle of Trafalgar ends the last serious challenge to its naval supremacy for the next hundred years.

1871 The unification of Germany leads to the creation of the Imperial German Navy.

AFTER
31 May–1 June 1916 At the Battle of Jutland, British and German dreadnoughts clash for the only time.

1922 The Washington Naval Treaty halts a naval arms race, as Britain, the US, France, Italy, and Japan accept limits to the size of their fleets.

1923 HMS *Dreadnought* is broken up at a yard in Scotland. Its scrap value is one-fortieth of what it cost to build.

Throughout the 19th century, Britain had the world's biggest navy and by far the largest merchant ship fleet. Government policy followed the "two-power standard" – the Royal Navy was to be stronger than the next two largest navies combined (meaning those of France and Russia). Before 1900, the Imperial German Navy was too small to pose any real threat. But all this changed in the years leading up to 1914.

A new German menace

The German emperor, Wilhelm II, longed for a large navy to support Germany's ambitions as a world power and found an ally in Admiral Alfred von Tirpitz, who was made state secretary of the Imperial Naval Office in 1897. Tirpitz's process of increasing naval power began with two Navy Laws in 1898 and 1900, which established ambitious warship plans – including the building of 38 new battleships.

Tirpitz developed a "risk theory", calculating that Britain would need a 3:2 ratio of naval superiority

HMS *Dreadnought* revolutionized battleship design but took part in only one significant action, ramming and sinking the submarine *U-29* in March 1915.

See also: The war at sea begins 88–93 ▪ The Battle of Jutland 160–65 ▪ The U-boats on the attack 200–05 ▪ Naval war in the Mediterranean 242–43

Dreadnought building

From 1906, Britain and Germany were in a race to build giant battleships. At first, Germany produced more vessels, but by 1914 Britain had secured a significant numerical superiority.

Key
 British ships (total 29)
German ships (total 17)

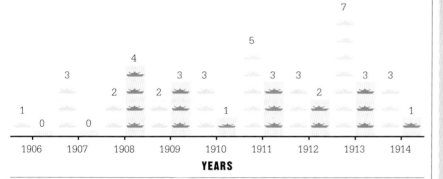

YEARS

Alfred von Tirpitz

Born the son of a Prussian lawyer in 1849, Alfred von Tirpitz was the architect of Germany's transformation into the world's second-largest naval power. He joined the Prussian Navy in 1865 and from 1877 commanded torpedo boats, developing their tactical use by the Imperial German Navy. Promoted to rear admiral in 1895, he commanded the German cruiser fleet in East Asia before becoming the de facto navy minister in 1897. The five Naval Laws that Turpitz introduced enabled Germany's rapid naval enlargement, and in 1911 he was awarded the rank of grand admiral.

With the onset of war and the clear superiority of Allied ship numbers, Turpitz began to champion all-out submarine warfare. Facing mounting opposition, he resigned in 1916 and co-founded the far-right Fatherland Party in 1917. From 1924 to 1928, Turpitz represented the right-wing German National People's Party in parliament, before retiring to Bavaria, where he died in 1930.

over Germany to maintain its preeminence, and would rather reach an agreement than build a fleet so large. Britain responded to the threat by moving into closer alliance with France and Russia between 1904 and 1907. This allowed the Royal Navy to divert ships from colonial duties and the Mediterranean Sea to home waters, where its most modern ships were increasingly concentrated.

The arms race begins

Sir John Fisher, who became Britain's First Sea Lord in 1904, oversaw improvements to the Royal Navy, such as the building of submarines and the conversion from coal to oil power. In 1906, he commissioned the building of the first of a new class of battleship, HMS *Dreadnought*, which could out-gun and out-run any other battleship afloat. This prompted Germany and other countries, including France, Italy, Russia, and Japan, to begin building their own "dreadnoughts".

Work began on the first German dreadnought, *Nassau*, in 1907, and in 1908 Tirpitz established a new Navy Law to build four big ships a year up to 1911. This arms escalation took Britain – which in 1908 had ordered only two more dreadnoughts – by surprise and provoked a public outcry for more ships. "We want eight and we won't wait" became a popular slogan, driven by the "Navalists", a powerful naval lobby that included industrialists, journalists, and members of the royal family. The government was forced to concede and ordered eight dreadnoughts.

The shipbuilding race continued, and when war began, in August 1914, Britain had 29 dreadnoughts to Germany's 17. The consensus was that big ships were the best measure of a nation's naval power and that they would inevitably face each other in set-piece battles. In practice, they acted more as a deterrent, with new naval threats emerging from mines, torpedoes, submarines, and aircraft. ▪

ATTACK IS THE BEST DEFENCE

PLANNING FOR WAR (1905–14)

IN CONTEXT

FOCUS
Military strategy

BEFORE
1871 Prussian victory against France and the subsequent unification of Germany forces European powers to plan for a future major conflict.

1874 Military engineers build a set of fortifications – the Séré de Rivières system – along France's borders and coasts, and in some of its colonies. The defences are later used during World War I.

1899–1902 Tactical failings during the Boer War – and the conflict's high human and financial cost – persuade Britain to pursue reform of both its military leadership and planning.

AFTER
2 August 1914 Official mobilization orders are posted in public spaces throughout France, the day after Germany declares war on Russia.

4 August 1914 Britain condemns the German invasion of Belgium, whose neutrality had been formally guaranteed by European powers, including Prussia, in the 1839 Treaty of London.

14 September 1914 Helmuth von Moltke is sacked as chief of the German general staff after his offensive on the Western Front is brought to a halt by the Allies at the Battle of the Marne.

In 1914, Europe was polarized into two rival armed camps, and the war plans of the great Continental powers reflected this division. The strategic balance was geographically determined: Germany and Austria-Hungary held the centre of the continent, surrounded by France to the west and Russia to the east. Britain – not a formal member of any military alliance – was on the periphery.

While the Central Powers of Germany and Austria-Hungary held the advantage of operating from the heart of Europe against outside forces attempting to converge on them, Germany faced the prospect of a war on two fronts against resurgent enemies. France

The enemy's front is not the objective. The essential thing is to crush the enemy's flanks.
Alfred von Schlieffen

Massed French infantry charge enemy positions in the Franco-Prussian War. The principle of attacking in huge numbers became a standard feature of French military planning.

had remained its chief potential opponent following the Franco-Prussian War of 1870–71, but a new threat was emerging in the east. The rise of Russia as an economic force was seen as a direct and possibly overwhelming threat to Germany's security. The German general staff had become so fearful of Russia's military potential that arguments were put forward to instigate a preventative war before Russia grew any stronger.

Germany and its strategy

Germany had developed various plans to defeat France and Russia, the most significant of which was one put forward by Alfred von Schlieffen, chief of the German general staff between 1891 and 1906. The central tenet of the "Schlieffen Plan", adopted in 1905, was to deliver a swift and massive blow to France before German forces were turned eastwards to deal with Russia. Schlieffen knew that it would take Russia far longer than France to mobilize and deploy its armies in the field. Although

See also: The situation in Europe 18–19 ■ The rise of Germany 20–23
■ Crisis in Russia 24 ■ The Alliance System 30–31 ■ The naval arms race 32–33

modified several times after 1905, the fundamentals of the Schlieffen Plan remained unchanged in 1914.

The Franco-German border region was narrow, and following defeat in the Franco-Prussian War, France had pioneered new defensive systems that both impressed and concerned their German opponents. To circumvent the defences, the plan proposed an outflanking advance through neutral Belgium, whose sovereignty had been guaranteed by Prussia and Britain in 1839. German chancellor, Theobald von Bethmann-Hollweg, however, dismissed the treaty as merely "a scrap of paper". Blinkered by an obsession with operational matters, Germany disregarded the wider international ramifications of a blatantly illegal act.

An inflexible plan

Chief of the German general staff, Helmuth von Moltke, planned to deploy the bulk of the German forces in the west. Nearly 1.5 million men, organized into seven armies, were to be in position along Germany's western frontier by the start of hostilities. The Sixth and Seventh armies at the southern end of the German line would act in a »

Alfred von Schlieffen

Born in Berlin into a Prussian aristocratic family in 1833, Alfred von Schlieffen studied first at the University of Berlin and, from 1858–61, received advanced officer training at the War Academy in Berlin. He fought in the wars against the Austrian Empire in 1866 and France in 1870–71 and rose steadily through the ranks of the German general staff, an elite corps responsible for the direction of German military strategy. He became its chief in 1891.

Schlieffen was pessimistic about Germany's chances of winning a war against France and Russia, whose combined forces greatly outnumbered those of Germany, and argued, without much success, for an expansion of the army. His 1905 memorandum – subsequently known as the Schlieffen Plan – was an attempt to show what might be possible if the army was expanded as proposed. This never happened, however, and his successor, Helmuth von Moltke, was forced to modify the plan to take this shortfall into account. Schlieffen retired on New Year's Day 1906 and died in 1913.

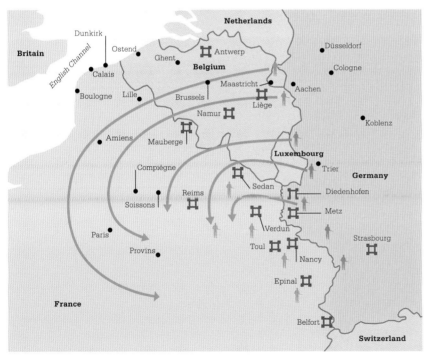

The Schlieffen Plan, Germany's strategy to defeat France, was based on a large-scale offensive through neutral Belgium, the Netherlands, and Luxembourg. German forces would envelop the French armies. The plan's 1914 version avoided the Netherlands.

Key:

⊞ Fortified towns

↑ German armies

↑ French armies

→ Planned routes of German armies

▨ Germany

▨ Allies

▨ Neutral territories

defensive role, while the main strike force would advance through Luxembourg and southern Belgium, then turn to rout the French armies.

German success depended on the speed of its mobilization, the completeness of the victory over France, and the slowness of Russia's reaction. A more fundamental problem was the plan's inflexibility as, regardless of where the threat originated, Germany had to invade France as soon as war was declared.

The diplomatic crisis deepened towards the end of July 1914, prompting more moderate members of the German government to raise doubts about attacking France when the source of conflict lay in Eastern Europe and the Balkans. The German general staff crushed all dissent, however, arguing that changing the rail schedules to enable rapid mobilization would throw the army's plans into disarray, leaving it vulnerable to attack. Senior German commanders insisted that their plan should not be modified.

French *élan* and *cran*

France's strategy to secure victory against Germany was designated Plan XVII, and consisted of a major

> [Britain] had never contemplated the preparation of armies for warfare of the Continental type.
> **Richard B. Haldane**
> *Before the War,* 1920

push into Lorraine, supported by a subsidiary offensive through Alsace. Previous plans had been more cautious, beginning with a defensive phase that relied on France's strong border defences to hold the line and break up a German attack. This would be followed by a French counterattack against an expectedly disorganized opponent.

The solely aggressive nature of Plan XVII was a result of two factors: a desire for speed to help Russia with its own attack in the east; and a largely erroneous belief in the inherent superiority of the offensive.

In the years leading up to the outbreak of war, French military theorists had virtually reduced strategy to transporting the army to the front. Once there, it was believed that French *élan* ("impetus") and *cran* ("grit") would lead to victory. In fact, the stark defensive realities of the modern battlefield, with its quick-firing artillery and machine guns, would come as a devastating blow to the French army in the war's opening clashes.

Changing British focus

Britain had traditionally remained aloof from martial affairs in Continental Europe, but the rise of German militarism pushed it into a covert relationship with France. Its military planners had agreed with their French counterparts that a British Expeditionary Force (BEF) would cross to France in the event of a German attack in the west.

The British plan was kept secret from both the parliament and much of the government, but it would

Tsar Nicholas II inspects Russian officer cadets in 1907. Defeat in the Russo-Japanese War of 1904–05 had led to major reforms of Russia's military.

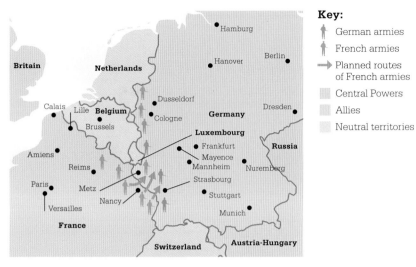

Key:
- German armies
- French armies
- Planned routes of French armies
- Central Powers
- Allies
- Neutral territories

By 1914, France had developed Plan XVII, its tactical plan for war in Europe. It involved a massive attack driving into key German industrial areas, through Alsace and Lorraine. This took no account of Germany's full-scale invasion of Belgium, however.

need their support if it was to go into operation. During the summer of 1914, there was strong opposition within the British government to committing its forces to European affairs. The likelihood of the British plan being realized, however, remained in the balance until the German invasion of Belgium swayed the antiwar party in favour of military involvement.

The Eastern Front

Austria-Hungary's plan in the east involved an offensive to drive northwards from Galicia to cut off Russian forces in the Polish salient (a projection into enemy territory). This was an over-ambitious plan, well beyond the capabilities of the cumbersome, multinational Austro-Hungarian army. The strategy also relied on close cooperation with Germany, but this was not forthcoming as the German tactical plan for 1914 required its forces in the east to remain on the defensive until troops could be released from

the Western Front. Only one German army was posted in the east, its role to guard East Prussia.

Russia had the advantage of large reserves of manpower, but the sheer size of its empire and its relatively poor rail communications hindered mobilization, as well as making the transport of reserves between fronts a slow process. Compounding such geographical problems were the incompetence, corruption, and departmental rivalry endemic in Russia's military and civilian bureaucracies.

Russia had envisaged that the main weight of its 1914 offensive would be directed against Austria-Hungary. However, Russia's French ally was desperate to divert German troops away from the Western Front, so the plans were modified to include an immediate invasion of East Prussia. The offensive against Germany was assigned to General Yakov Zhilinsky's forces. His First Army would attack East Prussia from the east, and the Second Army

would cross the German region's southern frontier – a simple and sensible plan, if the ramshackle Russian army could carry it out.

A bloody inevitability

The last great European war had ended in 1815, and a century later there was much debate as to what form future hostilities might take. The popular view was of a short conflict, with a few massive battles that would decide the outcome along the lines of the war between Prussia and France in 1870–71. A number of economists and political commentators supported this view on the logical basis that a modern war would be so destructive and expensive that there would be insufficient material resources to sustain it beyond a few months.

Other experts – both civilian and military – foresaw a longer struggle of attrition, in which economic strength and endurance would be key. Moltke, chief of the German general staff, certainly hoped for a short war – and a German triumph over France in a matter of weeks – but he also planned for a lengthier conflict. All commentators believed the war would be vast, chaotic, and bloody – and in this, at least, their forecasts were proved correct. ∎

No war in Europe can bring us much.
Bernhard Prince von Bülow
German chancellor, 1908

DEATH TO THE TYRANT!
THE ASSASSINATION OF FRANZ FERDINAND (28 JUNE 1914)

IN CONTEXT

FOCUS
Volatile Europe

BEFORE
1867 Austria-Hungary, or the Dual Monarchy, is formed as an alliance of two sovereign states – Austria and Hungary.

1908 In October, Austria-Hungary unilaterally annexes Bosnia-Herzegovina, which antagonizes Serb nationalists.

1911 Bosnian Serb student Gavrilo Princip joins the pan-Slav revolutionary group Young Bosnia.

AFTER
28–29 June 1914 Anti-Serb rioting breaks out in Sarajevo and other towns in Bosnia.

28 July 1914 Austria-Hungary declares war on Serbia.

28 October 1914 Princip is found guilty of assassinating Franz Ferdinand and receives a 20-year prison sentence. He dies of tuberculosis in 1918.

On 28 June 1914, Archduke Franz Ferdinand, heir to the Austro-Hungarian throne, arrived in the Bosnian provincial capital of Sarajevo to inspect local military manoeuvres. Six years earlier, Austria-Hungary had annexed the former Ottoman province of Bosnia-Herzegovina, whose mixed ethnic population

included Serb nationalists who were working towards a political union with the neighbouring Slav kingdom of Serbia.

Accompanied by his wife, Sophie, Franz Ferdinand travelled to the town hall in an open-topped motor car. Dispersed within a large crowd of onlookers were several Serbian revolutionaries from the Young Bosnia group, intent on assassinating him. They had been armed and trained by a secret society called the Black Hand, controlled by Colonel Dragutin Dimitrijević, head of Serbian military intelligence. Although the Serbian government as a whole did not want to risk antagonizing Austria-Hungary, rogue elements within the Serbian administration were linked to the attempt on the archduke's life.

Fatal wounding
One of the Serbian terrorists, Nedeljko Čabrinovič, threw a bomb at the archduke's car on

Gavrilo Princip, a Serb nationalist, fires two shots, hitting Franz Ferdinand in the neck and the archduke's wife in the stomach. The couple die within minutes of each other.

See also: The situation in Europe 18–19 ▪ The Balkans 25 ▪ The Alliance System 30–31 ▪ Planning for war 34–39 ▪ War is declared 42–43 ▪ Austro-Hungarian failures 82 ▪ The end of the Serbian campaign 140–43 ▪ A lasting peace? 312–17

Franz Ferdinand

Born in Graz, Austria, in 1863, Franz Ferdinand was the son of Archduke Karl Ludwig – Emperor Franz Joseph's younger brother. Only after the deaths of Crown Prince Rudolf and his own father did he become heir to the Austro-Hungarian throne. He earned royal disfavour in 1900 through his marriage to Countess Sophie Chotek, who, as a non-royal, was not considered a suitable choice of wife for a potential emperor.

Franz Ferdinand's relationship with Franz Joseph was tense, and he was often excluded from the higher reaches of government,

especially because of his efforts to reduce the strong Hungarian influence within the Dual Monarchy and promote better relations with the other minorities, including Slavs. His pro-Slav stance threatened the Serbian dream of bringing Austria-Hungary's Croatians, Slovenes, and Bosnians under Serbian rule, thereby making him a target for assassination. The archduke's death on 28 June 1914 removed what would have been a moderating voice for peace in the days leading up to the outbreak of war.

the morning of 28 June, which failed to hit the royal couple but injured some of the party in the vehicle behind them. Following a scheduled stop at the town hall, the couple continued with their plans, now amended to include a stop at Sarajevo Hospital to visit those who had been caught in the earlier bomb blast. However, en route their driver accidentally took a wrong turn. On discovering his mistake, he stopped to turn the car around, but stalled the engine. By sheer coincidence, another of the terrorists, 19-year-old Gavrilo Princip, was standing nearby. Seeing the stationary vehicle, he raced forward and fired his Serbian army pistol, fatally wounding the archduke and his wife.

Even before the archduke's assassination, Austrian foreign minister, Count Leopold von Berchtold, and his hawkish colleagues had been looking for ways to launch a limited war that would crush Serbia, whose pro-Slav agitation seemed a threat to the delicate multiethnic balance within

the Austro-Hungarian Empire. Although the immediate reaction to the deaths of Franz Ferdinand and his wife was muted – both were generally disliked within Austro-Hungarian government circles – the assassination provided an ideal justification for military action.

German support

Before Berchtold could act, he had to ensure that Russia would not intervene on Serbia's behalf. Russia had strong links to its fellow Slav state, and was also determined to prevent further Austro-Hungarian expansion into the Balkans. As a result, Berchtold felt obliged to win the support of his German ally, in the belief that the threat of German military involvement would deter Russian interference. By 6 July, Austria-Hungary had received repeated assurances of backing from Germany, giving it full authority to attack Serbia, in what became known as a "blank cheque". Germany knew that this could provoke Russia into coming to Serbia's aid, but believed that

Russia, still weakened from its defeat by Japan nine years earlier, would not risk a European war. To avoid making Austria appear as the aggressor, Berchtold began to prepare for Serbia a series of diplomatic demands – known as the "July Ultimatum". He knew the demands would be unacceptable. According to Berchtold's plan, once Serbia had failed to meet these conditions, Austria would have a solid justification for going to war. ▪

We must clear the Serbians out of the way.
German emperor Wilhelm II
in support of Austro-Hungarian action against Serbia

WAS THE TREATY NOT A SCRAP OF PAPER?

WAR IS DECLARED (JULY–AUGUST 1914)

IN CONTEXT

FOCUS
Declarations of war

BEFORE
1908 In October, Austria-Hungary annexes Bosnia-Herzegovina, enraging the state of Serbia.

28 June 1914 Archduke Franz Ferdinand, heir to the Habsburg throne, is assassinated in Sarajevo by a Bosnian Serb.

6 July 1914 Germany issues a "blank cheque" to Austria-Hungary to deal with Serbia as it wishes.

AFTER
23 May 1915 Italy declares war on Austria-Hungary.

9 March 1916 Germany declares war on Portugal.

6 April 1917 The US declares war on Germany.

14 August 1917 China declares war on Germany.

The Austro-Hungarian government issued an ultimatum to Serbia on 23 July 1914, demanding it to investigate the assassination of Archduke Franz Ferdinand and suppress all "terrorist" activity. Austria-Hungary had taken more than three weeks to deliver its ultimatum, partly to gain German backing for war and also to follow the advice of Franz Conrad von

Crowds of cheering people in Berlin celebrate Germany's declaration of war on Russia on 1 August 1914. Kaiser Wilhelm II gave the order to mobilize German troops the same day.

Hötzendorf, the chief of the general staff, that the earliest possible start for military operations should be 25 July, after the summer harvest.

Punitive action
German generals and politicians actively, if covertly, encouraged Austria-Hungary to take punitive action against Serbia, hoping that this might draw Russia into the conflict. Germany could then justify war against Russia, before it grew stronger militarily.

Serbia was given just 48 hours to reply to the July ultimatum, but enough time to start mobilizing its forces. Initially, Russia advised

See also: The Alliance System 30–31 ▪ Planning for war 34–39 ▪ The assassination of Franz Ferdinand 40–41 ▪ Austro-Hungarian failures 82–83

Who declared war on whom in 1914

Austria-Hungary ↓	Germany ↓	Britain ↓
Serbia 28 July	**Russia** 1 Aug	**Germany** 4 Aug
Russia 6 Aug	**Belgium** 3 Aug	**Austria-Hungary** 12 Aug
Belgium 28 Aug	**France** 3 Aug	**Ottoman Empire** 5 Nov

Montenegro ↓	Serbia ↓	France ↓
Austria-Hungary 6 Aug	**Germany** 6 Aug	**Austria-Hungary** 12 Aug
Germany 8 Aug	**Ottoman Empire** 2 Dec	**Ottoman Empire** 5 Nov
Ottoman Empire 3 Dec		

Japan ↓	Russia ↓	Ottoman Empire ↓
Germany 23 Aug	**Ottoman Empire** 1 Nov	**Russia** 11 Nov
Austria-Hungary 25 Aug		**Britain** 11 Nov
Ottoman Empire 5 Dec		**Japan** 11 Nov

Franz Conrad von Hötzendorf

Born in a suburb of Vienna in 1852, Franz Conrad von Hötzendorf rose steadily through the ranks of the Austro-Hungarian army, taking up both staff and field commands until reaching the post of chief of the general staff in 1906. A former war college professor and prolific military writer, he had a deep faith in offensive warfare that did not match his army's capabilities. He argued for a punitive campaign against Serbia after the assassination of Archduke Franz Ferdinand. He was also an advocate of war against Italy.

Conrad's aggression as a soldier-statesman was not matched by strategic talent. Austro-Hungarian failures against Serbia and Russia in 1914 led to him becoming increasingly sidelined by the German high command in the East. In March 1917, he was demoted from his post as chief of staff and served as a field commander on the Tyrol front until he was dismissed in July 1918. Conrad retired from military life in December 1918 and died in 1925 in Germany.

Serbia to take a conciliatory approach, while also putting the Russian army on full alert in the hope of deterring Austro-Hungarian military action.

Austria-Hungary remained undaunted. The failure of the Serbian government to meet all demands by 25 July was considered sufficient cause for action, and on 28 July Austria-Hungary invaded Serbia. A few last desperate attempts were made to stop the war spreading from the Balkans, but the momentum for conflict had become unstoppable.

Germany mobilizes

On hearing the Russian army had started to mobilize, German generals pushed for a full preparation of German forces. Diplomatic confusion reigned between the two countries, the supporters of war on each side wanting the other to be the first to signal that they were organizing for conflict.

On 30 July, Tsar Nicholas II ordered a general mobilization for the next day, then rescinded it before Russian generals forced him to reinstate the order – all on the same day. This gave the Germans the justification they were looking for. On 1 August, Germany declared war on Russia and began to marshal its troops. On 3 August, Germany invaded Belgium and declared war on France. The following day, Britain declared war on Germany. World War I was now underway. ▪

WHO'S FOR THE GAME?

PUBLIC OPINION (JULY–AUGUST 1914)

IN CONTEXT

FOCUS
Patriotism and propaganda

BEFORE
1848 The spread of nationalism fuels popular revolutions across Europe.

1877–78 During the Russo-Turkish War, a coalition of Balkan nationalists receive support from Russia. Under the subsequent Treaty of Berlin, Montenegro, Serbia, and Romania gain independence.

1898–1912 Expansion of the German navy threatens Britain's naval supremacy and increases British public hostility towards Germany.

AFTER
April 1917 After German attacks on American merchant ships, the US enters the war.

November 1918 The Armistice is celebrated with patriotic fervour in Allied cities. Reality for soldiers on the front is one of weary confusion.

The outbreak of World War I was anticipated by the major European powers, but it dismayed their citizens. For the first time, all participating governments used mass media to counteract unease about the war and shape public opinion. Newspapers, cinema newsreels, pamphlets, and posters justified aggression, encouraged patriotism, stoked hostility towards the enemy, and urged men to join the fight and women to dedicate themselves to

IS **YOUR** HOME WORTH FIGHTING FOR?

IT WILL BE TOO LATE TO FIGHT WHEN THE ENEMY IS AT YOUR DOOR
so **JOIN TO-DAY**

the home front. Later, the same media were used to raise morale and share news from the battlefield.

Germany and its allies
The increasingly influential Social Democratic Party (SPD), a vocal German critic of Kaiser Wilhelm II, had little desire for war. Thousands of SPD members supported an anti-war demonstration in July 1914. On 30 July, however, Tsar Nicholas II ordered a general mobilization of the Russian army, prompting Germany's leaders to declare war on its eastern neighbour as a "defensive" measure. On 4 August, SPD parliamentary members voted to support the war.

German propaganda portrayed Britain as a bully asserting its imperial power while attempting to constrain that of Germany. Swelling the ranks of its standing army and conscripted soldiers, thousands of untrained young men volunteered.

Austria-Hungary, by contrast, was ill-prepared for a major conflict when it declared war, and relied on

This alarming poster appeared in Ireland in 1915. Such propaganda emphasized the threat of war and its effect on families to urge men to volunteer to fight for their country.

See also: The rise of Germany 20–23 ▪ The naval arms race 32–33 ▪ Planning for war 34–39 ▪ The secret war 96–99 ▪ Society under strain 184–87 ▪ The February Revolution 192–93 ▪ Replacing the fallen 198–99 ▪ The home front in 1918 250–53

Order of the White Feather

White feather notes were a source of humiliation. No man wanted to be shamed into enlisting and many volunteered – at least initially.

In August 1914, British Admiral Charles Penrose Fitzgerald recruited a group of women in the coastal town of Folkstone to hand out white feathers to men not in uniform. He favoured conscription and hoped the feathers would shame recipients into volunteering for the war. The initiative, which was highly effective and spread rapidly around Britain, was inspired by A.E.W. Mason's 1902 novel *The Four Feathers*, whose officer protagonist quits the army and is sent four white feathers by his comrades and fiancée to signify his cowardice.

The campaign's supporters, including suffragette Emmeline Pankhurst, were fierce patriots, but their approach was often aggressive and unjustified. Many of the men targeted were civilians working for the war effort or, later, soldiers on leave and wounded veterans. Industrial and public workers wore official badges to prevent such harassment. In 1916, the British government also began to issue silver war badges for former servicemen to wear that read "For King and Empire" and "Services Rendered".

support from Germany. After an initial flood of patriotism, fanned by aggressive promotion from Vienna, tensions among its citizens quickly surfaced as food supplies dwindled.

Russia and France

Imperial Russia did not have a united population. In 1912, tsarist government troops had shot hundreds of workers protesting against conditions in Siberia's Lena gold mines, leading to widespread strikes up to July 1914. At the outbreak of war, much of Russia's workforce was conscripted, producing further rioting and violence exacerbated by soaring food prices. Yet an initial wave of patriotism also pervaded all classes, temporarily suppressing revolutionary zeal.

In France, the largely pacifist urban public supported mass peace demonstrations in July 1914; those in rural areas were mostly unaware that war was looming. All this changed in August 1914 when Germany invaded Belgium and Luxembourg. An army of 2.9 million

men was swiftly assembled, and France became united in a general mood of anti-German fervour.

Mobilizing Britain

A peace demonstration in London on 2 August 1914 attracted around 10,000 citizens, but the nation rallied patriotically two days later when Britain declared war. Most pacifists

were shamed and silenced. Britain's professional army of around 250,000 regulars, augmented to 700,000 with reservists and territorials, was dwarfed by that of Germany. Via news channels and a vast poster campaign, secretary of state for war, Field Marshal Lord Kitchener, called for volunteers. In two months, more than 750,000 men had signed up. ▪

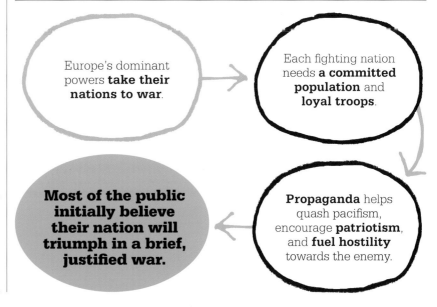

Europe's dominant powers **take their nations to war**.

Each fighting nation needs **a committed population** and **loyal troops**.

Propaganda helps quash pacifism, encourage **patriotism**, and **fuel hostility** towards the enemy.

Most of the public initially believe their nation will triumph in a brief, justified war.

THE WA
BEGINS
1914

R

Archduke Franz Ferdinand of Austria-Hungary is **assassinated** in Sarajevo, Bosnia, by a member of an extreme Serbian nationalist group.

Germany declares war on Russia and begins to ready its armed forces. **France mobilizes against Germany** in response.

British troops invade the German colony of Togoland in West Africa, which falls to them on 27 August.

Japan, which has a mutual defence agreement with Britain, **declares war on Germany** and helps close down German possessions in the Far East.

28 JUN 1914

1 AUG 1914

7 AUG 1914

23 AUG 1914

28 JUL 1914

4 AUG 1914

21 AUG 1914

26 AUG 1914

Austria-Hungary refuses the offer of international mediation. After declaring war on Serbia, it **prepares** a punitive expedition **to attack** the Serbian capital of **Belgrade**.

German forces invade Belgium, prompting Britain, a co-signatory to Belgian neutrality, to declare war on Germany.

France's Fifth Army is severely defeated at the Battle of Charleroi, marking the beginning of an overall **French retreat**.

The **Battle of Tannenberg** begins on the Eastern Front, with a German army destroying a large Russian force.

Before World War I, the last great, sustained European conflict had ended in 1815 with Napoleon's decisive defeat at the Battle of Waterloo. In the hundred years that separated the wars, two transformative factors had come into play.

As the size of European nations grew in the 19th century, so did their armies. By 1914, each state could typically deploy a relatively small standing army ready for immediate action, which could then be boosted by a larger well-trained reserve of men. Germany, for example, had a regular force of some 800,000 men, which in 1914 grew to around 3.5 million with the call-up of reserves.

Armed forces were also now equipped with powerful new weapons of mass destruction,

an arms technology revolution that had gathered pace in the two decades prior to 1914. The dramatic improvements in the arsenals of land armies, augmented by new ways of waging war in the air and under the sea, were to have a huge impact on the conduct of the war.

Firepower and first blows

The introduction of machine guns, magazine rifles, and quick-firing artillery gave defensive firepower an enormous advantage over manoeuvre and offensive operations. Such new battlefield realities were only partially understood by the generals in command of vast armies. Some insisted on the primacy of aggressive, offensive tactics and rejected the dominance of firepower as a dangerous fallacy that could fatally undermine an army's morale.

The French army, in particular, zealously pursued the primacy of the offensive – a gulf between military dogma and battlefield experience that had brutal consequences. Along France's eastern border on 22 August 1914, 27,000 French soldiers were killed – the highest fatality figure for a single day's fighting in the entire war. The casualties from these initial battles included many of the finest soldiers in the French army; their loss would be keenly felt in the battles to come.

The initial clashes between French and German troops in August 1914, known as the Battle of the Frontiers, saw five French armies collide with an advance of similar-sized German forces. The French attacks were repeatedly repulsed by the German troops, with heavy losses on both sides.

The **First Battle of the Marne** begins in northern France, marking the **end of the German advance** towards Paris.

The **First Battle of Ypres** begins, as a **combined Franco-British-Belgian force defends** the city against the main German army.

The **Battle of Coronel** takes place off the coast of Chile. A German naval force inflicts a decisive defeat on a British squadron.

The **British navy** replies to the defeat at Coronel by **destroying the German naval force** at an engagement off the Falkland Islands.

5 SEPT 1914   **19 OCT 1914**   **1 NOV 1914**   **8 DEC 1914**

14 SEPT 1914   **29 OCT 1914**   **22 NOV 1914**   **24–25 DEC 1914**

The **German army retreats** in good order to a defensive line on the River Aisne, the first stage in the **development of trench warfare**.

The **Ottoman Empire**, which enters the war on the side of Germany and Austria-Hungary, launches a **surprise raid against Russian ports** on the Black Sea.

Indian troops take the city of **Basra** in Mesopotamia (Iraq) as part of a British action to **protect oil fields in Persia** from Ottoman attack.

During the **impromptu Christmas truce** on the Western Front, British troops fraternize with their German opponents, exchanging gifts and singing carols.

The German army gained early territorial advantages, taking most of Belgium and parts of northeast France. During the First Battle of the Marne in September, the French – aided by the British Expeditionary Force – recovered and pushed back the German troops. The battle was a triumph for French generalship, which at the highest level proved more than a match for its opponents.

After the First Battle of the Marne, the war of movement came to an end. The conflict developed into a static, attritional struggle, with lines of trenches stretching from Switzerland to the North Sea.

The Eastern Front

Another major war zone covered vast areas of Eastern and central Europe. There, the conflict was much more fluid than on the geographically confined Western Front. Trench-bound deadlocks were few and temporary, allowing for strategic manoeuvres over open terrain. Yet paradoxically, the great distances that armies had to traverse made it hard to overcome an enemy outright. A defeated army could always retire deep into its own territory and regroup. As in the west, the war became one of attrition.

After a catastrophic defeat at the Battle of Tannenberg in August 1914, the Russian army recovered. It forced the Austro-Hungarian army back to the Carpathian Mountains while threatening German forces in Silesia. The fortunes of battle swung to and fro. The Russian forces lost momentum through shortages of supplies and munitions, and in November a German attack around Łódz pushed them back to the Vistula river. Major offensives then halted as both sides prepared for new military ventures in 1915.

A truly "world" war

Although this was a conflict begun in Europe by European powers, their global interests carried the fighting to other continents in 1914. Germany lost its colonies in West and Southwest Africa to the Allies, but resisted in East Africa. German outposts in the Pacific fell to New Zealand and Australian forces, while Japan's entry into the war ended Germany's presence in China. In Mesopotamia, Indian troops fought Ottoman forces to protect British oil resources, while even further from Europe, Germany and Britain locked horns in sea battles in the southern reaches of the Pacific and Atlantic oceans. ■

MURDER, LUST, AND PILLAGE
THE INVASION OF BELGIUM (AUGUST–OCTOBER 1914)

IN CONTEXT

FOCUS
Neutrality and its violation

BEFORE
1839 The Treaty of London formally establishes Belgian independence and neutrality, with Britain and Prussia among the signatories.

1899 Russian leaders instigate the Hague Convention, which seeks to set rules for land, sea, and air warfare.

1905 The first draft of the German Schlieffen Plan proposes an advance through Belgium to defeat the French.

AFTER
October 1914 A Belgian government in exile is set up in Le Havre, France.

May 1915 The Bryce Report condemns German actions in the 1914 invasion of Belgium.

1916–18 At least 2,500 Belgian men perish while imprisoned in German labour camps.

Early on the morning of 4 August 1914, the German army crossed the border into neutral Belgium. Although little resistance was expected from the Belgian army – 117,000 front-line troops under the command of King Albert I – the powerful fortresses of Liège and Namur were potential obstacles to the swift transit of German forces through the country.

Liège, astride the main route through Belgium, was a problem for which the German planners had made special provision. By 16 August, their army's 30.5 cm (12 in) Škoda and 42 cm (17 in)

We shall wipe it out, not one stone will stand upon another! We will teach them to respect Germany.
German officer
on the destruction of Leuven

Krupp super-heavy howitzers had reduced the city's steel-and-concrete fortifications to rubble. On 20 August, German troops marched into Brussels, and after Namur fell five days later, the remainder of the Belgian army retired north to the relative safety of the major port city of Antwerp.

The speed of the German advance and the apparent ease with which the much-vaunted fortifications had been destroyed partly hid the many problems faced by the German forces. As Belgian troops retreated, they demolished bridges and railway tunnels, which then had to be repaired. This disruption would hamper the reinforcement of German armies during critical stages of the First Battle of the Marne in September.

Total destruction
The need for vigilance against civilian snipers or *francs-tireurs* (literally "sharpshooters") featured prominently among lessons the German army learned from the Franco-Prussian War (1870–71). To discourage such resistance in Belgium, German troops cowed the population into submission through the semi-official policy

See also: Planning for war 34–39 ▪ The Battle of the Frontiers 52–55 ▪ The Race to the Sea 70–71 ▪ Shattered by war 310–11 ▪ War-crimes trials 318–19

of *Schrecklichkeit* ("frightfulness"). The destruction of property, and the rape, torture, and killing of civilians, took place throughout Belgium from the very beginning of hostilities.

The atrocities culminated in the sacking of Leuven (Louvain). On 25 August, German troops set the university library on fire, burning 230,000 books and nearly 1,000 manuscripts. Increasing numbers of civilians were shot, and over six days the city was razed and 10,000 inhabitants were forced to flee. In less than a month, more than 5,000 Belgian civilians were killed.

International outcry

Although the brutalities carried out by the German army succeeded in subduing the people of Belgium, there was an international outcry at such premeditated barbarity as soon as news of them reached the wider world. Although the Germans did their best to cover up their actions, journalists from neutral countries, including the US and Sweden, soon revealed the true extent of the massacres. Although the Germans attempted to justify their conduct, the Allies were the clear winners of the propaganda war that ensued. The battle for the hearts and minds of the neutral nations would continue to play an important role as the war developed. ▪

The sacking of Leuven by German troops left the city in ruins. Some 2,000 buildings were destroyed by soldiers on the pretext that they were forestalling attacks from civilians.

Edith Cavell

Born in 1865 in the village of Swardeston, Norfolk, Edith Cavell trained as a nurse in London and went on to work in several hospitals across Britain. In 1907, she took up the post of nursing director at the Berkendael Medical Institute in the Belgian capital of Brussels.

When the institute became a Red Cross hospital after the outbreak of war in August 1914, Cavell began to help Allied soldiers escape to the neutral Netherlands. In August 1915, after helping some 200 Allied soldiers, her actions were discovered by the Germans and she was arrested, tried, and sentenced to death. An international outcry and pleas for clemency went unheeded, and Cavell was executed by firing squad on 12 October 1915.

The night before her execution, Cavell declared: "Patriotism is not enough. I must have no hatred or bitterness for anyone." Her death was widely condemned, and she became a symbol of the bravery and sacrifice of Allied nurses during the war, and an important element of anti-German propaganda.

THE PRICE WAS A GENERATION OF FRENCHMEN

THE BATTLE OF THE FRONTIERS (7–24 AUGUST 1914)

IN CONTEXT

FOCUS
France at war

BEFORE
1871 The Treaty of Frankfurt confirms the German annexation of parts of French-held Alsace and Lorraine.

1911 General Joseph Joffre is appointed head of the French Army, replacing the more defensively minded General Victor-Constant Michel.

4 August 1914 German troops cross into Belgium and Luxembourg, beginning the war on the Western Front.

AFTER
26 August 1914 General Joseph Gallieni takes charge of the defence of Paris against approaching German forces.

2 September 1914 The French government moves from Paris to Bordeaux.

9 September 1914 German armies begin to retreat from the outskirts of Paris.

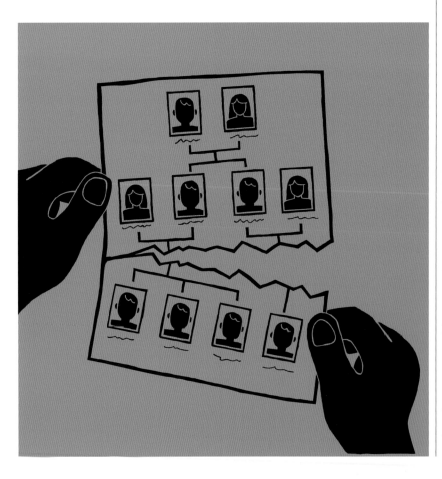

While the German army's main forces in August 1914 were enacting the first stage of the Schlieffen Plan by overrunning eastern and northern Belgium, the French army was implementing its own strategy, Plan XVII. Drawn up in 1913, this called for the mobilization and deployment of the main French forces to the eastern border with Germany.

The French commanders believed they would have numerical superiority over their opponents, who were fighting on two fronts, and could confidently plan to attack

See also: Planning for war 34–39 ▪ The invasion of Belgium 50–51 ▪ The Great Retreat 60–63 ▪ The First Battle of the Marne 64–69 ▪ Artillery 228–29

and overrun them. Some French soldiers chalked "*À Berlin*" ("To Berlin") on their troop trains, but this was never their generals' intention during these early battles. Instead, French commanders hoped to recover parts of Alsace and Lorraine lost to Germany in 1871 and keep the German forces busy until Russia's huge army was able to develop its full strength on the Eastern Front.

French shortsightedness

On the battlefield, French tactics called for all-out attacks as the only way to overcome the German army. Reconnaissance to discover the German positions and strength, and plans for heavy artillery fire to prepare for and support French attacks, were not deemed essential. The misguided belief within the French army was that massed troops charging with fixed bayonets would prove irresistible.

Recent wars, including the Russo-Japanese War (1904–05), had featured trenches and other

The French infantry uniform in 1914, with its dark-coloured tunic, trousers, and cap, made few concessions to battlefield camouflage. From spring 1915, uniforms changed to blue-grey.

fortifications, guarded by barbed wire and defended by machine guns. However, the French army largely disregarded these warfare developments and had little of the relevant equipment, weapons, or training. German troops had three times as many machine guns and were taught to dig in to defend a new position. Their rifles were also more accurate and faster to reload.

The French troops were easy targets, too, wearing the same kind of colourful uniforms as they had a hundred years before, while officers also donned white gloves and brandished swords. In contrast, German soldiers wore uniforms of an inconspicuous grey-green, known as *Feldgrau* (field grey).

Push and retreat

French mobilization started on 2 August 1914 and was swift and efficient, aided by an extensive railway network. Within days, hundreds of thousands of troops, »

[The French army] no longer knows any other law than the offensive.
General Joseph Joffre

Alsace and Lorraine

In 1914, many French people wanted revenge for what they saw as their humiliating defeat in the Franco-Prussian War (1870–71) and especially for the resulting loss of part of Lorraine and most of Alsace – historical regions of eastern France. These areas had long been part of France, but most of the inhabitants spoke dialects of German as their first language.

As the only place where Germany and France shared a border, the region was destined to be a focus for military action in the event of war. Both sides had built fortifications here before 1914. Germany regarded it as an eastern buffer zone, where French attacks could be held off while the Schlieffen Plan was put into action further west. France wished to regain lost territory and aimed to restore the "natural frontier" on the River Rhine. It also coveted the region's rich iron ore reserves and associated heavy industry.

French troops take up their firing positions in August 1914 – across Alsace fields that had been German territory since 1871.

The "Black Butchers"

Most French artillery batteries in 1914 were equipped with 75 mm (3 in) calibre guns. These had been designed for use against opposing troops manoeuvring in the open – the sort of battle that French strategists envisaged in a war against Germany.

French soldiers knew the gun as the *soixante-quinze* ("seventy-five"). German troops called it the "Black Butcher", inspired by the puff of black smoke given off when its anti-personnel shrapnel shells exploded above their heads, each one blasting 290 lead balls (the shrapnel) at the area below.

The guns, capable of firing 15 rounds per minute, proved very effective against German attacks in the early months of the war but of limited value in other aspects of combat. Their small shells had little explosive power to smash trenches and other fortifications, and in rough terrain, such as the Ardennes, their flat-trajectory fire could not strike the hidden far side of enemy-held hills.

French soldiers fire a 75 mm gun on the Western Front in 1914. To the left, a two-wheel cart, known as the limber, holds the artillery shells.

German infantry troops advance through fields of flowers towards French positions during the Battle of the Frontiers, in August 1914.

carried on thousands of trains, were at the German Alsace border. On 7 August, part of the First Army attacked the Alsace line near the Swiss border. French troops reached the town of Mulhouse on 8 August, but were driven out the next day and by 11 August had retreated to where they started. French chief of staff General Joseph Joffre dismissed the corps commander, General Louis Bonneau – the fate of many senior officers in the following weeks – and now concentrated on a broad offensive, planned for 14 August in Lorraine and the Ardennes forest of southern Belgium.

Battles of Lorraine

In the first stage of Joffre's main attacks, units of the First and Second armies advanced across the Lorraine frontier towards the towns of Morhange and Sarreburg. They pushed forwards for four days, not realizing that the German Sixth and Seventh armies, led by Crown Prince Rupprecht of Bavaria, were luring them into a long-planned trap, and weakening them as they did so with their longer-range artillery guns. The idea was that the more troops the French committed in this sector the fewer would oppose the main German drive through Belgium.

Behind the scenes, the German commanders urgently sought permission to change plan and to counterattack, believing that this would help the main German advance in Belgium. After several days of argument, German chief of general staff Helmuth von Moltke agreed to a counteroffensive.

At first, the German attack prospered, smashing into the French front line on 20 August. General Ferdinand Foch, a corps commander in the French Second Army, and a strong supporter of attacking tactics, had recklessly sent his units too far ahead into an exposed position. The now disorganized French line was thrown into retreat and confusion.

In some areas, the retreat turned into a headlong flight, with the French pushed back into their own territory. By 23 August, the French armies were defending a new front line along the River Meurthe, mainly in an area south of the city of Nancy known as the Trouée de Charmes. Although, thanks to successful French resistance, the front line in this sector would remain more or less unchanged until the final weeks of the war, France's initial attacking plans on its eastern borders had certainly been defeated.

Ardennes and final retreat

While battle was raging in Lorraine, other French attacks and similar bloody defeats took place further north, in the dense woodlands of the Ardennes, on the borders of France, Belgium, Luxembourg, and Germany. Joffre had ordered this advance to begin on 20 August. Taking part were the French Third and Fourth armies – 350,000 men in all – who expected both to surprise and outnumber their opponents. However, German reconnaissance aircraft had spotted the French advance and alerted the German Fourth and Fifth armies already pushing into Belgium. The message from French army headquarters – relying for reconnaissance on its cavalry – was that "no serious opposition need be anticipated".

The climax came on 22 August, a day that began in the Ardennes with dense fog, hiding the soldiers of each side from their opponents.

Some French units launched repeated charges against dug-in German positions they could hardly see, and were slaughtered by the firepower of the German artillery and machine guns. Some 27,000 French soldiers are believed to have died on that one day – the bloodiest in French military history. The victors were the German Fourth and Fifth armies, the latter commanded by Crown Prince Wilhelm – heir to the German throne – who reported the capture of thousands of French prisoners.

The concluding episode in the series of frontier battles took place further west into Belgium. Here, the German Second and Third armies were surging south across the River Sambre to the area around the city of Charleroi, opposed by the French Fifth Army, commanded by General Charles Lanrezac. These battles followed the general pattern of those to the east. French soldiers attacked on 22 August but failed to make headway, and German forces pushed them back the next day. To the west of Charleroi, Lanrezac's army was supported by the newly arrived British

Expeditionary Force (BEF), which fought a delaying action at Mons before retreating on 24 August.

End of the French offensive

With all the French armies now well beaten and in retreat, General Joffre recognized the obvious – that the French offensive laid out in Plan XVII had failed. On 25 August, he issued an order for the Allied armies to regroup to the south, with some units redeployed from Alsace and Lorraine to strengthen the line further west, where it was clear the enemy threat was most serious. Meanwhile, two German armies were now tied up on the Alsace and Lorraine borders – weakening the forces meant to be sweeping through Belgium. The scene was set for the next phases of the war on the Western Front – Allied retreat and counterattack, followed by attritional stalemate. ■

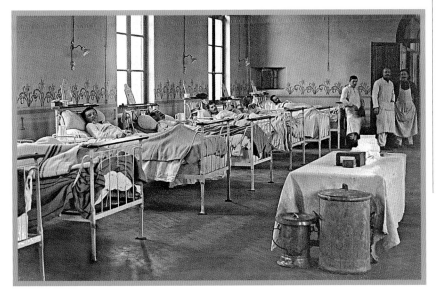

Wounded soldiers line the "Germans' room" at a military hospital in Nancy, the historic capital of Lorraine. French forces held the city against further German attack in September 1914.

THE LAMPS ARE GOING OUT ALL OVER EUROPE
THE BRITISH ARRIVE (AUGUST 1914)

IN CONTEXT

FOCUS
Britain at war

BEFORE
1905 British and French army officers informally discuss military cooperation.

1908 In April, a new Territorial Force is created in Britain to boost the number of British army reservists.

29 July 1914 British army units are given notice of a "precautionary period", the first step before mobilization.

AFTER
1920 Conscription ends. It is reintroduced in Britain in 1939 at the outbreak of World War II.

1941 The National Service Act calls up single women aged 20 to 30 to fill the labour shortage created by male conscription.

1949 National Service, a form of peacetime conscription for men aged 17 to 21, comes into force. It continues until 1960.

At 11pm, on 4 August 1914, Britain declared war against Germany. The following day, mobilization orders were issued to the armed forces to prepare for war. Around 250,000 regulars (army professionals) and 200,000 reservists (army-trained civilians) were ordered to barracks. Weapons and kit were distributed to the troops, 120,000 horses were requisitioned from civilian owners, and railway routes were redirected to despatch units to the English Channel ports.

The first troops sent to France were members of the highly trained British Expeditionary Force (BEF), led by Field Marshal Sir John French, which began to leave for France on 9 August under the protection of the Royal Navy. The initial force was made up of one cavalry division and four of the BEF's six infantry divisions (another was sent later, and one was retained for home

The BEF's cavalry division arrives in Belgium before the Battle of Mons. The cavalry played a key role in locating the German First Army, enabling the BEF to take up its defensive positions.

See also: Public opinion 44–45 ▪ The Great Retreat 60–63 ▪ The Race to the Sea 70–71 ▪ The Somme 172–79 ▪ Replacing the fallen 198–99

Western Front forces in August 1914

At the outbreak of war, Germany and France each mobilized more than a million men to fight on the Western Front. Britain sent some 90,000 men (five initial BEF divisions, plus one sent later), while seven Belgian divisions added 120,000 troops.

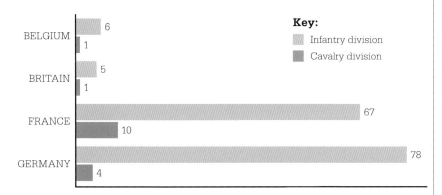

Key:	
░	Infantry division
▓	Cavalry division

BELGIUM 6, 1
BRITAIN 5, 1
FRANCE 67, 10
GERMANY 78, 4

Sir John French

Born in Kent, England, in 1852 to an Anglo-Irish family, John French joined the 19th Hussars at the age of 22. He served in several campaigns in Egypt, Sudan, and India and achieved distinction as a cavalry commander during the Second Boer War (1899–1902). His career went from strength to strength on his return to Britain: in 1912, he was appointed chief of the Imperial General Staff, and he was promoted to the rank of field marshal the following year.

In 1914, French was given command of the British Expeditionary Force (BEF). Its defeat at the Battle of Mons, subsequent retreat, and later devastating casualties appeared to unnerve him. He fell out with Joseph Joffre, the French commander-in-chief, and British secretary of state Lord Kitchener among others.

French was replaced in December 1915 and made commander-in-chief of the British home forces (1916–18). He was created a viscount in 1916 and became 1st earl of Ypres in 1921, when he retired from the army. In 1923, he was appointed captain of Deal Castle, where he died in 1925.

defence). The troops were divided into two corps – I Corps commanded by Lieutenant General Sir Douglas Haig, and II Corps under General Sir Horace Smith-Dorrien. Assembling around Maubeuge, a town near the Belgian border, the BEF advanced north into Belgium.

First encounter at Mons

The BEF took up its position on the left of the French Fifth Army, which placed the British troops in the path of the German First Army, whose greater numbers were not initially known. On 21 August, after being told that the French Fifth Army was under heavy attack from the German Second and Third armies, Field Marshal French agreed to hold a defensive line along the Mons-Condé canal to protect the otherwise exposed left flank of the Fifth Army.

On the morning of 23 August, the British came under German artillery fire from the First Army,

commanded by General Alexander von Kluck. The brunt of the German attack would be directed at the two divisions of General Smith-Dorrien's II Corps. An initial German assault was repulsed by accurate British rifle and machine-gun fire (the BEF was renowned for its rifle skills). However, a loop in the canal by the town of Mons left British defences vulnerable to attack, and the Germans exploited this weakness with increasingly accurate artillery and machine-gun fire. By mid-afternoon, as more German units arrived, the British forces realized that they would soon be outflanked. Smith-Dorrien ordered a withdrawal to a safer position a short distance to the south.

The retreat begins

Most British units retired in good order, and by nightfall they had successfully disengaged from the battle. Meanwhile, Field Marshal French discovered that the French »

Fifth Army had withdrawn, leaving both flanks of the BEF dangerously exposed. The British commander had no alternative but to order a general retreat.

Mons was the first World War I engagement for British troops and part of a larger series of battles along the Franco-Belgian frontier. The BEF suffered what would later seem modest losses – just over 1,600 killed, wounded, or missing – while German casualties were close to 5,000.

For the next two weeks, the BEF retreated through northern France, fighting a series of rearguard actions, including the Battle of Le Cateau on 26 August. There, the Germans attacked Smith-Dorrien's exhausted II Corps, which fought

Scores of British men queue outside the Whitehall Recruiting Office in London, some of the many who rushed to join up at the start of World War I.

We were stirred … by the atrocities, or the alleged atrocities, when the Germans invaded Belgium and France.
Private F.B. Vaughan
12th Battalion, Yorks and Lancs

it out alone as Haig's I Corps had retreated faster and further inland. This was a heavy artillery battle, with the Germans firing effectively from concealed positions, almost causing the collapse of II Corps' right and left flank before the arrival of French cavalry troops allowed

the British corps to slip away. The BEF retreat continued until French and reinforced British forces were redeployed in early September as part of the First Battle of the Marne.

A much smaller army
In 1914, Britain was the only major European power that did not have conscription. Traditionally, entry into the British Army was voluntary, and this continued to be the case when the fighting began. However, army numbers had fallen before the war, and intensive recruitment was needed to encourage more men to sign up. Many believed the fighting would be over in months. However, Lord Kitchener, secretary of state for war and a veteran of colonial conflicts in South Africa and Sudan, predicted it would last for at least three years and could only be won by overwhelming manpower. He instigated a mass recruitment campaign, calling initially for

Women at war

In most of the combatant nations, women were not allowed to fight. This frustrated British women who wanted to play an active role in supporting the conflict. Some – especially those of the middle- and upper-classes – joined paramilitary organizations, such as the First Aid Nursing Yeomanry (FANY), which had been formed in 1907. They worked on the front line, driving ambulances, evacuating wounded men, and setting up and running first-aid centres.

Other women joined the Voluntary Aid Detachment (VAD), a military nursing organization. As early as 1914, women also set up their own voluntary female paramilitary organizations, such as the Home Service Corps. Probably the best known of these was the Women's Volunteer Reserve (WVR). Its members ran canteens for soldiers, transported those who were injured, provided first aid, and drove cars and motorcycles. To the annoyance of the War Office, they wore khaki uniforms, learned to parade and drill, and formed local battalions.

Members of the British Women's Volunteer Reserve (WVR) practise a fire drill and emergency evacuation of patients from a hospital.

100,000 men, then another 100,000, to create huge, well-trained army units. They became known as Kitchener's Armies.

Enthusiastic recruits

Fired up by patriotism, a sense of duty, and excitement, or simply the desire to escape poverty, thousands of men responded to Kitchener's call. By the end of September 1914, more than 750,000 men had enlisted, and by January 1915 the number had reached 1 million. The response was so overwhelming that the War Office struggled to equip, house, and train recruits. Some 2.5 million men eventually volunteered to fight.

Posters played a significant role in recruitment. Some featured Kitchener himself, while others carried images of women and children urging their men to defend Britain. By April 1915, there were 90 different designs, and more than 2.5 million posters were displayed around the country.

Lord Kitchener "Wants You", one of the best known images of World War I, first appeared in September 1914 on a poster designed by Alfred Leete.

The poster campaign, backed up by music-hall stars such as Vesta Tilley (dubbed "Britain's best recruiting sergeant"), encouraged men to enlist with friends or workmates so they could serve together in so-called Pals' Battalions. Men from the same towns and villages volunteered together, as did footballers, artists, stockbrokers, and postal workers. The 23rd (Service) Battalion – a football battalion – included Walter Tull, who had played for Tottenham Hotspur. Thought to be the first

Black officer to lead British combat troops into battle, he was killed in action in March 1918. The shocking losses suffered by Pals' Battalions, some of which were virtually wiped out on the first day of the Battle of the Somme in 1916, so devastated local communities that the system was eventually dropped.

Compelled to enlist

As the British death toll mounted on the Western Front, the number of volunteers dropped sharply. More were needed and conscription was discussed but faced parliamentary opposition. In October 1915, the government introduced the Derby Scheme, inviting every eligible male to enlist immediately or promise to sign up later if required.

The new scheme still failed to raise enough recruits to join the war. On 27 January 1916, the Military Service Act was passed, imposing conscription on single men aged between 18 and 41. In May, the Act was extended to married men. The medically unfit, essential industrial workers, teachers, farmers, and clergymen were exempted, while conscientious objectors were given civilian and non-fighting roles. ∎

HOPELESS RESIGNATION TO UTTER FATIGUE

THE GREAT RETREAT (24 AUGUST–5 SEPTEMBER 1914)

IN CONTEXT

FOCUS
Tactical withdrawal

BEFORE
401 BCE After the Battle of Cunaxa, 10,000 Greek fighters withdraw across more than 5,000 km (3,100 miles) of enemy territory. The March of the Ten Thousand becomes the archetypal fighting retreat.

14–18 August 1914 After the capture of Liège by invading German troops, Belgian forces withdraw north to Antwerp.

AFTER
November 1915 More than 100,000 soldiers and civilians escape a German-led army in the Great Serbian Retreat.

March 1917 As Allied troops prepare the Nivelle Offensive on the Western Front, German forces withdraw from their forward positions to the newly completed Hindenburg Line.

When Europe went to war in August 1914, many expected that attack and retreat – the two-beat rhythm of battle – would characterize the campaigns. After a series of setbacks on the Belgium–France border, however, the Allies began an extensive withdrawal covering more than 250 km (160 miles). This began to foster a belief that the war would be brief, with German forces soon occupying Paris.

It was Allied commander-in-chief General Joseph Joffre who took the decision to order a huge retreat across the entire fighting front on 24 August 1914. Whatever his reluctance at such an early

See also: Planning for war 34–39 ▪ The Battle of the Frontiers 52–55 ▪ The British arrive 56–59 ▪ The First Battle of the Marne 64–69 ▪ The Race to the Sea 70–71 ▪ Russia retreats 138–39 ▪ The Second Battle of the Marne 270–73

Helmuth von Moltke

Although he was already 66 years old when war broke out in 1914, chief of the German general staff Helmuth von Moltke would never shake the nickname "Moltke the Younger" to distinguish him from his uncle and namesake "Moltke the Elder", a brilliant Prussian soldier and strategist. Born in the Grand Duchy of Mecklenburg in 1848, "the Younger" was cited for bravery in the Franco-Prussian War (1870–71), and in 1880 he was promoted to the German general staff. He was appointed personal adjutant (administrator) to its chief, his uncle, before he was 35.

By 1891, Moltke had become aide-de-camp (chief assistant) to Kaiser Wilhelm II, ensuring he was ideally placed to succeed Alfred von Schlieffen as chief of the general staff when he retired in 1906.

Inheriting Schlieffen's plan for winning a future war on two fronts – Russia to the east and France to the west – Moltke's task was to adapt it as required. His errors of judgement in the opening weeks of World War I cost him his position as chief of staff. Replaced in September 1914, he died two years later.

stage of the war, Joffre had no other choice. After defeat at the Battle of the Frontiers, his army's left wing was in danger of being outflanked, forcing him to fall back on his reserve units.

The long tramp south

Known as the Great Retreat, the two-week-long withdrawal of three French armies and the British Expeditionary Force (BEF), closely pursued by two German armies, involved hundreds of thousands of troops. The men were forced to march south in the blazing August heat, covering up to 50 km (31 miles) a day on a front 193 km (120 miles) wide in places. Woollen overcoats and heavy packs were discarded, cluttering roads already jammed with wagons and artillery pieces. Civilians, too, were fleeing and travelling with any furniture

and keepsakes they had managed to retrieve, having heard rumours of the atrocities German forces had committed in Belgium.

Small delaying rearguard actions were fought across the countryside. Yet by 27 August, the main German advance, which had swept across most of Belgium, was well into northern France. The region was threaded with rivers, large and small, flowing from east to west,

which hampered the progress of both sides. French sappers also destroyed every bridge they crossed in a bid to slow their opponents' advance, but German engineers simply deployed pontoons, and the close pursuit continued.

The Allied retreat was no rout, however, as chief of the German general staff Helmuth von Moltke soon realized. Despite the pace and the heat – horses were soon »

British troops are depicted fighting a rearguard action against German forces in the French town of Landrécies on 25 August 1914, during their retreat after the Battle of Mons.

dropping in the wagon tracks – the withdrawal was remarkably well-handled. The Allies gave up few prisoners and seldom abandoned equipment. Meanwhile, German supply and communication lines grew longer with each passing day.

The French Fifth Army, under the command of General Charles Lanrezac, launched counterattacks on 29 and 30 August at Saint-Quentin and nearby Guise. They blunted the momentum of the German troops but could not stop their advance. Joffre was forced to withdraw his forces to the Marne, a northern tributary of the Seine, flowing through the countryside east of Paris. From there, he decided that the Allies would regroup and prepare to defend the French capital. For some battalions, the Great Retreat had already covered nearly 240 km (150 miles).

General versus general

By now, there were also tensions between the various commands. In early September, Joffre sacked Lanrezac, accusing the general of overcautiousness bordering on insubordination. Days before the Great Retreat, Lanrezac – reluctant to commit his encircled troops to certain death – had angered Joffre by rejecting instructions to attack. To replace Lanrezac as commander of the Fifth Army, Joffre appointed General Louis Franchet d'Espèrey, who would soon play a key role in the great battle taking shape on the banks of the Marne.

Lanrezac's poor relationship with BEF commander Field Marshal Sir John French had also troubled Joffre, who feared the growing rift between the British and French commanders. While friction was unavoidable on a joint retreat in the heat and along the overcrowded roads, Joffre required Allied unity. After the Battle of Le Cateau, a rearguard action fought by the BEF on 26 August, Sir John had informed Joffre's headquarters that the British losses in that clash would cause only "bitterness and regret" in Britain.

A few days later, when the French Fifth Army launched the counterattacks at Saint-Quentin and Guise, Sir John kept the BEF out of the fighting, pushing his men southwards and merely sparring with pursuing German cavalry. Sir John warned Joffre that the BEF

> This awful exodus includes every kind of vehicle imaginable, overloaded with furniture, linen, children, and old people. Able-bodied people follow on foot …
> **Mme Brunehant**
> **resident of the Aisne region in France**

needed to pull out of the line to rest and refit south of the River Seine, if not actually retreat to the ports of the Channel coast. That provoked impassioned protests not only from Allied commander-in-chief Joffre but also from French president, Raymond Poincaré. It also brought British secretary of state for war, Lord Kitchener, to Paris. There, he met Sir John, who protested that his actions were in accord with earlier instructions to avoid excessive casualties without

A 1914 illustration in *The Graphic*, a British newspaper, depicts Parisians crowding onto a train at the Gare du Nord in a bid to escape to Britain.

Panic in Paris

In 1914, as late August turned to September, panicked civilians began to stream out of Paris. A mood of optimism at the start of the war had turned to fear as the battlefront crept closer to Paris and a German plane dropped the first bombs on the capital. By 2 September, when the French government completed its move to Bordeaux, taking the country's gold reserves, the numbers of refugees had soared. Special trains were scheduled to carry them away from the city.

The motivations to flee were varied. Germany appeared to be on the verge of victory, and older residents had not forgotten the 1870–71 Franco-Prussian War, when Paris was shelled during a bitter four-month siege that forced people to feed on rats and dogs. Belgian refugees, newly arrived in Paris, had also reported that German authorities would execute the innocent as readily as the guilty in response to any hostile actions directed against their forces. As a result, at least half a million Parisians fled the city.

Defensive trenches were built across Paris streets in September 1914 in response to the threat of advancing German armies. The scene here is at Porte Maillot in the west of the city.

explicit government authority and that his depleted ranks remained too weak to repulse a German attack. Kitchener ordered the BEF to return to the line and fight in conjunction with Joffre's divisions.

Meanwhile, the German high command became overconfident. On 30 August, Moltke and his German general staff followed the kaiser into occupied Luxembourg, and spent several days establishing new quarters in the Hôtel Staar. Not only was Moltke too far away from the Allies to assess the action and clinch victory, but he was also dependent on wireless transmission for intelligence, which was easily jammed by a powerful transmitter on the Eiffel Tower in Paris.

Defence and stretched lines

The armies were crawling ever closer to Paris, which braced itself for battle, surrounded by a ring of fortifications. As the national government prepared to relocate to Bordeaux, the defence of the city was entrusted to Joseph Gallieni, a 65-year-old retired general who had once been Joffre's commander.

As military governor of Paris, Gallieni prepared for a siege, emplacing nearly 3,000 pieces of artillery, cutting down trees, and making plans to demolish buildings to improve his gunners' lines of sight. He was even prepared to sacrifice the Eiffel Tower, despite its importance as a wireless transmitter. Gallieni also needed a garrison, so Joffre lent him the Sixth Army, newly formed around Amiens under the command of General Michel-Joseph Maunoury.

Under Gallieni's direct command, the Sixth Army would be styled the "Armies of Paris".

Maunoury's men were exhausted after a trek of some 150 km (93 miles) back from Amiens, but the Great Retreat had also taken its toll on the pursuing German troops. By late August, their marching infantry had outstripped their horse-drawn supply vehicles, causing food and ammunition shortages. Between 31 August and 2 September, which

… the greatest strain … worse than any physical discomfort or even hunger was the gut-wrenching fatigue. Pain could be endured, food scrounged, but the desire for rest was never-ending.
Ben Clouting
4th Dragoon Guards

would prove to be a critical period, Moltke and his German general staff in Luxembourg were often out of touch with their front-line divisions. At this point, General Karl von Bülow's German Second Army, approaching Paris from the north, was unexpectedly slowed by French rearguard attacks. As a result, General Alexander von Kluck, commander of the German First Army far to the west of Bülow, abandoned his intention to envelop Paris, as set out in the Schlieffen Plan, in favour of pushing east of the French capital to help the Second Army. On 2 September, Moltke approved the revised plan.

Allied aircraft spotted both the shift and the considerable gap opening up between the two oncoming German armies. The Great Retreat had not been an intentional feint, designed to draw an opponent into a trap on ground of the Allies' choosing. However, the position of the German armies as they moved into the valley of the Marne would give Joffre's armies the opportunity to launch an effective counteroffensive at the First Battle of the Marne. ■

ALL THAT MEN CAN DO, OUR FELLOWS WILL DO

THE FIRST BATTLE OF THE MARNE (1914)

IN CONTEXT

FOCUS
Decisive battle

BEFORE
1815 Just before Napoleon's final defeat at Waterloo, the Congress of Vienna agrees new political frontiers to redistribute power in Europe.

1871 At the end of the Franco-Prussian War, France cedes territory in Alsace and Lorraine to the new German Empire.

1905 The Schlieffen Plan envisages a swift German victory in Belgium, France, and Luxembourg before Russia is tackled in the east.

AFTER
1918 At the Second Battle of the Marne, Allied troops repel Germany's last major offensive. Further Allied victories bring World War I to an end.

1940 After the violent German blitzkrieg, France submits to German rule in World War II.

The Marne then was not a 'miracle' … but a brilliant advantage, rapidly snatched from the enemy's errors.
C.R.M.F. Cruttwell
A History of the Great War,
1934

German armies pursue retreating French and British troops into France and **advance on Paris**.

French general Joseph Joffre **recalls French troops** from the Alsace and Lorraine offensive to form a **new French Sixth Army** to defend Paris.

Having sent 11 divisions elsewhere, General Helmuth von Moltke **abandons the Schlieffen Plan to encircle the city**.

The **German positions to the north and east** of Paris leave them **vulnerable to attack** from the French and other Allied troops.

A strategic victory for the Allied forces dashes German hopes of a swift victory in the west.

Ever since Field Marshal Alfred von Schlieffen conceived his strategy in 1905 for winning a two-front war in Europe, German leaders had been planning how they could defeat rival powers to the west and east. The First Battle of the Marne, on the Western Front in September 1914, was a key test of their ability to carry out the strategy's central idea of quickly subduing France before attacking Russia. The German army's failure to achieve this objective would set the remorseless course of the war.

A change of tactics

By the end of August 1914, German armies had swept through Belgium and northern France, sending their Anglo-French opponents on a gruelling 240-km (150-mile) retreat south. Germany was poised to clinch a definitive victory. On 2 September, however, from headquarters in the Hôtel Staar, Luxembourg, Helmuth von Moltke, chief of the German general staff, issued a directive changing the order of battle.

The new directive abandoned the modified Schlieffen Plan, which had called for a vast encirclement of Paris. Moltke lacked the forces to carry this out after releasing seven divisions to reinforce the troops in Belgium and four more to strengthen the Eastern Front against Russia. Instead, he redirected his First and Second armies to the east of Paris to attack Allied forces drawing up along the Marne river. The new plan, however, left a gap between the two German armies that French commander-in-chief Joseph Joffre would quickly seek to exploit.

See also: The Battle of the Frontiers 52–55 ▪ The Great Retreat 60–63 ▪ The Race to the Sea 70–71 ▪ The First Battle of Ypres 72–73 ▪ Trenches take over 74–77 ▪ The Second Battle of Ypres 110–15 ▪ The Second Battle of the Marne 270–73

French troops load their 75 mm (3 in) field gun during the battle. The quick-firing weapon was used to devastating effect against German infantry.

The same day – 2 September – the French government evacuated Paris for Bordeaux, leaving the defence of the capital in the hands of its newly appointed military governor, 65-year-old retired general Joseph Gallieni. For his garrison, he was given the newly raised French Sixth Army under the command of General Michel-Joseph Maunoury.

Allied counterattack

In the revised German plan, General Karl von Bülow's Second Army, advancing from the north, was to be the main strike force. However, the position of General Alexander von Kluck's First Army – further west and closer to northeast Paris – was somewhat vulnerable as its right flank was open to a possible assault from the French Sixth Army – as the Allied high command noted on 3 September. To Kluck's dismay, Moltke downplayed the danger.

By this stage, the German columns were tiring after the long pursuit of Allied troops retreating back into France. As straggling increased, the gap between the two German forces presented an opportunity for the long-awaited Allied counterattack.

The arena of battle would be the 260-km (160-mile) stretch of countryside between Paris and the city of Verdun in the east. Joffre's divisions were south of the River Marne, which flows westwards into the Seine, just east of Paris. The German armies were beginning to cross the Marne. After much argument, the Allied leaders agreed a plan. Their divisions would attack and defeat the German First and Second armies individually, before »

Joseph Joffre

Born in Rivesaltes, southwest France in 1852, Joseph Jacques Césaire Joffre trained as a military engineer and graduated from the École polytechnique in Paris in 1870. After serving at the siege of Paris in the Franco-Prussian War (1870–71), he worked in French colonies in the Far East and Africa. He was promoted to major in Mali, then to brigadier-general under Joseph Gallieni in Madagascar.

In 1911, Joffre was appointed chief of staff of the French army – despite his lack of experience in such a role. After heavy French losses in August 1914, the First Battle of the Marne was an important success. He was made commander-in-chief of the French armies in 1915 but struggled to break the deadlock on the Western Front. On 26 December 1916, Joffre resigned and was awarded the title Marshal of France and given an advisory role. Sent to the US in 1917 as a military consultant, he was well received and later welcomed the US troops to France. Joffre received many honours and undertook various diplomatic missions after the war. He died in Paris in 1931.

> Every effort must be made
> to attack and drive back the
> enemy. Troops which can
> no longer advance must
> at all costs keep the ground
> they have won, and die
> rather than fall back.
> **General Joseph Joffre**
> General Order No. 6, 1914

they could join forces, while additional French troops held the eastern frontier near Verdun.

Using Allied transportation lines and the efficient French railway system, Joffre had amassed over a million soldiers, while the opposing Germans numbered only 750,000, so the plan had an excellent chance of success. However, Joffre had to beg for assistance from the overly cautious Sir John French, head of the British Expeditionary Force (BEF), which had lost more than 14,000 men – nearly a tenth of its landing force – the previous month.

The battle begins

At 8:30pm on 5 September, General Gallieni launched the offensive, ordering Maunoury's Paris-based Sixth Army to advance. In a thunder of artillery, it attacked Kluck's First Army near the Ourcq river, some 60 km (37 miles) northeast of Paris. At Verdun, much further east, artillery from the German Lorraine-based armies was challenging French forces. A few hours later, at 10pm, Joffre ordered a general Allied offensive for the following day.

By this time, Kluck had started to turn around the German First Army, recrossing the Marne to face the French Sixth Army on the northern side of the river. The move increased the gap in the converging German lines, which would soon be 48 km (30 miles) wide. On 8 September, the French Fifth Army, under the new command of General Louis Franchet d'Espèrey, would launch itself at Bülow's Second Army, forcing it to retreat north across the Marne river the next day. The Fifth Army, followed by the BEF, then moved into the widening gap.

Meanwhile, the French Sixth Army, still battling with the German First Army, had met such stiff resistance that Maunoury, its commander, called for help from Gallieni in Paris. The old general requisitioned nearly 1,000 vehicles, including some 600 taxicabs,

marshalling them at the Hôtel des Invalides. Under cover of darkness, the improvised transport corps, with only their rear lamps lit, ferried reinforcements to Maunoury. After this – the first-ever transfer of troops by motor vehicle – the Sixth Army withstood each subsequent German assault.

A sprawling conflict

The Battle of the Marne, like most of the war's major clashes, was a wide-ranging offensive, fought over a vast area of rolling, river-laced, largely open country dotted with farms and villages – all overrun by the week's fighting. It was a battle of movement, characterized by the slow retreat of the German First and Second armies as they backpedalled north, unable to coordinate satisfactorily because of the expanding gap between

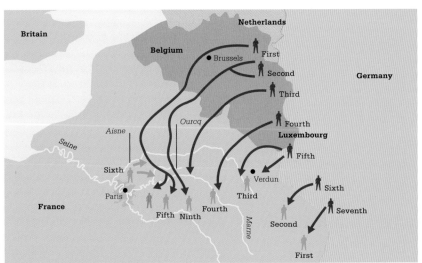

German armies had advanced to the Marne river in northern France in pursuit of retreating Allied forces. On 5 September, the French Sixth Army hit back. In five days of fighting, the reinforced French armies and the BEF would push the German troops back over the Aisne river to a new front line.

Key:

- Allies
- Central Powers
- German-occupied territory
- Neutral territory
- → German advance
- → French counterattack
- German forces
- French forces
- British Expeditionary Force (BEF)

Exhausted French soldiers – their vehicles and equipment scattered around them – seize some rest in woodland during a lull in the fighting at the First Battle of the Marne.

them. Driving that division were the northward thrusts of the BEF and the French Fifth Army, expertly led by General d'Espèrey.

For much of the battle, Moltke and the German commanders were not in touch. On 8 September, the third day of fighting, Moltke had finally sent his intelligence officer Richard Hentsch to investigate rumours of impending defeat. After meeting Bülow and Kluck's chief of staff, Hentsch ordered both armies to retreat more than 32 km (20 miles) north to behind the Aisne river. The German Supreme Army Command reaffirmed the general retreat on 10 September. Soon all the German armies, including those around Verdun, were withdrawing.

The aftermath

Scooping up German stragglers and abandoned equipment along the way, the Allied armies pursued their battered enemy. The French alone took nearly 12,000 prisoners, 30 field guns, and 100 machine guns. North of the Aisne river, German military engineers selected commanding positions and began to entrench. German forces would remain there for the next four years.

By this time, Moltke was unwell and depressed. On 14 September, Kaiser Wilhelm II appointed Erich von Falkenhayn to succeed him as chief of the German general staff. A war of entrenchment and attrition began, only ending a few months after the Allies repelled a last major German offensive in July 1918 – also between the Marne and the Aisne.

The First Battle of the Marne was an Allied triumph – largely due to Joffre's leadership – but resulted in over 480,000 casualties. More than 67,000 German, 80,000 French and some 7,000 BEF soldiers are thought to have died in the battle. In the melee, some had no formal burial. Near the Marne, a monument recalls 3,740 BEF members who died with no known grave between late August and early October 1914. ∎

Railways

In 1914, Europe's railways proved essential for mobilizing vast numbers of conscripts. Thanks to its superbly efficient network, Germany had quickly amassed 462,000 troops on the French frontier, outstripping France's 270,000-strong army. Four major, roughly parallel east-west lines crossed Germany, facilitating the movement of troops and goods from the Rhine to the Russian border. Russia, despite its huge area, had a sparse rail network and had also stripped out railway infrastructure from most of its border areas, hoping to delay a German invasion; in the event, this hampered its own offensives.

For its supplies to the trench-bound Western Front, Germany soon had the added advantage of a four-track railway from Lille to Koblenz that mirrored the arc of its trench system. France also had a sophisticated, efficient railway system, which, unlike Germany's, was centred on one city – Paris. General Gallieni used this network to quickly assemble a new army – the Sixth – which played a prominent role in the Battle of the Marne victory.

Allied soldiers ride on a small ammunition train carrying supplies to the Western Front. The railways played a key role during World War I.

THE LAST DITCH IN BELGIUM

THE RACE TO THE SEA (SEPTEMBER–OCTOBER 1914)

IN CONTEXT

FOCUS
Flanking manoeuvres

BEFORE
1905 Alfred von Schlieffen, chief of the German general staff, proposes a plan to rapidly defeat France in the event of war by outflanking and enveloping its forces.

4 August 1914 Germany attempts to avoid a head-on clash with French forces by invading from Belgium, but Belgian resistance is much greater than expected.

5 September 1914 The French Sixth Army attacks the right flank of the advancing German First Army, launching the First Battle of the Marne.

AFTER
1 September 1939 At the start of World War II, German armies sweep into Poland from the north, south, and west – outnumbering and outflanking the Polish forces.

O nce Allied forces had ended their Great Retreat and halted the German advance at the First Battle of the Marne in early September 1914, a two-month running fight between the Allied and German armies followed. This "swoop and counter-swoop", as Winston Churchill described it, became a race north to control the Channel ports of northern France and Belgium. At its end, the fighting would result in a stalemate, and entrenchment would prevent further flanking manoeuvres on the Western Front.

German troops stand ready in a trench overlooking the Aisne river, a front line that remained contested until the last few weeks of the war.

First Battle of the Aisne

On 12 September, immediately after the Marne victory, the British and French forces pursued their German opponents north to the new battlefront – the Aisne river. Pressing his advantage, Allied commander-in-chief Joseph Joffre hurled his armies uphill against the German entrenchments on the heights beyond the river.

After two fruitless weeks, however, fierce fighting that again produced thousands of casualties

See also: The Battle of the Frontiers 52–55 ▪ The Great Retreat 60–63 ▪ The First Battle of the Marne 64–69 ▪ The First Battle of Ypres 72–73 ▪ Trenches take over 74–77 ▪ The Somme 172–79 ▪ The Battle of Amiens 274–77

Belgian soliders ride in an armoured car, adapted from a Belgian-made Minerva motor car, on a West Flanders street in 1914.

Armoured cars

Among the forces defending Antwerp and the Channel ports was the British Royal Naval Air Service (RNAS), which possessed a squadron of armoured cars. Although intended to protect communications or find downed pilots, the vehicles so appealed to First Lord of the Admiralty Winston Churchill that he formed the Royal Naval Armoured Car Division. Lanchester and Rolls-Royce cars were stripped of their coachwork, armoured, and fitted with a turret and machine gun.

During World War I, every combatant nation adapted cars for war. The Belgians first used their Minerva armoured cars in August 1914. By September, Canada had its own Automobile Machine Gun Brigade. Generally used for reconnaissance work, armoured cars were rarely taken offroad, to avoid them getting stalled in streams or stuck in mud. The need for vehicles that could travel over a shell-torn battlefield gave birth to the prototype tank. Tanks were first used by British troops at the Battle of the Somme in 1916.

lapsed into a lull. As both sides dug in, frontal attacks became impossible. What followed was a series of outflanking attempts, as each army tried in turn to attack the other from the side – generally the weakest point in a battle line. Joffre decided to outflank the right wing of the opposing German forces, deftly moving one of his armies from his eastern flank well to the west, passing it south by road and rail behind his front. The new chief of the German general staff, Erich von Falkenhayn, mirrored the French move and threatened to outflank it in turn, as the frenzied campaign of swoop and counter-swoop began.

North to the sea

Each side's attempts to outflank its opponent pushed the battlefront northwards, towards the coast and the Channel ports. Falkenhayn's ultimate goal was to secure the coastline and ports, cutting off reinforcements and supplies to the British Expeditionary Force (BEF). Aware of this objective, the French forces and the BEF were equally

intent on defending the coastline. The BEF was moved from the Aisne front to Picardy, to a position from which it might outflank the oncoming Germans – only to find its own flank attacked and nearly repelled by German cavalry.

Battle of the Ypres

On 10 October, Antwerp fell to besieging German forces, some of whom were sent northwest towards the Channel ports. Ostend and Zeebrugge fell on 15 October as the Germans pressed on towards Dunkirk. The Belgian army, led by King Albert I, withdrew behind the Yser river to a front that stretched 35 km (22 miles) from Nieuport on the coast south to Zuydschoote, a village close to the city of Ypres.

German divisions battered the Belgian line. Those that pushed on through the coastal resorts were themselves shelled by British Royal Navy ships and repulsed. Largely thanks to British reinforcements, the Belgians held their line. As their ammunition supplies dwindled, however, their engineers blocked

22 culverts under a railway elevated above the lowlands. On the night of 28–29 October at high tide, the engineers opened the sluices at Nieuport. The North Sea poured through, creating an impassable artificial lake 16 km (10 miles) long and at least 5 km (3 miles) wide, which halted the German advance.

The Allies, skilfully coordinated by French general Ferdinand Foch, had saved the Channel ports, but would soon fight the First Battle of Ypres. There, flank attacks by both sides ended in stalemate, and prolonged trench warfare began. ▪

No retirement. Every man to the battle!
Ferdinand Foch
French general

THE MASSACRE OF THE INNOCENTS
THE FIRST BATTLE OF YPRES (1914)

During the summer and early autumn of 1914, the conflict on the Western Front leapfrogged north in the Race to the Sea, as each side tried to outflank the other. After the fall of Antwerp on 10 October, the Belgian army – covered by British and French forces – retreated west to the River Yser, 23 km (14 miles) north of the Flanders city of Ypres. Reinforcements for the British Expeditionary Force (BEF), including Indian and territorial divisions, arrived and began to take up positions around Ypres, in an area that over the next few years would become the site of some of the war's fiercest battles.

Reciprocal assaults
Fought between 19 October and 22 November 1914, the First Battle of Ypres was a series of assaults and counter-assaults. General Erich von Falkenhayn, chief of the German general staff, was set on launching an immediate, decisive assault to clear his way to the Channel and North Sea before the French, British, and Belgian lines solidified. Simultaneously, British and French

Trained French, British, and Belgian troops **fight together for the first time** against German forces.

With fighting largely in the open, **powerful artillery inflicts more than 100,000 casualties** on both sides.

The gunning down of German student volunteers is later immortalized as the **Massacre of the Innocents**.

The "Innocents" are the vanguard of **thousands more young volunteers sent to their deaths** in World War I.

See also: The British arrive 56–59 ▪ The First Battle of the Marne 64–69 ▪ The Race to the Sea 70–71 ▪ Trenches take over 74–77 ▪ The Second Battle of Ypres 110–15

The Christmas Truce

On Christmas Eve, 1914, German soldiers on the Western Front began to sing carols and put up Christmas trees along their trenches. This continued into Christmas Day, when soldiers on both sides spontaneously started to walk into no-man's-land. Groups of men mingled together, exchanging food, alcohol, and small gifts, such as buttons and cap badges. While most common in the west, similar truces occurred in parts of the Eastern Front.

Troops on the Western Front held joint religious services and sung carols. In a number of places along the line, football matches were organized. The truce also gave soldiers an opportunity to carry their dead back from no-man's-land for burial. Fraternization continued for several days on some parts of the front, but senior officers disapproved, afraid that it could affect fighting spirit, and orders were soon issued to resume hostilities.

A shallow, makeshift trench shelters British soldiers dug in along the road to Ypres on the Belgian front in November 1914. Powerful artillery took its toll on both sides, making deeper trench warfare inevitable.

forces, working in tandem under French general Ferdinand Foch, attempted an offensive designed to outflank the German troops. However, faced with superior numbers and a far greater weight of German artillery, the Allied offensive ground to a halt.

From 20 October onwards, the Allies were fighting a desperate defensive battle against the German Fourth and Sixth armies. On 30 October, the arrival of the French Ninth Corps to relieve the beleaguered British First Corps narrowly prevented a German breakthrough west of Ypres.

Holding the line

The German attacks continued with unrelenting ferocity, but stubborn British resistance and the timely arrival of more French reinforcements were sufficient to weather the German storm. On 11 November, the German units made their final breakthrough attempt. More than 12 of their most skilful divisions, including the Prussian Guard, were held by the remnants of the Allied line. From then on, the fighting subsided as winter set in.

Losses were heavy on both sides. At an early stage, trying to overwhelm a perceived weak spot in the Allied line around Langemarck, a village north of Ypres, the German army had committed reserve divisions that included student volunteers with little training or experience, making them easy targets for the regular French and British troops. The Germans later called this the *Kindermord* ("child murder"), or more loosely, the Massacre of the Innocents. By the end of the battle, German casualties numbered more than 130,000 men. The BEF suffered at least 50,000 casualties, severely weakening its strength, the French a similar number, and the Belgians up to 20,000.

Stalemate – a new phase

The First Battle of Ypres ended the 1914 campaign on the Western Front. Germany's inability to break through the Allied line underscored a larger strategic defeat – the failure to secure a swift victory over France. The German high command now knew that their country faced a long war on both its Western and Eastern fronts. The battle also marked the end of mobile warfare. Each side was now building vast defensive trench networks, stretching from Switzerland to the North Sea. ▪

Soldiers on both sides pose for a photograph during the unofficial truce of Christmas 1914. Up to 100,000 men took part along the Western Front.

HELL IS MUD

TRENCHES TAKE OVER (1914–15)

The war unleashed on Europe in August 1914 was unlike anything else the continent had seen – a conflict dominated by the deadly power of magazine rifles, machine guns, and quick-firing artillery. The same kind of weapons had been tested 10 years before in the Russo-Japanese War, as had the use of trenches as a defensive and protective system – but neither on the huge scale that came to define the Western Front. Such was the level of firepower, that soldiers had to dig for their very survival, and once the early German offensives had ground to a halt at

See also: The Race to the Sea 70–71 ▪ The First Battle of Ypres 72–73 ▪ The Gallipoli Campaign 122–29 ▪ Tank warfare 150–51 ▪ The Battle of Messines 214–17 ▪ Artillery 228–29 ▪ Trench warfare transformed 254–57

A British sniper takes up position beside a river and a ruined village near Verdun, on the Western Front.

Snipers

The static nature of trench warfare encouraged sniping – firing at an enemy with a rifle from a concealed position. Early snipers ranged from bored officers taking pot shots at enemy troops to skilled marksmen who knew about fieldcraft. The German army excelled at sniping, deploying former forest guards equipped with specially adapted service rifles fitted with telescopic sights. During 1914–15, German snipers on the Western Front caused huge damage, especially to units that failed to maintain good trench discipline, such as keeping heads below the parapets.

The Allies were slow to respond to the danger of sniping. It was only in 1916 that they made a concerted effort to overcome German sniper superiority. The British set up sniper schools to train recruits in shooting, fieldcraft, and tactical awareness, and sent experts into the trenches to teach front-line soldiers the practicalities of sniping.

the River Aisne in mid-September 1914, a new form of trench-bound warfare swiftly developed.

Levels of preparedness

The German army was already far advanced in the materials and techniques for waging trench warfare. The Allied soldiers faced an enemy not only well-equipped with large-calibre howitzers – big guns that could fire shells in a high, curved trajectory – but with trench mortars, grenades, rifle grenades, illuminating flares, searchlights, and an array of entrenching tools.

The French were also relatively well-equipped for trench fighting, but the British had arrived in 1914 with little more than sandbags, some coils of barbed wire, and new supplies of picks and spades to add to the infantryman's simple trench-digging tool. Shallow trenches were

German soldiers stand on their trench firestep, looking over the sandbag parapet, as they prepare to carry out an attack in Flanders, near the Yser river, in autumn 1914.

clearly insufficient. To keep men protected against artillery and other fire, trenches needed to be at least 2.5 m (8 ft) deep and 2 m (6½ ft) wide – and built to last for an unprecedented length of combat.

Trench systems

Front-line soldiers were instructed to dig trenches, not straight, but with traverses – zigzag or U-shaped sections that prevented the blast and fragments from an artillery shell travelling far along a trench. Traverses also prevented an enemy soldier from firing down the length of a trench. Lines of barbed wire were staked out in front of the trench to slow down an enemy attack; soldiers entangled in barbed wire were easy targets for a well-sited machine gun. »

Western Front trench system

Forward listening post

No-man's-land

Barbed wire

Sandbag parapet

Communication trench

Front-line trench

Support trench

Route to reserve trench

Dugout

The system of front-line, support, and reserve trenches was 200–500 m (650–1,640 ft) deep. Communication trenches carried soldiers, food supplies, equipment, and ammunition, while dugouts provided some space for rest and battle planning.

By the end of 1914, a basic trench system emerged of three roughly parallel lines interconnected by communication trenches. The front trench, directly facing the enemy, had a firestep, which lifted soldiers to parapet level, so they could fire while remaining concealed. Behind this was the support trench, which contained the bulk of the troops, ready to rush to the front-line trench in case of attack. The third line – the reserve trench – also held large numbers of men and acted as a further line of resistance. Soldiers strived to make the mud-filled, often waterlogged trenches more comfortable by installing rudimentary drainage and making dugouts in the trench sides to provide rest and shelter.

Geography played a key part in defining trench systems. The low-lying ground of the Flanders region in Belgium was prone to flooding and turned into a virtual swamp in wet weather once artillery fire had destroyed ditches and drainage channels. Trenches immediately filled with water, forcing troops to build chest-high sandbag fortifications above ground level.

The Vosges region of the Western Front, near the Swiss border, posed different problems. Its mountainous terrain meant that trenches had to be carved out of rock or thick forested slopes rather than flat expanses of soil.

No-man's-land

The strip of ground between the front-line trenches of opposing armies became known as no-man's-land. Its width could vary greatly from less than 12 m (39 ft) to almost 460 m (1,500 ft), with an average of around 230 m (750 ft). In the early days of the war, no-man's-land often included haystacks, farm buildings, and woods, where those operating between the lines could hide. It was the scene of sporadic infantry attacks and also more regular patrols and trench raids – usually at night. The aim of both was to gain information – especially from the capture of prisoners. Aggressive trench raids were also used to frighten the enemy and encourage a ruthless spirit among troops.

On the Aisne front and around the narrow Ypres salient in Flanders, Allied trench raids were conducted to dissuade German snipers from adopting forward positions, as their accurate fire chipped away at a battalion's strength and morale. Even more dangerous were the German artillery observers on lookout in no-man's-land for any Allied advance from cover; a signal from them would trigger a swift and accurate German bombardment.

Special weapons

Fighting the enemy during chance encounters in no-man's-land or in organized trench raids demanded its own specialized weaponry. Rifles with fixed bayonets were too cumbersome for the close-quarter combat typical of trench fighting,

No Man's Land under snow is like the face of the moon, chaotic, crater-ridden, uninhabitable, awful, the abode of madness.
Wilfred Owen
British lieutenant and poet

French soldiers prepare to fire a mortar from their trench on the front line. The mortars were given the nickname *crapouillot*, from *petit crapaud*, meaning "little toad".

so soldiers began to create their own weapons, including iron maces, wooden clubs, daggers, hatchets, and spears. German troops adapted entrenching tools, giving them a sharp edge that could both cut and stab. They were used alongside more conventional weapons, such as grenades and pistols.

Trench warfare also prompted the development of devices that could throw grenades further than by hand. Early catapults and spring-powered mechanisms proved highly inaccurate and were replaced from 1915 by rifle grenades. A variety of launch systems were used, with the much-copied French V-B cup launcher capable of propelling a grenade up to 180 m (590 ft).

Of all trench weapons, the mortar was perhaps the most important. It consisted of a metal pipe that could fire small shells at a steep angle – avoiding obstacles and dropping on the enemy from above, not unlike heavier artillery. The Germans had pioneered trench mortars before the war, so in 1914

they could deploy the fearsome *Minenwerfer* ("mine thrower") series, the largest of which was capable of firing a 97 kg (214 lb) shell up to 878 m (2,880 ft). The British and French had to start from scratch and preferred lighter, more mobile weapons. The British Stokes 81 mm (3 in) mortar, first used at the end of 1915, fired 4.5 kg (10 lb) shells up to 730 m (2,400 ft). Despite its relatively lightweight shell, the Stokes proved highly effective and was adopted by most Allied forces.

Trench rotation and relief

Commanders were soon aware of the strain that trench life placed on soldiers, and a rotation system was adopted by all sides. British soldiers, for example, would spend between four and eight days in a front-line trench, followed by around four days each in a support and a reserve trench. From 1915, 10 days' home leave was granted around every 12 months.

Engagement in offensive operations was rare in trench warfare, and for most of the time a soldier's life was relatively peaceful. This encouraged a phenomenon called the "live and let live" system, where soldiers on both sides refrained from opening fire to avoid retaliation from the enemy. It was easy, however, for commanders to break this peaceful equilibrium, whether through the deployment of specialist snipers, the installation of trench mortars with large supplies of ammunition, or the resumption of night raids.

An unbreakable line

The defensive trench system – resilient even in the face of the huge explosive and destructive power of modern weapons – proved so effective from late 1914 that it totally paralysed any hope of a war of movement on the Western Front. The Allies, however, were determined to break the trench deadlock and launched repeated offensives from 1915 onwards, all of which failed to break through the German lines. In the end, it took slow, steady attrition to turn the war against the German army and in favour of the Allies. ∎

Communications

A range of communication methods emerged to help commanders remain in contact with their troops. At the tactical level, commanders could use well-tested methods such as lamps and signal flags, or even animals, including dogs and pigeons, to carry written orders. Soldiers, called "runners", were also used as messengers.

By far the most important system of communication was the telephone, which enabled direct verbal interaction over

long distances from command headquarters to officers in front-line trenches. However, telephone cables could be easily cut, especially by artillery fire. During an offensive, even cables laid deep in the ground could be destroyed by heavy shelling. As troops advanced forwards from their trenches, signallers went with them, carrying compact field telephones in shoulder bags and reeling out cables. These were even more vulnerable to artillery fire and had to be constantly repaired – a highly specialized and risky job.

FLUSHING THEM OUT LIKE ANIMALS

THE BATTLE OF TANNENBERG (AUGUST 1914)

IN CONTEXT

FOCUS
Russian military action

BEFORE
1815 At the Congress of Vienna, the partition of Poland is reaffirmed, giving Russia a portion between Austrian Galicia and East Prussia.

1905 The Schlieffen Plan sets out how Germany could win a war against France to the west and Russia to the east.

AFTER
February 1915 German forces expel Russian troops from East Prussia. With Austro-Hungarian support, Germany invades Russian Poland in May.

March 1918 Bolshevik Russia withdraws from World War I after the signing of the Treaty of Brest-Litovsk.

W hen the first battles of World War I erupted in August 1914, France called on Russia – its ally since 1894 – to attack Germany in a bid to drain German forces eastwards. Although Russia mobilized quickly, it was not prepared for an offensive, through poor logistics and a lack of arms and equipment. It could, however, call on forces already defending its Polish salient – a bulge of territory projecting west between German East Prussia and Austrian Galicia.

Compromise strategy
The only German army on the entire Eastern Front was the Eighth Army under General Maximilian von Prittwitz in East Prussia. The

See also: Crisis in Russia 24 ▪ The battle for Poland 83 ▪ Russia retreats 138–39 ▪ The Brusilov Offensive 166–69 ▪ German victory in Eastern Europe 258–59

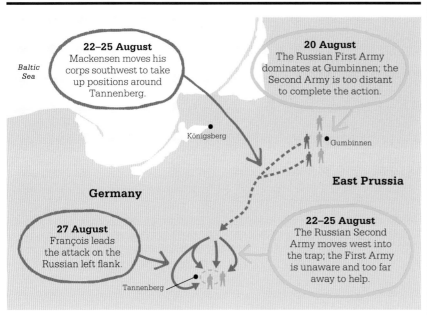

22–25 August
Mackensen moves his corps southwest to take up positions around Tannenberg.

20 August
The Russian First Army dominates at Gumbinnen; the Second Army is too distant to complete the action.

Baltic Sea

Königsberg

Gumbinnen

East Prussia

Germany

27 August
François leads the attack on the Russian left flank.

22–25 August
The Russian Second Army moves west into the trap; the First Army is unaware and too far away to help.

Tannenberg

The trap around Tannenberg is set as the Russian Second Army, unaware of the German generals' plan, moves west to pursue the German Eighth Army. Now isolated from the First Army, the Russian Second Army is cornered and destroyed.

Key:
- ▪▶ German retreat southwest
- ▶ German attack
- - - - Russians outflanked
- ♟ German soldiers
- ♟ Russian soldiers

Russian high command ordered its First and Second armies to shadow the German force from positions within the Polish salient and further northeast, and then set about planning a quick attack.

The Russian commanders devised what seemed like a winning strategy. Russia's First Army, commanded by General Paul von Rennenkampf, would drive west into East Prussia and attack the Eighth Army, while the Second Army, under General Alexander Samsonov, would advance north from Poland and hit Prittwitz in the flank, setting two Russian armies against one German force.

A labyrinth of forests and lakes, including the chain of Masurian Lakes stretching 80 km (50 miles)

along the East Prussian frontier, stood between the two advancing Russian armies. That natural feature and poor roads hindered military cohesion and communications between the two armies as they attempted to converge. Samsonov was also delayed in the Polish borderlands, which Russia had stripped of road and rail networks to deter invaders. While Rennenkampf entered East Prussia on 17 August, Samsonov did not arrive in southern East Prussia until two days later. This left his Second Army forces too far away to support the First Army.

The opening guns
On 19–20 August, the first major clash between Rennenkampf's First Army and the German forces »

Paul von Hindenburg

The son of an aristocratic Prussian officer, Paul von Hindenburg was born in 1847 in Posen, Prussia (now in Poland). Aged 11, he became a military cadet and fought in the Austro-Prussian War of 1866 and the Franco-Prussian War of 1870–71. Although he was Field Marshal Alfred von Schlieffen's choice to succeed him as chief of the German general staff in 1906, the post went instead to General Helmuth von Moltke.

Hindenburg retired as a general in 1911 and lived quietly in Hanover until he was despatched to East Prussia in 1914. The victory at Tannenberg elevated him to near godlike stature. With his leonine dignity and massive, ramrod-straight frame, the general was perceived as an incarnation of the noble Teutonic spirit. Within two years he had become the commander of all Germany's land forces. After the war, Hindenburg was twice elected president of the Weimar Republic. In 1924, he dedicated the Tannenberg Memorial, and was buried beneath it when he died aged 86 in 1934.

occurred around the East Prussian railway town of Gumbinnen. A long day of attack and repulse along a 48-km (30-mile) front was conceded to be a Russian victory. However, the flank attack from Samsonov's Second Army that could have dealt the Eighth Army a fatal blow was never delivered as the force was still several days' march away.

Fresh German leaders

At this stage, Prittwitz – unaware of the delay – thought the Russian Second Army might be about to encircle him and began to panic. Unknown to his staff, he telephoned Germany's Supreme Headquarters in Koblenz, outlining his intention to retreat to the fortified cities along the Vistula river, more than 160 km (100 miles) to the west. His deputy chief of staff, Max von Hoffmann, persuaded Prittwitz to hold his ground and advised him to move to a strategic position from where he could attack either Russian army.

Germany's Supreme Command were, however, unaware of the reversal of the retreat and, horrified at the thought of surrendering East Prussia to the scorched earth tactics of the Russians, dismissed Prittwitz

on 22 August. The new commander of the Eighth Army, General Paul von Hindenburg, and his chief of staff, General Erich Ludendorff, then approved a plan for attacking and defeating each Russian army before the two could unite.

Superior intelligence

Wireless technology was still in its infancy, and the Russians often broadcast without encoding their messages, allowing German intelligence to listen to them. On 26 August, German operators learned from one intercept that Rennenkampf, believing that the

Russian soldiers flee from a cavalry charge at the Battle of Tannenberg, in this German coloured lithograph produced in 1916.

German Eighth Army was now retreating to Königsberg, had plans to besiege that city. The Germans also learned that the Russian high command had ordered Samsonov to swing his Second Army west and block any German units retreating behind the Vistula river. Thus, the two Russian armies were now diverging, rather than converging, and would be unable to come to each other's aid.

Russian prisoners of war were taken in their tens of thousands by train towards Berlin after the Battle of Tannenberg.

Prisoners of war

After the Battle of Tannenberg, more than 90,000 Russians were taken prisoner. Together with captured supplies, equipment, and weapons (which alone required 60 trains), the prisoners were transported to Germany and initially held in barbed-wire stockades. German officials were quite unprepared for the challenge of feeding, clothing, and housing such an influx. Near-starvation rations, a mattress shared by four men taking turns to sleep, and similar hardships were the norm.

Deaths as a result of disease (especially typhus), malnutrition, and exposure soared. Schools, farms, factories – any buildings that could be converted to hold prisoners were seized.

By 1915, the construction of around 300 prison camps across Germany had been completed, each with rudimentary shelters and facilities. Officers were held in special camps, and transit camps were established to regulate the flow of men. When war ended in 1918, the number of prisoners held in Germany was close to 2.4 million.

> The Emperor trusted me. How can I face him again?
> **General Alexander Samsonov**

Hindenburg and Ludendorff promptly sent most of the Eighth Army southwest by train to trap Samsonov's Second Army, still making its way through East Prussia. The two corps under generals Hermann von François and Friedrich von Scholtz were deployed to the west of the Second Army, while General August von Mackensen's corps was sent to a position northeast of the Russians.

Into the trap

Over the next three days, the Russian Second Army marched into the trap. Samsonov attacked the two German corps to his west, but under heavy bombardment the Second Army's front and flanks were drawn into an increasingly chaotic and bloody conflict. The German pincers, still up to 65 km (40 miles) apart, then started to tighten. Mackensen, coming from the northeast, was ordered to close and deliver the main attack. The Russian divisions were still engaged with Scholtz and François to the southwest. Sensing disaster, some formations retreated back into Poland before 29 August, when François snaked around south of the Russian army, and closed the escape hole.

On 30 August, Mackensen's assault drove most of Samsonov's Second Army into an area 24 km (15 miles) wide and 8 km (5 miles) deep. Now surrounded on three sides and under a fierce artillery barrage, most Russian troops surrendered. Samsonov walked into the forest with his immediate staff and turned aside alone into the trees. A single shot was heard; German troops later found his body. The Russians had suffered around 30,000 dead or wounded, and the Germans 13,000.

The glory of Tannenberg

Reinforced by two army corps from the Western Front two weeks after Tannenberg, the German Eighth Army went on to defeat Rennenkampf's Russian First Army. The following year, German troops expelled all Russian forces from East Prussia; Russia did not attack German lands again in World War I.

The Tannenberg Memorial – here photographed from a zeppelin around 1931 – was demolished in 1945 to avoid its destruction by the Soviet Army at the end of World War II.

Hindenburg and Ludendorff became national heroes. Their 1914 victory was named Tannenberg after a nearby hamlet to redress a defeat there in 1410, when the Teutonic knights had been crushed by largely Slavic forces. The Tannenberg Memorial was completed in 1927 to mark the strategic triumph. ■

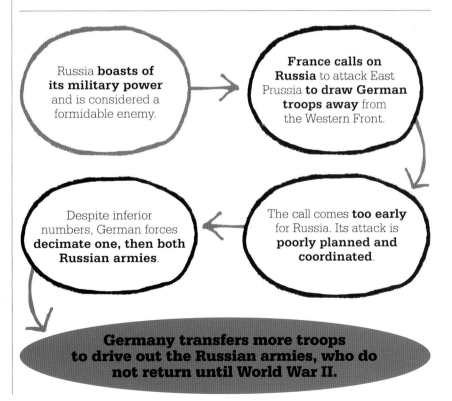

Russia **boasts of its military power** and is considered a formidable enemy.

France calls on **Russia** to attack East Prussia **to draw German troops away** from the Western Front.

The call comes **too early** for Russia. Its attack is **poorly planned and coordinated**.

Despite inferior numbers, German forces **decimate one, then both Russian armies**.

Germany transfers more troops to drive out the Russian armies, who do not return until World War II.

THIS MONSTROUS FRONT WILL DEVOUR US ALL
AUSTRO-HUNGARIAN FAILURES (1914)

IN CONTEXT

FOCUS
Austria-Hungary at war

BEFORE
1817 After two uprisings (1804 and 1815), the new Principality of Serbia gains independence from the Ottoman Empire.

1867 The Habsburg Empire, following defeat in the Austro-Prussian War of 1866, becomes the Austro-Hungarian Empire.

1912–13 After two Balkan Wars, Serbia emerges as an aggressive state on Austria-Hungary's southern border.

AFTER
1915 Austria-Hungary, Germany, and Bulgaria join forces to attack and defeat Serbia. Atrocities against Serbs provoke international censure.

1918 The break-up of Austria-Hungary results in states that later become Austria, Hungary, Yugoslavia, and Czechoslovakia.

In the summer of 1914, Franz Conrad von Hötzendorf, chief of the Austro-Hungarian Empire's general staff, faced the prospect of war on two fronts – against Serbia and Russia. Yet his army mirrored his divided, multiethnic nation: the Austrians and Hungarians were barely on speaking terms, while the Czechs, Slovaks, Slovenes, Croats, and Romanians, who made up nearly half the regiments, had little incentive to fight the governing pair's battles. Like the empire, the Austro-Hungarian army would soon be broken by war.

A year of setbacks
Austria-Hungary's war plans called for 13 of its 16 army corps to head east in case of war with Russia, but in August 1914 Conrad sent seven corps to crush Serbia, ignoring likely Russian intervention. Two of the corps were eventually redirected to the east, but the indecision caused them to miss the opening battles on both fronts. In Serbia, invading troops committed atrocities against civilians, and

they met stiff resistance before eventually taking Belgrade. In September, meanwhile, the Russians won a series of battles in Galicia around Lemburg (Lviv), then advanced quickly to the Carpathian Mountains. The retreating Austro-Hungarian forces suffered around 250,000 casualties, with a further 100,000 taken prisoner.

As a further humiliation, Serbian forces counterattacked in December 1914, and swept every Austro-Hungarian soldier from their land. ∎

The Austrians had rushed in, and had been flung out.
Winston Churchill
The World Crisis, **1923**

See also: The Balkans 25 ▪ The Alliance System 30–31 ▪ The assassination of Franz Ferdinand 40–41 ▪ The end of the Serbian campaign 140–43

DAYS OF SEE-SAW BATTLE
THE BATTLE FOR POLAND (1914)

IN CONTEXT

FOCUS
Eastern Front

BEFORE
1795 In the third Partition of Poland, Prussia is allocated western portions, including Warsaw, Austria gets Galicia in the south, and Russia takes a vast section in the east.

1812 Napoleon I, emperor of France, launches an invasion of western Russia from Polish soil, assisted by Polish troops.

1815 After the fall of Napoleon, the Congress of Vienna grants Russia most of the Kingdom of Poland, including Warsaw.

AFTER
1918–19 Poland regains its independence after more than 100 years of Prussian, Austro-Hungarian, and Russian occupation.

1939 Poland is invaded once again – by Nazi Germany and the USSR.

While French, British, and German armies became stuck in trench warfare on the Western Front in autumn 1914, a huge battle was being fought on the Eastern Front in Russian Poland. Grand Duke Nicholas Nikolaevich, commander-in-chief of the Imperial Russian Army, saw the collapse of Austro-Hungarian forces in Austrian Galicia in September 1914 as a chance to advance west and deliver a fatal blow to Germany's industrial heartland in Silesia.

Advances and retreats

The Germans, recognizing Silesia's vulnerability, assembled the new Ninth Army there, commanded by General Paul von Hindenburg. In late September, the army advanced into Russian Poland as far as Warsaw, but Russian troops forced them back.

Grand Duke Nicholas then renewed the Russian push towards Silesia. On 11 November, however, his right flank was hit suddenly by the German Ninth Army, driving them towards Łódz. For more than

Russian troops are pictured close to Warsaw in December 1914. Exhausted after the battle around the city of Łódz, they had withdrawn to the east.

three freezing weeks, at least 600,000 troops fought a titanic and bloody battle, each side in turn outflanking the other.

Finally, the Russians broke off and retreated east towards Warsaw. The Ninth Army followed, then both sides dug in for the winter. Between May and September 1915, German forces would drive Russia out of Warsaw and all of Poland. ■

See also: Russia retreats 138–39 ▪ The Brusilov Offensive 166–69 ▪ The Kerensky Offensive 224–25 ▪ German victory in Eastern Europe 258–59

LET THE VICTORY BE SACRED
OTTOMAN TURKEY ENTERS THE WAR (1914–15)

Between 1911 and 1913, military humiliations in the Balkans and North Africa had exposed the vulnerability of the vast and sprawling Ottoman Empire. Russia, to the north, had vowed to control the Turkish Straits on which the empire's capital Constantinople (Istanbul) stood, which was the only route between Russia's Black Sea ports and the Mediterranean. To the south, the British and French empires were eager to seize Ottoman territories in the Middle East. The priority for the Young Turk triumvirate of Talaat Pasha, Enver Pasha, and Cemal Pasha, who dominated the Ottoman government after a 1913 coup, was to keep the great European powers at bay and play them off against each other. Part of this strategy involved seeking military aid from Germany and naval advice and ships from Britain.

Taking sides
On 1 August 1914, the Ottoman War Ministry in Constantinople ordered the call-up of men of fighting age – 20 to 45 years old. The next day, the Istanbul government signed a secret defensive treaty with Germany, but did not at this point enter the war. The same month, the British government infuriated the Ottoman rulers by requisitioning two dreadnought battleships built in Britain for the Ottoman navy and already paid for. In September, the Ottomans closed the Straits by laying mines at each end – at the Bosphorus and Dardanelles.

The arrival of two powerful warships, *Goeben* and *Breslau*, from the German navy's Mediterranean Squadron then helped shift the balance of power. The ships were escorted through the Dardanelles and transferred to the Ottoman navy.

… those who sacrifice their lives to give life to the truth will have honour in this world, and their latter end is paradise.
Sultan Mehmed V
declaring holy war,
14 November 1914

See also: The Gallipoli Campaign 122–29 ∎ The Armenian Genocide 132–33 ∎ The Arab Revolt 170–71 ∎ The Battle of Megiddo 286–87

Outside the Ministry of War in Beyazit Square, Constantinople (Istanbul), in December 1914, crowds celebrate the Ottoman Empire's entry into World War I.

In October, the Germans offered Turkey significant funds in return for its support in the war.

On 27 October, an Ottoman flotilla led by the two former German warships set sail into the Black Sea. Two days later, with no previous declaration of war, they bombarded Odessa, Sebastopol, and other Russian ports and sank a gunboat and minelayer. Russia declared war on the Ottoman Empire on 2 November, and three days later, France and Britain followed suit. On 14 November Sultan Mehmed V proclaimed a call to jihad (holy war) in Constantinople.

War on land

By the time war was officially declared, the Ottoman army was also engaged. In the Caucasus, the Russian forces had launched an immediate offensive, blocked in mid-November by Ottoman resistance. In Mesopotamia, British Indian troops took Basra, thus securing key oil installations.

In late December, Enver Pasha, the war minister, personally led the Ottoman Third Army in an offensive in the Caucasus. He was hoping to outflank and encircle the Russians at Sarikamish but was defeated largely by freezing winter weather. Of more than 100,000 Third Army troops, tens of thousands froze to death, while others succumbed to an outbreak of typhus.

Further south, Cemal Pasha, commander of the Ottoman Fourth Army, launched a surprise raid across Sinai on the British-controlled Suez Canal. His troops reached the canal and, on 2 February 1915, established a bridgehead on its west bank, but were then driven back. The Ottoman offensive plans were by now in ruins, but some notable victories still lay ahead. ∎

The Suez Canal

For the British, control of the Suez Canal was vital to ensure the flow of shipping not only from India and South Asia, but also from Australia and New Zealand. Any threat to the canal was a threat to the war effort. Aware of this, Ottoman commanders and their German advisors had been discussing a possible attack on the canal since September 1914. Even an unsuccessful onslaught, they reasoned, would oblige the British to keep troops in Egypt, preventing them from being deployed to the Western Front or elsewhere.

When the Ottoman Empire entered the war, the British tightened their grip on Egypt and the canal zone. They had controlled the territory since the 1880s, but officially Egypt was still an Ottoman realm with a *khedive* (hereditary ruler) whose loyalties lay with the Ottoman sultan. On 18 December 1914, the British deposed Abbas II, the reigning, pro-Ottoman *khedive*, replacing him with a more pliant relative. At the same time, they proclaimed Egypt a British protectorate.

British artillerymen dig in and build strong defences along the Suez Canal to help counter the Ottoman attacks in early 1915.

WE DON'T WANT TO DIE FOR NOTHING
THE WAR IN AFRICA (1914–18)

Africa had not played a major part in European powers' pre-war plans. But once conflict erupted, the combatants quickly turned it into a battleground. Around 2.5 million Africans took part in the war – more than a million as soldiers, while others were labourers or porters, often carrying supplies in areas lacking transport.

Creating a regional force
To build their African armies, the European nations used a combination of volunteers and

War is a sad thing for the native population. The troops occupy the country for a bit, take what food there is, leaving nothing for the natives.
Captain Alexander Wallace
Medical officer
British South Africa Police

conscription or forced recruitment. In West and North Africa, the French often recruited via local chiefs, who volunteered their domestic servants and other lower-class individuals rather than friends and relatives. In British East Africa, a compulsory service order in 1915 made all males aged 18 to 45 years liable for service. Resistance to forced military service was rife and was a catalyst for major rebellions against the French and British during the war.

Organized into units and always commanded by European officers, African soldiers, known as "Askaris", were segregated from European or Africa-born white troops. They were often issued with older or inferior uniforms and weapons, and were sent into combat first.

Battles in West Africa
In August 1914, within days of the opening clashes on Europe's Western Front, British forces from the Gold Coast (Ghana) and French troops from Dahomey (Benin) invaded German Togoland (Togo), meeting scant resistance. The British expected a similarly easy victory when they attacked German Kamerun (Cameroon)

See also: Europe's colonies and empires 28–29 ▪ Ottoman Turkey enters the war 84–85 ▪ The war in East Africa 244 ▪ Post-war conflicts 320–21

Paul von Lettow-Vorbeck

Born into a military family in Saarland, Prussia, in 1870, Paul von Lettow-Vorbeck joined the Imperial German Army in 1890 and was later posted to China to help suppress the Boxer Rebellion. In 1904, he was sent to German Southwest Africa to quell a revolt. There, he acquired the bush survival skills necessary for guerrilla warfare, which served him well in German East Africa, where he led the Schutztruppe throughout World War I.

Lettow-Vorbeck's tactics enabled him to neutralize enemy forces 20 times larger than his own. Fighting Portuguese, British, and Belgian contingents on several fronts, he and an army of fiercely loyal, mainly African Askari, troops remained active until the end of the war and were never fully defeated.

Returning to Germany in 1919, Lettow-Vorbeck was hailed as the *Löwe von Afrika* ("Lion of Africa") and elected to the Reichstag. After refusing to collaborate with the Nazis, however, he was marginalized by Hitler and played no part in World War II. He died aged 93 in Hamburg in 1964.

later in the month. However, they were defeated at Garua and Nsanakong by the Schutztruppe – a colonial force comprising German officers and locally recruited soldiers – and pushed back into Nigeria with heavy losses.

East Africa

War broke out in East Africa in several different forms, including a British naval bombardment of Dar es Salaam in German East Africa (Tanzania), Schutztruppe raids into British East Africa (Kenya), and a gunboat battle on Lake Nyasa (Malawi and Tanzania). There were also short-lived German invasions of Nyasaland (Malawi) and Northern Rhodesia (Zambia). Skirmishes continued throughout the region until 1918, with the German forces, led by General

Paul von Lettow-Vorbeck, and their Askaris mostly proving a match for far larger Allied forces.

Southwest Africa

The Allied invasion of German Southwest Africa (Namibia) was led by the Union Defence Force (UDF), consisting mainly of white South African troops. Crossing the Orange river in 1915, the UDF army, led by Boer War heroes Jan Smuts and Louis Botha, easily routed the

Schutztruppe and captured Windhoek, forcing German troops to surrender the colony.

World War I involved almost every African country. More than 150,000 African soldiers and porters lost their lives and many more were wounded. Tens of thousands of Africans were caught in the crossfire, afflicted by famine, or displaced from their homes. At the war's end, the continent's borders were redrawn by the victors. ▪

Allied fighters, including African recruits, march through Togoland, West Africa, in 1914. The German colony was invaded on 9 August by French and British forces. By the end of the month, they had captured it.

THEY HAVE NO GRAVE BUT THE CRUEL SEA

THE WAR AT SEA BEGINS (AUGUST–DECEMBER 1914)

IN CONTEXT

FOCUS
Naval warfare

BEFORE
1889 In Britain, the Naval Defence Act introduces the "two-power standard", by which the strength of the Royal Navy must always match that of the world's next two biggest fleets.

1908 Germany passes a new German naval bill that vastly accelerates its rate of battleship construction.

AFTER
1915 Germany expands its attacks against Allied ships. In May, U-boats sink the cruise liner *Lusitania*, killing almost 1,200 people, including 128 American citizens.

1916 The Battle of Jutland exposes weaknesses in British ship design after the catastrophic destruction of three battle cruisers.

1917 The sinking of four American merchant ships by German U-boats in March and April prompts US president Woodrow Wilson to ask Congress to declare war on Germany.

When war broke out in 1914, more than a century had passed since the last major naval battle between European powers. Britain dominated the world's seas and had set the standard for modern warships with the launch in 1906 of HMS *Dreadnought*, spawning a new class of battleship – the "dreadnought" – with its long-range guns and ever-more-destructive shells, massive armour, and steam-turbine-fuelled speed. The number of battleships a navy possessed became a simple shorthand for a nation's sea-going strength. In August 1914, Britain had 29 dreadnoughts to Germany's 17, and the public perception in both countries was that these gigantic warships facing each other across the North Sea would slug it out in the greatest naval encounter since the Battle of Trafalgar in 1805.

Game-changing technology

In practice, naval commanders were cautious, due in part to the bewildering pace of technological advances. The long-range guns of modern battleships, which by 1914 were capable of firing further than 16 km (10 miles), rendered close combat obsolete. Paradoxically, as the battleship increased its striking power, it became more vulnerable to submarines and small surface vessels equipped with torpedoes, whose gyroscopic accuracy had greatly increased since the 1890s.

Germany's *U-14* submarine sank two ships – both from neutral countries – during its brief career. It was sunk off Peterhead on 5 June 1915.

A torpedo boat could, in theory, sink a 18,144-tonne (20,000-US ton) battleship. To counter this threat, the vessels were provided with a defensive screen of cruisers (heavily armed, but lighter and faster than dreadnoughts) and lightly armoured destroyers, which emerged as potent and flexible warships. Destroyers could steam

I must plough the seas of the world doing as much mischief as I can, until … a foe far superior in power succeeds in catching me.
Maximilian von Spee
German vice admiral

See also: The naval arms race 32–33 ▪ The sinking of the *Lusitania* 106–07 ▪ The Battle of Jutland 160–63 ▪ The U-boats on the attack 200–05

at a speed of more than 15 metres per second (30 knots) and were armed with guns and torpedoes, the latter capable of hitting a target more than 5 km (3 miles) away.

The submarine – first used in naval warfare in 1776 during the American Revolution – came of age in World War I, when all the major world navies included the vessel in their fleets. Britain was slow to accept the submarine but in August 1914 still had around twice as many as the German navy, which had poured most of its resources into building massive and expensive battleships. The sheer number of Royal Navy vessels, however, offered German submarines, known as U-boats – "U" for *Untersee* ("undersea") – easy targets. Their first victim was the cruiser HMS *Pathfinder*, destroyed on 5 September 1914 by *U-21* off the coast of Scotland. This was followed on 22 September by the sinking by *U-9* of three British cruisers near the Dutch coast, with nearly 1,500 sailors lost.

Listening in

A revolution in communication technology also transformed the nature of naval warfare. Developed from the 1890s onwards, wireless telegraphy – the transmission of messages using radio waves – allowed navies to liaise across great distances. It also enabled them to overhear their opponents, and a great deal of effort went into gaining telegraphic advantage. In one of the first acts of the war, Britain cut all but one of Germany's undersea telegraph cables. In turn, Germany attacked British telegraph stations and cables in the Pacific and Indian oceans.

> There was a terrific crash, and the ship lifted up, quivering all over. A second … later another and duller crash, and a great cloud of smoke, followed by a torrent of water.
> **Crew member**
> Survivor of a U-boat torpedo attack on HMS *Hogue*

Messages sent by the Germans were encrypted, but by October 1914 the British had acquired two codebooks seized from German ships, and in November intelligence officers established a decoding centre in London, known as Room 40. This gave the Royal Navy a priceless advantage: it was now virtually impossible for the German navy to make a move without British naval intelligence knowing.

A global navy

In August 1914, the Royal Navy was faced with a daunting array of tasks. It acted as the nation's shield, providing protection from assault and invasion, while also safeguarding extensive commercial interests around the world. No other country relied so heavily on maritime trade, and an effective Royal Navy was vital to British survival. So long as the Royal Navy retained its preeminent position, it could extend its role to the direct help of its allies and the hindrance of Germany and its allies. However, »

Coronel and the Falklands

The most powerful German cruiser force in 1914 was Vice Admiral Maximilian von Spee's East Asia Squadron in the Pacific Ocean. This consisted of two heavy cruisers, *Scharnhorst* and *Gneisenau*, plus three light cruisers. Spee was, however, faced by larger Australian and Japanese forces, and this led him to attempt an escape to safer Atlantic waters via Cape Horn on the southern tip of South America. He set course across the Pacific and on 1 November 1914 his heavy cruisers sank two obsolete British cruisers without loss off Coronel on the coast of Chile.

The British response was swift and devastating. Two battle cruisers, *Invincible* and *Inflexible*, under Vice Admiral Doveton Sturdee, were despatched to the Falkland Islands to bar Spee's passage into the Atlantic, and on 8 December the rival forces met. After a long-running fight, all the German vessels, except one light cruiser, were sunk. Spee and both his sons died in the action, as did nearly 2,000 German sailors.

The East Asia Squadron leaves Valparaíso, a Chilean port, in the aftermath of its victory in the Battle of Coronel – the first British naval defeat since 1812.

Seamen onboard a British warship watch as the German light cruiser SMS *Mainz* sinks in August 1914 during the Battle of Heligoland Bight.

if Germany gained control of the seas, Britain would face disaster. The commanders of the Imperial German Navy knew they could not match the size of the British fleet. Instead, by means of prolonged harassment, they sought to wear down the Royal Navy to a point where its supremacy at sea would be irretrievably lost.

One early priority for the Royal Navy was to safely transport millions of men from Britain and its empire to various theatres of war around the globe. The French navy carried out a similar role in the Mediterranean, transporting troops from North Africa. The Royal Navy then had to sweep the world's oceans of German ships in order to protect Britain's vital maritime trade and deny Germany any global advantage. It was equally important to stifle German trade and starve the nation of food, equipment, and other essential goods.

The kind of close coastal blockade used by Britain against French ports in the Napoleonic Wars in the previous century was impossible in 1914, thanks to the dual underwater threat of German mines and submarines. The solution was to impose a "distant" blockade alongside close observation of the English Channel and North Sea, policed by the bulk of the British fleet based in Scottish ports nearly 1,000 km (620 miles) from German naval harbours. This patient tactic was largely successful and became an important factor in the collapse of Germany in 1918.

Early naval encounters

Despite the lack of a big set-piece naval battle between the British and German navies in 1914, and the increased threat to shipping from submarines and mines, some surface conflicts took place. The British public was cheered by news of a successful Royal Navy action in the North Sea on 28 August 1914. Supported by the battle cruisers of Rear Admiral David Beatty, Commodore Reginald Tyrwhitt's

Karl von Müller – "gentleman pirate"

Born in Hanover, Germany, in 1873, Karl von Müller joined the Imperial German Navy in 1891. He served in various capacities before being given command of the light cruiser SMS *Emden* in 1913. Once war began in August 1914, Müller and his crew set about causing significant damage to Allied forces in the Indian Ocean, destroying two warships, sinking or taking 16 merchant ships, shelling Madras harbour, and raiding Penang. Müller's skilful tactics and daring forays earned him a reputation as a formidable opponent, although he also earned the soubriquet "gentleman pirate" for his chivalrous treatment of captured prisoners.

Müller's luck ran out on 9 November 1914 when the *Emden* was ambushed off the coast of the Cocos Islands – near the Indonesian island of Sumatra – and heavily damaged by the Australian cruiser HMAS *Sydney*. Müller managed to beach his ship on some rocks but he and his surviving crew were captured and imprisoned. After the war, Müller returned to Germany and lived there quietly until his death in 1923.

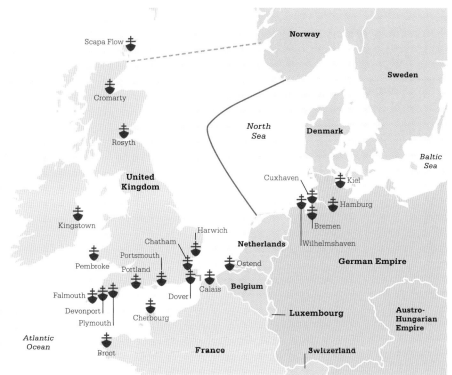

Allied blockades of Germany in late 1914 sought to close off the Atlantic Ocean to German trade. "Observational" vessels patrolled the North Sea. Bases on England's south coast protected the Dover Straits and northern France. The furthest blockade policed the route between northern Scotland to Norway.

Key:

- Central Powers
- Allies
- Neutral territories
- ⚓ Naval base
- --- Allied distant blockade
- — Allied observational blockade

Harwich Force of light cruisers and destroyers trapped a flotilla of German light cruisers in the Heligoland Bight off the German coast. Three German light cruisers and a destroyer were sunk, with more than 1,000 men killed or captured; the British lost no ships and only 35 sailors. The victory seemed impressive but was a minor action and concealed alarming errors of signalling and command on the British side. These failings were glossed over in the victory celebrations, but reappeared more damagingly later in the sea war.

The German navy scored its own North Sea "publicity" victory on 16 December 1914, when its raiding squadrons bombarded the towns of Hartlepool, Whitby, and Scarborough on the northeast coast of England and escaped with impunity. More than 100 people

were killed and nearly 600 wounded. The knowledge that German warships had stood off the English coast, shelling the defenceless civilian population, suggested to the British public that there were serious holes in Britain's defences. Supported by photographs in the popular press of devastated buildings, the casualty lists led to uproar. For the first time, modern war had directly touched the public consciousness.

The wider picture

While the Royal Navy dominated the seas around Britain and northern Europe, raiding parties of German light cruisers took advantage of the greater safety of distant waters, harrying merchant vessels and attacking Allied communications. In particular, the SMS *Emden* under Captain Karl von Müller had great success

in the Bay of Bengal and the Indian Ocean, disrupting shipping and destroying onshore wireless stations. But the sinking of the *Emden* in November 1914 marked the beginning of the end of German raiders as a trading threat. The light cruisers of the German East Asia Squadron were gradually picked off by British ships, with the last, *Dresden*, scuttled in March 1915. On the surface, at least, Britannia still ruled the waves.

By the end of 1914, the two main battle fleets of Britain and Germany lay for the most part idly at anchor. German shipping – naval and mercantile – had been steadily swept from the seas, seemingly enabling the British merchant fleet to go about its business unhindered. However, the British were soon to face an increasingly deadly threat from the German navy's most potent weapon, the submarine. ∎

A GRACE FROM HEAVEN
THE WAR IN ASIA AND OCEANIA (1914–19)

IN CONTEXT

FOCUS
War in the Pacific

BEFORE
1884 Germany declares the northeastern part of New Guinea in the Pacific its protectorate and names it Kaiser-Wilhelmsland.

1898 China leases more than 520 sq km (200 sq miles) of land to Germany, forming the Jiaozhou Bay Leased Territory, with Tsingtao as its capital.

1899 Germany, Britain, and the US sign the Tripartite Convention, which leads to the partitioning of the Samoan islands between Germany and the US.

AFTER
June 1919 The League of Nations mandate system splits control of Germany's former Pacific territories between Australia, Japan, and New Zealand.

The Pacific and Asian theatre was the largest geographical area of conflict in World War I, but one of the least bloody. Apart from naval warfare, most of the fighting took place near the coast and on islands.

The South Pacific
One of the first Allied objectives was to capture Germany's colonial possessions in the South Pacific; their wireless stations and port facilities made them key targets.

Soldiers of the Imperial Japanese Army 18th Division in an abandoned German army trench observe the enemy during the Siege of Tsingtao. Japan was keen to expand its sphere of influence.

Australia and New Zealand took on the task, keen to support Britain and to play a greater role in the region. From 29 to 30 August 1914, New Zealand forces invaded and captured German Samoa – the first enemy territory in the region to fall to the Allies – with no blood spilt.

See also: Europe's colonies and empires 28–29 ▪ The naval arms race 32–33 ▪ The war at sea begins 88–93 ▪ Naval war in the Mediterranean 242–43 ▪ The Great Influenza 308–09 ▪ A lasting peace? 312–17

During the span of the past two years Japan has secured a place in the sun, and she has become one of the happiest countries in the world.
The Asahi Shimbun
Osaka newspaper, 1 January 1917

Occupation of Samoa

The day after World War I began, New Zealand accepted a British request to send an expeditionary force to take German Samoa. The force of 1,400, under Colonel Robert Logan, landed on 29 August and seized key positions on the island. Facing little resistance, Logan declared the occupation the next day and raised the Union Jack. The New Zealand government had long-standing designs on the colony, believing it should be part of the British imperial sphere of influence in the South Pacific. Logan was made the area's military administrator and served out the war there. German citizens were given the choice of staying or going home; most remained.

In late 1918, the mishandling of quarantine rules by Logan led to an outbreak of the Great Influenza that killed a fifth of the population. The blunder caused considerable discontent, but German Samoa would stay under New Zealand's rule. It finally won independence as Western Samoa in 1962.

Australian forces captured the island of Nauru on 9 September, destroying wireless equipment and arresting its German administrator. Taking German New Guinea took a little longer. Australian troops landed on 11 September and overcame an outnumbered German force at the Battle of Bita Paka. The defeated Germans retreated to the port of Toma, which the Australians captured after a three-day siege.

By the end of 1914, most of the German forces remaining in New Guinea had surrendered. The exception was a small group led by officer and surveyor Hermann Detzner, who withdrew to the island's rugged interior and evaded capture. He finally surrendered in January 1919.

Siege of Tsingtao
Japan had formally declared war on Germany on 23 August 1914 – and on Austria-Hungary two days later. That October, Imperial Japanese naval forces captured Germany's remaining colonial possessions in the South Pacific.

Much earlier, on 27 August, Japan had sent ships carrying more than 20,000 troops to blockade Tsingtao, a fortified port in China's eastern Shandong province and Germany's most strategically important base in the Far East. The German East Asia Squadron, which supported its Pacific colonies, was based at the port, but when war broke out, most of its cruisers were elsewhere, leaving its garrison of 4,000 German, Austro-Hungarian, and Chinese defenders vulnerable to attack.

New Zealand soldiers display a German war flag captured after their seizure of German Samoa, which had been secretly planned before war was declared.

The Japanese were joined by 1,500 British and Indian troops. Allied forces landed on 2 September and besieged Tsingtao. Led by the Japanese, who suffered the bulk of casualties in numerous skirmishes, the Allied offensive forced a German surrender on 7 November. In the first-ever sea-launched air raids, Japan's seaplanes from its carrier *Wakamiya* had also made their mark. Japan occupied the port, and it remained in their hands until 1922.

Neutral powers turn
China would maintain its neutrality for much of the war. However, on 17 February 1917, a German U-boat sank a French ship carrying Chinese citizens – and tensions began to increase. On 14 August, China declared war on the Central Powers and occupied Austria-Hungary's concessions within its territory. The Chinese did not fight in Europe, but thousands served there as labourers, mostly in France. Siam, also neutral, joined the war on the Allied side on 22 July 1917, and sent troops to fight in France. ▪

THE ENEMY HAS EARS EVERYWHERE

THE SECRET WAR (1914–15)

IN CONTEXT

FOCUS
Intelligence gathering

BEFORE
1850 Austria's *Evidenzbureau* becomes the first military intelligence service.

1901 The German navy founds the *Nachrichten-Abteilung* ("News Department") to gather information on naval rivals.

AFTER
January 1917 British cryptographers decipher the Zimmermann Telegram, sent by Germany to Mexico. It promises American territory to Mexico in return for its military support in the war.

May 1918 The Sedition Act is passed in the US, imposing fines and imprisonment on any American citizen who is found guilty of conspiring against their country.

he tense political situation in the years before 1914 encouraged an appetite for novels and tales of espionage. With the outbreak of war, such literature, along with conspiracy stories in the popular press, fostered a spy mania that touched all warring nations.

In Britain, the prolific Anglo-French writer William Le Queux had a pivotal impact on public opinion – and, ultimately, on official policy. His novels – several, such as *Spies of the Kaiser* (1909), concerning a supposed invasion of Britain – were presented as fact dressed up as fiction. Le Queux even hinted that he had official documents to support his claims. There were no

See also: War is declared 42–43 ▪ Public opinion 44–45 ▪ The Battle of Tannenberg 78–81 ▪ The war at sea begins 88–93 ▪ Society under strain 184–87 ▪ The US enters the war 194–95 ▪ War-crimes trials 318–19

Mata Hari

Margaretha Geertruida MacLeod was a Dutch exotic dancer turned courtesan. Better known by her stage name, Mata Hari, she was born Margaretha Zelle in 1876 in Leeuwarden, Friesland. After her family lost their business, she left home to become a teacher.

In 1895, Zelle married Dutch army officer Rudolph MacLeod and went to live in Java and Sumatra. They were soon divorced, and she had to abandon her daughter. Moving to Paris, she worked as a dancer, used the name Mata Hari, and entered into liaisons – often paid – with military men.

In 1915, Zelle moved again, this time to the Hague, where she is thought to have agreed to supply information about France to the Germans. However, she may also have become a French spy, in return for being allowed to visit a wounded lover.

Even though Zelle supplied little more than gossip to either side, in 1917 she was seized in Paris, accused of being a German spy, and sentenced to death by firing squad. The possibility remains that she was treated as a scapegoat for France's military failures.

such papers, though his books did inspire plenty of correspondence from readers suspicious of people with German connections.

Le Queux passed the letters on to the British government. The Committee of Imperial Defence took the claims seriously, and in 1909 the Secret Service Bureau – forerunner of MI5 and MI6 – was born.

Secret services

Other countries already had similar agencies, founded in earlier times of tension and conflict. In Belgium, the *Administration de la Sûreté Publique* investigated espionage. Russia had the *Okhrana* (secret police) while Austria-Hungary's *Evidenzbureau* worked with the state police. In Germany, the *Abteilung III b*, founded in 1889, focused its attention on Russia and France, and its navy's secret service, the *Nachrichten-Abteilung*,

spied primarily on Britain. In France, military intelligence was handled by the *Deuxième Bureau*, founded in 1871 after France's defeat to Prussia.

Clampdowns and reprisals

On 8 August 1914, four days after declaring war on Germany, the British government passed its Defence of the Realm Act "for securing public safety". From then,

all communications were censored, pub opening times were restricted, and discussion of military and naval matters became illegal. Bonfires were banned as possible signals to the enemy; and whistling for a taxi was also forbidden for fear it might be confused with air-raid warnings.

Similar legislation was rolled out across the British Empire. Australia's War Precautions Act, Canada's War Measures Act and New Zealand's »

German soldiers escort a Russian spy caught cutting telephone wires behind German lines, during the opening year of the conflict.

Sabotage

Espionage in World War I took many forms, including sabotage – the targeting of munitions, factories, and ships to prevent supplies from reaching the front. As well as causing loss of life, property, and goods destined for the war effort, sabotage lowered public morale.

Sabotage was also used against non-combatants, including the US before it entered the war. On 30 July 1916, an explosion at the Black Tom railway depot in New Jersey, close to Manhattan, destroyed 910,000 kg (2,000,000 lb) of munitions, packed into rail trucks and destined for Allied use. The blast The blast caused over $20 million worth of damage.

An investigation blamed German agents, including men guarding the depot. The neutral US immediately created the Espionage Act and established intelligence agencies to tackle espionage on home soil. Public opinion turned against Germany, fuelling general support for the declaration of war in 1917

American policemen inspect sabotaged rail trucks in July 1916 at the Black Tom depot on a landfill peninsular in New York Harbor.

> ## Military intelligence in most countries takes three forms.

Signals intelligence (SIGINT) Intercepting signalling communications and code breaking.	**Imagery intelligence (IMINT)** Gathering visual information, including aerial reconnaissance.	**Human intelligence (HUMINT)** Obtaining information from human sources, including spies, prisoners, and deserters.

War Regulations Act were also designed to secure public safety and defend the Commonwealth.

The first wartime spy executed in Britain was Carl Hans Lody on 6 November 1914. British intelligence agents had detected German-born Lody trying to pass on military data. He was arrested, convicted, and shot by a firing squad at the Tower of London – the first execution there for 167 years. The British Army hoped the historic location would impress the public; instead Lody's brave comportment aroused a wave of sympathy. Ten more spies died at the Tower during the war.

Extreme wartime deprivation fuelled the hunt for spies and traitors; often suspicions alone could be enough to secure a death penalty. Austria-Hungary executed some 80,000 civilians caught on the wrong side of the shifting front lines; most were Galician Ukrainians and Bosnian Serbs who had welcomed enemy troops as liberators.

Spy networks

All the combatant nations deemed military intelligence essential. Networks of French, Belgian, and British intelligence agents penetrated France and Belgium and were often aided by citizens who resented the privations of living in German-occupied territory.

The port of Rotterdam in the Netherlands, which remained neutral, became the centre of spying activity, with German and British agents both operating there. It was home to the British Secret Service Bureau's main European station, which worked with Dutch citizens who were free to travel to Germany. Despite little or no

Tomorrow I shall be shot here in the Tower. I have had just judges, and I shall die as an officer, not a spy. Farewell. God bless you.
Carl Hans Lody
German spy,
final letter to his family,
November 1914

training, these agents and Belgian resistance groups could report from behind the Western Front. Germany, which convicted a total of 235 Allied spies during the war, also recruited Dutch citizens to spy on British naval ports.

All sides in the war employed counter-espionage, too. The German *Abteilung III b* formed its counter-intelligence section, *Spionageabwehr*, in the autumn of 1914. It had offices in Denmark, whose geographical location, good cable communications, and neutrality made it a centre of operations for the German, British, French, and Russian secret services.

Evolving technology

France, Germany, and Italy all had air photo-reconnaissance units before the war. From 1914, Britain also began using observation planes and aerial photography to gather military intelligence. As the interpretation of such imagery improved, camouflage for troops and equipment became important.

New technologies were vital to intelligence gathering but could also be exploited by spies. The wireless, in particular, was believed to be a security risk, and most countries prohibited its private use. Encrypted telegrams, sent via the newly completed global network of telegraph cables, were widely used. Consequently, codebreaking evolved rapidly among both the Allies and Central Powers.

One major success in the secret war was Britain's naval intelligence-gathering unit, Room 40, named after the room in the Old Admiralty Building in London's Whitehall that

its team occupied in November 1914. With the British acquisition of three German naval codebooks in the first four months of the war, the unit was soon decoding numerous wireless and telegraph messages, passing on its intelligence to the British navy.

Meanwhile the domestic section of Britain's Security Service Bureau (known as MI5 from September 1916) expanded nearly fiftyfold, to

a staff of 844 members during the four years of conflict. The section oversaw significant developments in techniques of observation and intelligence gathering, such as cable and postal censorship and creating (and breaking) complex codes. If fewer spies were apprehended after the early months of the war, it was because so many of them had been stopped at source. ■

118 - GUERRE EUROPÉENNE 1914

Un espion Français fusillé près de Reims

Shot by French troops, an alleged spy is left dead in public view under a sign denouncing him as a traitor, near Rheims, France, in October 1914.

DEADLO

1915

CK

Germany declares that from 18 February the **seas around Britain** will be considered **a war zone** with **unrestricted U-boat attacks**.

Opening the Battle of Neuve Chapelle, British forces **fire more shells in a day** than its armies fired in the whole of the Boer War (1899–1902). A **severe ammunition crisis looms**.

In the first **Gallipoli landings**, ground forces from France, Britain, Australia, and New Zealand **try to seize the Dardanelles** from the Ottomans but make limited progress.

A **German U-boat sinks the British liner RMS *Lusitania*** off the Irish coast without warning. Among the 1,198 dead are 128 Americans, which causes **outrage in the US**.

 4 FEB 1915

 10 MAR 1915

 25 APR 1915

 7 MAY 1915

FEB–MAR 1915

22 APR 1915

26 APR 1915

31 MAY 1915

French and British ships bombard Ottoman forts along the Dardanelles in a bid to capture the strait by naval means alone, but are forced to retire.

The German army launches **the Second Battle of Ypres**, in which **poison gas is used for the first time** on the Western Front. The offensive achieves little.

Italy signs a secret treaty with Britain, France, and Russia. It agrees to side **with the Allies in return for territorial gains** from Austria-Hungary and the Ottoman Empire.

German zeppelins target London for the first time, dropping incendiaries and bombs, which destroy buildings and **kill seven people**.

As 1915 dawned, hopes that the war might be brief were consigned to the past. It became clear that victory would go to the side that could keep fighting for the longest time. This meant mobilizing the civilian population, including women, to manufacture arms and munitions to support military operations.

Britain soon faced an acute shortage of munitions, however, and other war-related goods that led to a dependence on the US, which – although neutral – was prepared to supply the Allies with financial services and military materials. Ships carrying munitions across the Atlantic were quickly targeted by German U-boats. A concerted U-boat campaign that began in February 1915 led to attacks on passenger liners, too.

Mounting numbers of Americans killed in these attacks set Germany on a collision course with the US.

Civilians became increasingly involved in the war, whether suffering under occupation, in bombing raids, or during the mass internment of "hostile" foreign nationals in concentration camps.

Allied strategy
On the Western Front, the strategic initiative lay with Germany; its armies held Belgium (except for a narrow area around Ypres) and France's industrial centres in the northeast. Creeping German occupation enraged the deeply patriotic French. The strategy for France and its close ally Britain was to pursue offensive action at all levels to regain the French territory that had been lost

The major French spring assault of May 1915 – the Second Battle of Artois – was initially successful at Vimy Ridge, before repeated German counterattacks halted it. British efforts to support the French failed due to a shortage of guns (especially those of heavy calibre) and ammunition. The French autumn offensive in Champagne was larger, involving 35 divisions, but in the end achieved little. The British Army, attacking Loos, used gas for the first time – although unsuccessfully – and was, again, deficient in artillery and munitions.

Looking east
Even before these failures, Allied planners wondered if other theatres of war might offer more success. Strategists argued, as "Westerners" considered the decisive war front

The **Italian army launches** the first of 12 **offensives** to dislodge Austro-Hungarian forces from defensive positions **along the River Isonzo**.

Allied offensives open in **Champagne** and **Loos** on the Western Front. **Casualties are heavy on both sides** and territorial gains for the Allies are limited.

Despite being **neutral**, Greece allows **Anglo-French troops** to land at the port city of **Salonika** to **counter** the threat of **Bulgaria** (allied to the Central Powers).

British forces in Mesopotamia (Iraq) are **forced** from a position close to Baghdad **back to the city of Kut al-Amara**, where they are besieged by the Ottoman army.

23 JUNE 1915   **25 SEP 1915**   **5 OCT 1915**   **3 DEC 1915**

5 SEP 1915   **28 SEP 1915**   **24 OCT 1915**   **28 DEC 1915**

In the face of heavy losses on the Eastern Front, following the Gorlice–Tarnów Offensive, **Tsar Nicholas II takes personal command of the Russian army**.

American banks announce a **$500 million loan to Britain and France**, one of many such financial agreements that bind the US to the Allies.

Turkish authorities begin a series of **genocidal massacres** against their **Armenian minority population**. Up to an estimated 1.5 million Armenians are killed.

The **British cabinet** overrules the tradition of voluntary recruitment in favour of **compulsory military service, initially for single men only**.

---

was in France and Belgium, but the "Easterners", who urged attacks on Austria-Hungary and the Ottoman Empire, were winning the argument.

With trench deadlock in the west, the Ottomans' engagement in the war seemed an opportunity for Anglo-French sea power to gain ground in the east. The Allies decided to try to force a passage through the Dardanelles and Bosphorus, the two straits between the Aegean Sea and the Black Sea. If secured, Constantinople, the Ottoman capital, would fall.

The campaign to capture the Dardanelles in April 1915 focused on the Gallipoli peninsula but never progressed beyond a narrow coastal strip. The Ottoman forces held their positions, creating an impasse, and the Allied forces covertly withdrew during the winter of 1915–16. An unrealistic British attempt to invade the Ottoman Empire along the River Tigris in 1915–16 also failed.

Russian forces had routed Ottoman troops in the Caucasus in the winter of 1914–1915. Ottoman anger and fears of further Russian incursions, led to the scapegoating and massacre of thousands of Armenians, judged suspect because their ancestral homeland spanned areas of both Russia and Turkey.

German victories
In spring 1915, the German high command decided that its army should concentrate on the east and stay mainly on the defensive in the west. General Erich von Falkenhayn, Chief of the German General Staff, planned an offensive to relieve the hard-pressed Austro-Hungarian troops while also threatening Russian forces in the Polish salient. Falkenhayn's offensive succeeded; the Russians fell back in disarray, surrendering Warsaw on 5 August and withdrawing from Russian Poland by early September. In October, Falkenhayn launched an offensive against Serbia and crushed it, using combined armies of the Central Powers.

Dashed hopes for the Allies
As the year drew to a close, the German High Command could take some satisfaction from the success of its strategy. Allied assaults had been contained in the west, while on the Eastern Front, the German army now controlled much of Russia's western territories. For the Allies, 1915 was a year of dashed hopes and ongoing stalemate. ∎

PILE UP THE MUNITIONS!
RAMPING UP PRODUCTION (1915)

Women in a German state-run munitions factory work at a press for grooving artillery gun barrels. Nearly 1.4 million German women were employed in war work.

A t the start of 1915, the quick war predicted in August 1914 had been replaced by one of increasing attrition. Armies required vast quantities of raw materials, and a mighty manufacturing drive to transform them into supplies and munitions for the front.

Strategies and challenges

The war was going to be won as much by the combatants' industrial and agricultural capacity as it was by troop numbers. The objective of the British naval blockade of Germany, which began in August 1914, was to wreck Germany's economy and weaken its population. Industrial supplies vital to Germany, such as metals and coal, were intercepted and seized at sea, as were fertilizers for crop production. By 1915, imports to Germany had fallen by 55 per cent from pre-war levels, and a system of rationing in major cities was introduced.

Yet Germany still outstripped Britain and France in industrial strength. It produced twice as much steel as Britain, and its advanced chemical industry could synthesize ammonia to make explosives. Its government also controlled the supply and use of raw materials and exploited factories and mines in occupied Belgium and France.

Boosting resources

In March 1915, British forces fired more shells in one day at the Battle of Neuve Chapelle than in the whole of the Boer War (1899–1902). By spring, a severe shortage of ammunition – the "shell crisis" – prompted the Munitions of War Act and the building of more than 70 new armaments factories by the end of the year. Chemist Chaim Weizmann – president of the British

See also: Public opinion 44–45 ▪ Society under strain 184–87 ▪ The home front in 1918 250–53 ▪ Mutiny and revolution in Germany 288–89

Explosives production in Britain and Germany

From 1914 to 1916, Germany's explosives manufacturing capacity was far superior to that of Britain, but shortages of raw materials and the weakness of its allies later drained it. Britain's capacity increased rapidly from 1915, boosted by new factories and its vast empire's resources.

Zionist Federation and future first president of Israel – had recently discovered a fermentation process that sped up the production of acetone, a key ingredient of the explosive cordite. From 500,000 in 1914, Britain's shell production rose to 16.4 million in 1915.

Retaining key workers
All combatant countries were hit by the conflicting demands of their armed forces, industry, and agriculture. The mass mobilization of troops left industries and farms short of labour. In August 1915, Britain introduced a national register to ensure that key workers, such as miners and shipbuilders, were kept in place. France pulled hundreds of thousands of skilled workers back from the front and, by the war's end, had recruited almost 200,000 labourers from its colonies.

Governments also turned to women to do factory and field work. By late 1918, around two million women had replaced male workers in Britain; in Germany women made up half of the total workforce.

Inequalities and unrest
The huge financial and social costs of the war bore heavily on all home fronts; inflation soared and wages stagnated. In Britain, accusations of industrial profiteering in 1915 prompted a profit-curbing Treasury Agreement. Russia was riven by strikes – more than 300 in Petrograd alone in 1915 – while German cities saw their first food riots in the autumn. French citizens remained supportive of the war, although pacifist voices grew louder from 1916. Social solidarity was just about holding firm, but popular discontent simmered as governments battled to feed their populations and arm and supply their forces. ▪

The consumption of munitions … has been so great that we must employ all means possible to draw upon and make use of every potential source for munitions production.
German War Department memorandum, 13 August 1914

The Women's Land Army

In 1915, as more land workers left Britain to fight on the front, food production began to suffer. In February 1916, the Women's Farm and Garden Union appealed to the Board of Agriculture and Fisheries to fund a campaign to recruit women to work on the land. The initial Women's National Land Service Corps (WNLSC) quickly gained 2,000 recruits.

In early 1917, the WNLSC helped the government launch the Women's Land Army – with uniforms and awards to acknowledge their service. Training included the use of farm tools, milking, the care of livestock and horses, and, for some, hay-making, mole trapping, and driving tractors. By July 1917, 2,000 women had joined. When the Land Army was wound up in 1919, 23,000 women had served in it – overcoming some early male resistance to become a small part of a crucial workforce.

A 1917 poster by British artist Henry George Gawthorn urges women to join the Land Army to boost Britain's agricultural output.

SHE NEVER HAD BEEN ARMED
THE SINKING OF THE *LUSITANIA* (7 MAY 1915)

IN CONTEXT

FOCUS
U-boat attacks

BEFORE
October 1914 German U-boats begin attacking Allied merchant ships.

November 1914 Britain declares the North Sea a war zone, thereby threatening German merchant ships.

March 1915 The U-boat *U-28* sinks the passenger ship RMS *Falaba*. An American citizen is among the 104 lives lost.

AFTER
June 1915 The Royal Navy arms Q-ships – merchant vessels intended to lure and then destroy U-boats.

February 1917 Germany resumes "unrestricted" U-boat warfare – on hold since 1915.

April 1917 The US enters the war, fuelled partly by ongoing anti-German feeling caused by the sinking of the *Lusitania*.

Britain's status as an island, and its dependence on munitions and supplies from the US and its other trading partners, made the sea war a crucial aspect of the conflict. German naval commanders were determined to disrupt the Allies' transatlantic supply chain. To that end, on 4 February 1915, Germany declared that it would regard the sea around the British Isles as a war zone. Starting from 18 February,

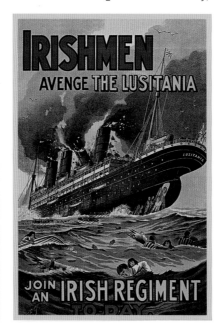

any shipping in the area – whether military or civilian – could be sunk without warning.

On 22 April, the German embassy in Washington, DC, placed a notice in American newspapers to remind travellers that Britain's waters had been designated a combat zone. It appeared beneath an advert featuring the timetable for the British-owned luxury liner RMS *Lusitania*. On 1 May, the ship left New York bound for Liverpool, carrying almost 2,000 passengers and crew. Unbeknown to those passengers, it was also carrying a small amount of munitions, mainly rifle ammunition, in its hold.

A fateful attack
On the afternoon of 7 May, Captain Walther Schwieger, commander of *U-20*, spotted the *Lusitania* off the coast of Ireland. The submarine was submerged, and would have been too slow to attack the liner had not the *Lusitania* turned into its path. Without warning, Schwieger fired a single torpedo. It hit the

The *Lusitania*'s destruction
was swiftly incorporated into Allied propaganda as a rallying cry, as this recruitment poster from 1915 attests.

See also: The naval arms race 32–33 ▪ The war at sea begins 88–93 ▪ The secret war 96–99 ▪ The US and World War I 134–35 ▪ Germany's war machine 182–83 ▪ The US enters the war 194–95 ▪ The U-boats on the attack 200–05

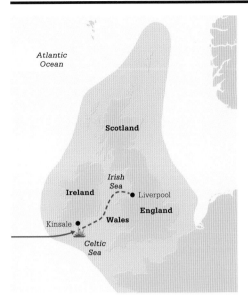

Key:

— Route from New York

⚜ Explosion

--- Route from the point of the wreck

▨ German submarine warfare zone, operational from 18 February 1915

The *Lusitania* liner was just a few hours short of Liverpool when it sank on 7 May 1915. It was struck at 2:10pm, about 18 km (11 miles) off the Irish coast, near Kinsale. Two months later, the SS *Arabic* was torpedoed 80 km (50 miles) south of Kinsale.

Maritime law

At the start of World War I, Germany adhered to a system of internationally accepted laws for commerce raiders known as "prize rules". These dictated that submarine commanders had to surface before stopping a ship, and warn its passengers and crew of their intention to destroy the vessel, thereby allowing them time to board lifeboats.

The submarine campaign of 1915 threw out prize rules, and U-boats sank enemy ships without warning. British merchant ships began flying the flags of neutral countries, as U-boats had orders to avoid sinking any neutral vessels (largely to avoid enraging opinion in the US). The British decision to arm merchant ships – in order to entice U-boats and then destroy them – further threw the prize rules into disarray.

centre of the ship and blew up, followed by a second explosion. The ship sank in just 18 minutes, before the lifeboats could be launched, killing 1,198 of the people onboard, including 128 American citizens.

The deaths caused outrage around the world. Germany argued that the *Lusitania* had been a legitimate target because it was carrying munitions, but the Allies flatly denied its claims. Instead, Allied propaganda presented the incident as cold-blooded murder, provoking an outbreak of anti-German feeling. In Britain, rioters looted German-owned businesses and there was a noticeable increase in the number of men volunteering to join the army.

A measured response

In the US, many Americans who had previously remained neutral now turned against Germany. There were calls to avenge the deaths and a general expectation that the US would declare war

on Germany. Instead, President Woodrow Wilson denounced the attack to the German government as illegal and counter to "the rights of humanity".

Another U-boat sank the British liner SS *Arabic* in August 1915. Germany claimed that it had acted in self-defence, as the ship had been zigzagging (a manoeuvre intended to deter U-boats in pursuit), leading the submarine's commander to believe his vessel might be struck. Three Americans were among the fatalities. This time, Wilson made it clear that if the attack was found to have been unprovoked, the US would cut diplomatic ties.

Germany was left in no doubt that the US would be pushed into entering the war if it continued to target unarmed ships. At the start of September 1915, the German government took the decision to suspend its submarine campaign, although it would be resumed two years later. ▪

There was a submarine on the surface watching us. I saw those sailors watching all those bodies of people and wreckage. The sea was as calm as a pond.
Alice Drury
English nanny who sailed on the *Lusitania*

ALL THE WORLD'S A CAGE
CONCENTRATION CAMPS (1915–18)

IN CONTEXT

FOCUS
Violation of human rights

BEFORE
Late 19th century Barbed wire and automatic weapons are invented – both later used to control interned people.

1896 In Cuba, the Spanish army starts to herd civilians into *reconcentración* camps.

1900 During the Boer War, Britain forces Boer civilians and displaced Africans into "concentration" camps.

AFTER
1919 In Russia, the Soviet authorities introduce a system of forced-labour camps.

1933–45 Nazi Germany creates more than 1,000 concentration camps and six extermination camps.

1942–45 In the US, around 120,000 Japanese Americans and Japanese nationals are interned during World War II.

In 1915, British prime minister Herbert Asquith locked up tens of thousands of German and Austro-Hungarian "aliens" – the legal term for those resident in one country but born in another. In times of war, paranoia over the presence of nationals from "enemy" countries was far from new; people feared they might prove a threat to national security. At the start of the Napoleonic Wars, the last great conflict before World War I, all British male subjects living in France were detained.

Internment spreads
Germans suspected of spying had been rounded up since the start of the war. However, the rising tide of public anger, rioting, and attacks on German shops and families that followed the sinking in May 1915 of the passenger liner RMS *Lusitania*, impelled Asquith's government to do more. The tools for mass incarceration – mainly barbed wire and guards with rapid-fire guns – were available, and soon thousands of arrests were made. By the end of 1915, more than 30,000 foreign-born male civilians aged between 17 and 75 years had been interned in camps across Britain.

Internees at Knockaloe camp on the Isle of Man pause for a moment during gardening duties. The largest British internment camp, Knockaloe held nearly 24,000 "enemy aliens".

See also: Public opinion 44–45 ▪ The secret war 96–99 ▪ The sinking of the *Lusitania* 106–07 ▪ The Armenian Genocide 132–33

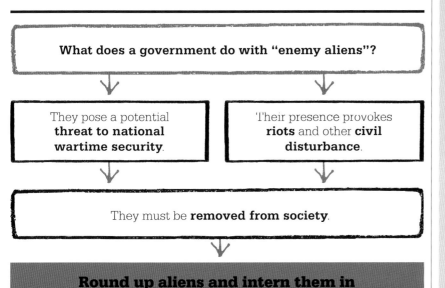

What does a government do with "enemy aliens"?

They pose a potential **threat to national wartime security**.

Their presence provokes **riots** and other **civil disturbance**.

They must be **removed from society**.

Round up aliens and intern them in "concentration camps".

Asquith's internment policies soon spread across the British Empire, to Canada, South Africa, Australia, and New Zealand – and to any British possession where a German or Austro-Hungarian expatriate might be found. German policy was the same; any foreign national residing in Germany but born in Britain or the British Empire was subject to arrest and imprisonment.

An extreme idea evolves
Xenophobia flourished during the war. Any foreign national from an enemy nation was considered potentially dangerous and often interned in camps for the duration of hostilities. There, they performed daily work duties under a degree of duress that varied from country to country. Some governments also seized the personal assets of internees. In October 1917, for example, the US government created an Office of Alien Property Custodian whose official duties involved the confiscation of property owned by resident aliens, often under the flimsiest of pretexts.

Internment proved to be an easy solution to the minimal problem of a relatively small number of enemy citizens living within a wider native population. Britain housed internees in a variety of buildings including disused factories, schools, stables, and castles. When space ran out in 1915, nine transatlantic liners provided further accommodation.

By the end of World War I, nearly 800,000 citizens had been interned worldwide. The camps ranged from the relatively lenient, such as Ruhleben in Germany or Fort Oglethorpe in the US state of Georgia, to the horrifying Deir ez-Zor open-air camp in the Syrian desert, into which Armenians were herded by Ottoman troops and denied food and water. The "death camps" of World War II would later become the tragically logical end point of the concentration camp's evolution. ▪

Ruhleben camp

Located in a western suburb of Berlin, Ruhleben was unlike most concentration camps. It was built around a former horse-racing track and its 5,500 detainees were largely well-educated British civilians intermixed with the crews of captured ships and fishing trawlers. Although housed in crowded stable blocks, the inmates were able to pass their time by playing cricket, football, rugby, and tennis. They also gave music recitals, printed and published a camp magazine, grew their own food, held mock elections, established a postal service, and even set up a Ruhleben Horticultural Society and Arts and Science Union.

Some detainees tried to escape, but few succeeded. One promptly recaptured escapee was British academic, author, and sportsman John Cecil Masterman. He exacted his revenge nearly 30 years later, when he ran the Double-Cross System that wrecked Nazi espionage efforts during World War II.

Civilian prisoners queue for Christmas lunch at Ruhleben in 1917, painted by Anglo-Dutch internee Nico Jungmann.

AS UNDER A GREEN SEA, I SAW HIM DROWNING

THE SECOND BATTLE OF YPRES (APRIL–MAY 1915)

IN CONTEXT

FOCUS
Chemical warfare

BEFORE
August 1914 French troops deploy ethyl bromoacetate (tear gas) grenades.

January 1915 German forces fire xylyl bromide tear-gas shells at Russian positions on Poland's Rawka river. The freezing, windy conditions render them ineffective.

AFTER
September 1915 The British use poison gas at Loos, but it blows back to their own lines.

July 1917 German troops use sulphur-based "mustard gas" – generally not lethal but acutely disabling and disfiguring.

November 1917 British forces deploy mustard gas at the Battle of Cambrai.

1925 The Geneva Protocol bans the use of chemical or biological weapons in war.

There is no idea of merely taking a trench here and there. My object is to surprise the Germans ... The keynote of the work is offensive action.
General Sir Douglas Haig

A woman operates a machine on a British artillery shell production line around 1915. As more men went to war, women were drafted into the munitions workforce, and production was stepped up to meet a desperate shell shortage.

By the end of 1914, both sides found the stalemate on the Western Front frustrating. With neither force making major advances, the fight seemed set to go on indefinitely. On 17 December, the Allies had tried to break the deadlock. The French Tenth Army attacked German forces outside the village of Auchel, starting the First Battle of Artois. A few days later, France's Fourth Army made a push a little to the south, which developed into the First Battle of Champagne. After three weeks of fighting, the Artois offensive ended inconclusively. As March 1915 began, the struggle in Champagne was ongoing, with no sign of victory on either side. It was at this point that the Germans decided to deploy a new lethal weapon – chlorine gas.

Fresh tactics
It had been evident for some time that a new approach was needed. Commanders on both sides were looking for something to give their forces an extra edge. From early 1915, General Sir Douglas Haig, commander of Britain's newly created First Army, and fellow Allied generals started to draw up detailed tactical plans to attack and break through the German lines at Neuve Chapelle, near Lille in northern France, close to the Belgian border.

The Allies took full advantage of new technologies. A sophisticated telephone network was set up to enable the infantry and artillery to coordinate their efforts, and the Royal Flying Corps (RFC) carried out a systematic survey of the battlefield. Aerial photography facilitated detailed maps of an area extending 1.4km (almost a mile) in advance of the Allied front line. Officers on the ground now knew exactly what they would be leading their soldiers into. The RFC would be airborne for the attack, using wireless transmitters and other signals to provide infantry officers with up-to-the-minute information and help the artillery fine-tune their shell bombardments.

Artillery bombardment had also evolved, with shrapnel shells largely replaced by high explosives. There were exceptions, as testing had established that shrapnel was more effective for cutting barbed wire and smashing fence posts, while large blasts tended to lift up the wire and wooden posts and deposit the debris roughly where it had been before. The Allies had also decided to attempt a fast and furious "hurricane bombardment" in place of the long hours (or days) of unrelenting shelling they had earlier relied on to weaken the opposing German forces.

Failures and recriminations

Early on 10 March, General Haig's First Army launched a surprise attack just west of Neuve Chapelle, with a huge barrage of shells that breached the German trenches. Haig's forces advanced, but the

> A cynical and barbarous disregard of the well-known usages of civilized war.
> **Field Marshall Sir John French**
> **on the use of chlorine gas at Ypres**

attack was soon thwarted by a lack of ammunition. In the heat of battle, the Allied forces' telephone system also failed under heavy German artillery fire, leaving different sections of Haig's army unable to communicate with each other.

Although the German troops were rocked by the first assault, they managed to regroup and recover much of their lost ground. The Allied plan had been to secure a swift victory, then attempt to

rush the German positions some 5km (3 miles) northeast of Neuve Chapelle on Aubers Ridge. After losing the early advantage afforded by intensive bombardment, the Allies could no longer gain from such surprise tactics.

The shortage of shells would also hinder later spring offensives, leading to a "shell crisis", a scandal stoked by British newspapers, such as The Times and Daily Mail. Chancellor of the Exchequer David Lloyd George used the uproar to pressurize the British government over its lack of a centralized plan for armament manufacture and distribution. Weeks later, he was made minister of munitions.

Chemicals and Ypres

The search for some kind of special edge in the conflict continued – and not only on the Allied side. The German commanders were just as desperate to find a breakthrough. In September 1914, artillery expert Major Max Bauer had proposed that Germany should embark on a chemical-weapons programme. »

David Lloyd George

Born in Manchester in 1863, David Lloyd George had Welsh roots and a Welsh upbringing. A Liberal, he became MP for Caernarfon in 1890 and rose through the party ranks, attracting attention with his opposition to the Second Boer War (1899–1902). His calls for restraint during the dreadnought arms race went unheeded, but he was taken seriously as a statesman.

When war broke out in 1914, Lloyd George had been chancellor of the exchequer for six years. He worked hard to foster better cooperation between government, employers, and trade unions. By

1915, he had become minister of munitions, and by 1916 secretary of state for war. His views often clashed with those of senior army and naval officers, but he oversaw a crucial surge in armaments production.

The British public became increasingly disillusioned with prime minister Herbert Asquith's handling of the war, and in December 1916, Lloyd George replaced him and later took a leading role in the Paris Peace Conference. In 1922, he resigned from office, but remained an MP until his death in 1945.

By spring 1915, a team of scientists led by German chemist Fritz Haber had found a way of weaponizing chlorine gas, ready for deployment at the Western Front.

For either side to secure victory, there was one key location where the deadlock had to be broken – the Ypres salient in Flanders. Here, the presence of the British Second Army and two French divisions was, for the Germans, both a temptation and a challenge. The position of the Allied armies left them dangerously exposed, with German forces on three sides. Their occupation of higher ground that overlooked German-held territory, however,

French soldiers struggle against the shocking effects of chlorine gas as German troops, equipped with rudimentary gas masks, advance towards them during the Ypres battle.

represented a continuing threat. It was this higher ground that the German forces would choose for their next offensive.

The Allies were not expecting an attack of any kind and were completely unprepared for chlorine gas. When troops saw the wispy cloud of vapour advancing up the slopes of the Gravenstafel Ridge towards them, on the evening of 22 April, they regarded it with no more than mild curiosity. Their complacency was short-lived. No sooner had they come into contact with the chlorine than their flesh burst out into burning blisters; as they breathed it in, the men felt the insides of their throats and lungs erupt. So traumatizing were the effects of the gas that it overrode all normal instincts; brave, experienced soldiers simply panicked. For the most part,

> Men ... exhausted, gasping, frothing yellow mucus from their mouths, their faces blue and distressed.
>
> **Lieutenant Colonel G.W.G. Hughes**
> **Royal Army Medical Corps**

they broke and ran, all discipline forgotten. Within 10 minutes, 5,000 Allied troops had been killed by chlorine inhalation; 5,000 more would die over the next few hours. Another 2,000 staggered around, sickened or blinded, until they were captured. Wide gaps opened up in the Allied line. The advancing Germans simply sauntered through.

Diminishing returns

Ironically, the effects of their new weapon had so far exceeded the expectations of the Germans that they were unable to press their advantage as they might have done. The air into which troops walked was lethally contaminated. While they gained some protection by breathing through cotton cloths soaked in sodium bicarbonate solution or urine, the conditions were not conducive to digging in effectively, nor to bringing up all the artillery and ammunition they would need to hold the ground.

Although the German army had the initiative, the Allied soldiers got the measure of the new weapon to a certain extent and quickly learned to mitigate its effects with wet rags. They rallied and put up

The French satirical magazine *Le Rire Rouge* dubs Germany *La Bête Puante* ("The Stinking Beast") on its May 1915 cover, condemning the use of gas as a chemical weapon.

fierce resistance. Casualties were terrible on both sides. Gas may have made the headlines, but the Second Battle of Ypres saw men killed and wounded in their tens of thousands by more conventional weapons.

Despite unflagging defiance from British, French, and Belgian troops, the German armies pushed southwest towards Ypres, taking the village of St Julien in the first week of May. Advancing up the nearby Frezenberg Ridge, they were thwarted by a brave last stand from Princess Patricia's Canadian Light Infantry on 13 May. The German attack was losing momentum. Gas was once more deployed against British positions around the village of Bellewaerde, but their defenders managed to hold on. The German offensive was abandoned on 25 May.

Countermeasures
By late May, British physiologist John Scott Haldane had developed a reasonably effective gas mask, known as the Black Veil Respirator, which covered the nose and mouth. This was quickly followed by the British Hypo Helmet, or "Smoke Hood", which protected the whole head and could be tucked under a

jacket collar. More than 2.5 million masks would be manufactured over the next three months.

These measures could not wholly neutralize the threat of gas, but they did provide some degree of defence. Despite its initial deadly impact, chlorine gas did not change the course of the conflict as the Germans had hoped. The British government was vociferous in its condemnation of what it saw as an outrageously inhuman (and illegal) weapon, but quietly set about building its own capabilities for gas warfare. Soon British and French forces would be able to compete on equally cruel terms.

Inconclusive but significant
The Second Battle of Ypres may not have been decisive, but it had a significant impact. Around 70,000 Allied combatants had been killed or wounded – troops not just from Britain and France but also Belgium, Canada, India, Algeria, and Morocco. The German side suffered around 35,000 casualties.

The Belgian city of Ypres (evacuated at an early stage in the battle) had been razed to the ground under heavy bombardment by German artillery. On the wider Ypres salient, the situation remained largely unchanged. The German forces had achieved some minor territorial gains, but the Allies were still in control of the all-important higher ground. The introduction of chlorine gas as a weapon, however, had changed the terms of the war and begun a debate around the morality of using chemicals in any kind of warfare. ∎

Chlorine gas
Scientists under the direction of German chemist Fritz Haber had been researching the use of chemical weapons on the battlefield since September 1914. They succeeded in developing a range of non-lethal noxious gases before settling on chlorine. As well as an irritant, it was so corrosive that inhalation could damage the throat and lungs badly enough to cause death by suffocation. The gas was also readily available as a by-product of the industrial manufacture of dye.

Stored under pressure, then discharged through siphons, chlorine caused havoc among the unprepared Allied troops at the Second Battle of Ypres, but would never again be quite so effective. Even ad hoc measures, such as wet cloths, reduced its impact, and gas masks soon offered good protection. However, gas remained a potent threat. Troops caught unawares were extremely vulnerable, and it was regarded with a terror that conventional weapons could not match.

Padded cotton respirators, worn here by the Argyll and Sutherland Highlanders in 1915, provided some protection against gas attacks.

THE CAVALRY OF THE CLOUDS

WAR IN THE AIR (1914–15)

In the years leading up to the outbreak of war, armed forces throughout Europe had been exploring the military potential of aircraft, and by 1914 all the major powers had fledgling aviation divisions. Although the overall usefulness and performance of aircraft was initially questionable, as the war progressed and technology advanced, it became clear that they could play key roles in warfare.

A giant of the sky
Germany explored the potential of airships, dubbed "zeppelins" after Count Ferdinand von Zeppelin, who invented them in 1900. More than 150 m (490 ft) long, the fabric-covered

See also: Europe's colonies and empires 28–29 ▪ The German bombing campaign begins 136–37 ▪ The German bombing campaign continues 222–23 ▪ Tactical flying 238–39 ▪ Trench warfare transformed 254–57

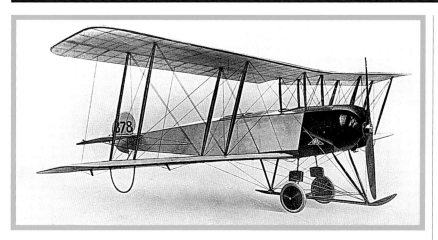

The British Avro 504 made the first ever strategic bombing raid. On 21 November 1914, three planes flew 400 km (250 miles) to attack the zeppelin sheds at Friedrichshafen, Germany.

craft had a light metal frame fitted with hydrogen-filled cells. Powered by at least three engines, they could fly at around 135 kph (85 mph) and carry a large bomb payload.

A German zeppelin carried out the first air raid of World War I. On 6 August 1914, as part of Germany's invasion of Belgium, it dropped artillery shells on the city of Liège, killing nine civilians. After limited success with airships on the Western Front, the German military used them to attack the British mainland. In January 1915, airships began a series of bombing raids against military and industrial targets in London and towns on England's east coast, but poor weather and navigation meant that bombs fell indiscriminately. In a total of 52 zeppelin raids on Britain during World War I, over 550 people were killed and more than 1,300 were injured. Germany deployed 115 airships and lost 77 to enemy fire or accident. Ultimately, the craft

proved too fragile, cumbersome, and flammable to be an effective weapon of war. By 1917, planes were preferred for bombing campaigns.

View from the air

The German army and navy also used airships to carry out aerial reconnaissance – observing enemy positions and movements – as did Britain's Royal Naval Air Service (RNAS), especially to counter German U-boat attacks. Airships were particularly useful for spotting enemy vessels beyond the horizon.

From 1914, reconnaissance was also carried out by early planes. They were not much faster than airships but considerably more manoeuvrable and cheaper to build and maintain. At the Battle of Tannenberg, on the Eastern Front, in August 1914, German planes accurately reported the movement of Russian forces, enabling the German army to take appropriate countermeasures. Similarly, pilots of the British Royal Flying Corps (RFC) and the French air service observed weak points in the German attack on French and British troops at the First Battle of the Marne in September 1914, »

At the start of the war, airships and early planes are **peripheral to the main military action**.

As **trench warfare develops**, both sides recognize that aircraft are **essential for gathering information** about their opponents' movements.

Once **planes become armed**, they can **attack enemy aircraft** as well as **scout and drop small bombs**.

Both sides build **bigger planes** that can carry **larger quantities of explosives** to drop on **strategic targets**.

Aircraft become ever more powerful weapons of war.

helping the Allies outflank the German forces and thwart their rapid advance through France.

The fighter plane emerges

Once reconnaissance aircraft became a regular feature over the battlefield, action was taken against them. At first, air crews on opposing sides merely waved to each other to acknowledge contact, but this changed with the arrival of revolvers, shotguns, and rifles in the cockpit. In these primitive attempts to arm aircraft lay the beginnings of the fighter aircraft and the concept of air superiority.

German and French aviation designers led the race to transform the plane's simple observation platform into an attack area. The most effective aircraft weapon was a flexibly mounted forward-firing machine gun. Some aircraft followed the "pusher" design, with the engine and propeller located at the rear of the fuselage. These could be easily adapted to take

A British war poster warning civilians of the type of aircraft that might attack reveals the range of German and British aircraft circling the skies in 1915.

a forward-facing machine gun. Most aircraft, however, were of the "tractor" type, with the propeller mounted conventionally at the front end of the fuselage, where its wide arc of movement obstructed bullets fired directly forwards.

Attack breakthrough

The problem of the front propeller impeding the machine gun was solved by French pilot Roland Garros and aeronautical engineer Raymond Saulnier. By March 1915, the pair had developed a system that synchronized a gun's rate of fire with the propeller's spin, so that pilots could fire through the gaps between the rotating blades. Because the system was not completely foolproof, they fitted steel deflector plates to the propeller to protect its blades. Garros downed several German aircraft before his own plane was shot from the sky in April 1915 and he was taken prisoner.

Fokker planes were dreaded by British pilots, but this Fokker E-III was brought down intact on the Western Front, giving the Allies a chance to study the plane's advanced design.

The propellor and gun from Garros's aircraft were sent to Berlin. There, 25-year-old Germany-based Dutch aviation designer Anthony Fokker studied them and within days developed a more sophisticated design – the interrupter gear system. This ensured a machine gun would stop firing if a propeller blade passed directly in front of it. Fokker combined the system with his own monoplane – the Eindekker, "single deck". This, in its E-III version, used from December 1915, became arguably the world's first true fighter aircraft.

The Fokker planes played havoc with the slow-moving aircraft of the Allies in what became known as the "Fokker Scourge", which lasted from summer 1915 until early 1916. The Allies countered with the arrival of improved aircraft, notably the British FE2b, a pusher model with a front-firing machine gun that entered service in September 1915.

> Of course it [the Fokker Eindecker] was bound to have a demoralizing effect on us … Several squadrons got so badly shot up that the whole of their morale crumbled.
> **Cyril Gordon Burge**
> **12 Squadron, Royal Flying Corps**

It was followed by the Airco DH2 and the French Nieuport 11, which helped swing the balance of air power in favour of the Allies until autumn 1916, when the German series of Albatros biplanes – with two machine guns and capable of 175 kph (109 mph) – became the preeminent fighter aircraft.

Aces and new tactics

A fighter pilot who recorded five or more aerial victories – or "kills" – was awarded the accolade "ace".

The cover of the May 1915 edition of the British *Boy's Own Paper*, featuring combat between two planes, shows that aerial exploits captured the imagination of children as well as adults.

All the major combatants produced aces, whose bravery and almost inevitable death captured the public imagination. The French Les Cigognes ("Storks") Squadron included Georges Guynemer, who had 53 kills before he died in combat in 1917, and the top-scoring French ace René Fonck (75 kills), who was a rare pilot survivor of the war. Among Germany's elite fighter units, the most famous was the Jagdgeschwader I ("Fighter Squadron 1"), created in 1917. Its commander was Baron Manfred von Richthofen (the "Red Baron"), who achieved 80 kills before he died in action in April 1918.

As the first nation to develop an effective fighter aircraft, Germany also pioneered aerial tactics. These included blinding an enemy pilot by attacking his plane from the direction of the sun, fighting in pairs for mutual support and protection, and performing an Immelmann turn – named after

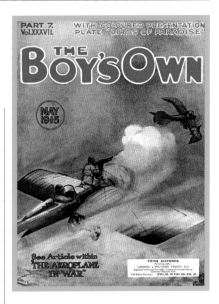

fighter ace Max Immelmann – a steep climb followed by a loop to bring the plane behind and level with an enemy craft.

Britain and its empire generated the greatest number of pilot aces, including Canadian Billy Bishop (72 kills) and Irishman Mick Mannock (61 kills). Englishman Albert Ball (44 kills), who died in May 1917 aged just 20, epitomized the spirit of the air ace with his good looks, natural daring, and superb solo flying skills. ∎

A British pilot prepares a Thornton Pickard Type C aerial aircraft camera attached to the side of his BE2c two-seater biplane in 1915.

Eyes in the sky

Aerial photography proved vital in mapping static, trench-bound fronts, tracking the movement of troops, and helping artillery to coordinate and direct their fire.

Tethered balloons provided a stable platform for aerial observation and were used by both sides, but they were unable to see far into enemy-held territory and were relatively easy to shoot down. More effective was the two-seater aircraft, carrying a glass-plate camera and roaming at will. Once a target area was

selected, the pilot flew repeatedly over it, while his observer made sketches and took photographs to create a detailed mosaic picture of enemy trench positions.

At first, individual film plates were changed by hand, often in freezing conditions. However, the introduction of the "Type C" camera in summer 1915 allowed up to 36 plates to be changed mechanically, producing a rapid succession of images. By 1916, it was possible to take pictures and deliver them to army commanders within the hour.

A NEW AND TREACHEROUS ENEMY

ITALY ENTERS THE WAR (MAY 1915)

IN CONTEXT

FOCUS
Italian ambitions

BEFORE
1861 The unification of Italy leaves some Italian minorities resident within the borders of neighbouring states.

1911–12 Italy is victorious in the Italo-Turkish War, taking the Dodecanese Islands and much of what is now Libya, but is left with a depleted army and financially drained.

AFTER
1918 At the war's end, poet and patriot Gabriele D'Annunzio says Italy has won a "mutilated victory".

1919 American, British, and French objections at the Paris Peace Conference deny Italy much of the land promised to it in the 1915 Treaty of London.

1936 With the conquest of Ethiopia, Benito Mussolini launches his plans for a new Roman Empire.

Italy is **united in 1861**, but some Italians feel the **new nation is incomplete**.

Italy's **alliance with Germany and Austria-Hungary does not help** it achieve its territorial ambitions.

A nationalist movement known as *Italia irredenta* ("unredeemed Italy") emerges in the country.

In World War I, Italy concludes that only the **defeat of Austria-Hungary** will further its expansionist aims.

Italy joins the Allies in exchange for the promise of unredeemed territory.

Irredentism – the belief that Italian-speaking areas in nearby countries should belong to Italy – became a national cause in the late 19th century. Many such areas lay within Austria-Hungary, Italy's partner, together with Germany, in the Triple Alliance concluded in 1882. Italy had joined the alliance primarily for protection against France, its rival in a quest for territory in North Africa. By 1914, however, with little to show for its allegiance, Italy opted for neutrality rather than fighting alongside its allies.

Italian prime minister Antonio Salandra argued that the Triple Alliance was a defensive agreement, which did not oblige Italy to support partners who were the aggressors in the war. Nor was Italy yet ready to fight again after its recent Italo-Turkish war. Its

See also: The situation in Europe 18–19 ▪ The Alliance System 30–31 ▪ The final battles of the Isonzo river 212–13 ▪ The end of the war in Italy 284–85

artillery was antiquated, it had too few mortars and shells, and would need a mass mobilization of largely unskilled peasant conscripts to supplement its small, trained army. Under the liberalizing leadership of Salandra's predecessor Giovanni Giolitti, Italy had also developed closer relations with the Triple Entente powers (Britain, France, and Russia). Yet, in spring 1915, Salandra, keen to fulfil Italy's irredentist claims, began to weigh up what might be on offer from the war's two opposing sides.

An alliance of opportunity

On 26 April 1915, Italy signed the Treaty of London, committing it to join the Allies and declare war on the Central Powers within a month. Britain, France, and Russia wanted Italy's support but were aware that their new ally had been driven less by principle than by the prospect of gaining more territory in the event of victory. This included areas in Austria-Hungary, from the Trentino and South Tyrol region to Trieste and the Adriatic islands, and parts of Anatolia in the Ottoman Empire.

Italy officially revoked the Triple Alliance on 3 May 1915. On 23 May, it formally declared war on Austria-Hungary but did not declare war on Germany until 28 August 1916.

Mountain warfare

The plan was to attack Austria-Hungary over Italy's far northeastern border, across the Isonzo river and the rugged limestone Carso Plateau. Italian commander Luigi Cadorna viewed this as the fastest route through to Trieste – and beyond.

On 23 June, on a vertiginous battlefield of jagged crags and mountainsides, Cadorna's army attacked. His troops outnumbered the Austro-Hungarian forces but his opponents had occupied higher, more advantageous positions and were better prepared and better trained. Despite some early gains, by 7 July the Italians had been routed in the First Battle of the Isonzo, with some 15,000 casualties, compared to 10,000 on the Austro-Hungarian side.

Eleven days later, Cadorna launched a second attack, which exhausted ammunition supplies on both sides. Two more offensives in 1915 produced a stalemate and a further vast toll of casualties. ▪

Known as *Alpini* **("Alpines"),** Italian mountain troops haul an artillery gun up a snow-covered rock face in 1915. In the winter battles, troops were blasted by wind, ice, and snow, with avalanches a constant, deadly threat.

Luigi Cadorna

Born into a military family in the Kingdom of Sardinia in 1850, Luigi Cadorna studied at the Turin Military Academy. Commissioned as a second lieutenant at the age of 18, he rose through the ranks to become a colonel in 1892. Though near retirement age in 1914, Cadorna was made chief of the Italian general staff.

Given command of the Austro-Italian frontier when Italy entered the war in 1915, Cadorna exercised a harsh discipline and an inflexible approach during the battles of the Isonzo. The full-frontal attacks he favoured often proved fatal against fierce machine-gun fire on icy mountain terrain. Men who could not cope were subjected to show trials and firing squads, further damaging morale. Ground was won at a tremendous cost of lives and seldom held for long.

After Italy's defeat in the Twelfth Battle of the Isonzo at Caporetto in 1917, Cadorna lost his post and was sent to represent Italy at the Allied Supreme War Council in Versailles, France. Made a field marshal in 1924, he died in Bordighera, Liguria, in 1928.

A NAME THAT WILL NEVER DIE

THE GALLIPOLI CAMPAIGN
(APRIL 1915—JANUARY 1916)

IN CONTEXT

FOCUS
Amphibious landings

BEFORE
490 BCE An invading Persian army lands on the shores of the Greek mainland, before it is defeated by Greek forces at the Battle of Marathon.

11 September 1914 Troops of the Australian army make the first amphibious landing of World War I – on the German-controlled South Pacific island of New Britain.

AFTER
1923 The Dardanelles and Bosphorus straits are opened to all civilian shipping under the Treaty of Lausanne, signed by Turkey and the Allied nations of World War I.

1944 The success of the Allied powers' Normandy landings in World War II – the largest ever seaborne invasion – is due, in part, to lessons learned from the Gallipoli campaign.

I n late 1914, as war stalled on the Western Front, British politicians looked to the east and how they might support Russia against the Ottoman Empire, which had allied with the Central Powers (Germany and Austria-Hungary) and declared war on Britain, France, and Russia in November 1914. The British hoped to force a way through the Dardanelles – the narrow strait in northwest Turkey that leads from the Aegean Sea to the Sea of Marmara, the Bosphorus strait, and then the Black Sea. The plan was to secure the sea route,

capture Constantinople (Istanbul) on the banks of the Bosphorus, and work with the Russians to knock the Ottoman Empire out of the war.

After a failed naval attempt to break through the Dardanelles in February and March 1915, the Allies launched a military offensive to capture the Gallipoli peninsula on the western side of the strait. The campaign lasted almost nine months – from the initial invasion on 25 April to the final evacuation between 8 and 9 January 1916 – and failed in all of its objectives.

The British rationale

Given the stalemate on the Western Front, targeting the Ottoman Empire – the weakest member of the Central Powers – had seemed a logical strategy to the British. First Lord of the Admiralty Winston Churchill had championed such an attack on the Dardanelles, relishing a chance to use the Royal Navy in a major offensive. Attacking the straits, he and others argued, would draw attention away from the Suez Canal, a vital British link to India. Securing a passage through the straits would also ease the military

HMS *Irresistible*, assigned to the naval campaign in the Dardanelles in March 1915, struck a mine. Inundated by water, the ship sank with the loss of 150 crew members.

and financial pressure on Russia, enabling it to receive armaments from Britain and to resume grain exports from Ukraine.

Then part of the Russian Empire, Ukraine produced around a third of all wheat traded globally. The Ottoman's closure of the straits in September 1914 had blocked Russia's sea route from the Black Sea, depriving it of essential

A good army of 50,000 and sea-power   that is the end of the Turkish menace.
Winston Churchill
First Lord of the Admiralty

See also: The Balkans 25 ▪ The Ottoman Empire in decline 26–27 ▪ Ottoman Turkey enters the war 84–85 ▪ The war in the Caucasus 130 ▪ The war in Mesopotamia 131 ▪ The Armenian Genocide 132–33 ▪ The Battle of Megiddo 286–87

income from exported wheat. Britain was also eager to boost the global supply of wheat to avoid social unrest at home and across its empire as grain became scarce and food prices spiralled.

A multiethnic campaign

The first British attack in the Dardanelles in February and March 1915 was by ship alone, as Field Marshal Lord Kitchener, Britain's secretary of state for war, refused to release land forces. For Kitchener, the campaign was a distraction from the main business of fighting on the Western Front.

The naval attack, hampered by minefields, failed to destroy the Ottoman fortifications, forcing Kitchener to change his mind and form a multinational land army, the Mediterranean Expeditionary Force (MEF) under General Sir Ian Hamilton. The 75,000-strong MEF comprised British and Irish professional soldiers from the 29th Division, and naval reservists and volunteers in the Royal Naval Division. Also included were Gurkha and Sikh battalions from India, the French Corps Expéditionnaire d'Orient (CEO) – made up of French Europeans, colonial troops from Africa, and men from the Foreign Legion – plus the newly recruited soldiers of the Australian and New Zealand Army Corps (ANZAC), who became known as "Anzacs". The transport vessels assembled off the Greek island of Lemnos.

MEF troops crowd V beach in a photograph taken from SS *River Clyde*, a landing ship adapted from a coal-carrying vessel to confuse the Ottoman forces. The ship carried around 2,000 troops to Gallipoli.

By the time Hamilton had prepared his invasion, the Ottoman forces, commanded by German General Otto Liman von Sanders, were ready for them, positioned at points along the shores of the Dardanelles where attacks were expected. Most of the Ottoman troops were Turkish peasants, supported by Syrians and Kurds; their officers were mainly Turkish but also included some Albanians and North African and Mesopotamian Arabs.

The first landings

On 25 April, following a detailed plan drawn up by Hamilton, French soldiers led a diversionary attack at Kum Kale on the south shore of the mouth of the strait, while the Royal Naval Division led another at Bulair, well to the northeast of the other landings. To distract the Ottoman defenders, New Zealander Bernard Freyberg volunteered to swim

You have got through the difficult business, now you have only to dig, dig, dig.
General Sir Ian Hamilton
MEF commander-in-chief

ashore to light flares. Hamilton focused his main effort on Cape Helles at the tip of the peninsula, identifying five landing points – code-named S, V, W, X, and Y – for his most experienced soldiers. The toughest of these were V and W beaches. To get the men as close to V beach as possible, the troopship »

Mustafa Kemal Atatürk

Born in 1881 in Salonika (now Thessaloniki, Greece, but then part of the Ottoman Empire), Mustafa Kemal attended a secular school and later a military college in Constantinople (Istanbul). In 1905 he graduated as a captain.

Sent to the Gallipoli peninsula in the Balkan Wars (1912–13), Kemal helped the Ottoman Empire regain lost territory. In 1914, he took command of the 19th Division of the army, and played a pivotal role in thwarting the Allied attack on the Dardanelles in 1915.

From 1919 to 1922, Kemal led Ottoman forces in overturning the humiliating peace treaty imposed on the Ottoman Empire after World War I, expelled occupying Allied forces, and extended Ottoman boundaries, crushing Armenian resistance.

In 1923, Kemal became founder and first president of the Republic of Turkey. He adopted the name Atatürk, "Father of the Turks", enacted significant modern reforms, and ruled until his death in 1938.

SS *River Clyde* was run ashore and openings cut in its side. The men then jumped out onto a makeshift pontoon – a floating bridge to the beach. However, the ingenious scheme had a fatal flaw. Ottoman forces were waiting for them, and their machine guns cut down scores of MEF troops before they reached the narrow beach. Only at nightfall could the rest of the soldiers land. At W beach, meanwhile, the Lancashire Fusiliers stormed ashore but also came under fierce Ottoman fire. Of the 1,000 men who attacked and eventually took the beach, 600 were killed or wounded.

An equally brutal battle took place further north on the peninsula, at Z beach. In what was conceived as a bid to block Ottoman reinforcements, and considered supplementary to the main battles, Anzac troops were sent ashore at Ari Burnu – later known as Anzac Cove – which proved to be a death trap. Faced with steep ravines at their landing site, they scrambled forwards, only to be met by men of the Ottoman 57th Regiment led by the skilled commander Mustafa Kemal. With his guidance, the Ottomans held back the Anzacs and managed to maintain control of the highest positions. By the end of the day, the Anzacs had suffered 2,000 casualties out of the 16,000 who landed on the Gallipoli shores.

Deadlock and disease

The Gallipoli campaign became mired in a stalemate. By the end of the first week of May, the Allies

were firmly established on the peninsula but, unable to reach the high ground, could advance no further, nor could the Ottoman forces succeed in driving the invaders back into the sea. Both sides dug trench systems for shelter.

A series of Allied offensives at Cape Helles between late April and early June failed disastrously due to hurried planning, exhausted troops, inadequate artillery support, and unimaginative and overambitious tactics. Ottoman offensives were also unsuccessful. Between 18 and 19 May, Kemal's Ottoman troops launched a mass attack at Anzac Cove. They were mown down by Anzac rifle and machine-gun fire, leaving thousands of dead bodies thickly strewn in a strip of no-man's-land between the lines. In the heat of summer, the stench became intolerable, and a truce was agreed to clear the casualties from the battlefield on 24 May – the only official ceasefire of the entire war.

Australian troops are depicted storming ashore at Anzac Cove, then scrambling up cliffs, in a painting by American-born British artist Cyrus Cuneo (1879–1916).

Where corpses lay unburied and unreachable in no-man's-land elsewhere, flies bred in swarms, then spred to the latrines and the troops' food. A lack of clean water and the crowded conditions behind the Allied lines made it impossible to maintain sanitary conditions, and sickness rates spiralled. Two Canadian nurses died of dysentery, and 12 of the remaining 25 nurses were invalided home.

With no space for field hospitals, serious cases required evacuation, which was also problematic. The three hospital ships accompanying the campaign and seven converted transport ships were overwhelmed. Within the first 10 days of fighting, every hospital bed in Alexandria, Egypt – over 1,600 km (1,000 miles) from Gallipoli – had been filled. At least 150,000 Allied soldiers passed through hospitals in Egypt and Malta during the campaign. For the Ottoman troops, sickness was less of a problem as they had better supply lines and a number of field hospitals.

Renewed offensive

A month after the Gallipoli invasion, the British government fell and was replaced by a coalition. At this point, military decisions stalled, which delayed the dispatch of the substantial reinforcements and armaments troops required. A shortage of shells meant there were insufficient munitions to supply the Western Front, let alone Gallipoli. However, as soon as two new army divisions had been dispatched from Britain – volunteers who had responded to Kitchener's call for recruits – plans for a renewed offensive to break the Gallipoli stalemate were put into action. The main focus for the new offensive was to be three high points in the Anzac sector, with new landings at nearby Suvla Bay. »

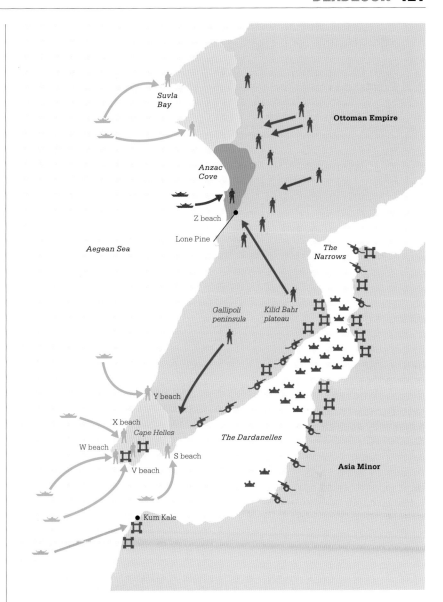

The main Allied offensive began on 25 April, with an attack on Cape Helles and at what became known as Anzac Cove, while the French led a diversionary attack at Kum Kale. Fierce Ottoman resistance resulted in deadlock, and a fresh Allied offensive in August around Suvla Bay could not break it. By 9 January 1916, all Allied troops had been evacuated.

Key:

Anzac landings	Land held by MEF troops
Anzac troops	Turkish troops
Land held by Anzac troops	Turkish army movement
French diversionary force	Turkish guns
MEF landings	Turkish minefields
MEF troops	Turkish forts

With **stalemate on the Western Front**, Britain seeks to make **headway in southeastern Europe**.

Perceiving the Ottoman Empire as **weaker after its Balkan War losses**, Britain **targets the Gallipoli peninsula** along the Dardanelles strait.

A mismanaged campaign that underestimates the Ottoman army's preparedness and skills **fails** – with **huge losses on both sides**.

The costly action has little impact on World War I, but the soldiers' bravery proves inspirational, especially for Ottoman and Anzac forces.

Night-time advances through difficult terrain and a series of coordinated attacks were planned for early August. The Ottomans had built improvised roofs to protect their trenches. To capture them, Australian soldiers were required to advance (some through a specially constructed tunnel) and then jump into the trenches to fight hand to hand. Although Turkish trenches were gained, one piece of high ground briefly held, and more territory captured, the offensive failed to deliver a decisive victory.

On 6 August, a diversionary attack by the First Australian Division at Lone Pine, on the southern end of Anzac positions, became one of the fiercest Gallipoli battles. Five days of brutal close combat resulted in 2,300 Australian and 6,000 Turkish casualties. For their bravery at Lone Pine, seven Australians won the Victoria Cross (the highest British military honour). Despite this and other

MEF guns and personnel are evacuated on a raft in broad daylight from Suvla Bay, after the mismanaged August offensive. Sir Frederick Stopford, the commander at Suvla, was dismissed.

heroic acts from Anzac troops, the attack had little impact on the Ottoman forces. The MEF never came close to capturing the high ground of the Kilid Bahr plateau, which would have enabled the Allies to dominate the Dardanelles strait. By 10 August, it was clear that the new initiative had failed.

The reckoning

Voices within the MEF's higher command continued to argue for further attacks, but they were gradually suppressed. Criticisms from within Hamilton's team of staff officers were shared in London, but the campaign's fiercest denunciation came from Australian journalist Keith Murdoch (father of Australian-American magnate Rupert Murdoch). He tried to smuggle out a critical account by British war correspondent Ellis Ashmead-Bartlett. When this was confiscated by military police, he rewrote it and sent his 8,000-word report to Australian prime minister Andrew Fisher and British government officials in London.

> God be thanked, the entire Gallipoli peninsula has been cleansed of the enemy.
> **General Otto Liman von Sanders**
> Commander of the Ottoman forces, 9 January 1916

On 14 October, General Hamilton was demoted. His replacement, General Sir Charles Monro, then recommended the evacuation of all Allied troops, a view confirmed by Kitchener the next month following a personal visit to the peninsular. Employing elaborate deceptions to maintain the illusion of a full military presence, the front lines were gradually thinned out. Anzac Cove and Suvla Bay were fully evacuated during the night of 19–20 December 1915, and a similar operation was carried out at Cape Helles by 9 January 1916.

Losses and legacy

Some 489,000 men fought in the MEF at Gallipoli. Opposing them were around 550,000 Ottoman soldiers, whose combat strength at any one time never numbered more than 315,500. Ottoman success came at an estimated cost of more than 250,000 casualties, while Allied failure left at least 132,000 killed or wounded. French and Australian deaths were roughly comparable – both close to 8,000 – with Britain losing more than 27,000 troops, New Zealand around 2,500, and India nearly 1,700.

Anzac troops contributed poems, stories, and images in response to the call from Australian war correspondent Charles Bean for material to create *The Anzac Book*, published in 1916 to commemorate the Gallipoli battles.

The Dardanelles campaign was the Ottoman Empire's only significant victory during World War I, and primarily remembered in Turkey for the emergence of Mustafa Kemal, who would go on to lead and create the modern state of Turkey. The MEF was hampered by indecisive political leadership, insufficient supplies of men and arms, and debilitating sickness. In Britain, the campaign was a political humiliation that prompted an enquiry – the Dardanelles Commission – which confirmed the campaign's poor planning and execution. The failure dogged the career of Winston Churchill, until he redeemed himself in World War II.

The Gallipoli campaign was remembered in Britain only in places where it held particular significance, such as Bury, home of the Lancashire Fusiliers, six of whom had won the Victoria Cross on the first day. In Ireland, which

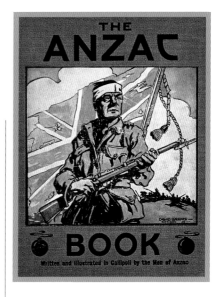

had provided 15,000 troops and lost 4,000 of those, the campaign's first anniversary was overshadowed by the Easter Rising armed rebellion of 1916. France had committed around 80,000 troops to Gallipoli and suffered as many as 27,000 casualities, but the campaign barely featured in the nation's collective wartime memories. In Australia and New Zealand, however, the dead of the campaign are still reverently honoured every year on Anzac Day, 25 April. ∎

Anzac troops

For the untested volunteers of the Australia and New Zealand Army Corps (ANZAC), fighting for the British Empire, Gallipoli was their first experience of battle. Just before dawn on 25 April 1915, Australian troops were the first to attack. War correspondent Ellis Ashmead-Bartlett described them as "a race of athletes". Some people attributed their bravery, mutual loyalty, and intolerance of fussy discipline to their practical experience of the rigours of life in the antipodean bush. While thought of as mostly of Anglo-Saxon heritage, the Anzac ranks included volunteers from Indigenous peoples and from those of Chinese, Indian, and even German backgrounds.

Anzac Day, first observed on 25 April 1916 with a march through London, celebrated the Anzacs' role at Gallipoli. The people of Australia and New Zealand mourned, but also felt huge pride and a new sense of national identity. Anzac Day remains a public holiday in Australia and New Zealand.

THE SCENES I WITNESS HAUNT ME

THE WAR IN THE CAUCASUS (1915–18)

ollowing the ill-conceived Ottoman campaign against Russian forces in the winter of 1914–15, the Caucasus Front was quiet for the rest of 1915. Then, on 10 January 1916, Russian troops launched a new offensive, taking the fortified Anatolian city of Erzurum on 16 February and the Black Sea port of Trabzon on 18 April. Ottoman counterattacks had some success in late summer, but by winter the Russians held much of eastern Anatolia. The Ottomans had failed to make the advances expected after victory at Gallipoli in 1915.

See-sawing fortunes

In 1917, revolution in Russia and the tying down of Ottoman armies in Palestine and Mesopotamia brought stalemate to the Caucasus. In February and March 1918, the Ottoman forces swept back into territories they had lost to the Russians in 1916 and in earlier conflicts. The Treaty of Brest-Litovsk, signed in March 1918 between Russia and the Central Powers, confirmed Ottoman gains.

In May 1918, the Transcaucasian nations Georgia, Armenia, and Azerbaijan declared themselves independent democratic republics. The final action was over Baku on the Caspian Sea – part of Azerbaijan, but still held by Russian Bolsheviks. On 15 September 1918, the Ottoman Caucasus Islamic Army stormed into the city, restoring Baku – and its vital oilfields – to Muslim Azerbaijani control. ■

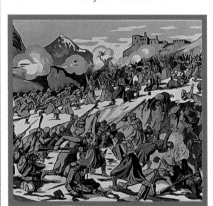

Russian troops clash with Ottoman forces in a print that celebrates the Russian victory at Erzurum in February 1916. Such prints were used to spread news of the war across Russia.

See also: The Ottoman Empire in decline 26–27 ▪ Ottoman Turkey enters the war 84–85 ▪ The Gallipoli Campaign 122–29 ▪ The Armenian Genocide 132–33

OUR ARMIES COME AS LIBERATORS
THE WAR IN MESOPOTAMIA (1914–18)

When the Ottoman Empire joined Germany and Austria-Hungary against the Allies in October 1914, Britain sent divisions of its nearly 240,000-strong Indian Army to protect British oil interests in the Ottoman province of Mesopotamia (Iraq). In early November, the Indian Expeditionary Force "D" sailed from Bombay and landed near Basra, taking the city on 21 November.

In 1915, one division advanced from Basra, up the Euphrates river, and took the Ottoman supply base of Nasiriya in July. Another division progressed up the Tigris river, and by September had captured Qurna and the cities of Amara and Kut al-Amara. This division, led by Major General Charles Townshend, then pushed on towards Baghdad but was defeated at Ctesiphon, southeast of the city, in November.

Siege of Kut
Townshend withdrew his troops to Kut al-Amara, where they were soon surrounded by Ottoman forces. After a siege of 147 days,

For the British Empire, Mesopotamia was, in terms of casualties, cost, and area, second only to the Western Front.
Edwin Latter
Journal of the Society for Army Historical Research,
1994

and several failed relief expeditions, Townshend surrendered. His army of around 13,000 were then marched into captivity, where more than one-third died.

After retaking Kut al-Amara in February 1917, British forces captured Baghdad in March. The Ottoman Sixth Army was finally defeated on 30 October 1918 and an armistice signed the same day. ■

See also: The Ottoman Empire in decline 26–27 ▪ Ottoman Turkey enters the war 84–85 ▪ The Arab Revolt 170–71 ▪ The Battle of Megiddo 286–87

THE GREATEST CRIME OF THE WAR
THE ARMENIAN GENOCIDE (1915–17)

IN CONTEXT

FOCUS
Armenian oppression

BEFORE
1880s As the Ottoman Empire crumbles, Armenians – who had enjoyed a degree of autonomy – are increasingly under threat.

1894–96 In response to tax protests, Ottoman authorities kill several hundred thousand Armenians across the empire.

1908 Seeking a more equal society, Armenians join the Young Turks revolution.

AFTER
1920 Thousands of Armenians who had returned to Cilicia, Anatolia, are killed by Ottoman troops when French occupying forces leave after their defeat at the Battle of Marash.

1991 After the collapse of the USSR, Armenia – a republic for two years after the end of World War I – finally regains its independence.

Once the Ottoman Empire allied with the Central Powers in 1914, the location of the ancient Armenian homeland put its mostly Christian people in jeopardy. From 1828 to 1917, most Armenians lived in six provinces of eastern Anatolia, ruled by Muslim Ottomans; others lived further northeast in the Christian Russian Empire.

In the late 19th century, Russian Armenian nationalists encouraged their Anatolian counterparts to protest against the financial and legal inequalities they suffered under the Ottoman Empire. The Ottoman authorities responded with mass killings of their Armenian subjects – a sign of events to come.

Armenian refugees await rescue on a beach in Musa Dagh in September 1915. After their banners alerted a French warship, more than 4,000 were taken in Allied ships to Port Said, Egypt.

When the Young Turks seized power in 1908, there were promises of equal rights for all Ottoman Empire citizens. However, a Turkish nationalist ideology soon took root, especially within the Committee of Union and Progress (CUP), which seized power in 1913. With the outbreak of war in 1914, anti-Armenian propaganda increased. A refusal by the main Armenian political party to persuade Russian Armenians to support the Ottoman Empire in the war fuelled fears that

See also: The Ottoman Empire in decline 26–27 ▪ Ottoman Turkey enters the war 84–85 ▪ The Gallipoli Campaign 122–29 ▪ The war in the Caucasus 130 ▪ The Battle of Megiddo 286–87 ▪ A lasting peace? 312–17

It is a gigantic plundering scheme as well as a final blow to extinguish the race.
Jesse B. Jackson
US consul in Aleppo, 1915

Anatolian Armenians had divided loyalties and might collaborate with other powers.

Expelled or killed

When the Russians defeated the Ottoman army in the Caucasus in the winter of 1914–15, Armenians serving in the Ottoman forces there were disarmed and in many cases killed by Ottoman troops. Retreating Ottoman forces then destroyed Armenian villages and murdered their inhabitants.

Armenians were now portrayed as a threat to national security, and on 8 April 1915 the first organized deportations began from Zeitun (Süleymanli), in southeast Anatolia. Victims were sent – often with no supplies – by train or on forced marches to Syria and Iraq; those who resisted were shot. On 24 April, Armenian intellectuals and civic leaders in Constantinople (Istanbul) were rounded up and either killed or imprisoned.

In June, across the empire, the Ottoman government ordered mass deportations and the confiscation of Armenian property. Various groups, including Ottoman soldiers, local

A poster from 1917 by American artist W.B. King promotes a fund-raising drive to aid and support refugees from Armenia and other countries, such as Greece and Syria.

militias, bandits, and Kurdish tribes, carried out massacres. Many thousands also died on the hard trek south. Some survived thanks to Ottoman neighbours who hid them, and in the northeast, Russian troops rescued others. For 53 days, from July to September 1915, more than 4,000 Armenians around Musa Dagh, on the Mediterranean coast, resisted Ottoman forces. When they ran out of ammunition and food, they were evacuated and taken to Egypt.

A contested history

By 1918, most of the Armenian population of Anatolia were dead or displaced. For those who survived or returned home, the persecution continued. Between 1914 and 1923, an estimated 1.5 million Armenians died, with survivors dispersing to more than 100 countries.

Turkey accepts many Armenians died but denies that the killings were state-sponsored and maintains that "resettlement" was essential for national security. Since 2017, it has criminalized any mention in its parliament of an Armenian genocide. However, in the face of archival evidence, most historians and more than 30 countries have formally recognized the Armenian deaths as a genocide. ▪

Aiding the Armenians

The plight of the Armenians spawned the first large-scale citizen-based international aid. In 1915, American businessman and philanthropist Cleveland Hoadley Dodge established the American Committee for Armenian and Syrian Relief (ACASR). Its aim was to rescue and aid minority survivors and help them recover, learn skills, and receive work training. Renamed first as the American Committiee for Relief in the Near East and then, in 1919, as Near

East Relief, the organization was backed by an intensive and highly successful public relations campaign, supported by high-profile figures, including US president Woodrow Wilson.

By 1930, Near East Relief had raised $110 million (around $1.25 billion today) to assist refugees in what had become the Turkish Republic. Its workers in Turkey, Syria, and Lebanon built food distribution centres, schools, and orphanages, helping affected Armenians to live better lives. The organization operates today as the Near East Foundation.

IMPARTIAL IN THOUGHT AS WELL AS IN ACTION
THE US AND WORLD WAR I (1915)

The war in Europe tested the United States' policy of neutrality as no previous crisis had. The country had strong financial and emotional ties to Europe. Its population was chiefly drawn from Europe's nations, as US president Woodrow Wilson noted in a speech to the American people on 19 August 1914. Declaring, however, that the US must strive to remain neutral, he urged its citizens to be impartial. He believed the US could act as a peacemaker in the world.

Many Americans favoured Wilson's neutral policy, but former president Theodore Roosevelt, among others, disputed Wilson's contention that the US could stand apart and urged preparedness for war.

Economic ties

The US's economic dealings with Europe challenged its neutrality from the start. Its booming economy in the late 19th century had boosted commerce with Europe. But when war broke out,

---

The US has considerable **financial connections** to Europe.

Large loans to the Allies make **Allied success important** to American investors.

Theodore Roosevelt and others urge **preparedness** and an **expanded US Army**.

American deaths in **U-boat attacks** spur the **military training of civilians**.

The US moves closer to entering the war on the Allied side.

See also: The sinking of the *Lusitania* 106–07 ▪ The US enters the war 194–95 ▪ Putting the US on a war footing 196–97 ▪ The Battle of Saint-Mihiel 278–79 ▪ The Meuse–Argonne Offensive 280–83 ▪ A lasting peace? 310–15

Woodrow Wilson

Born in Virginia in 1856 to devout Presbyterian parents, Thomas Woodrow Wilson studied political science and initially pursued a successful academic career. In 1910, he was made Democrat governor of New Jersey, where he battled against corruption and introduced progressive reforms.

In 1912, Wilson was elected US president. His new domestic policies earned him widespread approval, as did his neutral stance at the outbreak of war in 1914. However, his attempt to impose racial segregation in the federal government upset the Black American community, and his condemnation of lynching in 1918 was judged belated.

When the US entered the war in 1917, Wilson's intellect, oratory, and persuasive powers made him a highly effective wartime leader. At the Paris Peace Conference in 1918, he pressed the Allies for a fair, non-punitive peace; in 1919, he conducted a whirlwind tour to urge Americans to back his bid to join the League of Nations. Wilson then suffered a major stroke but did not leave office until 1921. He died in 1924.

Wilson ordered a ban on private loans to the belligerents so that the US would not appear to be favouring one camp.

By 1915, however, the warring nations had exceeded their cash reserves and, rather than limit trade, Wilson lifted the ban on loans. The move favoured the Allies as the British Navy had blockaded German ports to obstruct delivery of armaments and other goods. In two years, the Allies borrowed $2.25 billion, making their success in the war very much in the interest of financiers in the US.

Urging preparedness

Frustrated by Wilson's opposition to enlarging the small US Army, Theodore Roosevelt and his close friend Major General Leonard Wood encouraged voluntary military training for civilians and even suggested conscription. Wood had already helped set up two military training camps for college students in 1913. Four more were planned for 1914, and the outbreak of war gave the project a fresh urgency.

The drive came to be known as the Plattsburg Idea, after a camp in New York State where young businessmen first volunteered for military training in 1915. It gave rise to the Military Training Camps Association, established in 1916, which lobbied for preparedness for war. After the National Defense Act allowing for the expansion of the US Army was passed in 1916, the camps were incorporated into the US military training programme.

By now, German U-boat attacks had cost American lives, yet many people still favoured neutrality. In late 1916, Wilson's slogan "He kept us out of the war" narrowly won him a second presidential term. ▪

Workmen march through Washington, DC, in a Preparedness Parade, in 1916. Such marches rallied support for the participation of the US in the war.

BUILDINGS COLLAPSED LIKE HOUSES OF CARDS
THE GERMAN BOMBING CAMPAIGN BEGINS (JANUARY 1915)

IN CONTEXT

FOCUS
Aerial warfare

BEFORE
1909 French aviator Louis Blériot performs the first flight across the English Channel.

1911 An Italian pilot drops grenades on Ottoman troops in North Africa during the Italo-Turkish War – the first combat use of aircraft.

AFTER
1917 For bombing raids, Germany switches from zeppelins to Gotha aircraft.

April 1918 Britain forms the Royal Air Force, partly inspired by the slow response to the zeppelin threat in the war.

August 1918 Zeppelin L70 is shot down over the Norfolk coast during the final airship attack on Britain.

1919 The Treaty of Versailles bans Germany from possessing military airships.

At the start of the war, Germany had several zeppelins – rigid-framed airships that flew at a speed of around 135 kph (85 mph). The German army had employed a few of the airships to drop incendiaries and shells but used them mainly for reconnaissance of enemy positions and troop movements. In early 1915, when the conflict on the Western Front had ground to a stalemate, Germany decided to use its zeppelins to take the conflict to Allied civilians by attacking their homes – an unprecedented and frightening new move.

The first UK aerial bombing was in Great Yarmouth, carried out by a Zeppelin L3 on 19 January 1915. Here local officers assess the damage.

The new threat
German army zeppelins had bombed the Belgian cities of Liège and Antwerp in August 1914, killing around 20 people. In the earliest air raid on Paris, on 30 August 1914, a German Taube

See also: The secret war 96–99 ▪ War in the air 116–19 ▪ The German bombing campaign continues 222–23 ▪ Tactical flying 238–39

Parts of a zeppelin

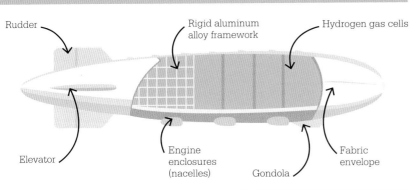

Rudder

Rigid aluminum alloy framework

Hydrogen gas cells

Elevator

Engine enclosures (nacelles)

Gondola

Fabric envelope

monoplane dropped four bombs, killing an elderly woman. In October, two more Taubes bombed the city centre but did minimal damage. Paris suffered again in March 1915, when two zeppelins dropped 2,000 kg (4,400 lb) of bombs, but there were no fatalities.

On 19 January 1915, zeppelins were used in the first bombing raid on the British mainland. Targeting the eastern coastal towns of Great Yarmouth and King's Lynn, they killed four people. The effect of the bombings in Britain was profound. People were terrified, particularly because the only warning of a zeppelin attack was the dull throb of its engines. With their engines turned off, zeppelins could glide almost silently at an altitude of around 3,350 m (11,000 ft), making their night-time attacks alarmingly unpredictable. Over the next few months, zeppelin raids continued to target towns on the east coast, causing six further deaths.

London attacked

On 31 May 1915, zeppelins attacked London for the first time. In the initial strike, one incendiary bomb hit a terraced house in the northern suburb of Stoke Newington; here the family within were unharmed. Within 20 minutes, however, the zeppelins had unleashed 1,360 kg (3,000 lb) of incendiaries and bombs, which started some 40 fires across the capital, destroying buildings and killing seven people. The deadliest and largest zeppelin attack, involving 16 airships, struck London on 8 September 1916 and caused 22 fatalities, with many more people injured.

An explosive response

Initially, the British had no effective way to counter zeppelin attacks, and public outrage grew, forcing the government to switch some resources from the Western Front to home defence. However, by 1916, a range of defensive measures included powerful searchlights, more guns, and exploding bullets that could ignite the gas-filled craft. Zeppelin raids slowed and by 1917, when 77 of a fleet of 115 had been destroyed, they stopped altogether.

In all, there were 52 zeppelin raids over Britain. Their bombs had killed more than 550 British citizens, injured more than 1,300, and terrorized the nation. ▪

Zeppelins

Germany's best-known airship was named after its inventor, Count Ferdinand von Zeppelin, and made its maiden flight in 1900 over Lake Constance. The cigar-like profile, enclosed by an envelope of tough fabric, concealed a rigid metal frame filled with hydrogen gas cells. A gondola on the underside housed the pilot, crew, and flying controls. War zeppelins also carried machine guns and "spy gondolas" – observation cars lowered 800 m (½ mile) from an airship hidden by clouds to report on enemy positions and targets.

After the war, zeppelins became passenger craft and regularly crossed the Atlantic. The giant Hindenburg, the largest-ever zeppelin, even included an elegant dining room. In May 1937, however, the Hindenburg burst into flames while landing in New Jersey, killing 35 of the 97 people on board.

Somebody said, 'Zeppelin! Zeppelin!' And way up in the sky and we looked and saw it floating along blotting the stars out. You see this trap door open and they threw the bombs out and shut it again.
George Walker
a young boy in Nottingham, watching from the ground as a zeppelin dropped its bombs

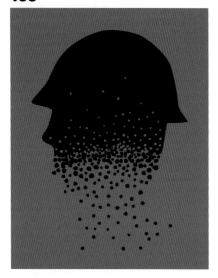

THEY MELTED AWAY
RUSSIA RETREATS (1915)

IN CONTEXT

FOCUS
The Eastern Front

BEFORE
1815 The Congress of Vienna reaffirms Austrian control of Galicia (now southeastern Poland and western Ukraine).

1905 Russia's defeat in the Russo-Japanese War erodes its military prestige and adds to growing domestic unrest.

1914 Germany defeats Russian forces in East Prussia, with a major first victory at the Battle of Tannenberg.

AFTER
1916 Russian forces, led by General Aleksei Brusilov, paralyse the Austro-Hungarian army in eastern Galicia.

1922 The borders of the Second Republic of Poland are formalized to include former Austrian Galicia and all of the Warsaw area; some is taken by the USSR after 1945.

During 1914, Russian forces had crushed the army of Austria-Hungary in its largest province, Galicia, in conflicts that cost hundreds of thousands of lives. However, in early 1915, Franz Conrad von Hötzendorf, chief of the Austro-Hungarian general staff, led a counterattack which, though unsuccessful, weakened the Russians and gave the general hope that, with the help of German reinforcements, his forces could repel the attackers.

In April, Conrad met Erich von Falkenhayn, chief of the German general staff, to discuss a strategy. They opted for a limited attack on the Russians – but one that would prove to be a spectacular victory for the Central Powers.

Mackensen's plan
General August von Mackensen was picked to command a new force made up of the German Eleventh Army and the Austro-Hungarian Fourth Army. His plan was to force a breakthrough of the Russian line so fast and deep that the enemy would have no time to stem it with reinforcements. At 6am on 2 May 1915, just east of Kracóv, Mackensen's artillery opened fire along a 45-km (28-mile) front bounded by the Galician towns of Gorlice and Tarnów. In the largest barrage yet seen on the Eastern Front, 610 guns fired 700,000 shells in only four hours, and then the infantry assault was underway. Gorlice fell within a day and Tarnów soon after, with tens of thousands of Russian troops taken prisoner. The battle became known as the Gorlice–Tarnów Offensive.

Russian soldiers abandoned their trenches and their guns and transport. A rout was inevitable but not instant. The offensive continued for 70 days as Mackensen's front widened and deepened, and the

This was rout, sanguinary rout. It looked as though it could never be halted.
Captain Neilsen
British attaché to the Russian Third Army

See also: Crisis in Russia 24 ▪ The Battle of Tannenberg 78–81 ▪ The battle for Poland 83 ▪ The Brusilov Offensive 166–69 ▪ The Kerensky Offensive 224–25

prisoner haul increased to 250,000. By the end of June, the Galician capital – Lemburg (now Lviv) – more than 300 km (186 miles) from the starting point, had been retaken. The Russian troops were ordered to leave Galicia.

The Great Retreat

In the wake of the defeat in Galicia, the entire Russian line, from the Baltic Sea to the Carpathian Mountains, withdrew up to 400 km (250 miles) – the Russian "Great Retreat". As the German army pursued them, Russian forces applied scorched earth tactics to the countryside, leaving nearly a million people homeless, many of whom later starved to death.

By September, when the great fortress cities near the Russian frontier were taken, the weary but triumphant Austro-Hungarian and German divisions had completed a summer of spectacular victories.

For the Russians, the retreat was a military necessity. Artillery shells and even rifles were so scarce that they had no choice but to fall back until supplies could be replenished. The defeats had cost them their Polish salient and some two million casualties. The soldiers were soon replaced, however, and the Russian heartland had not been breached. Under the command of General Aleksei Brusilov, the Russians would return and avenge their rout the following year. ▪

German troops seeking to reverse Austro-Hungarian losses in Galicia are watched by smiling residents as they pass through a town on their way to fight in the Gorlice–Tarnów Offensive.

August von Mackensen

Born in 1849 in the Prussian province of Saxony, Anton Ludwig Friedrich August Mackensen began his army career in 1869 and won an Iron Cross in the Franco-Prussian War (1870–71). In 1891, he was appointed to the general staff in Berlin, initially under Helmuth von Moltke and then under Alfred von Schlieffen. He impressed both them and Kaiser Wilhelm II, who gave him command of the First Life Hussars Regiment, later made him the royal adjutant, and ennobled him in 1899 as August von Mackensen.

In World War I, Mackensen first won acclaim for the 1915 Gorlice–Tarnów victory. After Germany's defeat, he was interned in Serbia for a year. Though he became a Nazi supporter, at heart he was a monarchist and wore the death's head uniform of the Life Hussars when attending functions with Nazi officials. In 1940, he denounced army atrocities in Poland in a letter to German army chief Walther von Brauchitsch. Mackensen would witness the destruction of Nazi Germany in 1945 and died the same year aged 95.

ALPINE WINDS WHISTLE THEIR SONGS OF DEATH

THE END OF THE SERBIAN CAMPAIGN (NOVEMBER 1915–JANUARY 1916)

IN CONTEXT

FOCUS
War in Eastern Europe

BEFORE
1882 The Kingdom of Serbia is proclaimed – the final stage in its bid to escape Ottoman rule.

1913 Bulgaria's defeat in the Second Balkan War results in territorial gains for Serbia, Greece, and Romania.

1914 After the assassination of Archduke Franz Ferdinand by a Serb, Austria-Hungary invades Serbia but is defeated.

AFTER
1 November 1918 Belgrade is liberated by Serbian and Allied forces. It becomes capital of the new Kingdom of Serbs, Croats, and Slovenes (later Yugoslavia).

1941 Nazi Germany invades and partitions Yugoslavia.

2003 Yugoslavia is abolished, and a new union of Serbia and Montenegro is founded. Each gains independence in 2006.

I n 1915, the Allies faced failure in Gallipoli and Mesopotamia, stalemate on the Western Front, and Russian losses in Galicia and Poland. Yet Serbia, a fourth member of the Allied bloc, located on Austria-Hungary's flank, was still in the fight and posing a threat. If the Central Powers could annihilate Serbia it would bring them dominance in the Balkans and a route to their Ottoman allies.

Taking sides

Germany wanted to keep the beleaguered Ottoman Empire in the war and, in order to supply it

See also: The Balkans 25 ▪ The assassination of Franz Ferdinand 40–41 ▪ War is declared 42–43 ▪ Austro-Hungarian failures 82 ▪ Greece and the Macedonian front 226–27 ▪ War-crimes trials 318–19

Milunka Savić

Milunka Savić was born in the Serbian village of Koprivnica around 1890. In 1912, she took the call-up papers of her sick brother Milun, cut her hair, put on men's clothes, and joined the Serbian army in the First Balkan War. Her bravery at the Battle of Bregalnica in the Second Balkan War in 1913 was rewarded with a medal and promotion to corporal. Her gender was revealed when she was wounded, but she remained in the Serbian infantry.

In one battle in 1916, Savić captured 23 Bulgarian soldiers single-handedly. Wounded nine times, she won further medals, including the Karađorđe's Star with Swords – Serbia's highest honour – the French Légion d'Honneur, and Russia's Cross of St George. Savić was the only woman in World War I to receive the French Croix de Guerre and is history's most decorated female combatant.

During World War II, Savić ran a Belgrade hospital serving wounded Yugoslav partisans and was imprisoned by the Nazis. After the war, she lived in relative obscurity and died in Belgrade in 1973.

with men, munitions, and supplies, needed a clear route for the Berlin–Constantinople Railway, which ran through hostile Serbia and neutral Bulgaria before reaching Turkey. Serbia, therefore, had to be defeated and Bulgaria persuaded to join the Central Powers.

The Allies, however, hoped to keep Bulgaria neutral and Serbia fighting on their side, although this seemed an increasingly unlikely scenario. Landlocked Serbia was flanked by Austria-Hungary to its north and neutral Greece to its south, and Bulgaria to its east was already leaning towards war. The Allies' recent defeat in Gallipoli had dampened any hope of persuading Greece or Bulgaria (Serbia's fierce rival) to join them.

Promised territory that it had lost to Serbia in the Second Balkan War (1913), Bulgaria was easily

won over by the Central Powers. On 6 September 1915, Bulgarian officials signed a convention obliging it to declare war on Serbia within a month. At the same time, Field Marshal August von Mackensen was sent to Austria to assemble a German and Austro-Hungarian army, now gathering on the Sava and Danube rivers to strike Serbia from the north.

As Bulgaria began to mobilize its army, Greek prime minister Eleftherios Venizelos agreed that 150,000 Allied soldiers could be based just south of the Serbian-Bulgarian border, in Salonika (now Thessaloniki), from where they could potentially assist Serbia. King Constantine I of Greece, who was married to Kaiser Wilhelm II's sister Sophia, hoped to maintain Greek »

German soldiers march through the town of Paraćin in central Serbia during the Austro-German Eleventh Army's advance against Serbian forces in October 1915.

Le Petit Journal

LE MAUVAIS FRÈRE

The cover of the French magazine *Le Petit Journal* from 10 October 1915 shows Serbia battling Austro-German forces, while its neighbour Bulgaria prepares to stab it in the back.

Within two days, the German and Austro-Hungarian troops were driving Putnik's men into the hills. Belgrade fell on 9 October, and several days later the Bulgarians attacked from the east.

From Salonika, French and British divisions pushed north to the Serbian border, hoping to open a path for the Serbian army to join the Allied forces. The French reached Krivolak and the British Kosturino (in present-day North Macedonia) but were blocked by Bulgarian forces. Outnumbered, the French and British troops were forced to disengage and retreat back to Salonika, repelling Bulgarian attacks all the way. With the Allies impelled to regroup and defend Salonika, the Serbs would have to fight alone.

The Great Serbian Retreat
By November 1915, the Central Powers' forces had driven the Serbian army into the valleys around Mitrovica and Pristina

… we saw the wreckage of all that had gone before. It seemed a veritable road of death.
Olive Aldridge
British volunteer nurse, witnessing the Serbian army retreat

in what is now Kosovo. Tens of thousands of refugees joined them. The conflict had heightened ethnic tensions, resulting in cruel reprisals and summary executions inflicted by both sides against civilians.

As winter set in, some 400,000 Serbian soldiers and civilians fled southwest across the mountains towards Albania and the Adriatic ports of Scutari and Durazzo – a daunting journey of 160 km (100 miles). At the ports, Allied shipping was assembling to take them to Greece. Every possible farm cart was requisitioned for the march,

neutrality, but Venizelos prevailed. Divisions over Greece's involvement in the war would continue until Constantine was deposed in 1917 in favour of his son Alexander.

As the Central Powers' forces gathered for the offensive, Field Marshal Radomir Putnik, who had led Serbia's effective resistance against Austria-Hungary in 1914, mobilized his troops. Their ranks, however, were depleted by typhus, and they had only 300 guns against Mackensen's 1,200.

Advancing south into Serbia, the German and Austro-Hungarian forces opened their campaign on 5 October with a bombardment by 170 large-calibre guns and 420 heavy mortars. That day, 13,000 British and French troops landed at Salonika, hoping to deter Bulgaria from joining the German and Austro-Hungarian attack on Serbia.

A German propaganda postcard shows the market square of Nish, in Serbia, captured on 9 November 1915. The occupation gave the Central Powers strategic control of the railway.

Serbian soldiers, including army general staff, cross the Viziers' Bridge over the White Drin river in Albania in bitter winter weather during the Great Serbian Retreat of 1915.

with soldiers front and rear, and civilians between them. Among those fleeing were the 71-year-old Serb king Peter and the ailing Field Marshal Putnik, both carried on stretchers. The march also included around 24,000 Austro-Hungarian prisoners-of-war together with British, French, and Russian diplomats and their staff, and American war correspondents.

The Serbian retreat followed three parallel roads through the snowy mountains. Each became lined with broken wagons and the carcasses of oxen, horses, and refugees who had died of starvation or exposure in the freezing weather. Although Albania was neutral, its people harboured a deep hatred for Serbs and often fired on them. Of the 400,000 who set out on the retreat in November 1915, more than half died during the journey. In January and February 1916, the survivors reached Scutari and Durazzo, from where the Allied fleet ferried them to Corfu and other Greek islands to rest and recover.

Intrepid British women

The escapees included a number of volunteer British nurses, although some medics opted to stay and help.

In the central Serbian city of Kruševac, 51-year-old Scottish doctor Elsie Inglis refused to leave the wounded at the military hospital where she worked. She had first proposed overseas medical units staffed by women in 1914, but the British War Office had told her to "go home and sit still". Inglis persisted, however, establishing units in France and Serbia. She was taken prisoner in 1915 and repatriated to Britain in February 1916.

Inglis's friend, Liverpool-born doctor Caroline Matthews, who was working with the Serbian Red Cross

in Užice, western Serbia, also stayed and was taken prisoner. When released in 1916, she published an account of her experiences – as did Flora Sandes, a volunteer ambulance driver who stayed on and joined the Serbian army, alongside Milunka Savić and other Serb women fighters. After suffering grenade wounds, Sandes was awarded the Serbian King George Star for her bravery. She was the only British female uniformed combatant to serve in World War I.

The fight goes on

After the Central Powers' success in Serbia, they dominated the Balkans north of Greece, with the Allies pushed back to the Aegean Sea. Yet Serbia never surrendered. The Serbian army began arriving in Salonika, where the Allied armies now occupied a huge encampment. Once rested and refitted, the Serbs were ready to resume their quest to liberate their homeland. ∎

Štip Massacre

After Bulgaria invaded Serbia in October 1915, atrocities were committed by both sides. The extreme brutality of Bulgarian units in areas they controlled, however, was most bitterly recalled. In November 1915, in the town of Štip, a member of a Bulgarian paramilitary group burst into a hospital and seized sick and wounded Serbian soldiers. Around 120 were then transported to the outskirts of a nearby village and shot. In the southern Serbian town of

Surdulica, in the Bulgarian occupation zone, an estimated 2,000–3,000 men were executed between 1916 and 1917. This and the "Štip Massacre", together with a number of alleged Bulgarian war crimes, were discussed at the Paris Peace Conference in 1919. Accusations flew back and forth. Serbia exhumed the bodies of the Štip victims and produced a list of perpetrators, including 500 Bulgarians; but the Bulgarian delegates denied it all. No Bulgarian was ever convicted of the war crimes in Serbia.

LIONS LED BY DONKEYS

THE ARTOIS–LOOS OFFENSIVE (SEPTEMBER–NOVEMBER 1915)

IN CONTEXT

FOCUS
Western Front

BEFORE
April 1915 German troops use gas for the first time, at the Second Battle of Ypres.

May 1915 In the Second Battle of Artois, French troops capture Vimy Ridge briefly but are later pushed back.

AFTER
December 1915 After criticism of the failure at Loos, Sir John French resigns as British commander. He is replaced by Sir Douglas Haig.

February–December 1916 In the Battle of Verdun, French forces repel a German advance, marking a decisive turning point in the conflict.

July 1916 The British attack at the Somme uses a more effective "creeping barrage", which moves forward slowly with infantry following behind.

The failure of the Allied spring offensives in 1915 left both sides dug in along the Western Front. The Allies had made some small territorial advances, but these were shortlived. The challenge was to consolidate gains and maintain pressure in the west, not least because of Russia's heavy losses on the Eastern Front.

General Joseph Joffre, French commander-in-chief, was fixed on a plan to force the Germans back from the Noyon salient – where their line bulged the furthest into France – by mounting offensives on two flanks: through Artois, to the north, and Champagne,

I could not see through the gas.
Second Lieutenant George Grossmith
on the British gas attack at Loos

to the southeast. Massive artillery bombardments would precede infantry attacks, with the Allied commanders enjoying a three to one advantage in troop numbers, thanks to the arrival of the first British volunteers and the transfer of many Germans to the east.

British forces, under the overall command of Field Marshal Sir John French, were committed to Joffre's plan. In a simultaneous advance eastwards along a 32-km (20-mile) front in Artois, the British First Army would attack at Loos – a coal-mining district north of the town of Lens – as the French Tenth Army advanced between Lens and Arras. Meanwhile, the French Second and Fourth armies alone were to attack the German lines in Champagne.

Two failed attacks
On 21 September, French field and heavy artillery in Artois began a preliminary barrage of German positions, firing a total of around 1.75 million shells. The defenders withdrew to their dugouts and waited. After four days, 19 divisions of the French Tenth Army advanced through the morning mist up Vimy Ridge – a strategic highpoint that dominated

See also: The British arrive 56–57 ▪ The Second Battle of Ypres 110–115 ▪ Russia retreats 138–39 ▪ The Battle of Verdun 152–55 ▪ The Somme 172–79

a broad sweep of the front – only to discover that the German defences had largely withstood the barrage. Although the 29th Division reached the top of the ridge, it could not get through the wire into the German rear lines. The retreating French suffered around 48,000 casualties.

To the north, it was a similar story for the six British divisions attacking under General Sir Douglas Haig. Although the first attack captured Loos, it proved impossible to hold. The volunteer soldiers thrown into their first major conflict were ill-trained for trench warfare, and the artillery shelling – although lasting four days – had proved ineffective, leaving swathes of barbed wire intact. The British effort was further hampered by

Half of the 72 battalions that fought on the first day at Loos were Scottish regiments. Here, with bayonets drawn, they bear down on the German trenches.

the refusal of Field Marshal French to release two divisions of reserves that Haig had requested.

The battle was also notable for the first British use of poisonous gas. However, a change in the wind blew the gas back over parts of the British lines, and it hovered above no-man's-land. German counterattacks then pushed the British back to their original positions.

Not a question of numbers

By mid-October, the offensive was all but over as exhaustion and heavy rain made fighting impossible. There were more than 100,000 French and British casualties, with Germany suffering only half that total. It was clear that superior troop numbers were not enough. Also, mass artillery barrages had not proved effective at softening up enemy defences. Allied commanders needed new ideas to capture and hold German positions. ▪

Kulbir Thapa

Born in Nepal in 1888, Kulbir Thapa was the first Gurkha to receive the Victoria Cross, Britain's highest award for bravery, for his actions during the battle at Loos. He was one of the soldiers from the British Indian Army, including the Gurkhas, who were sent to France and Belgium in 1914 to compensate for shortages of troops on the Western Front.

On 25 September 1915, Thapa found a wounded British soldier behind a German front-line trench. Despite being wounded himself, he guarded the man all night, before daylight and a cover of thick mist allowed him to drag the soldier to safety through the German wire. Then, under fire, he rescued two wounded fellow Gurkhas from no-man's-land before returning to finally retrieve the British soldier. It was reported that even the watching German soldiers stopped firing to applaud Thapa's courage as he made his final journey back to the British line. He was later presented with the Victoria Cross by King George V at Buckingham Palace. Thapa died in 1956.

TOTAL

1916

WAR

Britain passes the **Military Service Act**, which specifies that unmarried **men aged from 18 to 41** years are liable for service in the armed forces.

Russian artillery bombards German forces on the Eastern Front near Vilnius – a prelude to the **Battle of Lake Naroch**, a costly Russian defeat.

Britain and **France** conclude the **secret Sykes-Picot treaty** to divide up **Ottoman territories** after the war.

Russia opens the Brusilov offensive, a wide-ranging attack **against Austro-Hungarian positions** from the Pripet marshes in Poland south to Romania.

27 JAN 1916   **18 MAR 1916**   **16 MAY 1916**   **4 JUN 1916**

21 FEB 1916   **24 APR 1916**   **31 MAY 1916**   **10 JUN 1916**

The **German army** opens its **attack on French** positions around Verdun with the most devastating **mass artillery bombardment** yet known in warfare.

Irish nationalists revolt against British rule on Easter Monday. The **Easter Rising is suppressed**, but the execution of 16 leaders gains the nationalists new support.

Ships from the **British Grand Fleet engage with German** naval forces in a two-day operation, known to the Allies as the **Battle of Jutland**.

Emir of Mecca **Sharif Hussein bin Ali** kickstarts the **Arab Revolt** with attacks on Ottoman garrisons in Mecca and Medina.

German victories on the Eastern Front had boosted the authority of General Erich von Falkenhayn as chief of the German general staff. Planning his military strategy for 1916, his first task was to find a way to break the deadlock on the Western Front. He decided, in his own words, to "bleed France to death", attacking a section of the line French forces would have to defend, regardless of loss. It was the start of a year of attrition.

Holding the Western Front

Falkenhayn chose to attack in the salient around the fortress of Verdun so that the maximum amount of heavy artillery could be used against the French. Limited German infantry assaults were then to secure key points and draw out French reserves to be pounded by the guns.

At 7am on 21 February 1916, the Battle of Verdun began with a huge German bombardment of the French positions. Despite huge losses, the French forces stubbornly repelled the German advance. It was further hindered by heavy snowfall, which gave the French time to bring in reinforcements. German infantry divisions then became victims of French artillery fire. Falkenhayn's plan had clearly failed to produce the crucial breakthrough he hoped for. The battle would last 302 days, the longest of the war. In August, Falkenhayn lost his post as chief of the German general staff. Paul von Hindenburg replaced him, with Erich Ludendorff as his deputy.

With so many forces at Verdun, the French government needed British general Sir Douglas Haig to commit his army – most of them

volunteers – to a planned Allied offensive around the Somme river. Haig knew the battle would be attritional but had to agree.

The Battle of the Somme began on 1 July with disastrous losses for the British Army, whose attack stalled in the face of German artillery, machine guns, and barbed wire that an earlier bombardment by the British had failed to destroy. The offensive continued until mid-November, with little advantage ever gained by either side and more than a million casualties. By then the battleground was a sea of mud, bringing fighting to a halt.

Civilian hardship

The terrible death toll each battle inflicted had a damaging effect on the morale of civilians on the home front. Around a third of all soldiers

The opening day of the **Battle of the Somme** is marked by **heavy British casualties** for **almost no territorial gain** against the German defenders.

As a result of the **failed Verdun strategy**, Kaiser Wilhelm II **sacks Erich von Falkenhayn** from his post as chief of the German general staff.

General Robert Nivelle leads a major offensive against German forces at Verdun that helps secure a **French victory** in December.

US president **Woodrow Wilson** writes to the combatant nations in a **bid to find peace terms** acceptable to all. His **initiative fails**.

1 JUL 1916   29 AUG 1916   20 OCT 1916   18 DEC 1916

27 AUG 1916   15 SEP 1916   6 DEC 1916   30 DEC 1916

Lured by promises to extend its territory, **Romania joins the Allies** and declares war on the Central Powers.

During the **fight for Flers–Courcelette**, part of the Somme offensive, the **British use tanks for the first time**. Most break down.

Mounted on a white horse, **German Field Marshal August von Mackensen** rides triumphantly into **Bucharest, Romania's capital**.

The Russian monk **Grigori Rasputin is assassinated** by a group of aristocrats angered by his growing influence over the Tsar's family.

---

killed in World War I left widows and children, many of whom had to rely on charity to survive. Life for most civilians in affected countries was a daily round of queueing, shortages, and hard work. The Battle of Jutland between German and British fleets in late May 1916 had failed to end the Allied naval blockade, which drastically reduced Germany's food supplies. A poor harvest made things worse and, by autumn 1916, even the turnips people ate to survive were rationed.

On the Eastern Front
In Russia, extreme poverty caused widespread strikes, but its troops triumphed in a summer offensive, led by General Alexei Brusilov, a skilled commander. In June, he launched a surprise attack against Austro-Hungarian opponents on the Eastern Front in Galicia. The huge offensive, which stretched over a 480-km (300-mile) front was a spectacular success, with hundreds of thousands of prisoners taken and swathes of land seized. Finally, in September, German reinforcements brought the Russians to a halt.

Encouraged by Russia's summer victories and Allied promises of territory from Austria-Hungary, Romania declared war against the Central Powers on 27 August. This proved to be a fatal error; flanked by enemy nations, its position was highly vulnerable. After a spirited but futile defence against the two attacking Central Powers armies, the remnants of the Romanian army retreated east through Moldova to sanctuary in Russia in December 1916. For minimal losses, the Central Powers had gained control of Romania's important economic resources, including the vital commodities of oil and grain then under strict Allied blockade.

Fights for freedom
Elsewhere, nationalists used the distraction of war to pursue bids for independence. While aware of the unlikelihood of military success in their April uprising against the British, Irish republicans hoped to gain international recognition for their fight against British rule.

The British actively supported the Arab uprising against the Ottoman Empire in June 1916. From October, charismatic British officer T.E. Lawrence worked with the Arabs in a guerrilla campaign that would help Jordanian Hashemite and British Empire forces seize Damascus in 1918. ∎

HUGE MECHANICAL MONSTERS
TANK WARFARE

IN CONTEXT

FOCUS
Armoured attack vehicles

BEFORE
1886 German engineer Karl Benz builds what is generally considered to be the first practical automobile.

1907 Britain trials the Hornsby "Crawler" continuous-track tractor for military use.

1915 British naval officer Thomas Hetherington proposes a vehicle with outsized wheels to negotiate enemy trenches.

AFTER
1927 The British Army establishes an Experimental Mechanized Force to test technical developments.

1942 In World War II, tanks play a decisive role in the battles of El Alamein, Egypt.

1943 Soviet forces prevail in the Battle of Kursk, Russia – history's biggest tank battle.

The **technological innovations** needed to build tanks – the **internal combustion engine** and **continuous track** – have been in place for some time.

Individuals in **various countries** come up with the idea of **armoured vehicles** that run on **caterpillar tracks**.

Military commanders remain **sceptical about the idea**.

Deadlock on the Western Front leads to the adoption of a new attack weapon – the "tank".

The evolution of the internal combustion engine through the late 19th century and the development of continuous track in the early 20th century contributed to the emergence of the tank – but there was no sign of its appearance as World War I began. In 1911, Russian naval engineer Vasiliy Mendeelev proposed a vehicle propelled "on the caterpillar principle" and armoured with heavy steel plates in defence against enemy machine guns. However, Mendeelev's idea was rejected. In October 1914, British Army officer Ernest Swinton came up with a similar concept, but this too failed to find approval. Generals could not be convinced that a contraption like this had any place in modern warfare.

See also: Trenches take over 74–77 ▪ The Gallipoli Campaign 122–29 ▪ The Somme 172–79 ▪ The Battle of Cambrai 237 ▪ Trench warfare transformed 254–57 ▪ The Battle of Amiens 274–77 ▪ Breaking the Hindenburg Line 290–93

The problem was that battles were becoming near-impossible to win. Effective attack had been negated by troops defending from deep-dug trenches, protected by barbed wire and machine guns.

Protection on the move

Stalemate on the Western Front forced the British military to reconsider the potential of armoured vehicles, but support for the tank came from the Royal Navy – and Winston Churchill, who was its political head at the time – rather than the army. The navy had taken some responsibility for operating armoured cars on the Western Front and was more at ease with the idea of some kind of "landship" – hence the naval cannon fitted to the first completed prototype, "Little Willie", built by British engineering company Fosters in September 1915. Weighing around 16 tons, the tank stood 2.5m (8ft 3in) high.

Little Willie was not intended as an alternative to artillery. Its main function was to provide a moving bulwark to shield advancing

American soldiers of the 107th Infantry Regiment advance towards the Hindenburg Line from behind a British tank in September 1918.

infantrymen and flatten down the barbed wire in their path, spraying machine-gun fire before it to ward off would-be defenders. Tanks with cannons were designated "male", due to the phallic-looking nature of the weapon, while those with machine guns only were "female", and the pair would work in unison.

With a length of nearly 6m (20ft), Little Willie could take most trenches in its stride. The Mark IV

tank – from its introduction in 1917, the most widely deployed of the British fighting vehicles – was longer still, at about 8m (26ft). Even so, some trenches were simply too wide and too deep to be readily negotiated, especially as German troops became more conscious of the threat. Consequently, tank crews learned to carry fascines (tightly bound brushwood bundles) with them. These could be dropped into the deepest and widest trenches to provide a raised and springy floor on which the tank could more easily find traction.

Revolving turret

The French army introduced the revolving gun turret – later to be such a recognizable feature of a tank's outline – in its lightweight Renault FT, which first saw battlefield service in May 1918. In March of that year, Germany's A7V heavy tank was another late arrival at the Western Front. Only 20 were built, of which just 10 were armed; the others were used for carrying soldiers or supplies. ▪

Winston Churchill

The son of a British aristocrat and an American heiress, Winston Churchill was born at Blenheim Palace, Oxfordshire, UK, in 1874. He became a soldier in 1895 and used his personal connections to secure commissions in war zones, including India, Sudan, and Cuba. Later, he travelled as a journalist to witness the Second Boer War (1899–1902) before entering political life in Britain.

Serving first as a Conservative MP, then as a Liberal, in 1910 Churchill was appointed British home secretary, then First Lord of the Admiralty in late 1911. The improbability of the tank as an offensive weapon would have appealed to his restless and enquiring mind and sense of daring. His tenure at the Admiralty was marred by the disastrous Gallipoli Campaign (1915–16), but Churchill proved adept at bouncing back. He was British prime minister twice – 1940–45, during World War II, and 1951–55 – and died in London in 1965.

BLEED
FRANCE WHITE
THE BATTLE OF VERDUN
(21 FEBRUARY–18 DECEMBER 1916)

IN CONTEXT

FOCUS
Offensives and counteroffensives

BEFORE
1903 The French strengthen Fort Douaumont, one in a chain of modern forts around Verdun, with a reinforced-concrete bunker.

September–October 1914 Germany's victory at the Battle of Flirey leaves Verdun exposed on three sides.

July 1915 The railway line linking Verdun to Paris is cut by the German advance.

AFTER
August 1917 A renewed French offensive strikes north from Verdun, but a German counterattack means few territorial gains are made.

September–November 1918 The Meuse–Argonne Offensive results in an Allied victory.

The longest battle of World War I, at 302 days, Verdun was also among the most brutal. It is believed that as many as 300,000 combatants were killed between February and December 1916. The battle was also remarkable for the amount of back-and-forth action between French and German fighters as attack gave way to counterattack. French soldiers called the battle "the meat grinder".

A prestigious position

Verdun's importance was partly strategic. The German advance had so far bypassed this part of France, either sweeping through Belgium or Luxembourg to the north, or taking a more southerly route through Alsace–Lorraine. As a result, by early 1916, Verdun was at the centre of a salient jutting into German territory. Ringed by a chain of forts – part of the Séré de Rivières system built after the Franco-Prussian War (1870–71) and since partly upgraded – it represented a continuing threat to German forces. At the same time, surrounded on three sides by German positions, it was also a tempting target.

A print dated 1895 shows the small, ancient city of Verdun as it was before the war. Lying on the River Meuse close to the German border, the settlement was surrounded by a ring of 19 forts.

Verdun had a certain symbolic significance, too. A treaty signed here in 843 CE by the grandsons of the Emperor Charlemagne (747–814) had arguably brought about the birth of France. There had always been a front-line feeling about Verdun, close as it was to the German frontier and the long-disputed region of Alsace–Lorraine. It had also been the last fortress to fall after the German invasion of the Franco-Prussian War.

Erich von Falkenhayn

Born in 1861 into an aristocratic family in eastern Prussia, Erich von Falkenhayn spent most of his life in the military. An army cadet from the age of 11, he was serving as chief of staff for the German army's XVI Corps by 1907 and had earned the rank of *Oberst* (colonel) by 1908. In 1913, he was appointed Prussian minister of war.

Falkenhayn welcomed World War I, but he was sceptical about the strategy of bold aggression favoured by the German high command. Instead, he believed that victory would go to the side with the greater powers of endurance. As chief of the general staff from September 1914, Falkenhayn embraced the concept of attrition as a conscious military strategy. After his replacement by Hindenburg in August 1916, he commanded German troops in Romania and Ottoman forces in Palestine, where he intervened to prevent genocidal atrocities being perpetrated against the Jews. Falkenhayn died in 1922.

See also: Planning for war 34–39 ▪ The Battle of the Frontiers 52–55 ▪ The Great Retreat 60–63 ▪ The First Battle of the Marne 64–69 ▪ The Brusilov Offensive 166–69 ▪ The Somme 172–79 ▪ Artillery 228–29 ▪ Tactical flying 238–39

Erich von Falkenhayn believes Verdun will be **too important** for the French to **sacrifice it**.

Joffre starts **rebuilding Verdun's defences** – but belatedly and slowly.

Verdun becomes a symbol of **French resolve**.

General Joffre prepares to **abandon Verdun**, but he **changes his tactics** as the **Germans amass**.

Bad weather and a **heroic logistical effort** come to **France's rescue**.

Chief of the German general staff Erich von Falkenhayn had these considerations in mind when he fixed his sights on Verdun. He felt the city was too important to the French troops for them to abandon it, so they would send wave after wave of infantry to attack his entrenched Fifth Army – and be pulverized by his artillery in the process.

It barely mattered whether Falkenhayn's forces actually secured the city, as long as his opponents were willing to go on trying to lift the siege. France had already suffered 2 million casualties since the start of the war. The carnage would continue at Verdun, and slowly but surely, Falkenhayn believed, the attrition would bleed the French army white.

A pragmatic approach
Falkenhayn's cold and calculating logic of attrition was not supported by the facts on the ground, though. Far from seeing Verdun as a symbol to be protected at all costs, the French had been dismantling its defences since autumn 1914.

French general Joseph Joffre's thinking had been every bit as dispassionate as Falkenhayn's. Farther north on the River Meuse, the Belgian city of Liège was similarly ringed by 19th-century forts, but Germany's modern guns had made short work of such a supposed stronghold. Joffre concluded that the fortifications around Verdun were likely to be as ineffectual, so the troops and weaponry there should be sent to other parts of the Western Front.

France's Second Army would defend Verdun from positions on the east bank of the Meuse – but without support from the fortresses in their rear.

The battle begins
Some of Joffre's staff believed his decision was strategically short-sighted and protested. Possibly swayed by these objections, Joffre seems to have had second thoughts. At the start of February, as it became clear that the German troops had designs on Verdun, he threw the disarmament process into reverse. Even now, Joffre was convinced that they were only planning a diversionary attack. It soon became apparent how wrong he was. At dawn on 21 February, the German artillery opened up in what was then the biggest bombardment in history. That day alone, 1 million shells were fired.

More than 30 trains a day brought fresh munitions so the bombardment could continue with the same unprecedented level of intensity. Falkenhayn's force had 12,000 guns, half of which were »

The forces of France will bleed to death – for there is no retreat, regardless of whether we ourselves reach the target or not.
Erich von Falkenhayn
Message to Kaiser Wilhelm II, December 1915

large calibre. These included the 38 cm (15 in) SK L/45 Lange Max ("Long Max"), which fired 750 kg (1,650 lb) shells up to 34 km (21 miles). Originally designed for battleships, this gun had been adapted for installation in coastal batteries before its potential as a weapon on the Western Front had been realized.

"Step by step"

At noon on 21 February, the opening bombardment was briefly suspended so that elite German infantrymen could follow up. They moved swiftly through the French lines, where traumatized soldiers cowered in a shell-shocked daze. The German attackers cleared out trenches, blockhouses, and pillboxes with small arms and hand grenades. Making their combat debut in the hands of the Third Guard Pioneer Regiment, M.16. flame-throwers were used to devastating effect.

Lange Max guns were so large they had to be moved on rail tracks. The guns were devastating, but reloading them was slow and labour-intensive.

Initial progress was brisk: the German army advanced 5 km (3 miles) in the first 24 hours. The same pattern of artillery bombardment followed by infantry sweep was repeated again and again in the days that followed. Falkenhayn called this a "step-by-step" approach. Although the strategy was basically a cautious

one, in February 1916 it cut a swathe through inadequately prepared French forces.

The French artillery attempted to respond, but most of its guns were only just being moved into position, and none had the firepower of the large-calibre German guns. Without real artillery cover, the French infantry could offer no meaningful resistance. Even Verdun's mighty ring of fortresses were battered by heavy artillery fire, their defenders thrown about like rag dolls as the structures shook. Most of the protectors were forced to take refuge in cellars deep below the buildings they were nominally defending. Indeed, when German soldiers advanced on Douaumont – the biggest and most formidable of the forts – on 25 February, they were able to walk in unopposed.

In the days that followed, the French troops managed to slow the German advance. As commander

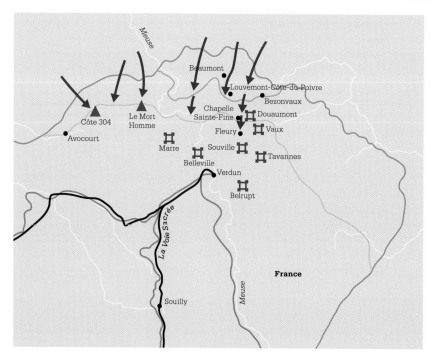

Falkenhayn's Fifth Army made rapid progress as it advanced south until 26 February, when it stalled, despite taking the formidable Fort Douaumont. Thereafter, progress was very slow, and the Germans did not reach their most advanced positions until early September. By that time, the tide of battle had turned, and in mid-December the French fought their way back to the villages of Bezonvaux and Louvemont-Côte-du-Poivre.

Key:

→ German attacks

— French front line, 21 February

— French front line, 26 February

— French front line, 9 April

— Railway

H Fort

> Yesterday, the 24th, I ordered that we hold the right bank north of Verdun. Any commander ordering a retreat will be court-martialled.
> **General Philippe Pétain**

of the Second Army, General Philippe Pétain gave orders that retreat was strictly forbidden. After the failure of a counterattack on Douaumont on 26 February, Pétain was quick to cut his losses. His men should defend the territory they held to the death, he said, but not – for now – attempt to take back what had been lost.

French reinforcements
Although Falkenhayn's initial reasoning – that the French had been planning to defend Verdun at all costs – had been flawed, he turned out to be right by accident. Once he had launched the attack, his prediction that the French army would feel compelled to keep pouring in reinforcements did prove well founded – though exactly why this was the case remains unclear. As important as Verdun was, more significant centres had been allowed to fall into German hands. A stand had to be made against the invaders for the sake of French morale.

Fortune suddenly favoured the French forces. On 29 February, heavy snowfall brought the German advance to a standstill and gave France time to bring in some 90,000 fresh troops, as well as munitions and supplies. The French infantry was now able to defend in depth, with successive lines, to hinder and then hold the German offensive. New French artillery units kept up a steady fire, increasing the pressure on the German infantry while easing it a little on the French. The problems the German soldiers faced were paradoxically compounded by the early gains they had made. Their southward advance upon the city had made them more vulnerable because it brought them within range of French guns on high ground above the west bank of the River Meuse.

The French troops were still very much on the defensive – and still sustaining heavy losses – but they did not look like an army that was "bleeding white". If anything, in the days that followed, it was the German soldiers who found the fight more draining. Falkenhayn considered halting his attack, but Verdun seemed to have taken on some symbolic significance for him, too. His men were going to have to fight on.

A reversal of fortunes
By early March, the fighting – while still extremely costly for France – was not as one-sided as it had been. Although the German advance continued, it took place under constant bombardment from French artillery. For every bit of ground gained, the German force sustained large casualties, though its superior heavy artillery still gave Germany an edge. Concentrated bombardments on specific positions, followed by brief infantry advances, enabled progress – but only sporadically, over short distances, across narrow fronts, and with steadily mounting casualties. Frustrated, German »

La Voie Sacrée
A stretch of road 72 km (45 mile) long between the town of Bar-le-Duc and Verdun was so vital for the supply of troops and ammunition and the provision of food and other supplies to the battlefront that it came to be known as *La Voie Sacrée*, or "The Sacred Way". Along this poorly paved route came the reinforcements that saved the French army from immediate collapse in the final days of February.

There was no alternative way to supply the salient. The Germans had already cut all the railway lines that might have brought support to the beleaguered city, leaving this road as the only viable way in or out. Constant repairs were needed to keep it open, but every day up to 6,000 trucks travelled back and forth. In the first month of the battle (21 February–22 March), the French brought in around 230,000 troops, 49,000 tons of ammunition, and 6,600 tons of other supplies.

Two endless columns of trucks plied *La Voie Sacrée* by day and night during the battle, with a vehicle passing every five seconds during the busiest periods.

generals in the field dispensed with Falkenhayn's step-by-step approach for bolder, more ambitious attacks, but all they achieved was a higher rate of deaths and injury.

As March progressed, the German troops did make advances, but they were painfully slow and hideously costly. By the month's end, Falkenhayn had lost more than 80,000 men in the attempt to take Verdun. Again, he found himself reviewing his whole strategy – and again he decided to persevere. Officers on the ground told him that the French men could not hold out much longer and that one final push might bring victory. However, as the French defence gradually grew in confidence, the German advance began to run out of steam.

Artillery above all

By the middle of April, although still struggling to hold the German troops back in some places, the French fighters were attempting counterattacks elsewhere. Neither side was making much headway overall, however. Along its main fronts, the battle appeared stalled, but still the fighting rumbled on. By convention ancillary to the main action on the field, where the infantry clashed, the artillery had taken on a leading role.

> Hell cannot
> be this dreadful.
> **Albert Joubaire**
> French soldier

A French artillery shell explodes near a group of German soldiers at Verdun, as they fight their way through barbed wire. About 143,000 Germans died during the battle.

A bitter game was played out as the two sides sought to neutralize each other's guns.

The placement of French guns on top of a hill – appropriately named Le Mort Homme ("The Dead Man") – 10 km (6 miles) northwest of Verdun was key to French resurgence. Thousands of men died as the German troops tried desperately to take this position. Many thousands more died in the fight for Hill 304. The sole significance of the hill, named for its height in metres (997 ft), was that it commanded a field of fire over Le Mort Homme's twin summits – hills 265 and 295. As wave after wave of infantry tried to rush Hill 304, the German forces pounded it relentlessly with their artillery. By the time they took the hill, on 6 May, its height had been reduced to 300 m (984 ft).

Airpower was also placed in the service of the artillery. Germany sent observers up in balloons and aeroplanes to help enhance their gunners' aim. When the French army deployed Nieuport 16 Bébé ("Baby") fighter planes to shoot them down or see them off – and, in turn, supply information to their artillery – Germany responded with Fokker Eindecker fighters. The contest in the air above Verdun became an important battle in itself. The French, flying in disciplined *escadrilles*, or small squadrons, eventually prevailed in what was a major setback for the German artillery.

Attack and counterattack

Throughout the rest of May the advantage seesawed, with each German attack prompting a French counterattack. On 22 May, after a terrifying bombardment, the French army went on the offensive, retaking Fort Douaumont – only to lose it again 36 hours later. So things went on through June. As the Germans pushed towards Fort Souville, the French continued to counterattack. Painfully slowly – and with huge loss of life on both sides – the German troops drove forwards. On 2 June, they took Fort Vaux. Then the weather intervened again, and days of torrential rain delayed the German advance on Fort Souville. A series of French counterattacks slowed them further but without finally halting them.

A French counterattack outside Chapelle Sainte-Fine on 23 June was more successful, and the Germans were held there. Further along the front, the back-and-forth continued, the village of Fleury changing hands 16 times up to 17 August. The German troops took Fort Souville for a few hours on 12 July, but they could not consolidate their hold.

Germany stretched thin

Despite the French army also enduring frustrated counterattacks, time was on its side, assisted by events elsewhere. The German army had to remove some big guns

Artillery at Verdun		
	60 million	Total number of shells fired by both sides between February and December.
	1,200	Number of artillery pieces on the German side at the outbreak of the Battle of Verdun.
	160	Distance in kilometres (99 miles) from which the German opening bombardment could be heard.
	26	Number of super-heavy long-range guns – up to 420 mm (17 in) calibre – the Germans had at Verdun.

to help against Russia's Brusilov Offensive on the Eastern Front and, closer to hand, it was fighting the Battle of the Somme, which had begun on 1 July. While both sides had to transfer troops to Verdun, the French forces could draw on their British allies. The German soldiers faced a critical reduction in their strength, while a discredited Falkenhayn lost his position as chief of staff to Paul von Hindenburg.

On 20 October, French troops mounted a massive offensive led by General Robert Nivelle, who eclipsed Pétain to become hero of Verdun.

After a preparatory bombardment of more than 850,000 shells, Nivelle's infantry was able to advance under a moving barrage. A group of Senegalese tirailleurs (riflemen) rushed Fort Douaumont, and by 2 November other key positions had been retaken. A lull ensued, but on 15 December, France launched a fresh offensive. After three days, the battle had been won, and Hindenburg's sombre conclusion was that Verdun had exhausted German forces "like an open wound". The French army was bowed but not broken. ∎

Tirailleurs Sénégalais infantry units fought with distinction at Verdun, Ypres, Dixmude, the Battle of Flanders, and the Dardanelles.

The tirailleurs of Senegal

France had about 600,000 soldiers from its colonies under arms in World War I. Of these, about 150,000 served in Europe, and some 135,000 of them were Black African infantrymen in the Tirailleurs Sénégalais corps. Originally formed in the 1850s to help keep order in French West Africa, the tirailleurs later supported colonial conquests in French Congo (now the Republic of the Congo) and Chad. In the 19th century, they served only the French colonial authorities, and despite being absorbed into the French army in 1900, they remained in a separate category as "colonial troops".

Masserigne Soumare, a tirailleurs sergeant, spoke of the pride he and his comrades felt at recapturing Fort Douaumont when the French had tried and failed many times. Approximately 30,000 tirailleurs died during World War I. Despite their achievements, racist attitudes later resumed, leaving many of the African soldiers embittered.

A TERRIBLE BEAUTY IS BORN

THE EASTER RISING (24–29 APRIL 1916)

IN CONTEXT

FOCUS
Irish nationalism

BEFORE
1801 The Act of Union comes into force, creating the United Kingdom of Great Britain and Ireland.

1845–52 The Great Famine in Ireland leads to the deaths of around 1 million people and the migration of a million more.

1913 Irish nationalists and republicans establish the Irish Volunteers military organization in response to the unionist Ulster Volunteers.

AFTER
1921 The Irish War of Independence, started in 1919, ends. Britain agrees to deliver independence to most of Ireland.

1922 The independent Irish Free State is formed. Protestant-dominated Northern Ireland decides to opt out and remain part of the UK.

The outbreak of World War I delayed the implementation of the 1914 Home Rule Act, which would have granted Ireland limited self-government. During the conflict, nationalist leader John Redmond backed the Allied war effort, calling on the Irish Volunteers to join the British Army. Although around 150,000 members supported this policy, more than 10,000 Irish Volunteers did not. They split off (retaining their original name), and their ranks swelled when they were joined by many members of Sinn Féin, a nationalist party advocating

The noise of bursting shells and tumbling walls and roofs was indescribable.
Éanna de Búrca
(aka Frank Burke)
Irish Volunteer,
Dublin, 27 April 1916

separation from Great Britain. Subsequently, the Irish Volunteers came under the control of the Irish Republican Brotherhood (IRB), since many of its leaders, notably poet, teacher, and republican Pádraig Pearse, were also IRB members.

With the British government occupied by the war, the IRB began to plan a major uprising, lobbying the German government for assistance. On 20 November 1914, Germany declared support for Irish independence and agreed to arm the rebels, although the shipment of German weapons sent in April 1916 was intercepted by the British in Tralee Bay. The uprising, also joined by James Connolly's Irish Citizen Army (ICA), was set for Easter 1916.

The Irish Republic
On 24 April, Easter Monday, more than 1,000 armed members of the Irish Volunteers, the ICA, and the all-female paramilitary group Cumann na mBan begun taking control of strategic points in the Irish capital, Dublin. They met little resistance at first, because the British had just 400 troops stationed in the city. At 12:45pm, Pearse read the Proclamation of the Irish Republic outside the General

See also: The situation in Europe 18–19 ▪ Europe's colonies and empires 28–29 ▪ Public opinion 44–45 ▪ The secret war 96–99 ▪ Replacing the fallen 198–99 ▪ The home front in 1918 250–53 ▪ Post-war conflicts 320–21

James Connolly

Born in Edinburgh, Scotland, to Irish parents in 1868, James Connolly enlisted in the British Army at age 14. Serving mostly in Ireland, he grew disillusioned with the military and deserted in 1889, returning to Scotland, where he became a key figure in the trade union and socialist movements.

In 1895, Connolly moved to Ireland and then, in 1903, to the US, all while continuing his left-wing activism. In 1910, he settled in Dublin, where he worked for the Irish Transport and General Workers' Union (ITGWU) and co-founded the Irish Labour Party in 1912. During the Dublin Lock-Out industrial dispute (1913–14), Connolly co-founded the Irish Citizen Army (ICA) to defend demonstrators and strikers against police violence.

By late 1914, Connolly was leading both the ITGWU and ICA, as well as opposing Irish involvement in the war. He helped plan and lead the Easter Rising, in which he was shot and captured by the British. He was sentenced to death; unable to stand because of his wounds, Connolly was placed before the firing squad tied to a chair.

Post Office (GPO), which would act as the rising's headquarters. The rebels then consolidated their control by seizing more buildings and erecting barricades.

The next day, British military reinforcements began to arrive, numbering more than 18,000 by the week's end. By Wednesday, the fighting had grown more intense, and the British began shelling the city, causing fires to break out. Despite mounting a brave resistance, rebel casualties rose. Outnumbered and outgunned, the rebels abandoned the GPO on Friday, when fire engulfed the building. The next day, Pearse issued an unconditional surrender. Nearly 500 people had been killed in the fighting and 2,600 wounded.

The rise of Sinn Féin

Following the rising, British officials arrested more than 3,500 people and held secret military courts for leading rebels, 16 of whom (among them Pearse and Connolly) were executed. This fuelled the belief that the British response was overly punitive, and it led to increased sympathy for Sinn Féin and its republican cause. Public support for Sinn Féin grew further in April 1918, when the British attempted to introduce conscription in Ireland.

In May 1918, based on thin intelligence reports, the British administration claimed that Sinn Féin was involved with Germany in a plot to start another uprising. This did not diminish Sinn Féin's popularity. In Britain's first post-war elections, in December 1918, Sinn Féin won the majority of seats in Ireland, paving the way for its declaration of independence in January 1919. ▪

Irish rebel forces	
Irish Republican Brotherhood (IRB)	A secret nationalist organization founded in 1858; its military council planned the Easter Rising
Cumann na mBan ("Women's Council")	An Irish republican women's paramilitary group founded in 1914
Fianna Éireann ("Soldiers of Ireland")	An Irish nationalist youth organization founded in 1909; before the Easter Rising, it had been involved in gun-running
Hibernian Rifles	A small nationalist militia associated with a fraternal organization called the Irish-American Alliance; it had begun recruiting from around 1912–13
Irish Citizen Army (ICA)	Co-founded by James Connolly in 1913 as the paramilitary branch of the Irish Transport and General Workers' Union
Irish Volunteers	A nationalist militia active since 1913; during the rising it was led by Pádraig Pearse

YOU HAVE STARTED A NEW CHAPTER IN WORLD HISTORY

THE BATTLE OF JUTLAND (31 MAY–1 JUNE 1916)

IN CONTEXT

FOCUS
War at sea

BEFORE
1914 A British force sinks three German light cruisers and a destroyer in the Heligoland Bight, just off Germany's northwest coast.

1915 British ships sink the German cruiser *Blücher* in the Battle of Dogger Bank in the North Sea.

April 1916 German battle cruisers bombard the British coastal towns of Lowestoft and Yarmouth.

AFTER
December 1916 Vice Admiral Beatty takes charge of the Grand Fleet after Admiral Jellicoe is made first sea lord.

1917 British and German ships skirmish inconclusively in the Heligoland Bight.

O n 23 February 1916, Admiral Reinhard Scheer took command of the German High Seas Fleet, following the death of his predecessor, Admiral Hugo von Pohl. Scheer, a critic of the ultra-cautious Pohl, had a new approach as commander. In a set of "guiding principles" issued earlier that month, he had acknowledged that the British Grand Fleet, based in Scapa Flow, in Scotland's Orkney Islands, outmatched the German fleet in size and firepower. Even so, pressure could be put on the British through U-boat attacks, mine-laying, airship bombing raids, and sorties by the High Seas Fleet.

See also: The naval arms race 32–33 ▪ The war at sea begins 88–93 ▪ The sinking of the *Lusitania* 106–07 ▪ The U-boats on the attack 200–05

The confrontation between the British and German fleets took place over two days off Denmark's Jutland peninsula. It was the only full-scale naval battle of the war.

Key:
- British fleet
- German fleet
- British route
- German route
- Area of battle

Sir John Jellicoe

Born in Southampton, UK, in 1859, John Jellicoe joined the Royal Navy as a cadet aged 12 and specialized as a gunnery officer in his early 20s. He was promoted to captain at the age of 37. In 1900, Jellicoe served in the expedition to rescue Europeans in Beijing during the Boxer Rebellion. Later, he became a keen proponent of modernizing the navy.

At the outbreak of the war, Jellicoe, now an admiral, was appointed commander-in-chief of the Grand Fleet. Unlike his rival David Beatty, he never underestimated the quality of German ships and sailors. As commander, he was popular and worked hard to mould the Grand Fleet into an efficient fighting force – none of which prevented criticism for his failure to secure a convincing victory at Jutland.

In late 1916, Jellicoe was appointed first sea lord, the Royal Navy's most senior post. A year later, he was dismissed for his opposition to the convoy system for protecting merchant shipping from U-boats. After the war, Jellicoe was made governor-general of New Zealand. He died in London in 1935.

Sections of the Grand Fleet would be forced to sea, allowing the German fleet to inflict real damage on these smaller forces. Slowly but surely, the German navy would wear down Britain's superiority.

Scheer's British counterpart, Admiral Sir John Jellicoe, was aware of the danger. The German fleet had to be kept in its North Sea bases, where it could do no harm to high-seas shipping, but Jellicoe felt no obligation to destroy it and risk his own ships in the process. Containment was enough.

Heading for the Skagerrak
German raids in the spring yielded inconclusive results, but by May 1916 Scheer was planning a bold strike against the shipbuilding port of Sunderland, in northeast England. Battle cruisers commanded by Rear Admiral Franz von Hipper would bombard the port, forcing British battle cruisers under Vice Admiral Sir David Beatty in Scotland's Firth of Forth to come out against them. Hipper would turn and lead the British first onto waiting U-boats, then against the might of the German High Seas Fleet.

In the end, weather conditions obliged the Germans to change their plan. At 1am on 31 May, Hipper set sail from Wilhelmshaven with five battle cruisers, five light cruisers, and 30 destroyers. They were due to steam north to the Skagerrak Strait between Denmark and Norway to threaten Allied shipping. An hour and a half after Hipper, »

There is something wrong with our bloody ships today.
Attributed to Sir David Beatty

Scheer also set sail with the High Seas Fleet, which included 16 dreadnoughts. The German thinking was that a British force would be despatched to deal with Hipper, who, once engaged, would turn and lead them to the High Seas Fleet, 80 km (50 miles) to the rear.

By this time, unknown to the German admirals, Jellicoe's Grand Fleet (including 24 dreadnoughts) and Beatty's Battlecruiser Fleet (with six battle cruisers and backup from four dreadnoughts) were already in the North Sea. British code breakers had intercepted signals indicating a major German sortie, and on the evening of 30 May, the Admiralty in London had ordered both fleets to sea. By early afternoon the next day, they were preparing to meet near the entrance of the Skagerrak.

At this point, Jellicoe believed the bulk of the German fleet was still in Wilhelmshaven. A little after 2pm, two of Beatty's light cruisers, HMS *Galatea* and HMS *Phaeton*, spotted a Danish tramp steamer and went to check on it. The steamer had also caught the attention of a light cruiser from Hipper's force, *Elbing*, which sent two destroyers to investigate.

At 2:20pm, *Galatea* sighted the destroyers and signalled, "Enemy in sight". Eight minutes later, the British ship fired the first shots of the Battle of Jutland.

The run to the south

At 3:30pm, Beatty's and Hipper's battle cruisers came in sight of one another. As planned, Hipper turned about to lure the British ships towards the High Seas Fleet. Beatty pursued, aiming to cut the Germans' line of retreat to their bases. In what came to be known as the "run to the south", the two lines of battle cruisers, following parallel courses, pounded each other with fire. The German

The wreckage of HMS *Invincible* protrudes from the water. There were just six survivors. This image was taken by a sailor on HMS *Benbow*, half an hour after the *Invincible* was shelled.

gunnery proved more effective. At 4pm, a shell from Hipper's flagship, *Lützow*, smashed into a gun turret on HMS *Lion*, Beatty's flagship. *Lion* survived a subsequent explosion, but battle cruiser HMS *Indefatigable* was less lucky: it sank with the loss of more than 1,000 crew.

At 4:26pm, a second battle cruiser, HMS *Queen Mary*, blew up and sank, with nearly 1,300 lives lost. Twelve minutes later, a British light cruiser sighted the

Smoke billows skywards from HMS *Queen Mary*. The British battle cruiser exploded after being hit by the German ship *Derfflinger*.

How the battle cruisers were lost

Britain lost three battle cruisers at Jutland, while Germany lost one, *Lützow*. Respective designs account for part of this disparity. Battle cruisers were built to be fast and carry big guns. British ships sacrificed heavy armour to increase speed; German cruisers had thick armour and watertight compartments, allowing flooding to be controlled if a ship was hit.

Another factor was gunnery. For faster firing, British gunners stacked ammunition outside the magazine (ammunition storage area) beneath each gun turret, and the magazine doors were often left open. If a turret took a hit, fire could spread to the magazine, causing an explosion large enough to sink the ship, as was the case for *Indefatigable*, *Queen Mary*, and *Invincible*.

British battle cruiser HMS *Lion* was saved by the action of Royal Marine Major Francis Harvey. Seconds before dying, he ordered the flooding of the magazine beneath the turret, forestalling an explosion.

approaching German High Seas Fleet. Beatty's four supporting dreadnoughts came into action as he ordered his fleet to turn about.

The run to the north

In the "run to the north" that came next, the tables were turned, with Beatty luring the Germans towards the Grand Fleet. British firepower was more effective, causing damage to *Lützow* among others. Support came from further battle cruisers under Rear Admiral Sir Horace Hood, despatched by Jellicoe. At 6pm, the Germans realized they had sailed into a trap. Minutes later, Jellicoe ordered his dreadnoughts to deploy for action in a single line. In a manoeuvre known as "crossing the T", they would steam across the front of the German fleet, creating a T-shape and bringing all their guns to bear on the Germans, who could return fire only with their forward guns. Hood's battle cruisers, meanwhile, engaged Hipper's, inflicting further damage on *Lützow*. At 6:32pm, however, a number of shells hit *Invincible*. The ship exploded, broke in two, and sank with more than 1,000 men, including Hood.

About-turns

At 6:33pm, Scheer, understanding the danger of his position, signalled his fleet to turn 180 degrees. To provide cover, he sent destroyers to torpedo the British ships. The about-turn completed, Scheer's fleet headed southwest. When he realized what was happening, Jellicoe, wary of the torpedoes, chose not to pursue closely. Instead, he ordered a southwards course, hoping (as Beatty had done earlier) to come between the German fleet and its bases. Just before 7pm, Scheer signalled another about-turn. He would later explain this as an

> The superior English armada eventually appeared … What happened? The English were beaten.
> **Kaiser Wilhelm II**
> **on a visit to the fleet, 5 June 1916**

attempt to "inflict a second blow" on the British ships to prevent them cutting his retreat lines. Within minutes, British sailors had sighted the returning Germans and were firing on them. At 7:13pm, Scheer ordered his battle cruisers to charge. He also signalled his destroyers to attack again with torpedoes and raise a smoke screen. Then he signalled yet another about-turn.

Jellicoe responded to Scheer's destroyers with attack of his own, using destroyers and light cruisers. At the same time, controversially, he ordered his fleet to turn away from the German vessels. His wariness of torpedoes, along with decreasing visibility and poor signalling, are believed to have contributed to the decision. Had the British pursued the Germans more vigorously, they might have inflicted decisive losses; certainly this is what Beatty would later maintain.

As night fell, Jellicoe was still confident of coming between the German warships and their line

Admiral Reinhard Scheer stands proudly, surrounded by crew members of *Friedrich der Grosse*, the flagship of his High Seas Fleet. Scheer skilfully outplayed the British at Jutland.

of retreat. Aware that his opponents were better trained and equipped for night fighting than his crews, Jellicoe decided against engaging overnight. He expected, however, to continue the fight the next morning.

Scheer escapes

Sporadic encounters between smaller ships continued into the night. When dawn broke, however, the seas around the British fleet were empty of German vessels. Jellicoe had assumed that Scheer would regain his bases via the Frisian Islands. Instead, he had slipped past the rear of the British fleet on a more easterly route.

At 11am, Jellicoe ordered a return to base. At 3pm, Scheer's flagship, *Friedrich der Grosse*, sailed into Wilhelmshaven. The High Seas Fleet had survived. Germany claimed the battle – the war's largest naval encounter – as a victory. In the event, although British losses were significantly greater – 14 British ships sunk against 11 German, more than 6,000 British dead against 2,500 German – the High Seas Fleet stayed in port for most of the rest of the war, and the Royal Navy retained control of the North Sea. ∎

OUR IRON ARMY WILL WIN A TOTAL VICTORY

THE BRUSILOV OFFENSIVE (JUNE–SEPTEMBER 1916)

IN CONTEXT

FOCUS
Russian fortunes

BEFORE
1914 While combat in France and Belgium sinks into trench warfare, more mobile battles are fought on the Eastern Front.

1915 The Central Powers use innovative tactics in the Gorlice–Tarnów Offensive to break through the front.

AFTER
1917 Low morale at the front is a key factor in fuelling the Russian revolutions.

1941 In World War II, tank-led attacks enable the German army to encircle and destroy massive Soviet formations.

1945 Returning to the "steamroller" strategy of the tsarist era, the USSR defeats Nazi Germany and overruns most of Eastern Europe.

The Eastern Front stretched 965 km (600 miles), from Lithuania to the borders of neutral Romania. As 1916 dawned on the front, the contending armies were still locked in the positions they had occupied at the end of the previous autumn. There was little hint that Russia's greatest victory of the war – the Brusilov Offensive – was just months away. Knocked out of Austrian Galicia, Russia had pulled back from its Polish salient.

A change of plan

Even though the front had stayed static, the quality of the Russian army had greatly improved. It had come through the 1915 munitions

See also: The Battle of Tannenberg 78–81 ▪ The battle for Poland 83 ▪ Russia retreats 138–39 ▪ The February Revolution 192–93 ▪ The Kerensky Offensive 224–25 ▪ The October Revolution 240–41 ▪ German victory in Eastern Europe 258–59

Aleksei Brusilov

The son of a Russian general and grandson of an officer who had fought against Napoleon I in 1812, Aleksei Brusilov was born in Tiflis (Tbilisi), Georgia, in 1853. His first posting was in the cavalry in the Dragoon Regiment. After his first military engagement – in the Russo-Turkish War (1877–78) – he rose through the ranks of the Second Guards Cavalry Division to become deputy commander-in-chief of the Warsaw Military District. At the start of World War I, the elderly cavalryman believed that cavalry was obsolete in an age of mechanized warfare. He adapted quickly, however, and his victory on the Russian Southwest Front won him the Sword of St George with Diamonds – an award that only eight Russian commanders received during World War I.

Surprisingly, given his privileged background, Brusilov sided with the Bolsheviks after the war. Following his death in Moscow in 1926, he was given a state funeral that was attended by representatives from both "old" and "new" Russia.

---

crisis that affected both sides, and shells and rifles were arriving daily. Its two military fronts north of the vast Pripet Marshes (straddling the Belarus–Ukraine border) were now preparing to launch an offensive against the German armies in Lithuania, which were close to the Russian capital Petrograd and only 110km (68 miles) from the Lithuanian city of Kaunas, where Field Marshal Paul von Hindenburg and his chief of staff, General Erich Ludendorff, had their headquarters.

A Russian probe commenced on 18 March, resulting in the Battle of Lake Naroch, near Vilnius in Lithuania, but it pulled back after losing upwards of 110,000 men. That costly failure had been an attempt to relieve the pressure on France, which was then locked in the desperate struggle for Verdun.

Following the defeat at Lake Naroch, the Russian high command planned a bigger and more detailed offensive for July, based on three sectors of the Russian front. The West Front, commanded by General Aleksei Evert, and the North Front, led by General Aleksei Kuropatkin, would work in tandem. The Southwest Front, to the south of the Pripet Marshes and facing Austro-Hungarian Galicia, would mount only diversionary attacks.

Once again, events on other fronts upset Russian plans and timetables. In May, Austro-Hungarian forces assaulted Italian positions in the Trentino region and threatened to break through into the plains of Lombardy. Now it was Italy's turn to plead for Russian assistance. Mindful of the terms of the Chantilly Conference of December 1915, which committed the Allies to simultaneous attacks against the Central Powers, Tsar Nicholas II pushed his commanders to begin the Russian offensive in order to relieve pressure on both France and Italy.

Evert and Kuropatkin resisted the demands – the best they could promise was to move their timetable to mid-June. However, the commander of the Southwest Front, General Aleksei Brusilov, said that his troops were ready to go.

Well, God be with you. Have it your own way.
Russian chief of staff Mikhail Alexeyev
speaking to Aleksei Brusilov

Shifting tactics

Brusilov knew that the Austro-Hungarian forces entrenched before him in Galicia had been thinned in order to reinforce the Italian front. The Austro-Hungarian command assumed that their defensive works were impregnable. Germany, too, had transferred much of its heavy artillery to the Verdun front, perhaps underestimating the resolve of the Russian army. »

Brusilov would undermine these assumptions with a unique set of tactical innovations. Rather than assaulting a particular point, he would attack along his entire Galician front, stretching 480 km (300 miles). Also, Brusilov's opening bombardments would be spaced well apart, sowing confusion about where the main thrust was coming from and forcing the Austro-Hungarian forces to thin their lines by dispersal.

The offensive begins

When the bombardments started, before dawn on 4 June 1916, they caught the Austro-Hungarian troops completely by surprise. In many places, the Russian infantry was in their opponents' trenches before the Russian artillery had ceased firing. Brusilov's engineers had dug tunnels close to the Austro-Hungarian lines so that his special forces did not have to cross 1.6 km (1 mile) of open no-man's-land.

The first Russian attack fell on the first Austro-Hungarian trench, while a second Russian wave headed for the second, or reserve, trench, in quick succession, and so on. The third and final trench nearly always surrendered en masse.

Brusilov's tactics turned out to be remarkably successful. The Austro-Hungarian line collapsed exactly where he had hoped it would. The commander of the Austro-Hungarian Fourth Army was Archduke Joseph Ferdinand, the emperor's godson. He lost 130,000 men in the first two days alone, a huge toll that eventually led to his dismissal. The Russian offensive also reaped huge hauls of prisoners along the immense front. In just one week, the Austro-Hungarian army on the Eastern Front lost about half of its troops.

The steamroller

With the whole front in motion, the much-vaunted "Russian steamroller" was never more in evidence. Its scale was enormous. Seemingly contiguous battles marked its wide approach, announced by rumbling artillery barrages; after the surprise start to the offensive, Brusilov reverted to the old pattern of sustained bombardments, followed by human-wave infantry assaults.

In the steamroller's wake lay shattered villages, snaking supply lines, and busy field-aid stations. Files of prisoners marched east, and heaps of corpses awaited mass burial. The success of the offensive

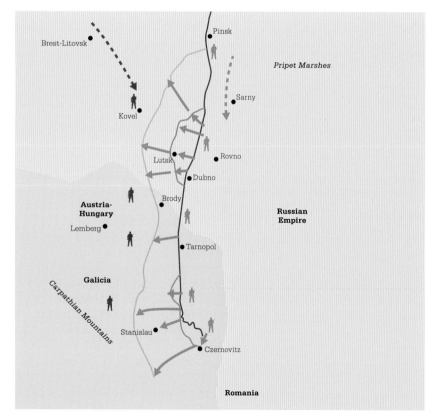

More than half a million men from four Russian armies were involved in the first thrusts of the Brusilov Offensive. A fifth army arrived in July, reinforcing the lines. The Austro-Hungarian armies were driven back, deep into their own territory, almost as far as the Carpathian Mountains. Brusilov's advances were held up after the arrival of German reinforcements from the west.

Key:

- Russian army
- Austro-Hungarian army
- Austro-German lines, 4 June
- Austro-German lines, 10 June
- Austro-German lines, 20 September
- Russian advance
- Russian reinforcements
- German reinforcements

Russian infantry troops charge towards an Austro-Hungarian position. During the Brusilov Offensive, General Brusilov used specialist forces to breach weaknesses in the opposing lines.

astonished even Brusilov himself. The efficiency of the German railway network, however, kept the Galician front from collapsing altogether. Seventeen German divisions from the Western Front set off to stem the rout. Additional Austrian divisions were stripped from the Italian front to assist.

The Central Powers were able to reinforce the beleaguered front line because of the relative inactivity of the Russian fronts north of the vast Pripet Marshes. General Evert did mount a half-hearted Russian offensive aimed at the city of Baranovichi (in modern-day Belarus), but that collapsed with heavy losses. Brusilov's own momentum also began slowing as he outran his supply lines.

The cost of success

On 27 July, Hindenburg was given command of all Central Powers troops on the Eastern Front north of Brody in eastern Galicia. By this time, however, the Russian juggernaut was again rolling forwards. Brusilov's greatest successes now lay in the south, where Russian divisions reached the Romanian border and the foot of the Carpathian Mountains, capturing all of the Bukovina, the southern prong of Austrian Galicia.

Brusilov's bloodiest repulse, however, was on his northern front, at Kovel (in modern-day Ukraine), near the southern reaches of the Pripet Marshes. Surrounded by swamp, the town was approached by radiating causeways. For nearly two weeks, in late July and early August, one Russian attack after another funnelled down these causeways, only to be wrecked by converging rifle and machine-gun fire. Even the elite Guards Division, usually held in reserve, was ordered forwards. Time and again, they charged down the causeways, and the slaughter was appalling. Suffering nearly 70 per cent casualties, the Guards Division was effectively destroyed.

Diminished reserves

By September, Brusilov's offensive had run out of steam. He had few reserves and even fewer supplies, and the autumn rains were imminent. However, his average depth of penetration was nearly 65 km (40 miles), over a front of 480 km (300 miles), resulting in huge swathes of conquered territory. As such, the Brusilov Offensive is widely regarded as the greatest Russian victory of the war. Apart from its territorial gains, Russia weakened Austria-Hungary so much that it ceased to function as a great power independent of Germany. Also, so many German divisions had been transferred east from the Western Front that the French troops could finally prevail at Verdun. Brusilov's success also brought Romania into the war on the Allied side, a disaster for that nation but a development that further diminished the Central Powers' military resources.

The success of the Brusilov Offensive came at a terrible cost. Up to a million men may have been killed or wounded. The survivors were exhausted, which sapped the morale of the whole Russian army, contributing to the rise of radicalism in the ranks and leading to the success, a few months later, of the Russian Revolution. ∎

Russia had sacrificed herself for her allies, and it is [unjust] that subsequent events should obscure the debt.
B.H. Liddell Hart
The Real War: 1914–18

WE REBELLED IN ORDER TO PLEASE GOD

THE ARAB REVOLT (JUNE 1916–OCTOBER 1918)

IN CONTEXT

FOCUS
War in Arabia

BEFORE
1915 Hussein bin Ali offers British high commissioner Arthur McMahon support against the Ottomans in return for Arab independence after the war.

May 1916 Secretly drafted by France and Britain, the Sykes–Picot Agreement divides the Ottoman territories of the Middle East into post-war spheres of European influence.

AFTER
1920 The League of Nations declares British mandates in Palestine and Transjordan, and French mandates in Syria and Lebanon.

1926 Abdulaziz bin Saud names himself ruler of the Kingdom of Hejaz and Nejd, an independent Arab nation that will later be called Saudi Arabia.

Having agreed to support the Allied war effort instead of joining forces with the Ottomans, in June 1916 Hussein bin Ali, emir of Mecca, sent his recently formed Sharifian Army and irregular tribal warriors to attack the Ottoman garrisons in Mecca and Medina. The operation, which spurred on the Arab Revolt, achieved mixed results: although Arab forces failed to breach the Ottoman defences of Medina, they seized Mecca, the port of Jeddah on the Red Sea coast, and also a handful of other cities.

It soon became evident that the inexperienced and lightly armed Arabs would be no match for the Ottoman army without further assistance from the Allies. To help train and organize the Arab resistance, both Britain and France deployed advisers to the region, including 28-year-old Captain T.E. Lawrence.

A partnership with Faisal

Lawrence discovered a strategic soulmate in Faisal bin Al-Hussein, son of the emir and commander of the Jordanian Hashemite forces. Using guerrilla tactics to offset the Ottoman advantage in troops and arms, the duo launched hit-and-run attacks on the Hejaz railway and other targets. These actions severely affected the Ottoman army's ability to resupply and reinforce Medina and other outposts; they also drew thousands of Ottoman troops away from the main Allied thrust in Palestine.

Astride camels and horses, the ad hoc Arab forces continued to push northwards. Without the knowledge of the British high command, in June 1917 Lawrence and Faisal staged a daring trek of 965 km (600 miles) across the desert to launch a surprise attack on Aqaba, an Ottoman port on the Red Sea. A battle on 6 July resulted in the surrender of Ottoman forces.

The best of you brings me the most Turkish dead.
T.E. Lawrence

From the start of 1917, Faisal led a unit of camel-riding troops known as the Ageyl Bodyguard through the Red Sea coastal desert to Aqaba.

Capture of the strategic port allowed reinforcement of the Arab army with small but highly efficient British and French units (including flying corps) and modern weaponry such as machine guns and armoured cars. This boost was much needed, because the Ottoman army was now assisted by German ground troops and Austro-Hungarian air support, as well as by local tribes opposed to the Hashemites.

The Palestine campaign

Through the remainder of 1917 and 1918, the Arab army aided the Allied advance across Palestine and the capture of Jerusalem by engaging against the Ottoman army. Technically a liaison officer between Arab and British forces, he became a de facto commander with Faisal bin Al-Hussein.

Ottoman forces in the Transjordan region. In January 1918, they enjoyed a tactical victory at the Battle of Tafilah, and in the spring they carried out incessant raids on the Hejaz railway.

In September 1918, as Allied and Ottoman armies clashed at the Battle of Megiddo, in Palestine, Arab forces led by Faisal, Lawrence, and others were distracting Ottoman forces east of the Jordan river. Their capture of the railway and communications hub at Daraa was a major blow to the Ottoman troops. Along with Allied victory at Megiddo, it opened the door to the capture of Damascus on 1 October.

The Ottomans and their German allies were now in complete retreat. The final large-scale battle of the Middle Eastern theatre took place over the course of 25–26 October, when Faisal's forces captured Aleppo in northern Syria. ▪

T.E. Lawrence

One of World War I's most renowned figures in the Middle East, Thomas Edward (T.E.) Lawrence was a highly skilled military strategist, diplomat, and communicator. Born in Tremadog, Wales, in 1888, he spent the pre-war years working as an archaeologist in the Middle East before joining the British Arab Bureau intelligence unit in Cairo. In October 1916, Lawrence was dispatched to the Arabian peninsula to assess the ability of Arab tribes battling against the Ottoman army.

A vocal advocate of Arab independence, Lawrence was disappointed by the post-war division of the Middle East. Returning to Britain after the war ended, he briefly worked at the Colonial Office, served in the Royal Air Force (RAF), and wrote about his wartime exploits in *Seven Pillars of Wisdom*. In 1935, Lawrence died following a motorcycle accident.

IT WAS A DANCE OF HELL

THE SOMME (1 JULY–18 NOVEMBER 1916)

IN CONTEXT

FOCUS
War of attrition

BEFORE
1566–1648 The Eighty Years' War between Imperial Spain and the Dutch Republic is a long attritional conflict.

1812 Russia uses attritional tactics to defeat Napoleon I's invading Grande Armée.

1864–65 In the final stages of the American Civil War, Union forces use attrition tactics to wear down entrenched Confederate armies.

AFTER
August 1918 In the Battle of Amiens, the Allies break the German line, ending the war of attrition and beginning their "Hundred Days" of victories.

1947–91 The Cold War is an undeclared war of attrition between countries of the West and the USSR.

[Victory] would not have taken place but for the period of ceaseless attrition, which used up the reserves of the German Armies …
Sir Douglas Haig

All wars follow the **same pattern** as a typical single battle – proceeding from manoeuvre, to **grinding attrition**, to final breakthrough.

The stage of **attrition**, of "wearing down", always produces **heavy casualties**.

If the ultimate result is victory rather than defeat, the casualties are considered justified.

In mid-December 1915, when Allied generals gathered in the Hôtel du Grande Condé in Paris, each knew that the war he had trained for – a quick campaign won in a decisive "battle of annihilation" – had been illusory. The conflict, especially on the Western Front, had instead become its opposite, a war of attrition.

The chosen battlefield

In an effort to break the deadlock, the generals agreed to mount simultaneous summer offensives – by Italy in the Alps, Russia on the Eastern Front, and Britain and France on the Western Front – so heavy and persistent that Germany and Austria-Hungary could not switch reinforcements from one front to another. The Central Powers would be stretched so thinly that, even if no breakthrough resulted, they would be progressively weakened. The strategy of attrition would then begin to triumph.

On the Western Front, locked in entrenchments, there could be no flanking manoeuvres, only more costly frontal attacks. British and French commanders agreed to jointly assault the German line between Flanders and Picardy, in the valley of the River Somme northeast of Paris.

Before the war, the rolling chalk hills bisected by the river were almost treeless, with occasional copses. They once ranked among northern France's most important arable regions but had not been ploughed for nearly two years at the start of the summer of 1916. The villages and farms dotted around the slopes were now fortified ruins, since the uplands had fallen to the German army during the "Race to the Sea". Chalk-white lines of entrenchments now scarred the hillsides.

When British troops replaced the French in this sector, they filed into fieldworks that ran along the base of the downs. A long, gently rising slope with rows of fortifications rose above them. This was reputedly the strongest part of the German line. The Somme sector was also where the British and French lines adjoined, a factor that would prove to be important. The old Roman road leading from the market town of Albert, in the British rear, ran

See also: The Race to the Sea 70–71 ▪ Tank warfare 150–51 ▪ The Battle of Verdun 152–59 ▪ The Battle of Passchendaele 230–35 ▪ The Spring Offensive 260–67

northeast across the downs for 18 km (11 miles) to Bapaume, a junction on the railway network running behind and parallel to the German lines. An advance along that axis might be decisive.

General Sir Douglas Haig, commander of the British Expeditionary Force (BEF) since December 1915, envisaged that a breakthrough by ground troops might then be exploited by hard-riding British cavalry. At the same time, during the weeks spent planning the assault, Haig had raised the spectre of a battle of attrition, warning the British government that the real purpose of the Somme offensive was to continue wearing down the German army so that it could be decisively defeated in 1917.

Difficult terrain

The British sector of the battlefield, north of the River Somme, was in turn bisected by the Ancre river, a small tributary flowing southwest through Albert. North of the Ancre was a complex of high, rounded hills that German forces had made practically impregnable. South of the Ancre and the Roman road, the chalk formed one continuous ridge, the lower slopes of which – covered with forts, salients, and redoubts – formed the German first line.

The looming battle would not be one of surprise. German observers in their chalk eyries would have seen the enormous dumps of ammunition and supplies piling up behind Albert. After dark, the new men of Kitchener's Armies – the British volunteers of 1914 – were fed into the line.

Constant bombardment

On Saturday 1 July, the weather in northern France was warm and cloudless. Along the battlefront, however, the entire German line was a wall of flashes and smoke, as it had been for the past seven days. The noise of the week-long British bombardment had been »

A British Royal Garrison Artillery 15 cm (6 in) heavy gun opens fire on German lines on the Western Front in June 1916, during the build-up to the Battle of the Somme.

Sir Douglas Haig

Born in Edinburgh, Scotland, in 1861 to a wealthy family, Douglas Haig graduated from the Royal Military Academy at Sandhurst in 1885. As a skilled cavalryman, he spent his early army years in key colonial postings: India; the Sudan, where he met Lord Kitchener and fought against Mahdist rebels; and South Africa, in the Second Boer War. Haig rose through the army ranks and commanded I Corps of the BEF in August 1914 and the First Army from early 1915. He was promoted to field marshal in late 1916.

Haig's leadership of the BEF through 1916–18 was capped by the breakthrough victory at Amiens, the "black day of the German army", which opened the road to Allied victory. In 1921, he was appointed president of the newly formed British Legion ex-servicemen's organization.

When Haig died, in 1928, he was hailed for his wartime leadership qualities. In the following decades, however, his judgement and character were questioned, and he became associated with the huge casualty tolls from the Somme and Passchendaele.

indescribable, as nearly 1,500 guns – one every 20 m (66 ft) – had systematically raked over the German trenches. During the final hour, it had doubled in intensity and then suddenly halted. Just before 7:30am, with cataclysmic cracks and booms, 19 subterranean mines exploded beneath sectors of the smoking German first line, the tremors even demolishing parts of the British parapets.

Over the top

The officers blew their whistles, and the infantry – 17 British divisions – climbed the ladders out of their trenches and began the uphill assault. After filing through the cuts in their own wire, the troops mostly deployed into waves and, nearly shoulder to shoulder, advanced across no-man's-land, each soldier burdened by 27 kg (60 lb) of gear and equipment. They would set their pace to that of the barrage moving ahead of them by 100 m (328 ft). For most of the front, which ran for 26 km (16 miles), the battalions advanced in unison.

No one expected any resistance from the thoroughly demolished German front line. In shows of

bravado, some men even dribbled footballs ahead of them. Yet they were soon cut down in their thousands. German machine-gun teams had been able to weather the bombardment in deep dugouts. They had also been drilled in racing into new positions and siting their weapons within just three minutes. On a single traverse, a machine gunner was able to cut down a long file of soldiers like a reaper scything corn.

The moving barrage had also started to outrun the infantrymen, who had no protection on the open

Young men of a Public Schools Battalion prepare for action at "White City", near Beaumont-Hamel. This sector of British trenches was named by troops for its banks of white chalk.

slopes. Worse still, when the British battalions encountered the German wire, they discovered that the bombardment had failed to cut through it. Men were shot dead while entangled in fields of barbed wire 1.5 m (5 ft) high.

In the opening 30 minutes of the grand assault, as many as half of the 66,000 soldiers in the first wave

A 2-tonne (2.2-ton) mine explodes under the German front line at Hawthorn Ridge Redoubt on the first day of the Battle of the Somme.

The role of mines

Long before the opening artillery bombardment on 1 July, the Battle of the Somme was already under way in the strong yet easily worked chalk below the trenches. The main job of the tunnelling companies from the Royal Engineers of the British Army was to lay charges beneath the German front line. German engineers sought to prevent that by undermining the miners and detonating their own explosives to break up the British tunnels. Between them, the British and

German soldiers detonated 227 subterranean explosions before the assault of 1 July.

British troops had managed to place 19 mines at carefully chosen positions beneath the German line. When detonated on 1 July, the explosions sent shock waves over the battlefield. Despite the destruction, the German front line easily repelled most British assaults. The miners also dug "Russian saps", communication trenches in no-man's-land, thinly covered with soil, although these largely went unused.

were hit and put out of the fight. By noon, the casualties were probably approaching the 50,000 mark.

Huge sacrifice

Little of this was known back at headquarters. Three cavalry divisions were still mounted and waiting to exploit the expected breakthrough, not realizing that knots of officers and men were fighting desperately from shell holes or even within the German lines. The Glasgow Commercials, a Kitchener's Armies unit, penetrated the formidable Leipzig Redoubt. The 36th Ulster Division pounded into the nearby Schwaben Redoubt, and parts of it stormed as far as Thiepval, a ruined fortified chateau on a bluff above the Ancre river that would take three months to seize.

Some assaults were tragically heroic. Opposite La Boisselle, another strongpoint just south of

the Ancre river, the 103rd (Tyneside Irish) Brigade, another Kitchener's Armies formation, attacked with 3,000 infantrymen. It crossed 1.6 km (1 mile) of open land in the face of machine guns until the men that were left crashed into the German trenches. Around 50 survivors made it as far as Contalmaison, another fortified village halfway up the slope, but they were all killed or captured.

Extraordinary courage was also demonstrated by the men of the Newfoundland Regiment, sent in to make a "diversionary attack" against the virtually impregnable fortress of Gommecourt in the far north of the front. They had to cross 275 m (900 ft) of open ground before reaching their own front, and then a similar distance of no-man's-land, all in the face of German machine guns. As they bunched up to get through the

gaps in their own wire, they were slaughtered by converging German fire. Of the 752 who launched the attack, 658 men and 26 officers were casualties, 91 per cent of the attacking force.

North of the old Roman road, the British assault was a horrible failure. South of it, five of the 17 assaulting divisions met most of their objectives, capturing or surrounding fortified villages and strongpoints along portions of the German first line. Adjoining the British right, the French divisions, too, met all of their objectives, largely because they massed more heavy guns during the opening bombardment and resorted more to stealth than bravado when mounting their attack.

According to the doctrine of attritional warfare, the opening day at the Somme was a qualified success. But after sunset, the »

The first phase of the battle saw the French Sixth Army and the right flank of the British Fourth Army making big advances around Maricourt. To the north, however, the British Army suffered its worst-ever daily losses. By mid-September, the German Second Army had been pushed back further in the north. When the battle was finally curtailed, in November, despite the Allies' biggest territorial gains since the First Battle of the Marne (1914), they had failed to take their main objectives: Bapaume and Péronne.

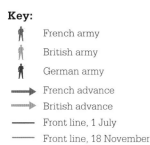

Key:

🧍	French army
🧍	British army
🧍	German army
→	French advance
⇒	British advance
—	Front line, 1 July
—	Front line, 18 November

thunder of artillery unceasing, the British medical services were utterly overwhelmed. Most of the ambulance trains had not arrived, and wounded men were strewn everywhere. Thousands more were still lying in no-man's-land, where most would die. Weeks passed before the final tally could be compiled. Of more than 100,000 who went over the top in various waves on 1 July, 57,470 became casualties, including a staggering 19,240 killed. Since most of the men listed as "missing in action" were also likely to have been killed, the real figure was probably more than 21,000. It remains the British Army's bloodiest single day.

Wearing down

The Battle of the Somme lasted another 140 days. The ceaseless thundering of the guns could be heard, some claimed, as far away as southeast England. This was the battle's "wearing-down" phase, war as constant frontal pressure, where neither side could gain the advantage – much less a vulnerable flank – over or around its opponent.

By 2 July, Haig had abandoned the carnage-strewn ground north of the Somme river and was now targeting a ridge south of the

The battlefields of the Somme were the graveyards of Kitchener's Army.
Winston Churchill

Wounded British soldiers trudge wearily from the Somme battlefield. More than half the British troops who took part in the offensive on 1 July were injured or killed.

Ancre river (a Somme tributary) that was easily seen from the British line. Every patch of ground would be contested. When Erich von Falkenhayn, chief of the German general staff, visited the Somme front a few days later, vowing that no territory would be willingly surrendered and every attack would be met with a furious counterattack, he was calling for a battle of attrition. He threw all the reserves he could spare at the British, increasing the size of his forces on the Somme to such an extent that they were split into two armies. France took more territory during the battle, but its divisions were not menacing the vital rail junction at Bapaume.

It took the British troops, hastily dug in, a full two weeks to reach Bazentin Ridge to the north, where the German second line ran, a distance that before the war could be strolled in 20 minutes. Even then, the British commanders resorted to a daring night attack that caught their exhausted opponents by surprise.

Much of the toughest fighting in this phase of the battle took place in the various copses or woods, especially Delville Wood, standing astride the ridge with a commanding prospect in every

direction. In the eight weeks from 15 July, the forest of mature beech and hornbeam trees was reduced to charred splinters. At times, 400 shells a minute rained down on "Devil's Wood", as it became known. More than 30,000 British men alone were killed or wounded there.

With the roar of battle continuous by night and day, both sides now fought over bite-sized chunks of territory. Haig, applying pressure across the front, called it "nibbling", another tactical expression of the wearing-down battle.

New strategies

As summer turned to autumn, two events changed the wearing-down dynamic. On 28 August, Field Marshal Paul von Hindenburg replaced Falkenhayn as German chief of the general staff. He reversed the strategy of holding ground at all costs in favour of defence-in-depth, a more flexible strategy that would curtail German losses. He was already planning a strategic withdrawal across the entire Western Front to what would become the Hindenburg Line.

The second event, in mid-September, was the introduction of the tank by the British. As Allied troops pushed across the ridge and onto the gentle reverse slope leading down to Bapaume, they mounted a third major drive. On 15 September, 32 new Mark I tanks, their noise drowned out by the roar of bombardment, joined them. The following dawn, when the attack was launched along the axis of the Roman road between the villages of Flers and Courcelette, only 24 of

A Mark I tank is flanked by men from the 122nd Brigade of the British Army, which it led into the eastern part of Flers on 15 September 1916.

The Mark I tank

Developed in 1916, the British Mark I tank was a bold attempt to break the stalemate on the Western Front. It resembled one of its early names, a "landship", made distinctive by its use of continuous-track propulsion, invented more than a decade earlier for tractors. The tank's role was to smash through barbed wire and bridge the welter of trenches behind enemy front lines.

Also intended as a movable gun platform, the Mark I was built to two specifications. One was the "male" model, armed with two 6-pounder (57 mm) guns and three Hotchkiss machine guns. The other was the "female", armed with heavy Vickers machine guns to protect "male" tanks against infantry attack. Although revolutionary, the tanks had weaknesses: their eight-man crews – in hot and cramped conditions – had only a narrow field of view, so could not always see where they were going; and their top speed of just 6 kph (3.7 mph) made them a slow – as well as large – target for enemy gunners.

the vehicles remained operational, with the other eight having already broken down. The week-long assault, which was the final British success on the Somme, claimed another 15 sq km (6 sq miles) of muddy ground.

Despite the tanks' dismal performance as a whole, they did prove their great battle potential. Only a handful saw actual combat and some of those were knocked out by German shelling. Others, however, as they clanked into view, terrified German infantrymen, who had never seen their like. The future of tanks on the battlefield was assured, while that of the cavalry remained in doubt.

The mud of the Somme

On 26 September, the German troops at Thiepval surrendered. The fort had been a thorn in the British side since 1 July. With its capture, most major fighting on the Somme subsided. The rains arrived, and the shell holes and the newly dug mass graves in no-man's-land became a mire. The all-devouring mud of the Somme became legendary, and a fitting metaphor for the futility of war.

Haig closed the offensive on 19 November. He would never calculate its ultimate cost, but others did so subsequently. The French forces, for all their extensive gains in the southern sector, suffered more than 190,000 casualties. German losses are estimated at 600,000 or more. The British – for whom the collective memory of the Somme still resonates deeply – lost around 420,000 men in exchange for a stretch of pulverized downland just 10 km (6 miles) long and 36 km (20 miles) wide. The Somme had, however, turned an army of British volunteers into a battle-hardened force and acted as a testing ground for new weaponry. ∎

A 15-cm (6-in) howitzer is hauled through the mud near Pozières, which was taken by Australian troops on 23 July 1916 after costly fighting.

EVERY MISERY BORNE AT ONCE

ROMANIA GOES TO WAR (AUGUST–DECEMBER 1916)

IN CONTEXT

FOCUS
The war in Romania

BEFORE
1861 The principalities of Wallachia and Moldavia unite under one monarch, leading to the formal creation of Romania.

1867 Transylvania becomes part of Hungary.

AFTER
10 November 1918 Romania re-enters the conflict on the side of the Allies – the day before the Armistice is signed.

1920 The Kingdom of Romania, which includes Transylvania, Bukovina, Bessarabia, and other territories, becomes known as Greater Romania.

1940 Greater Romania breaks up. Southern Dobruja returns to Bulgaria; Bessarabia and Northern Bukovina are ceded to the USSR; and Northern Transylvania is awarded to Hungary.

The **new nation of Romania** wants **stable borders**, including **Transylvania**.

↓

Romania **must fight Austria-Hungary** to **win Transylvania**.

↓

Joining the Allies offers **Romania** a chance for **territorial gains**.

↓

But pursuing its own agenda leads to the loss of 90 per cent of the country.

During the first two years of World War I, the Kingdom of Romania was courted by both the Allies and the Central Powers. It might have remained an island of neutrality for the length of the conflict had it not been for its territorial ambitions.

Romania was an inherently unstable country, its fluid borders subject to change with every new international agreement. In one matter, however, the Romanians always remained steadfast: they hoped one day to acquire Transylvania, a region beyond the Carpathian Mountains to the west, where three million ethnic Romanians lived under the rule of Austria-Hungary. They also wanted to hold on to the Dobruja region, a flatland between the Danube river and the Black Sea, which they had won from Bulgaria in 1913, after the Second Balkan War.

Romania bides its time

The extraordinary early Russian successes of the Brusilov Offensive across the border suggested that the moment to side with the Allies had now arrived. On 17 August 1916, Romania signed a convention with France and Russia that

See also: The Balkans 25 ▪ The end of the Serbian campaign 140–43 ▪ Greece and the Macedonian Front 226–27 ▪ A lasting peace? 312–17

promised the eventual realization of all those territorial ambitions. It proved to be a disastrous mistake.

Romania's declaration of war, on 27 August, was upsetting for Germany's Kaiser Wilhelm II. In addition to the family betrayal by King Ferdinand I, he feared that this intervention might lead to the demise of Austria-Hungary. Next day, the kaiser replaced his chief of general staff Erich von Falkenhayn with Field Marshal Paul von Hindenburg. He then dispatched Falkenhayn to Transylvania to shore up the region's defences.

Strategic error

The Allies suggested Romania delay its planned Transylvania operation, in favour of a combined attack on Bulgaria. In the capital Bucharest, however, the king and his generals wished to pursue their own priorities and instructed Romanian divisions to march through the mountain passes into Transylvania.

While Romanian forces were focusing on Transylvania, Field Marshal August von Mackensen led German, Austrian, Bulgarian, and Ottoman soldiers across Romania's

> Now that I have conquered the Hohenzollern who was in me, I fear no one.
> **King Ferdinand I**

southern border and into the Dobruja region. On 6 September, they seized the Danube fortress of Turtucaia, taking 25,000 prisoners and 115 heavy guns. Later that month, the end of the Brusilov Offensive allowed the redeployment of 12 German and Austro-Hungarian divisions, which Falkenhayn used to drive Romanian forces out of Transylvania. By early November, he had joined Mackensen in invading Romania.

After taking Constanţa, Romania's main Black Sea port, Mackensen headed to Bucharest, where he arrived on 6 December 1916, riding on a white horse. The same week, the British tried to sabotage the Ploieşti oil fields, north of Bucharest, but the derricks were soon pumping again.

The rest of the Romanian army ended the year holed up in a small enclave near the temporary capital of Jassy in the northeast. Within just a few months, Romania had lost control of almost the entire country. ▪

Commanding officers of a German auxiliary division consult maps and define strategies at the Bran Pass in the Carpathian Mountains of the Transylvania region in 1916.

King Ferdinand I of Romania

A member of the Prussian Hohenzollern dynasty and a cousin of Kaiser Wilhelm II, Ferdinand I was born in Germany in 1865. Due to a complex web of family relations, the Hohenzollerns sat on many thrones, including that of Romania, which was occupied by Ferdinand's childless uncle, King Carol I.

On Carol's death in 1914, Ferdinand acceded to the throne, his father and brother having renounced it. He swore to parliament that he would "reign as a good Romanian" – an oath he stood by despite the misfortunes of war and one that earned him the nickname "the Loyal One".

In 1922, Ferdinand was crowned king of Greater Romania, which included Transylvania, awarded to Romania by the Treaty of Trianon in 1920. A progressive monarch, Ferdinand was disappointed in his playboy son, Prince Carol, who would later, during his own reckless reign, lead Romania into World War II. Ferdinand died in 1927.

A SILENT DICTATORSHIP
GERMANY'S WAR MACHINE (1916)

Erich von Falkenhayn had been chief of the German Supreme Army Command since September 1914. However, by 1916, his leadership was being questioned. In August, Chancellor Theobald von Bethmann Hollweg persuaded Kaiser Wilhelm II to replace Falkenhayn with the commander of the Eastern Front, Paul von Hindenburg. The latter was joined by his chief of staff, Erich Ludendorff. The two men had overseen not just military strategy in Eastern Europe but also the occupation of Lithuania, Latvia, Poland, and other territories, exploiting their economic resources and imposing strict limitations on the population. The ultimate plan was to transform the area into a colonial region populated by ethnic Germans. This extension of military rule would become typical of the new leadership.

Hindenburg's policies

The assessment of the situation on the Western Front made by Ludendorff and Hindenburg was uncompromising. They believed the Allies were too strong to be defeated in an offensive war. However, Germany could grind them down in a war of attrition, achieved by retreating to a secure defensive position, the so-called Hindenburg Line, construction of which began in October 1916.

The two men then set about implementing the Hindenburg Programme, a policy that would transform both the German government and economy, making them completely focused on the war. In December, the Reichstag passed the Auxiliary Services Act, obliging men aged 17 to 60 who were not already in the military to undertake national service.

Every man must be put into service according to his skills, be it at the lathe, in the office, or in any other occupation where he best serves the state.
Hindenburg Programme
Extract from the original proposal

See also: The rise of Germany 20–23 ▪ The Battle of Tannenberg 78–81 ▪ Ramping up production 104–05 ▪ The Brusilov Offensive 166–69 ▪ Mutiny and revolution in Germany 288–89 ▪ The rise of fascism 322–23

Paul von Hindenburg and Erich Ludendorff discuss tactics over the German army's situation map at general headquarters in 1917. Kaiser Wilhelm II is pictured between the two men.

German industrial output – of machine guns and artillery in particular – increased, but it was falling behind that of the Allies. Thousands of skilled workers were reallocated from the front line to the factory floor, weakening the army. Moreover, a poor harvest and the British naval blockade led to the Turnip Winter of 1916–17, when millions of Germans relied on this root vegetable, traditionally used to feed livestock, as their staple food.

The German government had no choice but to introduce rationing and set price controls.

To starve the Allies of resources, Hindenburg and Ludendorff also resumed unrestricted U-boat warfare in February 1917, overruling Bethmann Hollweg's objections. That month, Operation Alberich – the withdrawal to the Hindenburg Line – began. It was completed on 20 March, with the German troops following a scorched-earth policy in the areas they abandoned. The new defences were formidable, with vast belts of barbed wire, reinforced concrete fortifications, and anti-tank obstacles.

Bethmann Hollweg resigns

There was some opposition to the new policies. To stifle dissent, the government increased its censorship and control of the press that had begun with the start of the war. Bethmann Hollweg found himself ever more marginalized as the Supreme Army Command grew in power. Lacking the support of the Reichstag, he resigned on 13 July, and was replaced the next day by Georg Michaelis. For the rest of the war, the Supreme Army Command would dominate the government, with Hindenburg and Ludendorff enjoying virtually dictatorial powers. ■

Erich Ludendorff

Born into a semi-noble Prussian family in 1865, Erich Ludendorff began his military service in 1885 and was appointed to the German general staff at just 29 years of age. When war broke out, he accompanied the German army to Belgium, where he led the capture of Liège in August 1914. He was then sent to the Eastern Front as Hindenburg's chief of staff. In August 1916, Ludendorff was named first quartermaster-general; in addition to extensive responsibilities in overseeing military operations, he had sweeping powers on the home front, especially over workers.

As Germany slipped towards defeat, Ludendorff lost public support. He resigned in October 1918 and fled to Sweden, where he wrote extensively, propagating the stabbed-in-the-back myth – which said Germany had lost the war due to a lack of patriotism at home. In 1923, he was a leading figure in Hitler's Munich Putsch; after its failure, Ludendorff became a marginal figure in German politics and died in 1937.

THE CITIES ARE HUNGRY

SOCIETY UNDER STRAIN (1916)

IN CONTEXT

FOCUS
The home front

BEFORE
1913 The Ottoman Empire suffers food crises, which are exacerbated by poor transportation infrastructure.

1913 The Allied nations aim to starve the Central Powers into submission in the event of war.

AFTER
1917 In Russia, hunger is a major cause of revolution, which leads to the founding of the USSR in 1922.

1918 Malnutrition caused by war weakens populations in many nations, making them more susceptible to diseases such as the Great Influenza.

1939 Nazi Germany ensures there are adequate home front supplies before embarking on World War II.

L ife for civilians on the home front was a combination of shortages, hard work, and boredom by 1916. When they were not working, people stood in queues and waited for news – of loved ones, the war, and supplies. Whole days might be taken up assembling a meagre basket of essentials, many of which would be poor quality.

Governments sought to keep up morale at home and on the fighting front by encouraging letter-writing between soldiers and their families. The British Army Postal Service alone delivered around 2 billion letters over the course of the war. The French government arranged for *marraines de guerre* ("war

See also: The home front in 1918 250–53 ▪ The end of the war in Italy 284–85
▪ Mutiny and revolution in Germany 288–89 ▪ Shattered by war 310–11

> Shortly after the war begins, **food inequalities** become apparent between the **Allies and the Central Powers**.

⬇

> The **Central Powers** lack food stocks or the **infrastructure** for equitable food distribution, risking **food security**.

⬇

> The **Allied naval blockade prevents imports** reaching the Central Powers' **military and home fronts**.

⬇

> The **inability to supply adequate food** causes **unrest** among the **civilian populations**.

⬇

> **Food shortages, failing crops, and increasing protests risk bringing defeat to the Central Powers.**

godmothers") to write letters to soldiers who had no family or whose family lived in occupied zones. The link with everyday life at home provided a glimpse of the world beyond the conflict and, it was hoped, reminded soldiers of what they were fighting for – home and country.

Growing shortages

The British naval blockade and the German submarine U-boat attacks limited imports to all warring nations. The value of US exports to the Central Powers fell from about $370 million in 1913 to virtually zero in 1916, for example. Shortages of food and other essentials became normal, and society had to adapt to what it could get. Lack of food came to symbolize a conflict many were unhappy to endure – and a conflict, too, between town and country, rich and poor.

"It is incredible to see how thin so many people are getting", wrote British governess Mary Thorp in her diary chronicling life in German-occupied Brussels through the summer of 1916. All occupied zones suffered shortages, and with large numbers of troops billeted in their towns and villages, life in these zones was completely upended. Some help came from humanitarian aid organizations. The International Committee of the Red Cross and »

War widows

Of all the military personnel killed in the war, one-third are estimated to have left a widow and children. Voluntary organizations such as the Soldiers' and Sailors' Families Association in Britain provided support for these dependants. In most belligerent nations, widows' practical needs were met with government pensions; however, these were often inadequate, and poorer women had to rely on charity to get by. Widows were also subject to government scrutiny: early 20th-century attitudes expected high moral standards from women if they were to be deemed deserving of state support. Society, too, believed women should live up to their husbands' sacrifice.

Beyond the protocol were human stories of intense loss. For example, Helen Thomas, the wife of British poet Edward Thomas, who was killed at Arras, France, in 1917, wrote about their relationship in *As It Was* (1926) and *World Without End* (1931), in a bid to cure her depression.

A war widow (right) wearing the distinctive uniform of the Woman's Mutual Aid Society advises a young mother.

the Commission for Relief in Belgium sent food and clothing parcels to prisoners of war and civilians.

Before the outbreak of war, one-third of all Germany's food, animal feed, and fertilizer was imported. When the British naval blockade started to take hold in 1915, the German government published posters calling on the country's farmers to produce more food and ease hunger across the land.

Prisoners of war were set to work on farms, but crop yields fell. In 1915, bread was rationed and inferior K-Brot (a bread made with potatoes and rye) was introduced, with pulverized straw sometimes added to make the dough go further. Food for the military was a priority, and price caps were imposed on all necessities.

Growing discontent

Anticipating a swift victory, Germany had made no plans for a long conflict. By 1916, food prices had doubled since the start of the war. And by June of that year, potatoes, butter, sugar, and meat were rationed. In towns and cities, women had to queue for hours for food that often did not materialize.

City parks were turned into fruit and vegetable gardens, and even balconies were given over to the rearing of rabbits and hens.

Urban citizens in Germany – mostly working-class women – began to lose faith in the state. In the summer of 1916, food protests were commonplace, with women marching on town halls to demand more and better food rations. Some city women made trips to the countryside to trade, purchase, or even steal from better-provided rural compatriots.

Hungry soldiers form part of a large crowd of German men, women, and children jostling for soup ladled out of vats in Berlin in 1916.

Bad weather in autumn 1916 led to the failure of Germany's potato harvest. As a result, turnips, which had traditionally been used to feed livestock, became rationed substitutes. While they provided vitamins, they had few calories, the daily per capita intake of which fell to below 1,000 on the home front. British intelligence revealed that, by April 1917, rations for German soldiers and horses had been reduced by 25 per cent.

The Turnip Winter of 1916–17 highlighted the inadequacies of the German authorities' economic decisions. Across the Central Powers, the military established postal censorship boards to study correspondence and gauge the public mood, for fear of growing unrest. Civilian morale fell as people grew weak from poor nutrition, and their susceptibility to disease increased. For many people, victory became a secondary concern; their main worry now was where to find food.

Illegal trade

Supply shortages and high food and fuel prices resulted in hoarding in most combatant nations, despite the practice being both illegal and socially unacceptable. In Britain, food control officers had the power to prosecute hoarders and confiscate their excess goods. If they deemed that a person already had enough food, these officers also had the authority to name and shame the culprits in the local press. Similar laws applied across Europe.

While sacrifice came to be seen as a moral obligation, illegal trade was rife. In rural areas, wheat and other cereals were sold to profiteers who would sell them on in the towns for higher prices. Profiteers also doctored food – something that could be difficult to detect. Butter was mixed with margarine, milk watered down, and cheese mixed with starch. For hungry people on the home front, this spoilage of staples made a bad situation worse. Much food was also "lost" in transit, even on its way to the front.

> All we had was a ration of … bread. I remember it was something very dark … It didn't taste like bread at all.
> **Helena Reid**
> Resident of the German-occupied city of Lille, France

In the Austro-Hungarian Empire, several factors led to a decline in agricultural production, including occupation of farmland by Russian troops, labour shortages, and the scarcity of imported fertilizers. Previously efficient distribution networks were disrupted, leading to food shortages, especially in the capital, Vienna, where there were long queues for staples from 1915. Similar problems developed in the Ottoman Empire, particularly in eastern Anatolia, northern Syria, and Lebanon.

Russia seethes

Shortages affected civilian life dramatically in Russia. In the countryside, people wanted land reform so that they could grow their own food. In 1916, just 20 per cent of households held a land title. In towns and cities, factory workers suffering low pay went on strike. The tsarist government attempted to introduce a form of rationing, but despite the issuing of bread cards, there was often no bread to be had, since it was difficult for the state to enforce the supply of low-priced grain for its production. Tensions between urban and rural areas increased, because manufactured goods – made in industrial centres – were purchased by urban citizens first. With no access to these goods, rural producers lost the incentive to provide raw materials for industry and sell food to industrial workers in towns and cities.

Anger towards incompetent governance increased among the Russian elite, too. The growing influence of a self-proclaimed holy man and mystic healer, Grigori Rasputin, on Tsarina Alexandra Feodorovna and the wider royal court was seen as symptomatic of this and a threat to the empire. Acting on their frustrations, a group of Russian nobles murdered Rasputin in December 1916.

Conscription and control

In Britain, conscription was introduced in January 1916. By that point, public opinion had begun to turn against the war, as it had in the rest of Europe. Poor weather led to a reduced wheat harvest, and the potato crop failed in England and parts of Scotland; staples became unaffordable for the less well off. In response, in December 1916, the government established a Ministry of Food to oversee the country's supply.

As 1916 drew to a close, the conflict appeared to be deepening. Germany had declared war on Romania, Italy had declared war on Germany, and two terrible battles had taken place – at Verdun and the Somme. On 12 December 1916, Germany called for peace negotiations. This proposal seemed to be based on confidence in its own strength, but it was partly motivated by fears that the effects of privation on its own population were becoming unsustainable. The German high command was also worried that the US would soon enter the war.

On 18 December, US president Woodrow Wilson sent letters to the foreign embassies of the belligerent nations on both sides requesting their terms for peace. He believed that a "peace without victory" was essential to end the conflict, and he highlighted the "uselessness of the utter sacrifices made". Wilson's idealistic appeal failed. So, despite the suffering and privations on both the front line and the home front, the war dragged on. ∎

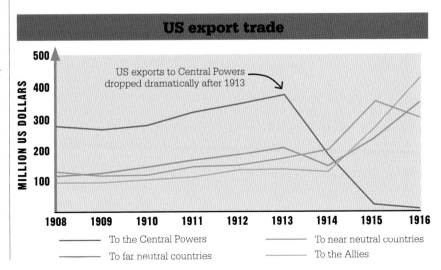

US export trade

US exports to Central Powers dropped dramatically after 1913

MILLION US DOLLARS

——— To the Central Powers
——— To far neutral countries
——— To near neutral countries
——— To the Allies

REVOLUTION AND EXHAUS

1917

TION

Germany adopts a programme of **unrestricted submarine warfare**. U-boats now attack with **no prior warning**.

11 MAR 1917

The **US Congress agrees** to President Wilson's request **to declare war on Germany**.

6 APRIL 1917

French forces assault the Chemin des Dames position overlooking the River Aisne, the **first part of the Nivelle offensive**.

16 APR 1917

The first contingent of troops from the **US Army begins training in France**.

27 JUN 1917

---

14 MAR 1917

The British-led Egyptian Expeditionary Force **suffers a defeat** to Ottoman forces at the **First Battle of Gaza** in Palestine.

9 APR 1917

The **Battle of Arras** begins. **Canadian troops** distinguish themselves during the hard-fought **struggle for Vimy Ridge**.

26 JUN 1917

Germany sends **21 Gotha aircraft** to attack the Channel port of Folkestone in broad daylight. Their bombs **kill 95 people and injure 260** more.

22 JUL 1917

With Greek king Constantine forced into exile, the **Greek government declares its support for the Allies**.

The cost of the great battles of Verdun and the Somme in 1916 profoundly shocked the governments of France and Britain. As the new year dawned, demands for change were in the air.

General Joseph Joffre was replaced as French commander in chief by General Robert Nivelle, an artillery specialist who had made his reputation during the Verdun counterattacks. In Britain, new prime minister David Lloyd George mistrusted his own commanders' focus on the Western Front, but Nivelle persuaded him that the trench deadlock could be broken.

Nivelle's offensive in April 1917 was a modest success but failed to produce an outright victory. Its heavy toll of casualties lowered morale across the French ranks. In May, some divisions refused to return to the trenches; others rejected orders to attack. Thanks largely to the careful handling of the situation by General Philip Pétain, who replaced Nivelle, the mutinies were shortlived.

Failure in Flanders

After the Nivelle offensive, the British Army concentrated its plans on Flanders. However, the Third Battle of Ypres (better known as Passchendaele), beginning at the end of July, achieved little, except heavy casualties on both sides. The innovative British tank attack at Cambrai in November lost momentum when tanks broke down, and the Germans countered with effective artillery and trench mortars.

The dull stalemate persisted elsewhere, too, including on the Italian front. There, costly battles around the Isonzo river culminated in an Italian retreat in November, but the Italians would regroup and fight on against the Central Powers.

War at sea and in the air

In early 1917, Germany's newly expanded fleet of 148 U-boats began to attack shipping without prior warning. Between February and April 1917, at a cost of nine U-boats, the Germans sank more than 500 merchant ships. The Allies started to send merchant ships in armed convoys, which afforded them some protection but never wholly eliminated the U-boat threat.

In the air, the race was on to perfect ever more advanced planes and weapon systems. Germany's control of the western skies ended when the Allies introduced superior aircraft in 1917, such as the French

The British **Women's Army Auxiliary Corps (WAAC)** is officially established to **take on non-combatant tasks** behind the front line in France.

Bolshevik forces storm the Winter Palace in Petrograd and **arrest members of the Provisional Government** taking refuge there.

In the final stage of the **Third Battle of Ypres**, **British and Canadian troops capture** the ruined village of **Passchendaele**.

A mass **British tank attack** opens the Battle of Cambrai. A **German counterattack** makes good use of **infiltration tactics**.

 15 OCT 1917

 2 NOV 1917

 7 NOV 1917

 20 NOV 1917

24 OCT 1917

Austro-German troops launch a surprise offensive against Italian forces on the **Isonzo** river close to the town of Caporetto, **forcing them to retreat**.

6 NOV 1917

The **Balfour Declaration** is issued, promising **a Jewish homeland in Palestine** without affecting indigenous Palestinian rights.

20 NOV 1917

Forced out of German East Africa by Allied troops, German commander **Paul von Lettow-Vorbeck and his Schutztruppe** enter Portuguese East Africa (Mozambique).

9 DEC 1917

British forces under General Allenby **expel Turkish troops from Jerusalem** – a **symbolic victory** for the Allies.

SPAD S.XIII and British Sopwith Camel. The US Army Air Corps added its strength and expertise at the end of the year.

Despite the lack of headway in Western Europe, the Allies could now be confident of sustaining their military effort, with the full support of the US government. Germany's ruthless U-boat strategy – and the subsequent loss of American lives at sea – pushed the US government to enter the war on 6 April. It was perhaps the best news for the Western Allies in an otherwise frustrating year, relieved only by the capture of Jerusalem in December.

Tending the wounded
The torrent of casualties after each battle had initially overwhelmed each army medical corps. Aided by teams of volunteers from the International Red Cross, however, effective triage systems evolved to treat those who could be rescued. Advances in areas such as plastic surgery and prosthetics also improved medical care, and shell shock became a recognized condition that could be treated.

Transformation in the East
While little changed on the Western Front, an era of change had begun in Russia. In spring 1917, mass protests and strikes in many Russian cities had prompted the abdication of Tsar Nicholas II and the end of the ruling Romanov dynasty which was blamed for food shortages and the continuing war.

On 14 March, a collection of opposition leaders set themselves up as the Provisional Government. It was still committed to the war and expected to strengthen Russia's efforts. Ground gained in July in the Kerensky Offensive – Russia's final stand – was soon lost, however, as the authority of the Provisional Government was undermined by radical Bolsheviks, with the support of peasants and soldiers exhausted by the conflict.

In November, the Bolsheviks seized power. Under the leadership of Vladimir Lenin and Leon Trotsky, they formed their own government and quickly sought peace negotiations with the Central Powers. The German High Command saw an opportunity to seize large areas of Russia, then to transfer the bulk of their army to the Western Front. On 15 December 1917, Russia and Germany signed an armistice, and peace talks followed in the new year. ∎

THE EMPEROR IS BLIND
THE FEBRUARY REVOLUTION (MARCH 1917)

IN CONTEXT

FOCUS
Russian Revolution

BEFORE
1867 Karl Marx publishes the first volume of *Das Kapital*, which argues that wage labour exploits the working class.

1905 A revolution in Russia is put down by the authorities, but Tsar Nicholas II enacts limited constitutional reforms, including granting his people freedom of speech.

1914 Partly as a result of anti-German feeling at the start of the war, St Petersburg is renamed Petrograd.

AFTER
November 1917 Bolshevik revolutionaries overthrow Russia's provisional government and take power.

1918 Russia signs the Treaty of Brest-Litovsk with the Central Powers, ending its involvement in World War I.

By January 1917, more than 700,000 Russian soldiers had died on the Eastern Front, and many more had been wounded. Discouraging reports of hardship at home had filtered through to troops on the front line, and news of the war's carnage, defeats, and chaos reached families back home.

Food shortages hit the working class hard, and angry workers went on strike in protest. Towards the end of February (early March in the Gregorian calendar, which was not adopted in Russia until 1918), mass protests began against the government of Tsar Nicholas II.

Initially, the tsar remained defiant, having already withstood an uprising in 1905. This time, however, he faced a mutiny by the Petrograd (St Petersburg) garrison, and most of his generals advised him to step down.

Worsening conditions
Authority was handed over to a provisional government led by Prince Georgy Lvov. His administration held dual power with the Petrograd Soviet, or workers' council. The working

Petrograd residents riot in the streets in 1917, protesting a scarcity of food. The city's army garrison initially attempted to suppress the uprising, but the soldiers later switched sides.

See also: Crisis in Russia 24 ▪ The Kerensky Offensive 224–25 ▪ The October Revolution 240–41 ▪ Post-war conflicts 320–21

A Soviet propaganda painting of 1935 shows a crowd greeting Lenin on arrival at Petrograd's Finland Station in 1917, after years of self-imposed exile.

class was represented to some degree – if only indirectly – by those educated radicals who claimed to speak for it. Even so, real power resided with the wealthy and educated men around the prince.

Crucially, conditions for most people continued to worsen. Many responded enthusiastically to the rhetoric of revolutionaries such as Vladimir Lenin, the leader of the far-left Bolshevik wing of Russia's Social Democratic Labour Party. Lenin, who had fled to Switzerland when the trouble started, was eager to get home and play his part. The German authorities were happy to help him, given the disruption they believed he could cause in Russia. The train on which he journeyed across Germany to the Baltic coast was supposedly sealed to prevent the country's "contamination" with his dangerous ideas.

A change of leadership
Lenin travelled with his wife and a few staff, arriving at Petrograd's Finland Station on 16 April 1917. Once there, he delivered an impassioned speech, denouncing Lvov's "bourgeois revolution".

In a country facing such desperate problems, Lenin's views seemed less extreme to many workers and peasants than they otherwise might have. A long, hot summer flared into open conflict when protests against food rationing were forcibly suppressed. Armed soldiers, sailors, and workers took to the streets of Petrograd in the "July Days" unrest. The provisional government's response was an attempt to quell the protests by force, and Lenin fled to Finland.

These tough measures failed to calm the mood. Its credibility lost, Lvov's government fell, to be replaced by a new provisional government led by Alexander Kerensky. A reformer who supported workers' rights and spoke against inequality, Kerensky also broadly accepted the capitalist model – something the revolutionaries saw as a feeble compromise. Neither the workers nor the peasants were satisfied when Kerensky refused to remove what they saw as the greatest obstacle to improving their lives: Russia's ongoing engagement in a tragic and costly war. ▪

The world thinks that the Russian Revolution is at an end. ... The Russian Revolution is just beginning.
Alexander Kerensky
Interview with John Reed, July 1917

Vladimir Lenin

Born in Simbirsk (later named Ulyanovsk) in 1870, Vladimir Ilyich Ulyanov adopted the famous codename Lenin – the meaning of which is unclear – as a young revolutionary. As a Marxist, Lenin believed capitalism was exploitative by its nature, and he wanted the whole system overthrown. He also believed that private property should be confiscated and redistributed, and that workers' representatives should direct the economy in a communist state.

His principles meant that Lenin lived his life on the wrong side of the law, leading to imprisonment and exile to Siberia in the 1890s. He then spent the years 1900–17 abroad, finally settling in Switzerland. The authorities there tolerated his presence, but he still had to live a semi-clandestine existence.

Lenin's uncompromising leadership ensured that Soviet communism prevailed, but it also led to bloody despotism. After being shot in Moscow in 1918 by Fanny Kaplan, a Jewish Russian woman who saw him as a "traitor to the revolution", Lenin had a series of strokes and died in 1924.

THE WORLD MUST BE MADE SAFE FOR DEMOCRACY
THE US ENTERS THE WAR (APRIL 1917)

IN CONTEXT

FOCUS
Declaration of war

BEFORE
1915 US Secretary of State William J. Bryan resigns when President Woodrow Wilson fails to condemn the British blockade as strongly as German U-boat warfare.

1915 *The Battle Cry of Peace*, a silent film, promotes the entry of the US into World War I.

1916 Wilson confidante Edward M. House makes a fruitless effort to mediate talks between Britain and Germany.

AFTER
May 1918 The first American soldiers enter combat under the US flag.

1921 The Veterans Bureau is created to coordinate benefits for American war veterans.

1948 President Harry S. Truman orders the racial integration of the US military.

Although US president Woodrow Wilson believed that a neutral United States could help steer the world away from balance-of-power rivalries to "an organized common peace", events steadily pushed his thinking towards active belligerence. The European war moved into the Atlantic in 1915, with the British blockade of the Continent and Germany's submarine warfare.

If truly neutral, the US could have condemned both sides equally; however, it really did matter to American interests who won.

The submarine challenge
Wilson condemned the new submarine technology as immoral and illegal, not acknowledging that the real danger was its threat to British sea power, which had protected US commerce for a

---

The United States **attempts neutrality** despite **threats to its commercial interests**.

The **British blockade** of European ports and German **submarine warfare** threaten US commerce.

Germany's **unrestricted submarine warfare** pushes the US Congress to a **decision**.

Wilson condemns **German submarines** as "immoral" but **mutes complaints** to Britain about the blockade.

Wilson declares war on Germany to make the world "safe for democracy".

See also: The war at sea begins 88–93 ▪ The sinking of the *Lusitania* 106–07 ▪ The US and World War I 134–35
▪ Putting the US on a war footing 196–97 ▪ The U-boats on the attack 200–05 ▪ The Meuse–Argonne Offensive 280–83

century. The considerable economic interests the US had in Britain, and British control of the war news crossing the Atlantic – often akin to propaganda – further pushed American sympathies towards the Allies.

On 7 May 1915, a U-boat (German submarine) sank the British passenger liner RMS *Lusitania* with the loss of 1,198 lives, including 128 Americans. In this case, and after the sinkings of SS *Arabic* in August 1915 and SS *Sussex* in March 1916, Wilson took a tough line with the German government. As he campaigned successfully for re-election in 1916, his supporters proclaimed "he kept us out of war"; the president knew, however, that American involvement in the fighting was increasingly likely.

Still hoping to end the war without US entry, Wilson outlined a plan for "peace without victory" on 22 January 1917. He sought to mediate negotiations and resolve any future conflicts through an international organization. His vision was bold and almost completely detached from the rage engulfing Europe. Then, on 31 January, Germany announced its intention to resume unrestricted submarine warfare – to win the war before the US sent troops.

The US declares war
In March 1917, British intelligence leaked details to the press about German foreign minister Arthur Zimmerman offering to help Mexico reconquer Texas and other territories lost to the US in the 1840s – in return for a wartime alliance. The Zimmerman Telegram inflamed anti-German sentiment in the US and increased Wilson's distrust of Kaiser Wilhelm II.

The sinking of four American merchant ships by U-boats the week of 12 March confirmed the impossibility of a policy of armed neutrality. Concurrently, the abdication of the Russian tsar made the British, French, and Russian alliance appear more democratic. Most important, however, was Wilson's conviction

A British cartoon from 1917 depicts a hand in a German gauntlet carving up the southwestern US – a reference to the Zimmerman Telegram, a factor in America's entry into the war.

that Europe could not endure its agony much longer. US entry into World War I could hasten an end to the fighting and strengthen US influence on a peace treaty.

On 2 April 1917, Wilson asked Congress to declare war on Germany, which he accused of "warfare against mankind". He called upon Americans to fight "to make the world safe for democracy" and freedom. ▪

The Harlem Hellfighters (369th Infantry)

In 1916, in preparation for war, civic leaders in Harlem secured the creation of the 15th New York National Guard Regiment. With a white commander and a mixture of Black and white officers, this otherwise entirely Black American unit trained in South Carolina, where the locals subjected them to racial abuse and harassment.

To ease tensions, the renamed 369th Infantry Regiment deployed to France in 1918, ahead of the American Expeditionary Forces. General John Pershing transferred the 369th to French command, and its members went on to perform heroically in the heaviest fighting. The Germans called them the "Hellfighters". France awarded the unit the Croix de Guerre, and 171 officers and men individually received the Croix de Guerre and Legion of Honour for gallantry in action. Official US recognition came in 2015, when President Barack Obama awarded a posthumous Congressional Medal of Honor to Private Henry Johnson, whose singular performance exemplified the spirit of all the Harlem Hellfighters.

I WANT YOU FOR THE US ARMY

PUTTING THE US ON A WAR FOOTING (1917)

IN CONTEXT

FOCUS
American home front

BEFORE
1892 The US opens Ellis Island, an inspection station that processes 12 million immigrants up to 1954.

1898 The US fields an army of 275,000 in the Spanish-American War; almost 80 per cent are volunteers.

AFTER
1929 Share prices crash on the New York Stock Exchange, signalling the start of the Great Depression.

1933 US President Franklin D. Roosevelt models the National Recovery Administration on President Woodrow Wilson's War Industries Board.

1941 In World War II, Roosevelt and British prime minister Winston Churchill draft the Atlantic Charter, a vision for a post-war world inspired by Wilson's Fourteen Points.

The US **enters the war in 1917** after more than two years of **neutrality**.

The **Allies are desperate** for **reinforcements**, but the US is **unprepared** for immediate deployment.

Thanks largely to conscription, the **US deploys more than 2 million soldiers** to France by autumn 1918.

Wilson proposes a **14-point peace plan** for a diplomatic **resolution to the war**.

US forces and peace proposals help to end the military stalemate.

Delaying entry into the war for more than two and a half years presented President Wilson's administration with several challenges: opinion in the US remained divided about the war (the economy had struggled but had also benefited in some ways), and the Allied armies desperately demanded more troops than the US had available. Moreover, Wilson insisted he could mediate a peace – even with the US as a belligerent.

Wilson's rhetoric had increased traditional mistrust of European politics among Americans. Many of them continued to believe that remaining neutral was the best course of action. Also, one-third of Americans were first- or second-generation immigrants, with direct connections to one or even both sides of the conflict.

To prepare the public for any potential participation by the US, the administration created the Committee on Public Information, headed by progressive journalist George Creel. It employed 75,000 speakers to promote patriotism in schools, churches, and other public places. Similarly, Congress established the War Industries Board to focus industrial production on the

See also: The US and World War I 134–35 ▪ The US enters the war 194–95 ▪ The Battle of Belleau Wood 268–69 ▪ The Battle of Saint-Mihiel 278–79 ▪ The Meuse–Argonne Offensive 280–83 ▪ A lasting peace? 312–17

Eugene V. Debs

One of the most influential and vocal opponents of American involvement in World War I, Eugene Victor Debs was born in Indiana in 1855, the son of French immigrants. He became a labour organizer – founding the American Railway Union in 1893 – and head of the Socialist Party of America. He was his party's candidate for US president five times between 1900 and 1920. In the 1912 election, won by Woodrow Wilson, Debs received more than 900,000 votes (6 per cent of the total).

Debs railed against the entry of the US into the war in 1917 and condemned conscription, saying that "the master class has always declared the wars; the subject class has always fought the battles". His views landed him in prison, stripped of his US citizenship, and Wilson refused his release after the war. Debs fought his final presidential campaign in 1920 while still incarcerated – convicted for violating the Sedition Act of 1918 – and died in prison in 1926. His US citizenship was restored posthumously in 1976.

war, using persuasion, incentives, and implied threats rather than centralized economic controls.

Conscription begins

In the American Civil War (1861–65), both sides had imposed a limited military draft. World War I was the first time the US relied primarily on conscription. The Selective Service Act – enacted by Congress on 18 May 1917 – authorized the government to raise a conscript army, the American Expeditionary Forces (AEF). The Selective Service System established by the Act operated on a huge scale, with a national headquarters and 4,000 local draft boards. Within a year, it had registered 23.9 million men and drafted 2.8 million. More than 70 per cent of the 3.5 million in the wartime army were draftees. About 350,000 Black Americans served in

segregated units. Some Americans evaded the draft, and more than 60,000 registered as conscientious objectors, but the system met the personnel needs.

The departure of men for war opened employment opportunities for female workers. About 1 million women entered the labour force, but most of them were forced out after the war. Some, such as

activist and social reformer Jane Addams, became outspoken pacifist opponents of the war.

The Fourteen Points

On 8 January 1918, President Wilson delivered his Fourteen Points address – a bold outline for peace. It was a response to the huge scale of casualties in the summer of 1917 – and a counter to the Russian Bolshevik vision of ending all war through a global revolution against capitalism. Point number one called for "open covenants of peace, openly arrived at", without secret treaties. Four general principles then followed: free navigation of the seas, removal of all trade barriers, arms reduction, and balancing colonial claims with the sovereignty of the populations concerned. Wilson's keystone, though, was "a general association of nations" to guarantee political independence and territorial integrity for all nations. At the post-war Paris Peace Conference, this concept was enshrined as the League of Nations. ▪

In this US Army poster, "Uncle Sam" urges young men to enlist. Created by James Flagg, it was based on a British poster of 1914, in which Lord Kitchener made a similar appeal.

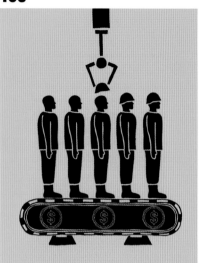

EVERY MAN AND EVERY DOLLAR
REPLACING THE FALLEN

B y 1917, front-line fighting had resulted in huge losses on all sides. While offensives began to use more tanks and aircraft and fewer personnel, all armies' strategies depended on replacing the fallen.

Before World War I, Germany, Austria-Hungary, Russia, and France already had in place systems of conscription, or compulsory

An army sergeant walks past a row of new British recruits still wearing civilian clothes but carrying their newly issued military uniforms.

enrolment, into the armed forces, which ensured a steady supply of trained combatants. Even then, however, French and German armies were suffering shortages, since agriculture and industry on their home fronts also required workers to provide critical supplies.

More men for the front
Britain had previously depended on volunteers, and at the start of the war it had an army of 733,500 – the smallest of the major powers. In 1915, 1 million men had enlisted on the strength of the "Lord Kitchener

See also: Public opinion 44–45 ▪ Putting the US on a war footing 196–97 ▪ The Battle of Passchendaele 230–35 ▪ The Battle of Cambrai 237 ▪ The home front in 1918 250–53

Wants You" propaganda poster, but as losses grew, volunteer numbers dwindled.

In January 1916, the British government introduced the Military Service Act, decreeing that every unmarried British man aged 18 to 41 was liable to be enlisted for the duration of the war. It was an unpopular move, and in April 1916 more than 200,000 people gathered in central London to demonstrate. These protests had little effect, and conscription was extended to married men in May. Many thousands appealed on medical, family, and economic grounds.

Canada's divisive law

With a promise of supplying more men to the Allies, but no volunteers in sight, Canada's government, led by Prime Minister Robert Borden, also decided to impose conscription. In August 1917, the Military Service Act was introduced, ruling that the government could call upon men aged 20–45, if necessary, making more than 400,000 men liable for conscription until the war's end.

> We don't tell the public the truth, that we're losing more officers than the Germans and that it's impossible to get through on the Western Front.
> **Lord Rothermere**
> **Owner of Britain's *Daily Mirror*, 1917**

Borden felt that conscription would extend Canada's influence in British decision-making and strengthen the two countries' alliance, but the law was divisive. British Canadians were largely supportive, but most French Canadians were not. Farmers demanded exemptions, which were first agreed, then overturned. First Nations leaders challenged the conscription, arguing that it violated treaties between its

people and the Crown and that those without voting rights should not be called into combat. The fight to be exempted from the act was successful, although about 4,000 First Nations soldiers did volunteer to serve alongside the Allies.

Conscription in the US

When the US declared war on Germany in April 1917, its peacetime army totalled 135,000 men. In a wave of patriotism, volunteers across the country quickly swelled its ranks, but more soldiers were needed. On 18 May, Congress passed the Selective Service Act, which required men aged 21 to 30 (later 45) to register for military service. The draft resulted in the registration of approximately 24 million men. Nearly 4.8 million would go on to serve in the war; of those, 2.8 million were conscripts.

On 26 June 1917, the first US infantry troops began training in France. The addition of these well-equipped troops marked a turning point in the conflict, shifting the advantage to the Allies. ▪

Women in uniform

The British Women's Army Auxiliary Corps (WAAC) was formed in 1917 to take on non-combatant tasks in France and free more men for service on the front line. Recruiting began in March 1917, and a total of 50,000 women volunteered.

At the time, women were prohibited from joining the army and other services, so they were enrolled rather than enlisted, and restricted to administrative, catering, and store work. By the end of 1917, more than

6,000 WAACs were serving in France. When the US entered the war, many were assigned to the American Expeditionary Forces (AEF).

By the war's end, 81 women had been killed in the fighting. In 1918, the WAAC was renamed Queen Mary's Army Auxiliary Corps, and many members remained in France to assist with the clean-up in the war's aftermath, until the unit was disbanded in September 1921. It was the first example of a western nation employing women in the armed services.

WAAC members march through London on a recruitment drive in 1915. The women wore uniforms but were not permitted military ranks; nor were they issued with weapons.

THE BEST AND SHARPEST WEAPON

THE U-BOATS ON THE ATTACK (1916)

IN CONTEXT

FOCUS
Submarine warfare

BEFORE
1776 In the first recorded use of a submersible craft in combat, a one-man vessel named *Turtle* attacks British warship HMS *Eagle* in the American Revolutionary War.

1864 The Confederate vessel *H.L. Hunley* becomes the first submarine to sink an enemy craft – the USS *Housatonic* in the American Civil War.

1868 British engineer Robert Whitehead manufactures a torpedo for the Austrian navy.

AFTER
1918 Britain introduces food rationing after the U-boat campaign leads to shortages and rising inflation.

1919 The Treaty of Versailles decrees that Germany should not be permitted to build or acquire submarines.

Submarines became a potentially useful weapon after the introduction of the self-propelled torpedo in 1868. During the decades that followed, improvements to the batteries that powered the vessels also enhanced their effectiveness. Several navies soon began to develop their own submarine fleets, but Germany was one of the last. At the start of the war in 1914, it possessed just 36 submarines (*Unterseeboote*, or U-boats), compared with 89 in the Royal Navy and 77 in the French navy. However, early successes against Allied merchant ships encouraged the German high command to expand its fleet.

Maritime law

According to the "prize rules" – the internationally accepted laws of war at sea – submarines had to follow the same guidelines as conventional warships, which prevented a surprise underwater attack. However, after Britain declared the North Sea a military zone as part of its blockade of enemy ports in 1914, pressure grew from the German high command for U-boats to be used for attack.

Our crews are like the sword-wielding brotherhoods of the Viking age.
Harald Busch
U-boat commander

On 4 February 1915, Kaiser Wilhelm II announced that the North Sea was a war zone and that all ships, including vessels belonging to neutral countries, could be sunk without warning. This particularly angered the US, whose merchant fleets nonetheless continued to carry supplies across the Atlantic Ocean to Britain.

Also, as stated in the prize rules, a submarine had to surface before attacking a ship, so the crew and passengers had time to escape. This rule was exploited by the British in late 1914 with the

Reinhard Scheer

Born in Obernkirchen, Germany, in 1863, Reinhard Scheer is credited with recognizing the importance of submarines in warfare from an early stage. He joined the German navy in 1879, becoming chief of staff of the High Seas Fleet under Admiral Henning von Holtzendorff before being promoted to commander of the German High Seas Fleet in 1916.

Convinced that the war could be won at sea, Scheer planned a naval battle to defeat the British. His strategy of dividing the larger British fleet and destroying its battle-cruiser division was the thrust of the Battle of Jutland, when his fleet achieved a tactical victory but failed to break the blockade. After the battle, he wrote to the kaiser to advocate unrestricted submarine warfare as Germany's only hope for victory at sea. After defeat was certain, he ordered a final, suicidal sortie against Britain, but his fleet mutinied in October 1918, precipitating the German revolution of the following month. He died in Marktredwitz, Germany, in 1928.

See also: The naval arms race 32–33 ▪ The war at sea begins 88–93 ▪ The sinking of the *Lusitania* 106–07 ▪ The Battle of Jutland 162–65 ▪ Naval war in the Mediterranean 242–43 ▪ The home front in 1918 250–53

Although dimly lit, crowded, and cramped, U-boats were highly effective, sinking more than 5,000 Allied and neutral merchant vessels and warships in World War I.

introduction of Q-ships – heavily armed decoy merchant vessels that began to sink surfaced U-boats. On 22 September 1914, a U-boat sank three obsolete Royal Navy warships manned by reserve forces. This was followed by the controversial sinking of the passenger ship RMS *Lusitania* in May 1915 and the English Channel ferry SS *Sussex* in March 1916, both with high civilian losses. Despite worldwide outrage, Admiral Reinhard Scheer, who took command of the High Seas Fleet in February 1916, decided to boost the number of U-boats and use them more aggressively. By February 1917, Germany would have 148 U-boats at its disposal.

Dwindling food supplies
At the start of the war, Britain used its numerically powerful navy to blockade German ports. The Royal Navy intended to starve the Central Powers into submission by making it impossible for neutral countries such as the US to send supplies. By the winter of 1916, the strategy was clearly working: Germany was suffering from widespread hunger,

and hunger riots were breaking out. For its part, Britain relied on food imports brought by merchant ships from around the globe.

A new strategy
In an attempt to break the British blockade – and also spurred on by Germany's failure to take back control of the seas in the Battle of Jutland (May 1916) – the German high command sought permission

for unrestricted submarine warfare. On 22 December 1916, chief of the Admiralty staff Admiral Henning von Holtzendorff sent a message to the kaiser explaining the rationale behind the request.

Typically, British merchant ships travelled singly across the Atlantic Ocean or North Sea. Holtzendorff reasoned that attacking these easy targets would disrupt food imports to such an extent that Britain would be starved into submission and forced to surrender within six months. He argued that the prize rules should be ignored since the British had already undermined these principles by committing a "war crime" when on 19 August 1915 the Q-ship HMS *Baralong*, sailing under a false American flag, sank the submarine *U-27*. As German crew members drifted in »

Unrestricted submarine warfare	
Pros	**Cons**
Destroys enemy ships and disrupts food supplies	Blatantly disregards international maritime law
Creates food shortages, forcing Britain to surrender	Incurs the wrath of neutral countries, most significantly the US
Could shorten the war	Could draw the US into the war, bringing extra troops and military hardware
The Central Powers are victorious	Allies are victorious

the sea, they were shot dead by British sailors on the orders of the *Baralong*'s captain.

The kaiser immediately agreed to Holtzendorff's proposal, and on 8 January 1917 the German military leadership adopted a programme of unrestricted submarine warfare: U-boats could now attack targets without any prior warning. The new campaign was launched on 1 February 1917, with Germany's greatly expanded submarine fleet.

Success at a price

The German high command decided to allow U-boats to operate as lone hunters, picking off and sinking merchant ships as they came into view in the crowded shipping lanes. The tactic was highly successful. Holtzendorff had calculated that U-boats would sink about 590,000 tons of merchant shipping each month, but his number proved, if anything, to be an underestimate.

The British response under naval commander Admiral Sir John Jellicoe was to hunt and destroy the U-boats. The Royal Navy

developed underwater listening devices called hydrophones to locate submarines, and depth charges to destroy them once tracked. However, it proved much more difficult to find the U-boats than anticipated – between February and April 1917, the British destroyed only nine U-boats, while the Germans sank more than 500 merchant ships. It was clear that without a rapid solution, the German navy would achieve its aim of bringing Britain to the brink of starvation.

One suggestion to counter the new German strategy was for the unarmed Allied merchant ships to travel in convoys, escorted by armed Royal Navy warships that could deter U-boat attacks. Jellicoe and the Admiralty staff rejected this plan in March 1917, arguing that the navy could ill afford to spare warships for escort duty. One of the more bizarre options put forward was to train circus sea lions to detect U-boats.

The US finally entered the war on 2 April 1917. That month, Allied losses escalated as U-boats sank

Submarine menace is a truly terrible one for British commerce and Great Britain alike.
Sir John Fisher
Admiral of the Fleet,
May 1913

430 Allied and neutral ships, with more than 850,000 tons of shipping lost. In the second half of April, an average of 13 ships were sunk each day; the most successful U-boat commanders sank several enemy vessels daily.

A slow response

Britain faced disaster unless something changed quickly. Under pressure from the British government, Jellicoe approved a trial convoy on 27 April, and it proved to be a success. Sixteen merchant ships crossed the Atlantic without a single loss. The system was duly introduced, although its roll-out remained slow. By the end of 1917, around half of all Allied merchant ships were travelling in convoys. With the U-boats finding it much harder to target and destroy groups of ships with armed escorts, merchant shipping losses fell to an average of around 400,000 tons per month. Meanwhile, U-boat losses had increased to between five and 10 per month. The convoy system continued into 1918, with the number of escort ships augmented by the addition of US destroyers.

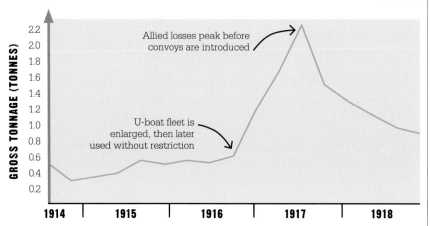

The tonnage of ships lost as a result of enemy action or marine risk during World War I rose sharply in the second quarter of 1917. This corresponds to the declaration of unrestricted submarine warfare by Germany on 1 February that year. The world's shipbuilding output increased steadily over the course of the war but could not compensate for the losses sustained.

The British troop ship RMS *Walmer Castle* was repainted in dramatic black-and-white "dazzle camouflage" in the Atlantic in 1917.

Dazzle camouflage

An artist and zebra stripes played a vital role in the Royal Navy's efforts to confuse U-boat crews and make it harder for them to target British vessels. Volunteer seaman Norman Wilkinson's civilian background as a graphic designer led him to a radical idea: if ships could not be hidden at sea, make them as conspicuous as possible.

Wilkinson suggested the painting of ships' hulls with black and white stripes, swirls, and abstract patterns more typically found in a gallery of Cubist art. He realized that when a U-boat's crew located a ship through its periscope, the complex patterns of intersecting shapes would distort its outline and make it difficult to determine the ship's size, distance, speed, and direction of movement. This made calculations for launching torpedoes much harder. The dazzle camouflage was used extensively, with great success, from August 1917.

The Allies were never able to completely eradicate the U-boat threat, despite dedicating huge resources to the task. Anti-submarine barriers of underwater nets and mines were created in the Dover Straits and in the North Sea between Scotland and Norway, and both stretches of water were patrolled by warships. U-boat commanders found ways to circumvent the defences, however. The British increased their use of air patrols, using blimps (non-rigid airships), which forced the U-boats to stay submerged until they had no choice but to surface, where they could be spotted and destroyed. The air patrols, too, ultimately failed to stop the German submarines.

German resistance

Despite all of the various Allied efforts – which included raiding U-boat bases in the German-occupied Belgian ports of Ostend and Zeebrugge on 23 April 1918 – the German submarine campaign continued until the Armistice in November of that year. Long-range U-boats were deployed in the Atlantic Ocean and even managed to sink ships in US coastal waters. In one notorious incident, *U-86* sunk the Canadian hospital ship HMHS *Llandovery Castle*, and the survivors were then fired on in their lifeboats. Only a month before the war officially ended, on 10 October 1918, the mail ship RMS *Leinster* was torpedoed by a U-boat, with the loss of more than 500 passengers and crew – the single worst maritime disaster ever recorded in the Irish Sea.

Germany deployed a total of 335 U-boats during the war and had another 224 under construction when it ended. They sank more than 11 million tons of shipping. Ultimately, 178 U-boats were lost, but only after the Allies spent considerable resources to contain the threat. While the undersea campaign ultimately failed, the prospects for success would lead Germany to try submarine warfare again in World War II. ∎

The crew of U-boat *U-58* surrenders to the American destroyers USS *Fanning* and USS *Nicholson* in the North Atlantic on 17 November 1917, shortly after sinking a British vessel.

I WITNESSED THE BIRTH OF A NATION

THE BATTLE OF ARRAS (9 APRIL–16 MAY 1917)

IN CONTEXT

FOCUS
Canadian troops

BEFORE
April 1915 Canadian troops fighting in the Second Battle of Ypres are among those subjected to the German army's first gas attacks.

November 1916 The Fourth Canadian Division takes the German trenches at Courcelette, France, in one of the final acts of the Battle of the Somme.

AFTER
September 1918 The Canadian Corps launches a series of attacks near Canal du Nord, France, eventually breaking through the Hindenburg Line and driving German troops out of Cambrai.

Autumn 1918 Between mid-August and mid-October, Canadian forces suffer more than 30,000 losses – killed, wounded, or taken prisoner.

The Battle of Arras was part of the wider Nivelle Offensive devised by the new French commander-in-chief General Robert Nivelle in early 1917 to break the deadlock on the Western Front. British soldiers, under the command of Sir Douglas Haig, were to stage a diversionary attack at Arras, while Canadian troops were tasked with capturing nearby Vimy Ridge. This diversion would tie down German troops, leaving them unable to reinforce the line on the Aisne river, where

Such a noise I never imagined in my life. Bedlam was sure let loose … The sights around the field are terrible looking. I hope I don't witness anything like it again.
Harry Chalmers
The Canadian Corps

Nivelle planned his main attack. He had promised his political superiors a rapid Allied victory that would bring the war to an end.

A relentless attack
The British attack at Arras was preceded by five days of heavy artillery bombardment, during which the British Army pummelled German lines with 2.5 million shells, 1 million more than had been used in the disastrous attack on the Somme in July 1916. Compared with the latter, the bombardment was more precisely targeted at German gun emplacements. Additionally, shells fitted with "graze fuzes" – which exploded even when striking the ground at oblique angles – destroyed barbed-wire defences rather than simply blowing craters in the ground.

The British attack began at dawn on a bitterly cold Easter Monday, 9 April 1917. The first morning saw impressive Allied gains. The infantry poured from forward positions that they had reached unseen via a network of tunnels and caves, and advanced only 50 m (164 ft) behind a creeping barrage of heavy explosives and gas shells.

See also: The Second Battle of Ypres 110–15 ▪ The Battle of Verdun 152–59 ▪ The Somme 172–79 ▪ Replacing the fallen 198–99 ▪ The Nivelle Offensive 208–11 ▪ Breaking the Hindenburg Line 290–93

Packed with troops and watched by crowds of onlookers, SS *Princess Sophia* prepares to leave Victoria, Canada, bound for Europe.

Canadians in World War I

The Battle of Arras was the first time that all four divisions of the Canadian Corps fought together, and their success at Vimy Ridge became a defining moment in Canadian history. Mindful of the political risks, Major General Arthur Currie, who had excelled during the Second Battle of Ypres in April 1915 and since been made commander of the First Canadian Division, planned the attack in minute detail. Determined not to waste a single Canadian life, he and the British commander of the Canadian Corps, Lieutenant General Julian Byng, made soldiers practise working with the creeping barrage. The meticulous planning and execution enabled three of the four divisions to achieve their objectives within hours.

Canada's involvement in the war remained controversial, however. Although half a million Canadians had volunteered to fight, there was still a shortage of men. Prime Minister Robert Borden introduced conscription in August, but his decision was met with widespread hostility.

By the end of the first day, the British infantry had advanced some 5 km (3 miles) in places, overcoming German strongpoints and machine-gun nests and capturing around 9,000 German prisoners.

Meanwhile, Canadian troops fought their way up Vimy Ridge, a long crest of land around 8 km (5 miles) northeast of Arras. Previous French attempts to capture the ridge had failed, losing several thousand lives, but by the late afternoon, Canadian troops on the captured ridge watched German soldiers retreat across the plain below. The victory had cost Canada 11,000 casualties.

Despite the advances gained on the first day, the prospect of a British victory soon diminished. General Sir Edmund Allenby, commanding the Third Army, was slow to press the advantage, and by the time he sent the cavalry forward on 11 April, the German army was deploying reserves that had been brought up from behind the lines. The fighting descended into a stalemate as the British troops lost their momentum. Haig insisted on continuing the operation, however, to support the French assault on the Aisne river, which was also faltering. The battle dragged on until 16 May, before it was finally called off.

Heavy losses

Despite the improved performance of the British artillery and infantry, and the Canadian troops' remarkable feat at Vimy Ridge, Arras was a failure for the Allies. They suffered about 158,000 casualties compared to the German army's 130,000. ∎

Soldiers of the Canadian Corps break through German barbed wire to take Vimy Ridge from the German Sixth Army – a key moment in the evolution of Canadian nationhood.

DOWN WITH THE WAR!

THE NIVELLE OFFENSIVE (16 APRIL–9 MAY 1917)

IN CONTEXT

FOCUS
The French army at breaking point

BEFORE
December 1916 French victory at Verdun comes at the cost of almost 400,000 men (either dead or wounded).

April 1917 The Allied forces and many French army commanders oppose General Nivelle's planned offensive.

AFTER
June 1917 French commander-in-chief Philippe Pétain opts to wait until US Army troops are ready before launching an Allied offensive, taking pressure off French troops.

1998 French prime minster Lionel Jospin says that the mutinous soldiers of May and June 1917 should be "wholly restored to our collective national memory".

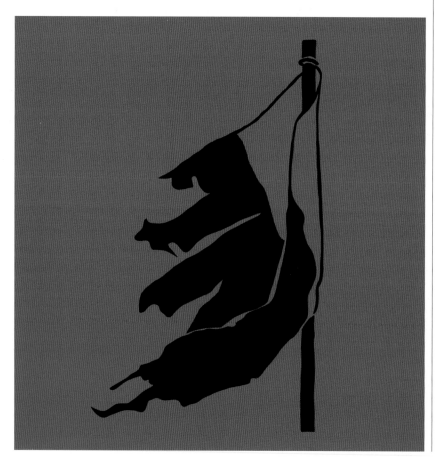

By April 1917, the Western Front had fallen into a pattern of short-lived advances by each side, which were contained and then pushed back by the other – often with huge casualties and little strategic advantage. Frustrated French army commanders and politicians were eager to take the war to the Central Powers and turned to their new commander-in-chief Robert Nivelle, who had replaced General Joseph Joffre in December 1916.

Towards the end of the heroic French resistance at the months-long Battle of Verdun, Nivelle – in command of the Second Army – had captured German fortified

See also: The Battle of Verdun 152–59 ▪ The Somme 172–79 ▪ The February Revolution 192–93 ▪ The Battle of Arras 206–07 ▪ The Spring Offensive 260–67

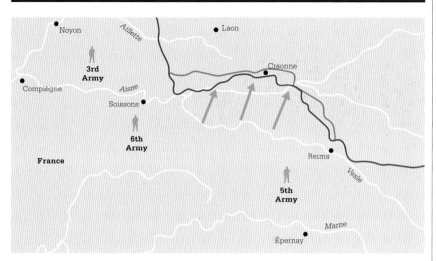

On 16 April 1917, the first day of the Nivelle Offensive, one division of the French Sixth Army advanced 2 km (1.25 miles) to the Chemin des Dames ridge, near Craonne, and took about 3,500 German prisoners of war. Elsewhere, little headway was made.

Key:

🚶 French army

➡ French Nivelle Offensive

—— French front line, 16 April

—— French front line, early May

---

positions by using the tactic of creeping artillery barrages to defend the advancing infantry.

An ambitious plan

A new government had recently taken charge in France, and Nivelle promised his political superiors a rapid victory with low casualties by using tactics similar to those used at Verdun. He had selected part of the German line on the Aisne river and its tributary the Vesle, between Soissons and Reims, for a French offensive. Nivelle planned a huge artillery barrage against German lines in the days before the infantry and their accompanying tanks – the first French tanks to see action in any numbers – punched a hole in the German front line. Waves of French troops would then pour through the breach, forcing the Germans to withdraw.

Nivelle was confident he could force a German retreat within 48 hours. His optimism persuaded not only his political superiors in France but also British prime minister David Lloyd George, who was so optimistic about Nivelle's plan that he considered putting the British Army under French command. That did not happen, although commander-in-chief Sir Douglas Haig reluctantly agreed that the British would launch an attack along the line at Arras to divert German troops from Nivelle's offensive.

When Nivelle first proposed his plan, the French envisaged that the offensive would be coordinated with a push by Russian forces in the east. The unfolding revolution in Russia, however, had left that hope in tatters. In March 1917, German forces withdrew from their forward positions to a new »

French mutinies

The mutinies in the French army that began in May 1917 were an immediate reaction to the failure of the Nivelle Offensive, but they were also the culmination of years of frustration for troops on the Western Front. On 3 May, the French Second Division refused to follow an order to attack. They were followed by other units throughout May and early June. The mutineers argued that their commanders kept launching offensives with little chance of success, while not allowing troops sufficient time to recuperate behind the lines or visit their families.

The mutinies took place almost entirely among the infantry, which had suffered most casualties. Other divisions helped arrest thousands of mutineers. Nearly 3,500 faced court martials, with many being sentenced to hard labour and 629 to death, though only 49 executions were carried out. By July, reassurances by Nivelle's successor had restored a fragile order to the ranks.

Exhausted French soldiers seek cover during an offensive on the Western Front. Battle fatigue could take both a physical and mental toll.

line of defences that they had just finished building, the Hindenburg Line. As they retreated, they used a scorched-earth policy, destroying supplies and infrastructure, and setting booby traps as they went.

This unexpected German move led the inexperienced leaders of the French ministry of war to propose a pause in planning for an offensive. Nivelle refused. For him, the German withdrawal was a source of frustration because he was worried they would drop back even further, not giving him a chance to launch his attack. At a meeting with French and British politicians, he threatened to resign if the attack was postponed. Given his popularity and confidence, and the fact that he had not yet lost a battle, he prevailed. The Germans had recently announced the resumption of unrestricted submarine warfare and Allied commanders felt pressure to take the battle to the Germans on the Western Front.

The offensive begins

While Haig planned his attack at Arras, Nivelle assembled a huge amount of artillery along the front and began a 10-day bombardment. However, the German withdrawal forced the French army to attack from south to north towards the River Aisne.

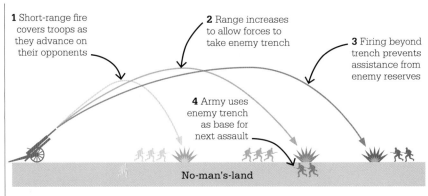

1 Short-range fire covers troops as they advance on their opponents

2 Range increases to allow forces to take enemy trench

3 Firing beyond trench prevents assistance from enemy reserves

4 Army uses enemy trench as base for next assault

No-man's-land

A creeping barrage is a technique of sustained artillery fire targeting a line, moving forward in increments. In World War I, it became the standard tactic to provide cover for an infantry attack.

This route had few roads to ease progress and only small towns with little infrastructure to support a large advance. On the north bank of the river, the land rose steeply to a ridge called the Chemin des Dames, near Craonne. The main German line was sheltered on the far slope of this ridge, supported by three reserve lines.

The strength and depth of the new German defences were enough to dilute the artillery power Nivelle had gathered along a front of 40 km (25 miles) – a field gun and a trench mortar for every 23 m (75 ft) of defences, and a heavy gun for every 21 m (69 ft). By breaching French intelligence, German commanders had ample warning of the offensive.

They kept their troops safely in deep dugouts and bunkers until the preliminary barrage was over.

Strategic failure

When the French advance finally began on 16 April, the German defenders left their bunkers and took up their positions: they had 100 machine guns for every 915 m (3,000 ft). The French soldiers thus advanced slowly into an artillery bombardment and fierce machine-gun fire. They were weighed down by three days' worth of rations, to support an expected advance of at least 8 km (5 miles). The creeping barrage that was supposed to pin down the defenders inside their shelters moved too far ahead of the infantry, who consequently advanced with little or no cover and suffered heavy losses. One officer observed, "At 6am the battle began. At 7am it was lost."

To make matters worse, the French Schneider CA1 tanks soon became trapped in mud or were

As a second wave of French soldiers of the 11th Colonial Corps prepares to advance (foreground), the first wave reaches the German trench on the Chemin des Dames ridge.

blown up by German artillery – on the first day, 64 of the 132 tanks became bogged down, and 57 were destroyed by shells. The tanks burned easily due to their petrol reserves and blocked the route of the attack, causing a huge traffic jam behind French lines and obstructing the advancing infantry. The offensive petered out, and was officially abandoned on 9 May.

National disappointment

The Nivelle Offensive was not a complete failure. The French had gained up to 7 km (4½ miles) of territory in one sector – less elsewhere – and had captured 28,000 German prisoners and some artillery. It had also drawn in and exhausted many German reserves. Those gains, however, came at the cost of 187,000 French casualties and fell a long way short of the strategic breakthrough Nivelle had confidently promised.

The result was a profound sense of disappointment among French civilians and the military. Morale was low. By this time, some French soldiers had spent more than two years facing the enemy and had become disillusioned with

[The French] soldiers … heard nothing but another terrible threat: new suffering, great dangers, the prospect of an awful death …
Corporal Louis Barthas
French 296th Infantry Regiment

the quality of their officers, the conditions under which they served, and the poor chances of success of any offensive they were ordered to undertake. The long defence at Verdun had sapped their energy, and the rate of desertion rose during the early part of 1917. That dissatisfaction now manifested itself in a series of mutinies along the Western Front that peaked in June 1917. About 40,000 troops from 68 divisions, mainly concentrated in the area of the offensive, between Soissons and Reims, disregarded

orders to return to the line. Most of them were not refusing to fight, however; they simply wanted more time to rest and recuperate.

In civilian life, too, strikes broke out among textile and munitions workers, mainly in response to a 40 per cent rise in the cost of living and a 10 per cent drop in real wages. When the French ministry of the interior surveyed civilian morale in June 1917, it found it to be "indifferent" or "poor" in 37 of 70 departments.

A change of commander

Given the collapse of the Russian army, French commanders were concerned that socialist agitation might instigate revolution among the French army, so they acted swiftly. On 15 May, Nivelle was removed as commander-in-chief and replaced by Philippe Pétain, who had orchestrated the defence of Verdun. Pétain had a reputation for being more cautious than his headstrong predecessor. He toured front-line military units to assure soldiers that their grievances were being addressed and that there would be no further futile attacks like the Nivelle Offensive. ■

Philippe Pétain

Born into a peasant family in northern France in 1856, Philippe Pétain was admitted to Saint-Cyr military academy in 1873. His career advanced slowly until the early months of World War I, when he quickly rose through the ranks. He led the French defence of Verdun and became commander-in-chief of the French army in May 1917, tasked with rebuilding it after the Nivelle Offensive. Pétain remained in command throughout the rest of the war, and was made a marshal of France in 1918.

In 1940, at the age of 84, Pétain agreed to lead the Vichy government set up by Nazi Germany, arguing that it helped prevent total German occupation of France. He collaborated closely with the Nazis, including in the deportation of Jewish people. As a result of this, after World War II, he was tried for treason and sentenced to death – commuted to life imprisonment due to his World War I service record. Pétain died in 1951.

TODAY I WOULD NOT WISH TO BE ITALIAN
THE FINAL BATTLES OF THE ISONZO (12 MAY–7 NOVEMBER 1917)

Italy's hopes to conquer the ethnically Italian border territories of Austria-Hungary were beginning to look a little unrealistic by the beginning of 1917. There had been no fewer than nine battles along the banks of the Isonzo river. The Italian forces had won four of them; the Austro-Hungarian army, three; and two had proved inconclusive.

Italian commander Luigi Cadorna had perseverance, but his resolve was close to becoming obstinacy. Nearly 340,000 of his soldiers had been killed, wounded, or taken prisoner, with very little to show for it. Cholera was rampant among his troops, who were camped out among the dead of previous battles, sourcing their drinking water from pools compromised by decaying bodies and raw sewage.

Cadorna's plan
Undeterred and unwilling to modify his strategy, Cadorna remained adamant that, if his troops would only be brave enough, a frontal attack could not fail. The Italian

Italian commander **Luigi Cadorna**'s forces fight **11 battles of the Isonzo**.

At best, **Italy advances 25 km (15 miles)** into Austro-Hungarian territory.

The Italian troops are **pushed back** 150 km (93 miles).

The **12th battle** brings **catastrophic failure** at **Caporetto**.

The armies of Prince Emanuele Filiberto and General Armando Diaz make a stand.

See also: The situation in Europe 18–19 ▪ Austro-Hungarian failures 82 ▪ Italy enters the war 120–21 ▪ The end of the war in Italy 284–85 ▪ A lasting peace? 312–17 ▪ The rise of fascism 322–23

Italian troops fighting in the Alps wore white uniforms in a bid to blend in with the snowy landscape and so camouflage themselves.

Mountain warfare

Even as they fought off an Italian assault through Slovenia, Austro-Hungarian forces advanced on Italy directly from the north. This meant crossing the Alps and the Dolomites, a landscape lying between 2,000 m and 4,000 m (6,500–13,000 ft) above sea level and a challenge for attackers and defenders alike. Snow cloaked the slopes year-round; temperatures could drop as low as -35°C (-31°F). A journey of just 2 km (1.25 miles) on the map could take hours or even days across glaciers, ravines, and icy rivers. Weapons and supplies had to be carried up by mules or by the soldiers themselves, despite the construction of new roads, tunnels, paths, and cableways by both sides.

In such harsh conditions, making contact with the enemy was difficult. Most of the many thousands of deaths were caused by exposure, disease, and exhaustion.

troops made modest gains in the Tenth Battle of the Isonzo (12 May–8 June 1917), then won a more significant victory in the 11th (18 August–12 September), but at a cost of nearly 310,000 more casualties. Fearing an Italian breakthrough, Germany sent General Otto von Below to the Isonzo with reinforcements trained in infiltration tactics, backed by artillery with poison gas.

Defeat at Caporetto

The 12th Battle of the Isonzo, at Caporetto, pitted Cadorna's troops against a much more formidable opponent. In the early hours of 24 October 1917, the Central Powers unleashed a gas bombardment of canisters secreted on the slopes above the Italian positions; this was followed by mortar fire and gas grenades. Some of the Italian troops had already fled by the time the regular bombardment began.

Austro-Hungarian troops tackle a sheer rockface on the Italian front. Such terrain presented a tough challenge to soldiers on both sides of the conflict.

Amid the ensuing panic, German stormtroopers moved deep into Italian lines, wreaking havoc. Their resistance soon broken, Cadorna's troops retreated hastily. The general himself was absent on leave when the battle took place; he was relieved of his command on 9 November. By then, his army had lost another 305,000 men, including 265,000 taken prisoner.

Further to the south, the Italian Third Army under the command of Prince Emanuele Filiberto, Duke of Aosta, was also forced to withdraw. However, the army managed to maintain its discipline and was able to halt the general retreat, albeit after the Italian line had fallen back 150 km (93 miles) to the banks of the Piave river.

Even this regrouping was only possible because the Fourth Army, led by General Armando Diaz, held the fortifications that Cadorna had built around the rocky summit of Monte Grappa. The army's victory at this, the First Battle of Monte Grappa (13–26 November), halted the Austro-Hungarian advance towards Venice and bought Italy some time. ▪

THE EARTH SEEMED TO VOMIT FIRE

THE BATTLE OF MESSINES (7–14 JUNE 1917)

When the Nivelle Offensive of spring 1917 ended in failure, the new French commander-in-chief Philippe Pétain decided to wait until American troops were ready to fight before launching further major offensives. Britain, however, was eager to keep up the pressure on the German army. The failure of the French offensive had convinced British commander-in-chief Sir Douglas Haig that his army should be less concerned with supporting French plans and instead create and implement its own strategy. Haig believed that Flanders, in Belgium, was the most logical place for an independent British offensive.

See also: The First Battle of Ypres 72–73 ▪ The Second Battle of Ypres 110–15 ▪ The Somme 172–79 ▪ The Battle of Passchendaele 230–35

> The German troops were stunned, dazed, and horror-stricken … Many of them lay dead in the great craters opened by the mines.
> **Philip Gibbs**
> **British war correspondent**

Still shocked by the high casualty figures of the Battle of the Somme, British politicians were wary of Haig's ambition, but General Sir William Robertson, the chief of the general staff, proposed a step-by-step offensive with limited objectives, meaning operations could be brought to a halt at any time. Robertson wrote to Haig, "… instead of aiming at breaking through the enemy's front, aim at breaking down the enemy's army, and that means inflicting heavier losses upon him than one suffers oneself". Robertson's approach, supported by Pétain, was more simply known as attrition.

Haig still wanted to smash the German line in Flanders. He believed a breakthrough could secure the railway junction at Roulers – a key German supply route – and even, with support

from the Royal Navy, the Belgian ports at Ostend and Zeebrugge. He believed such an advance could bring the war to an end in 1917. If the plan failed, it could still be defended as part of Robertson's attritional strategy.

Ypres salient

The British troops had been in the Ypres salient, a bulge in the front line, since 1915, but Haig aimed to strengthen their position south of the city ahead of a large offensive further north in Flanders. Britain had been planning an attack in the area for more than a year. As early as 1916, commander of the Second Army, General Sir Herbert Plumer, had identified a low ridge occupied by the German army that ran from Messines to Wytschaete, southeast of Ypres, as a promising position for an attack. He had begun a meticulous process of undermining the German positions facing him.

The German defences were formidable. There were four parallel systems of trenches guarded by »

British explosives

From 1916, the explosives the British Army laid on the Western Front were made of ammonal, a variation on the T-ammonal used in grenades and shells. It contains a combination of ammonium nitrate and aluminium powder, which acts as an oxidizer and was cheaper than pure TNT.

Ammonal can be spoiled by humidity, and it turns to liquid in the presence of air, so it was stored in metal cans or rubberized bags for protection. It was packed with guncotton, or nitrocellulose, which acted as a propellant. At Messines, the explosives were piled into chambers at the ends of tunnels and sealed off with walls of sandbags to direct the force of the blast upwards rather than sideways. Ammonal explodes with great force due to the high temperature generated by the burning aluminium dust. It is still used for mining and quarrying operations today.

Australian troops dig underneath Hill 60, on the southern edge of the Ypres salient. On 7 June 1917, around 55 tons of explosives were detonated there in two tunnels.

machine-gun nests and concrete pillboxes, with many troops held in reserve trenches ready to be brought forwards to push back attackers who managed to break into the front-line trenches. The sector was defended by soldiers of the German Fourth Army, commanded by General Friedrich Sixt von Armin.

Underground preparations

Most of the largely flat agricultural land in Flanders was both soft and waterlogged, which made it unsuitable for digging tunnels, but Allied military engineers discovered a seam of blue clay about 25–30 m (82–98 ft) beneath the surface at Messines that could be mined. Throughout 1916, more than 30,000 Allied troops dug an extensive network of tunnels towards the German positions on the ridge. Many of the tunnellers had been coal or gold miners in civilian life, so they were well accustomed to underground work, but even so, the tunnelling was difficult. The miners carried

> Nineteen giant roses with carmine petals ... rose up ... out of the ground, then split into pieces with a mighty roar.
>
> **German observer**
> Messines, 7 June 1916

oxygen tanks and used electric lights and mechanical diggers where they could, but much of the work had to be carried out by hand to avoid noise that would alert the German defenders above. At the end of the tunnels, beneath the German front lines, the Allies dug out large chambers, which they filled with explosives.

The engineers excavated a decoy network of tunnels closer to the surface to distract the German

troops, who dug their own counter-tunnels to try to disrupt the Allied efforts. German soldiers only discovered and destroyed one of the chambers of explosives. With tunnelling largely complete, Allied mining activity declined towards the end of 1916, and the German troops assumed that the underground threat had passed. They were in for a rude awakening. Another 19 chambers packed with explosives survived.

Plumer had a reputation as a thorough commander, and the whole offensive was carefully planned. He was also more protective of soldiers' lives than had been the case in previous assaults, such as the Somme or the Nivelle offensives. In addition to the tunnel network, Plumer commissioned infrastructure to support the attack, including light railways to take ammunition and supplies to the front, and pipelines to carry drinking water to the troops. He concentrated 2,200 artillery guns along a 16-km (10-mile) front ready for a preliminary bombardment.

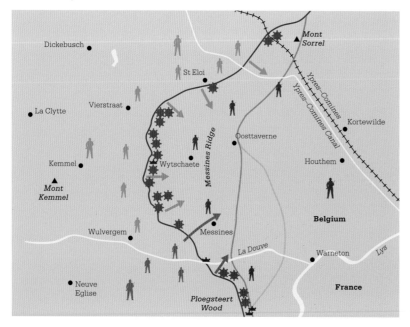

The near-simultaneous detonation of 19 huge mines (four failed to explode) beneath the German front line on 7 June 1917, followed by a creeping barrage, allowed Allied troops from the II ANZAC Corps (Australia and New Zealand), IX Corps (Ireland), and X Corps (Britain) to advance over the Messines Ridge. Along the southern part of the front, the actual territorial gain exceeded the objectives.

Key:

🚶 German army

🚶 British Army

🚶 ANZAC army

✸ Exploded mine

⚓ Unexploded mine

— Front line, 6 June

— Final objective

— Actual territorial gain, 7 June

➡ British advance

➡ ANZAC advance

Soldiers gaze into a crater 116 m (380 ft) across and 45 m (148 ft) deep caused by the largest underground explosion at Messines. All the mines were detonated within 20 seconds.

The first bombardment began on 21 May 1917. It was far more accurate than many previous bombardments, thanks in part to a new technique – sound ranging. This used microphones on the battlefield to calculate the precise location of an opponent's guns. British commanders also received information from reconnaissance aircraft flying above German positions to direct Allied fire. The front-line German defenders were trapped by the bombardment, with little food or water; the reserves in the rear trenches were pinned down and unable to come forward to relieve them. The bombardment continued for 17 days.

A huge explosion

The attack started in earnest just before dawn on 7 June. At 3:10am, engineers detonated the mines in the 19 chambers beneath Messines, causing a series of explosions so loud that they were said to have been heard in London: only the atomic bombs of World War II caused larger detonations. In all, the mines held more than 450 tons of explosives. The ground shook as sheets of flame erupted and smoke rose into the sky.

As many as 10,000 German soldiers on the front line died instantly, and dazed survivors wandered towards the British troops to surrender. Around 7,000 German soldiers were taken prisoner. The attackers found the front line virtually deserted.

Follow-up operations

There was a lull in the fighting before the advance on the second line of defences began around 7am.

The Allies crossed no-man's-land behind a creeping artillery barrage, with machine-gun fire from behind keeping the German reserves from moving forwards with a meaningful counterattack. A combination of Australian, New Zealand, and British divisions captured the village of Messines. Meanwhile, Irish solders captured the village of Wytschaete. The Irish troops included volunteers from both Protestant and Catholic militias, who as recently as 1916 had appeared likely to fight each other in an Irish civil war.

As Allied reserves were sent to the front later in the day, it was clear that the assault had been largely successful, despite fierce German counterattacks that cost thousands of casualties. Fighting continued for another week as the British forces consolidated their gains. Plumer's objectives, however, had always been limited in scope. Rather than achieving a general breakthrough, he had intended only to capture the high ground that would allow the British troops to control the Gheluvelt plateau – a strategically important high point and launch pad for further advances – ready for a more general future offensive. In that, he had been entirely successful. ∎

Underground war

Tunnelling was part of the war from December 1914, when German engineers destroyed an Indian brigade by laying mines beneath its position. That began an underground war in which both sides recruited expert miners to plant explosives under enemy lines while preventing their opponents from doing the same by digging counter-tunnels. Miners listened for enemy tunnellers by placing a stethoscope against the wall of the shaft. Allied miners could often hear Germans working and talking in their own tunnel nearby, and vice versa.

Tunnellers sometimes dug into an enemy's shaft and engaged in underground combat. If the opposition found a tunnel, they used explosives to destroy it – possibly burying the miners alive – or pumped in poisonous gas to asphyxiate them. Digging tunnels under such conditions was physically tough and mentally draining.

I CAN'T STOP WHILE THERE ARE LIVES TO BE SAVED

TREATING THE WOUNDED

The unprecedented nature and scale of World War I produced a torrent of casualties – and horrific wounds – that overwhelmed the medical corps of combatant armies in the early weeks of the conflict. Over time, however, advances in medical treatments, equipment, and transport, and the support of tens of thousands of volunteer nurses and the International Red Cross, helped them meet the gruelling challenge.

Until the 19th century, battlefield medicine hardly existed. The wounded were left where they fell and collected after the fighting, or, more often, died from blood loss or sepsis. Medics offered little more

See also: Society under strain 184–87 ▪ Replacing the fallen 198–99
▪ Artillery 228–29 ▪ Shell shock 236 ▪ The Great Influenza 308–09

Nurse Anna Rochester feeds a wounded soldier at the US Red Cross hospital in Souilly, France, in 1917 or 1918. Nurses bore the brunt of caring for severely injured and broken men.

Elsa Brändström

than bandages and amputations. Beginning in the Napoleonic Wars of the early 19th century, and continuing during the Crimean War (1853–56) and the American Civil War (1861–65), a new system developed for placing medical teams closer to the front line. Battlefield casualties were also prioritized according to the severity of their wounds – known as triage from the French *trier*, "to sort".

Battlefield demands

The powerful artillery employed in World War I inflicted most of the injuries. As many as 60 per cent of wounds were caused by exploding shells; their shrapnel – small lead balls released at high velocity – tore through flesh, killing and maiming. Some machine guns could fire more than 600 rounds per minute, fracturing bones and piercing organs with their lethal bullets. An estimated 91,000 people died from poisonous gas inhalation, and others suffered blindness and devastating lung damage. With the advent of trench warfare came

further afflictions, such as trench foot, lice, diarrhoea, pneumonia, and shell shock – the mental effect of the war's trauma.

As the war continued, doctors developed more effective antiseptic treatments and surgical techniques, and delivered increasingly efficient battlefield care. The International Red Cross, established in 1863 to provide "relief for the wounded", had branches in all combatant powers, except the Ottoman Empire, where the equivalent Red Crescent society flourished. Thousands of volunteers in both organizations provided essential nursing and other care. In Russia, whose army had no integrated medical service, the Red Cross played a crucial role.

Stages of care

Although local conditions differed, procedures for the collection and care of men wounded on the many »

I never knew what I was going to find; there were many missing limbs, horrible deep wounds.
Emma Weaver
US Army Nurse Corps,
from her journal

The daughter of a Swedish military attaché, Elsa Brändström was born in 1888 in St Petersburg, Russia. When World War I broke out, she volunteered to serve in the medical division of the imperial Russian army, but joined the Swedish Red Cross after seeing the poor treatment of German prisoners of war. She travelled to Siberia, where many Austrian and German prisoners were held, and there laboured tirelessly, often in camps rife with typhoid and typhus, soon earning the moniker the "Angel of Siberia".

After the war, the Bolshevik regime in Russia accused Brändström of being a spy and imprisoned her. On her release, she went to Sweden, where she raised funds for prisoners-of-war and their families and was five times nominated for a Nobel Peace Prize. German-American theologian Paul Tillich wrote that whenever she appeared, "despair was conquered and sorrow healed". In the 1930s, Brändström and her family moved to the US, where she assisted newly arrived German and Austrian refugees. She died in 1948.

battlefields were roughly similar. The first challenge for regimental stretcher bearers was to brave artillery or machine-gun fire to reach the seriously injured. They would bandage wounds as best they could, then carry casualties to a regimental aid post, just behind the front line, sometimes in a reserve trench or dugout. There, medical staff carried out emergency treatment, such as further bandaging or splinting, and administered morphine to relieve pain. Wounded men capable of walking were also treated at the aid posts, but there was no capacity for housing patients. Those needing further care were sent by horse-drawn wagon or motorized ambulances to dressing stations, where doctors gave anti-tetanus injections and performed urgent operations. Some patients were then sent to nearby field hospitals – often housed in tents – while more serious cases were transported to main hospitals further from the front.

The efficiency of battlefield care and the methods of transporting patients necessarily depended on the terrain. The Italian army used cable cars and mules to carry its wounded from the Italian Alps during the Battles of the Isonzo (1915–17). At Gallipoli, both the Allies and Ottoman forces had to evacuate sick and injured men by ship from the peninsula, and many died on the long journeys. Elsewhere, between 1915 and 1918, 13 Allied hospital ships were attacked and sunk.

Treating the wounded

The British military established casualty clearing stations (CCSs) – miniature hospitals, administered by the Royal Army Medical Corps (RAMC) – where more seriously wounded men were sent for surgery and nursing care. The clearing stations were located some 11 km (7 miles) from the front line and often near waterways or railway lines to facilitate the transportation of patients, if necessary, to larger hospitals. Two out of six surgical teams were always on duty, and the hundred or so personnel included many nurses, who assisted in round-the-clock operations and attended to the men on stretchers, changing bandages, inspecting wounds, and comforting the dying.

As wounds caused by shrapnel or machine-gun fire became septic within six or eight hours, the most common procedure in the CCS was a debridement – cleaning the wound of contaminants such as

Royal Army Medical Corps

Dealt with **9 million** cases

Administered **1,088 million** doses of drugs

Distributed more than **1.5 million** splints

Applied **108 million** bandages

Used **7,140 tons** of cotton wool

Ordered **22,386** artificial eyes

British nurses Mairi Chisholm and Elsie Knocker, also known as "the Madonnas of Pervyse", drive an ambulance in Belgium in 1917.

Ambulances

At the start of the war, seriously wounded men were transported in field ambulances that had changed little from those of the Napoleonic era a century earlier. Such conveyances were canvas-covered horse-drawn wagons fitted with racks for stretchers.

Motorized ambulances were initially deemed too unreliable to negotiate the blast-cratered roads, but were soon widely adopted as they moved so much faster than their horse-drawn counterparts. Ford, Daimler, and other leading automobile makers began to produce the new vehicles, which attracted a colourful crowd of volunteer drivers, including American writer Ernest Hemingway and British novelist Somerset Maugham.

Soon funds were being raised to send motorized ambulances to the Western Front. The Red Cross alone despatched more than 2,000 of the vehicles, of which some 90 were destroyed in battle. By 1918, standard US Army Ambulance Sections would have 12 horse-drawn and 36 motorized ambulances.

Wounded American soldiers lie amid the rubble of a bombed-out church in Neuvilly, northern France, waiting to receive medical care.

pieces of uniform, shell fragments, splintered wood, and the mud of the trenches. A tetanus shot was often given, and nurses would bathe the wound daily, usually with an antiseptic compound called Dakin's solution.

Gas attacks produced injuries that doctors had to learn how to treat. Chlorine and phosgene irritated the lungs, but with oxygen and bed rest, those affected could fully recover in time. Mustard gas, however, could blind and cause excruciating blisters and severe lung damage. Bathing in soap and hot water within half an hour of exposure proved an effective treatment, so portable shower units with specially trained medical staff were introduced to minimize the gas's blistering effects.

Developing plastic surgery

Around 9 million men in Britain, France, and Germany alone were wounded during World War I. Of these, as many as 280,000 soldiers were left disfigured by their injuries. Some chose to wear a facial mask, while others opted for reconstructive surgery – a new medical technique that developed quickly as a result of the war, largely thanks to New Zealand-born surgeon Harold Gillies.

Gillies had joined the RAMC at the outbreak of war. While stationed in Wimereux, France, he had watched French-American dentist Major Sir Auguste Charles Valadier employ early skin-grafting techniques while treating soldiers with jaw and other facial injuries. Inspired by this work, Gillies opened the first dedicated facial injuries ward in 1915 at the Cambridge Military Hospital in Aldershot, UK. In 1916, offensives such as the Battle of the Somme produced hundreds of thousands more wounded men, including many with severe facial injuries. As Gillies' existing facilities were overwhelmed, he persuaded the medical authorities to establish the first-ever hospital dedicated to facial reconstructive surgery – Queen's Hospital in Frognal House, a refurbished Jacobean mansion in southeast London. It opened in 1917.

Over the next four years, the facility would help reconstruct the damaged faces of more than 5,000 men, helping them gain the confidence to re-enter society as their wounds healed. In 1930, British king George V awarded Gillies a knighthood for his "wonderful work".

Artificial limbs

The war wounded also spurred improvements in prosthetics, which in earlier years had been wooden and so ill-fitting and painful to wear that they were seldom used. With so many men maimed and unfit for work, governments recognized the need for the mass production of prosthetic limbs, and designers and manufacturers rose to the challenge of making the fit precise and comfortable. Lightweight, more durable materials began to be used, such as the aluminium alloy duralumin produced by British manufacturer Desoutter Bros, whose co-founder Marcel had lost his leg in a flying accident.

For decades after the end of the war, men in wheelchairs, on crutches, or with empty shirt sleeves were familiar sights in Europe. That they managed to survive at all was a tribute to the successful partnership of civilian and military medical establishments of countries across the world. ■

One boy today, screaming to die, the entire top layer of his skin burnt from his face and body. I gave him an injection of morphine. …
Shirley Millard
American nursing volunteer in France

THE BROKEN THUNDER OF THE GERMAN DEATH

THE GERMAN BOMBING CAMPAIGN CONTINUES (MAY 1917–MAY 1918)

IN CONTEXT

FOCUS
Bombing civilians

BEFORE
August 1914 Zeppelin airship raids on Liège and Antwerp, in Belgium, kill several civilians.

1915 Germany launches its first strategic bombing campaign against Britain and France using zeppelins.

1915 Russian and Italian bombers enter service – the first large bomber aircraft.

AFTER
1939 The Luftwaffe (German air force) bombs Polish cities, with raids on Wieluń, Frampol, and Warsaw.

1942 The British RAF's first "1,000-bomber raid" destroys much of Cologne, Germany.

1945 Huge civilian casualties result from the atomic bombs detonated by the US Air Force over the Japanese cities of Hiroshima and Nagasaki.

I n 1917, Germany launched new bombing raids on London, Paris, and Britain's Channel ports. Instead of airships, these raids were carried out by planes of unprecedented size. Following its bombing campaign of 1915, Germany developed the Gotha G.IV, which could carry up to 500 kg (1,100 lb) of bombs. On 25 May 1917, Germany sent 21 Gothas from airfields in occupied Belgium to attack the Channel port of Folkestone and nearby army camps. Dropped in broad daylight, the bombs killed 95 people and injured 260 more. On 13 June, a daylight raid on the Liverpool Street Station area of London killed 162 people, including 18 schoolchildren in their classroom. No warning was given.

A shocked nation

Appalled by such bold attacks, people demanded a response from the British government. Unlike during the early German bombing

German airmen attach a 100 kg (220 lb) bomb to the underside of a twin-engined Gotha bomber before it embarks on a raid in World War I.

See also: The secret war 96–99 ▪ War in the air 116–19 ▪ The German bombing campaign begins 136–37 ▪ Tactical flying 238–39

campaign in 1915, the authorities were quick to divert fighter planes from the Western Front to attack the bombers, which defended themselves with machine guns.

The successful introduction of highly manoeuvrable Sopwith Camel fighters by Britain in the summer of 1917 forced the Gothas to fly only at night. From September 1917, the Gotha night raids were joined by Zeppelin–Staaken R.VI "Giants". These massive aircraft had four engines and a wingspan of 42 m (138 ft). Between May 1917 and May 1918, German bombers carried out 152 night raids on targets across Britain, killing 857 people and injuring 2,508. In one incident, in January 1918, a bomb penetrated a shelter in a London basement, killing 38 people.

Britain's response

The Allies established a network of observers to spot approaching bombers and raise the alarm. Fighter planes could then intercept them and civilians could take shelter – usually underground.

> … the report of a gun rattled through the air … Coming towards me from the northeast, like huge brown birds, was a flock of aeroplanes.
> **Georgina Lee**
> **British war diarist**

A German Zeppelin LZ 33, shot down over Essex in 1916 is inspected by local officers The airships carried a large bomb load, but their size made them easy targets for air-defence gunners.

Bombing at night was made more challenging for German aircraft after British cities introduced blackouts, forcing pilots to navigate by emitting signals to radio beacons on the ground in Germany; poor weather conditions also led to many raids being aborted. Such difficulties were reflected in the limited success of the final German bomber raid on London, which took place on 19 May 1918. Of the 43 bombers that left Belgium, only 19 penetrated the city's outer defences, although they still caused substantial damage, leaving 49 people dead and 177 injured.

A change of plan

In the final months of the war, Germany abandoned its strategic bombing campaign, diverting its bombers to support its troops in France. The British defensive systems had reduced civilian casualties and – for a short time – had diverted valuable German resources from the Western Front. However, concerns were raised at the failure of the UK government to better protect its citizens, and an inquiry was commissioned into the country's air defences. ▪

The Allied bombing response

The success of the German long-range bombing campaign in 1915 and then 1917–18 was later emulated by the Allies. The establishment of the Royal Air Force (RAF) in April 1918, which made Britain's airpower independent of the army and navy, was driven partly by the idea of carrying out a bombing campaign on German soil. In June 1918, the Independent Air Force – part of the new RAF – was formed in France, under the command of General Hugh Trenchard. Its bombers flew into Germany to target airfields and cities such as Frankfurt and Mannheim. Caproni and Handley Page aircraft attacked at night, while De Havillands and Bréguets flew during the day. The idea of bombing civilian targets was well established by the end of the war – and the tactic would play a much greater role in World War II.

A 1918 RAF recruitment poster advertises daily pay of up to £44 (2023 prices). By the war's end, the RAF had more than 5,000 pilots.

THE STEAMROLLER THAT COULD NOT CRACK A NUT
THE KERENSKY OFFENSIVE (1–19 JULY 1917)

Following the February Revolution and abdication of the tsar, it was unclear what part, if any, Russia would play on World War I's Eastern Front. To reassure Britain and France that Russia was still a dependable ally, Alexander Kerensky, the Provisional Government's minister of war, ordered a new offensive to be launched in the summer of 1917. His hope was that the move would lift national spirits and dampen enthusiasm for those Bolsheviks calling for an immediate peace.

The army's new commander-in-chief, General Aleksei Brusilov, was dubious. Munitions and his soldiers' morale were spent. Since the Great Retreat of 1915, millions had been killed, wounded, or captured in failed counterattacks. Weary for peace and recognizing their mutual hardship, front-line Russian and German troops had begun to fraternize. The Bolsheviks were also recruiting at the front, weakening the Russian army's field command system. As a result, Russian troops were becoming rebellious. Nevertheless, Brusilov amassed 31 divisions and more than 1,300 guns, planning, once again, to cross the fields of eastern Galicia.

A final offensive
The opening artillery salvoes started in late June, but it was on 1 July that the Russian infantry charged into view, attacking along an 80 km (50 mile) front. The Austro-Hungarians opposing them to the south near the Romanian border were hit hard, with 7,000 being taken as prisoners on the second day. German units were rocked, too, and General Erich Ludendorff ordered the transfer of six divisions from the Western Front. Many of the already battle-scarred towns and cities in the area once again changed hands,

The Russian army withdrew in disorder; the Revolution had destroyed its backbone.
General Erich Ludendorff
Ludendorff's Own Story, 1919

See also: Crisis in Russia 24 ▪ The war in the Caucasus 130 ▪ Russia retreats 138–39 ▪ The Brusilov Offensive 166–69
▪ The February Revolution 192–93 ▪ The October Revolution 240–41 ▪ German victory in Eastern Europe 258–59

Russian prisoners, captured in August 1917 near Czernowitz (now Chernivtsi) in Galicia, are escorted by German troops after the disastrous collapse of the Kerensky Offensive.

and the battle raged for two weeks. However, on 15 July, a five-day Bolshevik insurrection disrupted the city of Petrograd.

Masterminded by Bolshevik leader Vladimir Lenin and fellow Russian revolutionary Leon Trotsky, the July Days demonstrations were attacked by soldiers sent by the Provisional Government, now led by Kerensky as prime minister.

Amid this turmoil, the Germans in Galicia counterattacked. The Kerensky Offensive staggered to a halt and then collapsed.

The great desertion

With the offensive over, thousands of Russian soldiers deserted their posts. They abandoned their weapons and walked away, and hundreds of officers who tried to stop them were killed. The Central Powers military did not even try to take any more prisoners; there was no need – the Russian army had simply melted away. Its remnants fell back in disarray so quickly that, by early August, all the ground the Russian army had gained had been retaken. The advancing Central Powers were only stopped by a determined Romanian army stand – and by outrunning their supply chain.

The Kerensky Offensive had been Russia's final onslaught of World War I, and it resulted in 400,000 more of its troops being killed, wounded, or captured – and a similar number of desertions. Ultimately, it was all for nothing. The offensive had only weakened Russia, preparing the ground for the final stages of the Bolsheviks' march to power. ▪

Battalion of Death

In the wake of the tsar's abdication and the collapse of army morale, the Russian high command began considering a plan to raise battalions of women to fight. It was thought that this might shame the men into doing their duty. Nearly 20 such units were formed, including the most notorious – the First Russian Women's Battalion of Death.

While many of the Russian women's battalions served as communications specialists, the First Battalion of Death saw combat in the 1917 Kerensky Offensive and acquitted itself well. Its most renowned member was the formidable Maria Bochkareva, who was wounded in one of the Kerensky Offensive battles. When she travelled overseas in 1918, her notoriety led to audiences with US president Woodrow Wilson and King George V in Britain, before she returned home. In 1920, however, Bochkareva was executed by the Cheka, the Soviet secret police, for her connections with the anti-Bolshevik White movement.

An all-female combat unit was the idea of Maria Bochkareva (far left), who became the first Russian woman to command troops.

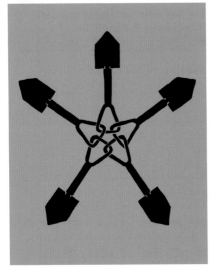

THE GARDENERS OF SALONIKA
GREECE AND THE MACEDONIAN FRONT (1917–18)

IN CONTEXT

FOCUS
Military cooperation

BEFORE
1913 Greece and Serbia defeat Bulgaria in the Second Balkan War.

1914 World war begins, but Greece remains neutral at the insistence of King Constantine I.

AFTER
December 1918 The newly liberated Kingdom of Serbia merges with several other southern Balkan states to form the Kingdom of Serbs, Croats, and Slovenes (renamed Yugoslavia in 1929).

1919 Greece attempts to take territory in west Turkey in the Greco-Turkish War.

1920 The Treaty of Sèvres hands Smyrna, Eastern Thrace, and other Turkish territories to Greece.

At the insistence of King Constantine I, Greece remained neutral at the start of World War I, but it joined the Allies in the summer of 1917. While the king – who had been educated in Germany and was the kaiser's brother-in-law – had pushed a policy of neutrality, Greek prime minister Eleftherios Venizelos supported the Allies, and this difference of opinion created a "national schism".

In February 1915, Constantine had forced Venizelos to step down, but the latter was re-elected five months later. Demonstrably the people's choice, the prime minister believed he was entitled to make decisions on their behalf. He

> **King Constantine I** insists on Greece's **neutrality** and dismisses prime minister Eleftherios Venizelos, who supports the Allies.

> The people **re-elect Venizelos**. He assists the Allies **against the wishes of the king**, who dismisses him a second time.

> After **Venizelos forms a rival government** at Salonika, the Allies force the king to abdicate. **Greece formally enters the war**.

> **Based in Salonika, the Allied Army of the Orient brings soldiers from a wide array of nations together to fight in a common cause.**

See also: The Balkans 25 ▪ The assassination of Franz Ferdinand 40–41 ▪ Austro-Hungarian failures 82 ▪ The end of the Serbian campaign 140–43

> Ammunition dumps were exploding … The city was full of fleeing and exhaust[ed] enemies, unable to fight.
> **French officer**
> **Skopje, 29 September 1918**

showed this in September 1915, when he authorized the Allies to use Greece's port city Salonika (Thessaloniki) as a base to assist Serbia's defence. Although their support came too late to save Serbia from defeat by the German, Austro-Hungarian, and Bulgarian armies the following month, the Allies remained. Driven from their homeland, most Serbian troops found their way back via Albania and Corfu and joined British, French, Italian, and Russian troops at Salonika.

Inaction at the front

The Macedonian Front extended from Albania to the mouth of the Struma river in Greece. It was so quiet for much of the time that French minister of war Georges Clemenceau dismissively described the Allied soldiers who defended it as "the gardeners of Salonika". The thick barbed wire protecting the Allied base gave rise to the British nickname "The Birdcage", conjuring up an image of being trapped in futile idleness.

The lack of military action did not mean that the men could take things easy. By the time the fighting on the Macedonian Front had finished, the British alone had lost more than 18,000 men killed or wounded in action. In addition, malaria and other epidemics tore through the Allied camps, and many more died or had to be evacuated due to severe illness.

The French contingent at the front was led by General Maurice Sarrail, who – unusually for a high-ranking French officer – was an outspoken socialist. In August 1916, he was put in charge of all Allied forces on the front – called the Allied Army of the Orient.

Greece goes to war

At the end of August, Venizelos formed his own government at Salonika, which the Allies recognized after failing to coerce Constantine to support their Macedonian Front. They finally forced him to go into exile in June 1917. Greece made its partnership with the Allies official and, in spring 1918, sent its troops with Sarrail's Allied army – now half a million strong – on an offensive aimed at Sofia, the Bulgarian capital. The city lay some 160 km (100 miles) away, over rugged mountains. Although ultimately a failure, the attack piled further pressure on the overstretched Central Powers.

Not until the autumn of 1918 did Sarrail feel ready for another offensive. This time, with Serbian troops well to the fore, the Allies pushed north and east up the Vardar Valley, deep into Bulgaria – whose surrender was received on 29 September. ▪

The Allied Army of the Orient

Critics in France muttered that socialist general Maurice Sarrail had been sent to Salonika as a kind of exile. To many western European troops, it certainly felt like a long way from home. The army assembled there was almost a world in itself, with troops drawn from a host of different nations. Along with those of France, Britain, and Russia, there were major contingents from Serbia and, eventually, Greece. There were also fighters from Montenegro and Albania.

France's Armée d'Orient was itself a multiethnic force. It included a sizeable contingent of light cavalry, the Chasseurs d'Afrique, descendants of European settlers in French colonies. Another light-cavalry corps was recruited from the Indigenous populations of Algeria, Tunisia, and Morocco. There were also tirailleurs (light infantry) from West Africa and Indochina.

A standard-bearer at Salonika leads a light cavalry contingent of Spahis – Arabs and Berbers from French North African colonies.

THE DIN, THE ROW, THE SWISHING OF THE SHELLS
ARTILLERY

Industrialization, innovation, and technological advances before World War I had a huge transformative impact on artillery. Tactical developments during the war also forced changes. The sheer power of the heavy weaponry, such as mortars and howitzers, led to the advent of trench warfare, which in turn briefly brought the value of artillery into doubt. Ultimately, the move to the trenches would change the type of artillery employed.

Despite technical advances that improved their loading, handling, and range, field guns still worked in roughly the same way as earlier cannons: a controlled explosion behind the projectile sent it flying out of the barrel towards the target. The projectile arced through the air, before hitting the ground at a shallow angle. Except in the unlikely event of a direct hit, soldiers who were well dug in were shielded from the blast.

The **destructive power of modern guns** sends soldiers on all sides into **trenches, dugouts, and bunkers**.

⬇

The **defensive success** of trenches, dugouts, and bunkers sends military planners **back to the drawing board**.

⬇

High-trajectory mortars and howitzers are used more often for their greater destructive capabilities.

See also: The Battle of the Frontiers 52–55 ■ The First Battle of Ypres 72–73 ■ Trenches take over 74–77 ■ The Second Battle of Ypres 110–15 ■ War in the air 116–19 ■ The Battle of Verdun 152–59 ■ The Somme 172–79 ■ The Battle of Cambrai 237

> We were under incessant bombardment. … Our dugouts crumbled … and we had to dig ourselves and our comrades out.
> **Stephen Westmann**
> **German medical officer**

More powerful explosives, aerial reconnaissance, and improved mapping enhanced the quality of artillery bombardments, while industrial production boosted the manufacture of munitions, such as shells. Gunners could rely on sheer firepower to break up the ground the enemy occupied, raining down shells in lengthy bombardments and gradually degrading the fabric of the enemy trench system. Even so, opposing troops that were dug in deeply – and able to hold their nerve – could expect to ride out an artillery storm.

More effective by far was the kind of indirect fire supplied by a muzzle-loaded mortar, a metal pipe that fired small shells at a steep angle striking opposing troop positions from above. The gunner calculated the direction and range but did not fire directly at the target. The large-calibre howitzer – such as Germany's mighty Big Bertha – fired projectiles in a high, curved trajectory; large shells from Big Bertha could bombard targets from a distance of almost 9 km (6 miles).

Sustained fire

Field-gun bombardments still had a part to play. Sustained barrages intimidated the enemy before an infantry advance. Barrages on the Western Front could could go on for days. They included any combination of high explosives, shrapnel, smoke, chemicals, and "star shells" – shrapnel shells adapted to carry tiny vials of

With its high elevation capability, the 42 cm (17 in) calibre German M-Gerät ("Big Bertha") howitzer was designed for firing on unseen targets, especially opponents' trenches.

incendiary material. Like shrapnel shells, they were timed to explode in the air above the ground.

Improving accuracy and rates of fire allowed "creeping barrages", with infantry advancing behind a wall of exploding shells. The British tried the tactic without success at the Somme, but Canadian forces used it to great effect in April 1917 at Vimy Ridge during the Battle of Arras. ■

Observation balloons fitted with powerful cameras, such as this German example, were used for gathering battlefield intelligence.

Sighting without seeing

As the range of powerful weapons increased, gunners were often firing at targets they could not see. Sightlines might be blocked by intervening high ground or targets were distant and well dug in. Advances, such as better weather forecasting and accurate measurements of air temperature, helped improve the accuracy of indirect fire.

Aerial reconnaissance evolved quickly in World War I and was supported by rapid advances in photography. By 1916, cameras could produce a fast succession of images, helping armies plot and map enemy troop positions and other targets.

Artillerymen also learned to locate their opponents' guns by monitoring the flashes in the sky as they fired ("flash-spotting"), triangulating their observations to obtain a precise position. This skill was supplemented by "sound ranging" – estimating distances by timing the delay between the flash of a gun and its sound.

HORSES, MULES, MEN, EVERYTHING DEAD

THE BATTLE OF PASSCHENDAELE (31 JULY–10 NOVEMBER 1917)

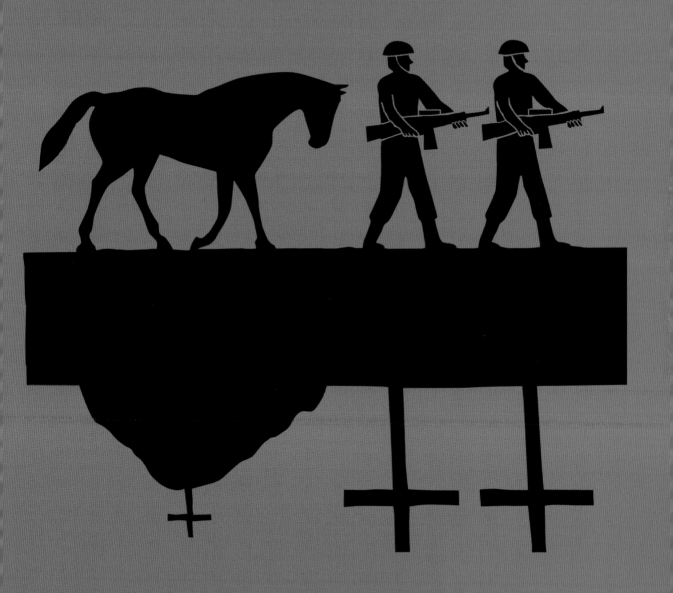

IN CONTEXT

FOCUS
Suffering under fire

BEFORE
1914 Field Marshal Sir Douglas Haig attributes his success at the First Battle of Ypres to the German army's failure to press home its advantage.

1916 British General Hubert Gough's impetuosity is highlighted by the scale of casualties at the Battle of Mouquet Farm, during the Somme campaign.

AFTER
March 1918 Gough is dismissed as commander of the British Fifth Army.

April 1918 As part of its Spring Offensive, the German army advances into the Ypres salient before being repulsed.

September–October 1918 In the Fifth Battle of Ypres, the German forces fail in a final effort to dislodge the Allies.

Passchendaele, a village just east of the Ypres salient – a bulge in the Allied front line thrusting deep into German-held territory in western Flanders – gave its name to the Third Battle of Ypres, the bloodiest and most futile battle in a long and brutal war. Driving rain and the mud it created were to prove enormously important in shaping the flow of the battle as it unfolded over the summer and autumn of 1917. The quagmire in which troops died in their thousands went on to become one of the most memorable and haunting images of the war.

The German troops had grown too comfortable in the sector, and their U-boat bases on the nearby North Sea coast, at Ostend and Zeebrugge, played a key role in the resumption of unrestricted submarine warfare. A breakthrough at Ypres was likely to force their evacuation. Two major battles had already been fought over the Ypres salient; early in 1917, British commander Sir Douglas Haig decided it was time to start a third.

The Ypres salient was a thorn in the side of the German army. The vulnerability of the British,

The Somme was bad enough, but this is a thousand times worse.
Jack Sweeney
Private, Second Battalion, Lincolnshire Regiment

French, and Belgian forces, who were all but surrounded here, made its capture an obvious and important goal. Conversely, the Allies were eager to expand the salient and consolidate their hold.

A contentious campaign
Not everyone agreed with a new offensive. British prime minister David Lloyd George was sceptical, and his war cabinet withheld approval until 25 July. France's General Ferdinand Foch favoured a succession of more limited and localized operations, at least until

War horses

Long after the invention of the internal combustion engine in the late 19th century, horses remained the primary source of motive power. Although armies were early adopters of new technology – and cars, trucks, and buses were widely seen on the Western Front – they also relied heavily on about 380,000 horses. Some still carried cavalry, but others pulled carts and field guns, or carried packs. Sometimes, they hauled railway trucks or tramcars behind the lines.

The Battle of Passchendaele highlighted the wretchedness of these animals' lives. Although they could cope in conditions where motorized transport failed, it was often at a terrible cost. Struggling through thick mud was exhausting enough for the laden animals, but many were literally worked to death. Many more had to be euthanized after breaking limbs; others were killed by bullets, bombs, or shells. Still more were drowned in flooded craters.

See also: The Race to the Sea 70–71 ▪ The First Battle of Ypres 72–73 ▪ Trenches take over 74–77 ▪ The Second Battle of Ypres 110–15 ▪ The Battle of Verdun 152–59 ▪ The Somme 172–79 ▪ The Battle of Arras 206–07

the American Expeditionary Forces arrived to lend support. Never lavish in his praise of Haig, Foch was frank in his condemnation of what he saw as a "futile, fantastic, and dangerous" offensive. Some, more sympathetic to Haig's plan, were nevertheless uneasy at his decision to place it in the hands of General Hubert Gough.

Bold or naive?

Gough divided opinion. Some maintained that this protégé of Haig's had been overpromoted under his command and that he was both reckless and naive. From the Ypres salient, Gough envisaged a bold advance into fresh territory on the first day, before the German forces had a chance to prepare their defences, but Haig's other generals foresaw a slow and painful grind from the outset.

As this wrangling continued, major mutinies in the French army threw uncertainty over the Allies' plans; then bad weather hampered preparations on the ground. Cloudy conditions made

aerial reconnaissance difficult and hindered the efforts of Allied artillery to soften up enemy positions (although millions of shells were still fired from 3,000 guns). It was not until the end of July that Gough finally felt his offensive could get under way in earnest.

Gough's plan was that Allied forces would push their way east to the ridge-top village of Passchendaele, then on to the railhead of Roulers, which German forces across western Flanders relied on for their supplies.

From deluge to disaster

On the morning of 31 July, Gough gave the order for his Fifth Army to advance up Pilckem Ridge, supported from the south by the

General Hubert Gough commanded Britain's Fifth Army from 1916 to 1918, but disappointing results in the Battle of Passchendaele saw him sidelined.

Allied soldiers seek cover in water-filled craters in the mudscape of Passchendaele. It was impossible to dig trenches in such conditions.

British Second Army and from the north by France's First Army. They made good progress, taking the higher ground as planned, crossing the ridge, and pushing on across the Gheluvelt plateau. Ominously, though, in the afternoon it started to pour with rain.

Initially, the rain was merely an inconvenience to be shaken off. However, night came, and the downpour did not ease. Haig noted in his journal on 1 August that it was "A terrible day of rain. The ground is like a bog." It would only get worse. The torrential rain failed to abate the following day. In fact, 63 mm (2½ in) of rain fell between 6pm on 31 July and 6pm on 4 August. The Allied advance slowed to a standstill, so » impassable was the terrain. Two earlier major battles – and the incessant artillery fire in between them – had stripped the landscape of the trees and undergrowth that had previously bound the topsoil. The resulting wasteland had been left cratered and churned up by further shelling. The clay-based soil held huge quantities of water. Shell craters turned to muddy pools – death traps for unwary men and horses. Overflowing streams spread to form vast bogs. Vehicles bringing up supplies from the rear stuck fast in the mud and had to be abandoned; field guns sunk to their axles and could not be moved.

On the orders of commander Erich Ludendorff, the German artillery maintained a constant bombardment across the Gheluvelt plateau. With the Allies' advance now stalled, the German infantry had the opportunity to regroup. Pushing back, they retook the village of Westhoek on 10 August.

> Many of the men can hardly speak. You see wild eyes gazing out of faces which are no longer human.
> **Rudolf Binding**
> German staff officer

Gough's enthusiasm was fading, and he subsequently claimed that he had advised Haig to abandon the attack. Despite Gough's apparent change of heart, Haig had refused to change his plans.

Haig could not have expected such a wet August in Flanders. At 127 mm (5 in), the rainfall was double the average for the month, and there were only three dry days in the whole month. Allied soldiers struggled on heroically but with limited success. A pattern was established of Allied advances quickly becoming bogged down and then, as often as not, thrown into reverse. The second main attack, launched in mid-August, was in some respects a replay of the first. On 18 August, outside the village of Langemarck, the German fighters recovered a great deal of the ground they had lost earlier in the month.

Limited progress

All was not completely in vain for the Allies. On 25 August, after 10 days of fierce fighting, Canadian troops captured the strategically important Hill 70, 48 km (30 miles) south of Ypres. More than 1,500 Canadians died and 8,000 were wounded in the process, but German casualties exceeded 25,000 – and the engagement delayed German efforts to relieve exhausted troops elsewhere.

Polygon Wood, named after its angular appearance on the map, had been occupied by the invading Germans in 1914 but hotly fought over since then. The struggle to secure it amounted to a small battle within the Battle of Passchendaele. An Anzac-led Allied offensive at the end of September was partially cancelled out by German counterattacks, but by 4 October Australian and British troops were pushing on towards Passchendaele.

Key:

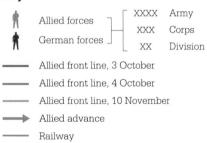

Allied forces
German forces

XXXX Army
XXX   Corps
XX   Division

——— Allied front line, 3 October
------- Allied front line, 4 October
——— Allied front line, 10 November
⟶ Allied advance
——— Railway

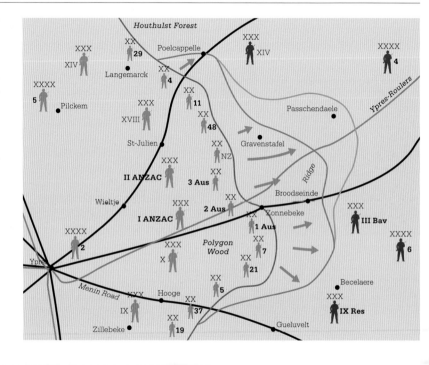

Joined by local children, troops of the Canadian Corps triumphantly march back to base after taking Hill 70 in August 1917.

The weather continued to thwart Gough's attempts to pursue a coherent strategy. The battlefield was a morass, and even tracked tanks struggled to make progress. Commanders mapped areas in which the ground was impassable for vehicles, and soon these covered much of the battlefield. When troops did have the chance to advance, they had difficulty finding their way across this featureless expanse of mud. Abandoned German trenches had more or less been obliterated, and rain and low-lying cloud reduced visibility, hampering the efforts of artillery observers, even those covering the battlefield from the air.

A change in the weather

September brought fine weather and the Allies took full advantage of the improved conditions to push forwards. Their dogged resistance had left the German troops exhausted and struggling to get supplies. They may even have thought that the battle was over and that the Allies had been defeated. It seems just as likely, however, that Ludendorff decided to concentrate on rebuilding his depleted forces, ready for a much larger counterattack.

Events continued to go the Allies' way. Gough had been sidelined, and his replacement, General Sir Herbert Plumer, pursued a more cautious strategy of "bite and hold". Instead of launching a wide, full-frontal assault, he attacked more limited sections of the enemy lines, pounding them with artillery, rushing them with infantry, and then digging in so that his men could not be dislodged.

On 25 September, the Allies took, and managed to hold, the Menin Road Ridge after five days' fighting. Ludendorff counterattacked, but the British troops were equal to this and, by 3 October, had advanced further, taking Polygon Wood.

More mud

The battle for Passchendaele itself began on 12 October. By now, autumn was well advanced, and the weather began to deteriorate. As in the summer campaign, the armies were lashed by rain and mired in mud. Brief Allied advances were thrown back by German counterattacks. Haig had learned to call a halt when his forces' actions were ineffective. The weather improved at the end of October, and on 6 November his troops resumed their advance against the German position, finally taking Passchendaele that day – but they were still 8 km (5 miles) short of Roulers, their target.

Although Passchendaele was technically a victory for the Allies, they had gained very little for their 300,000 dead and wounded. Indeed, there may even have been slightly fewer German casualties. ∎

Perverse persistence?

"Why has not Haig been recognized as one of England's great generals?" the *News Chronicle*, a British newspaper, asked in March 1935. "The answer can be given in one word – Passchendaele." Before the battle, some British army officers had questioned whether it made sense to fight there at all. Then, when the Allied attack faltered disastrously during the first few days of the offensive, Douglas Haig opted to press on blindly rather than recognize and adjust his tactics – a strategy that would ultimately cost the British Army dearly. September's successes went some way towards justifying the offensive overall.

Despite the fact that Haig was a talented and thoughtful general, Passchendaele underscored the reputation he had established at the Somme as one who favoured dogged determination over flair. The battle also set the perception of the wider war as a futile struggle between wretched armies, mired in mud.

TREMBLING LIKE A LEAF

SHELL SHOCK

The term "shell shock" first appeared in print in the February 1915 issue of *The Lancet*, a British medical journal. The author, Dr Charles Myers, had been treating a soldier who had broken down after extensive combat. During a lull in the fighting, the young man had suddenly gone blind and become overwhelmed by uncontrollable shivers, among other puzzling symptoms. His fellow soldiers, it seemed, were already calling such cases "shell shock".

There is no man on earth who can stick this thing forever.
Unidentified soldier

Initially, this seemed an apt description for a syndrome that also included paralysis, amnesia, nightmares, and hallucinations. Physicians thought this malady might be akin to concussion. Yet the disorder also resembled cases of hysteria and neurasthenia, or overwrought nerves, which were common among civilians, and which in extreme cases could translate into uncontrollable physical tics or movements.

It was Myers' former teacher, Dr W.H.R. Rivers, who made the next advance in understanding the condition. In February 1918, while serving at the Craiglockhart War Hospital outside Edinburgh, Scotland, he published an article in *The Lancet*, arguing that the symptoms resulted from attempts to bury the memory of overwhelming trauma. Recovery involved the "talking cure": talking through the traumatic memories to lighten their burden. While some fortunate soldiers were able to do so, hundreds of thousands of others were permanently damaged by shell shock. ∎

See also: The Somme 172–79 ▪ Treating the wounded 218–21 ▪ The Battle of Passchendaele 230–35 ▪ Shattered by war 310–11

HELL WAS LET LOOSE

THE BATTLE OF CAMBRAI (20 NOVEMBER–7 DECEMBER 1917)

British colonel J.F.C. Fuller had argued for a more widespread use of tanks, which – he maintained – could transform the battlefield, if the ground was good. Fuller urged an attack somewhere on the chalklands of northern France, such as those near Cambrai, a supply centre for the Germans on the Hindenburg Line.

Innovative tactics

Meanwhile, British major general Henry Hugh Tudor was looking into ways for infantry to attack with more precision – and less warning. Gunners had hitherto pinpointed their targets by taking trial shots, which excluded the element of surprise. Exploiting improvements in surveying and cartography, Tudor developed a system that enabled the gunner to aim accurately from the first shot, by "shooting off the map".

Advance artillery bombardment, which helped by shredding the barbed wire set up in front of the infantry's advance, also advertised the intentions of the attacking army. Tanks, trundling forward,

British tanks led a surprise attack against the German defences at the Battle of Cambrai, but they were soon beset by technical problems.

could flatten these barriers – and protect the infantrymen moving in their wake from machine-gun fire.

General Julian Byng combined the two approaches at Cambrai. The German troops were almost swept away, but the initial shock quickly faded. In addition, the British Army started losing momentum as its tanks broke down, leaving the infantry exposed. Field Marshal Sir Douglas Haig urged the troops to persevere in what turned into a battle of attrition. ∎

See also: Tank warfare 150–51 ▪ The Somme 172–79 ▪ Trench warfare transformed 254–57 ▪ The Battle of Amiens 274–77

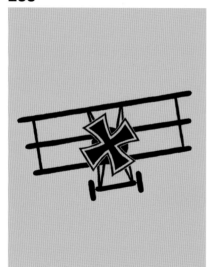

FIGHT ON AND FLY ON

TACTICAL FLYING

IN CONTEXT

FOCUS
Air war

BEFORE
1794 French troops use a balloon to monitor Austrian military movements during the Battle of Fleurus.

1909 The US Army Signal Corps purchases a Wright Model A, which becomes the world's first military aircraft.

1911 Italian aviation is the first to instigate reconnaissance and bombing missions in the Italo-Turkish War.

AFTER
1918 The British Royal Flying Corps (RFC) becomes the Royal Air Force (RAF), the first aviation service that is fully independent of the army.

1919 A converted Vickers Vimy bomber makes the first nonstop flight across the Atlantic, from Canada to Ireland.

In no other sphere of warfare was the pace of change as great as that seen in military aviation. An improvement by one side would almost immediately be countered by some form of development from its adversary. Change, innovation, and advance were the watchwords during this extraordinary phase of technological progress.

Military dominance shifted from one side to the other chiefly as the result of the introduction of a more advanced aircraft or weapon system. German pilots had gained a strong advantage in the summer of 1915 with the "Fokker scourge"; they were to gain the upper hand once more during the spring of 1917 as the latest Albatros D.III fighters

tore apart Allied planes, so much so that British pilots called the worst phase of the period "bloody April".

The German control of the skies over the Western Front was not to last. The Allies introduced a series of first-rate aircraft, including the French SPAD S.XIII (first action, May 1917) and the British Sopwith Camel (June 1917), both of which were very manoeuvrable. In addition, a further two rugged British planes would become, in their respective roles, deadly gun platforms: the Royal Aircraft Factory SE5a and the two-seat Bristol F.2 Fighter.

New tactics, new pilots

Another change occurred at the tactical level. The earlier style of single combat, in which victory went to the most skilful and daring ace, was now superseded by the introduction of large aerial formations. In this new approach, flights of six or more aircraft would work together using strength in numbers to overwhelm the enemy.

A German pilot sits in his Fokker E.III Eindecker fighter plane. These single-seat aircraft played a significant role in – and gave their manufacturer's name to – the "Fokker scourge" of 1915.

See also: Europe's colonies and empires 28–29 ▪ War in the air 116–19 ▪ The German bombing campaign begins 136–37 ▪ The German bombing campaign continues 222–23 ▪ Trench warfare transformed 254–57

> The main power of defence and the power of initiative against an enemy has passed to the air.
> **Billy Mitchell**
> **US Army officer, November 1918**

During the latter half of 1917, the Allies benefited from the arrival of the US Army Air Corps. American pilots had been flying for the Allies in a semi-official capacity for three years, since 1914. They did this either as independent volunteers or as part of the French air force, in the famous Lafayette Escadrille unit. Such pilots were subsequently transferred to official US service; as a key member of the 94th Aero Squadron, Captain Eddie

Rickenbacker achieved fame by shooting down 26 enemy aircraft in just four months, flying solo.

New types of plane
Although reconnaissance remained a key function of military aviation, other roles became increasingly important. Air-to-air combat planes, such as the British Sopwith Camel, were reassigned for the close support of ground operations, and new models, such as the German Junkers J.I, were designed. These planes were better armoured and fitted with machine guns and light bombs, enabling direct attack on ground targets, but pilot casualties were high in these low-flying craft.

At the opposite end of the spectrum was the arrival of heavy bombers, such as the German Gotha G.IV and Zeppelin-Staaken R.VI. These were designed for independent bombing missions deep behind enemy lines. Heavy bombers were seen as the future of military aviation; their use would come to influence the military thinking of every major nation. ▪

A fleet of Allied planes sits on a French airfield, ready for action at short notice. Despite the weaponry on board, the pilots were dangerously exposed in such small craft.

Eugene Bullard

Born in Columbus, Georgia, US, in 1895, Eugene Bullard stowed away on a cargo ship bound for Scotland while he was a child. There he worked as a boxer and music-hall act before travelling to Paris in 1914. When war was declared, Bullard joined the French Foreign Legion. He was wounded at Verdun in 1916 (receiving the Croix de Guerre) and volunteered for a French aviation unit in 1917.

Bullard was the first Black combat pilot, and over the course of 20 missions he shot down two enemy aircraft. He apparently flew with a small pet monkey tucked into his flying suit, and his plane bore the motto "All blood is red".

Refused a commission in the US Army Air Corps, almost certainly because of his colour, Bullard was returned to the infantry after an off-duty fight with an officer. After the war, he became a nightclub owner in Paris, and during World War II he worked for French intelligence; he was wounded in 1940 before escaping to the US. Although he received many French honours, Bullard died in relative obscurity in 1961.

PEACE, LAND, AND BREAD

THE OCTOBER REVOLUTION (NOVEMBER 1917)

IN CONTEXT

FOCUS
**Revolution and
counterrevolution**

BEFORE
1897 Russian Marxist agitator
Vladimir Lenin is exiled to
Siberia for three years.

1903 The Russian Social
Democratic Labour Party splits
into Bolsheviks ("majority")
and Mensheviks ("minority").

1905 The First Russian
Revolution begins. Tsar
Nicholas II is forced to carry
out democratic reforms.

AFTER
1922 Prominent Bolshevik
Joseph Stalin becomes
general secretary of the
Communist Party.

1929 Stalin exiles fellow
revolutionary Leon Trotsky
for urging more democracy
in the Communist Party.

1991 The USSR collapses
and is dissolved.

Russia's February Revolution had achieved dramatic change. It had brought centuries of tsarist oppression to an end and addressed important economic injustices. In principle, Alexander Kerensky's Provisional Government had transformed Russian society, but its realities were want, chaos, and a sense of drift. With continued chronic food shortages, the wage rises won by revolutionaries made no real difference to people's daily lives. The new factory committees and soviets (workers' councils) had nominally empowered people, but this meant little when everything else was spiralling out of control.

Capital, created by
the labour of the worker,
crushes the worker …
Vladimir Lenin

The Bolsheviks' demands – which included the abolition of private property and Russia's immediate withdrawal from the war – may have been extreme, but February's more moderate reforms had failed to solve the country's problems. The Bolsheviks' programme started to enjoy much popular support as a result. Their leader Vladimir Lenin argued that, in order to achieve change, a "workers' revolution" would be necessary, led by a band of committed activists.

A counterrevolution

In July 1917, Kerensky appointed General Lavr Kornilov commander-in-chief of the Russian army, replacing Aleksei Brusilov. Kornilov believed that discipline and a strict hierarchical structure – the principles that armies are built on – should guide society as a whole.

Fearing that the Bolshevik-dominated Petrograd Soviet was trying to sabotage his government, in August 1917 Kerensky gave cautious backing to Kornilov's plan to take back the city by force. The general needed no encouragement to attack the Bolsheviks in their stronghold in Petrograd, but he also hoped to sweep Kerensky

See also: Crisis in Russia 24 ▪ The Battle of Tannenberg 78–81 ▪ Russia retreats 138–39 ▪ The Brusilov Offensive 166–69 ▪ The February Revolution 192–93 ▪ The Kerensky Offensive 224–25 ▪ German victory in Eastern Europe 258–59

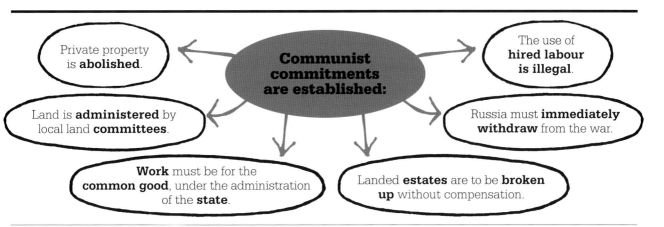

Communist commitments are established:

- Private property is **abolished**.
- The use of **hired labour is illegal**.
- Land is **administered** by local land **committees**.
- Russia must **immediately withdraw** from the war.
- **Work** must be for the **common good**, under the administration of the **state**.
- Landed **estates** are to be **broken up** without compensation.

aside at the same time. In the event, sympathy with the Bolsheviks among Russia's soldiers (and the railway workers that transported them) brought the army's advance to a humiliating halt. The failure of Kornilov's counterrevolution helped boost the prestige of the Bolsheviks still further.

Bolshevik victory

On 8 November (26 October in the Russian calendar of the time), Lenin's Bolshevik forces carried out a raid on Petrograd's Winter Palace, where the Provisional Government had taken refuge. From the nearby Neva River, the guns of the cruiser *Aurora* gave the signal, and the revolutionaries took the palace by storm, arresting those present in the name of the Russian people. Kerensky himself had already escaped into exile.

Inevitable backlash

The two Russian revolutions of 1917 had ended the tsarist monarchy, caused royalists to flee, and ousted the liberals. Next, the Bolsheviks targeted their former allies: the Mensheviks and other leftist groups. After marginalizing them within the Russian government, they expelled them completely.

Despite gaining power with little resistance, the Bolsheviks soon had to defend it in a bloody and bitter civil war (1917–23). Counterrevolutionary pressures came from both left and right. In Georgia, the Mensheviks rose up against the Bolsheviks' Red Army. Elsewhere, a broad coalition, including followers of Kerensky, monarchists, and extreme nationalists enlisted in a White Army of their own. ▪

The Winter Palace was stormed again in 1920, as seen here, in a dramatic re-enactment involving Vladimir Lenin and the Red Guards.

Soviet legend-building is born

The storming of the Winter Palace was to go down in Soviet history as a heroic moment – as was the shelling of the besieged building by the cruiser *Aurora*. However, in reality the assault met little resistance. Armed revolutionaries led by Trotskyist Vladimir Antonov-Ovseenko were able to walk straight into the building and arrest a group of government ministers who were meeting at the time. The *Aurora*'s crew only fired a blank round, to signal the start of the storming.

The most famous photographic representation of the episode was staged in 1920 as part of a third anniversary pageant, but it was claimed to be real by the regime for many years. This spin on the Winter Palace story presented the entry into the palace as a spontaneous uprising of the people against a glittering symbol of social inequality and tsarist power. Propaganda such as this was to become a major instrument of state power in the Soviet Union.

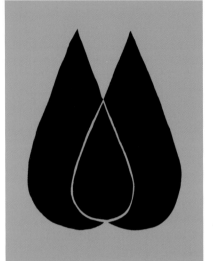

OUR ALLIANCE, CEMENTED IN BLOOD

NAVAL WAR IN THE MEDITERRANEAN

IN CONTEXT

FOCUS
Submarine warfare

BEFORE
1901 HMS *Holland 1*, the Royal Navy's first submarine, is launched in Barrow-in-Furness in northwestern England.

1906 The German Imperial Navy launches *U-1*, the first German U-boat. It is used as a training vessel in World War I.

1914 The German U-boat *U-21* sinks the British cruiser HMS *Pathfinder*, the first ship ever sunk by a submarine firing a self-propelling torpedo.

AFTER
1918 Under Article XXII of the November Armistice, 176 German submarines are surrendered to the British naval authorities.

1935 Karl Dönitz, the former U-boat commander in the Mediterranean, takes command of Nazi Germany's U-boat fleet.

The Mediterranean saw no major surface-fleet engagements during the war. Action came instead from German U-boats, responsible for sinking 3.6 million tons of shipping there between 1915 and 1918. The attrition began in May 1915, when a lone U-boat, *U-21*, torpedoed and sank the British battleships HMS *Triumph* and HMS *Majestic*, supporting the action against the Ottoman army in Gallipoli. The Dardanelles strait, separating Gallipoli from Asia Minor, was too well defended for further U-boat activity there, but the wider Mediterranean was open, its east–west routes crucial for Britain's trade with its colonies and dominions, and its north–south routes France's and Italy's link with their North African colonies.

A deadly waterway

The German admiralty based four large U-boats in the Austro-Hungarian Adriatic harbours of Cattaro (Kotor, Montenegro) and Pola (Pula, Croatia), and in October 1915 they sank 18 ships. Under the captaincy of Waldemar Kophamel, the Mediterranean U-boat flotilla then sank 44 ships in November.

During the winter of 1915–16, the U-boats wrought havoc on vessels carrying Allied troops to Salonika (Thessaloniki). By the second half of 1916, Allied losses were stark – 155 ships sunk between July and September, and 129 ships between October and December

The Allied response was confused. A barrage across the Strait of Otranto at the mouth of the Adriatic – which was intended to trap or impede submarines – proved to be ineffective. A series of Allied conferences proposed schemes to counter the U-boat menace, none of which reduced the

It was not easy for us to sink merchant ships, because we would have preferred to make the war against warships.
Franz Becker
U-boat commander

See also: The naval arms race 32–33 ▪ The war at sea begins 88–93 ▪ The sinking of the *Lusitania* 106–07 ▪ The U-boats on the attack 200–05

sinkings, especially after Germany resumed unrestricted submarine warfare on 1 February 1917.

By April 1917, the Germans had 14 U-boats in the Mediterranean. That month, they sank more than 250,000 tons of shipping, with Austro-Hungarian submarines sinking a further 23,000 tons. This was the peak of the Central Powers' submarine campaign.

Success on both sides

April 1917 brought reinforcements for the Allies in the form of eight Japanese destroyers based in Malta. At another conference, in Corfu, it was agreed to reorganize the Allied command structure and authorize a convoy system. In May, the British navy ran a successful convoy between Malta and

The Japanese destroyer *Sendan* stands in the Mediterranean port of Marseilles. *Sendan* began life as Britain's HMS *Minstrel* and was loaned to Japan from 1917 to 1919.

Alexandria, in Egypt. By October, they were running convoys between British waters and Port Said, at the northern end of the Suez Canal; four more Japanese destroyers had also arrived.

German successes continued – as late as May 1918 submarines sank more than 110,000 tons in the Mediterranean – but the drift was against them. On 9 November, *UB-50* landed a final blow when it torpedoed and sank the elderly British battleship HMS *Britannia* – off Cape Trafalgar, the scene of Lord Nelson's victory of 1805. ▪

The U-boat aces

Pioneers of a new form of warfare, U-boat commanders such as Lothar von Arnauld de la Perière, Walther Forstmann, and Otto Hersing destroyed more enemy ships than any submarine commander then or since. German-born, though of French ancestry, the unassuming Arnauld became the most successful submarine ace of all time, sinking 195 ships between January 1916 and October 1918. During his most deadly cruise, which took place off the coast of southern Italy from 26 July to 20 August 1916, his *U-35* sank 54 ships. Recalled to active service in World War II, Arnauld died in a plane crash near Paris in 1941 while on a secret mission.

Forstmann, commanding *U-39*, sank 149 ships, initially in the North Sea but mostly in the Mediterranean. Hersing's tally aboard *U-21* was more modest at 36 ships, but these included the British scout cruiser *Pathfinder* and the battleships *Triumph* and *Majestic*, earning him the nickname "destroyer of battleships".

U-boat commander Lothar von Arnauld de la Perière (second from left) stands on the deck of his submarine with his fellow officers.

Anatomy of a U-boat

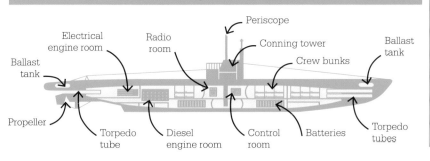

Electrical engine room — Radio room — Periscope — Conning tower — Crew bunks — Ballast tank

Ballast tank

Propeller — Torpedo tube — Diesel engine room — Control room — Batteries — Torpedo tubes

GRIP THE ENEMY BY THE THROAT

THE WAR IN EAST AFRICA (AUGUST 1914–NOVEMBER 1917)

IN CONTEXT

FOCUS
Guerrilla warfare

BEFORE
1885 German chancellor Otto von Bismarck grants a charter for the German East Africa Company to establish a colony along the coast of present-day Tanzania.

1890 Britain gains control of the German East African island trading island centre of Zanzibar.

1904 General Lettow-Vorbeck studies guerrilla warfare while posted to German Southwest Africa to crush a rebellion by the Indigenous Herero people.

AFTER
1919 The Treaty of Versailles divides German East Africa among Britain, Belgium, and Portugal.

1922 The new British colonial administration abolishes slavery in Tanganyika, formerly part of German East Africa.

Paul von Lettow-Vorbeck, commander in 1914 of the Schutztruppe (colonial troops) in German East Africa, soon realized that his combined force of 3,000 German troops and 11,000 local Askari soldiers could not forestall an Allied invasion using traditional combat. Flanked by British, Belgian, and Portuguese colonies, and with the Royal Navy likely to control the Indian Ocean, he concluded that an irregular, disruptive warfare was the only way to prevent defeat and syphon Allied soldiers from the European theatre.

To gain all
we must risk all.
**Paul von
Lettow-Vorbeck**

Lettow-Vorbeck used ambush, sabotage, and hit-and-run raids to compensate for vastly inferior numbers. A week into the war, the Schutztruppe staged its first raid into British East Africa to disrupt transport via the Uganda Railway. These clandestine cross-border attacks continued into early 1916.

Evading pursuit
After South African general Jan Smuts took command of the British East Africa Expeditionary Force in February 1916, the Allies went on the offensive. By the end of the year, they had occupied Dar es Salaam, Moshi, Mwanza, Iringa, and other German colonial cities.

In November 1917, Lettow-Vorbeck relocated his troops further south, in Portuguese East Africa. Living off the land, the Schutztruppe evaded its pursuers for eight months before marching into British-held Northern Rhodesia. When he learned of the German capitulation in Europe, Lettow-Vorbeck surrendered on 25 November – two weeks after the Armistice. ∎

See also: The rise of Germany 20–23 ▪ Europe's colonies and empires 28–29 ▪ The war in Africa 86–87 ▪ A lasting peace? 312–17

THE SOLDIERS OF THE LAST CRUSADE
JERUSALEM FALLS (NOVEMBER–DECEMBER 1917)

IN CONTEXT

FOCUS
The war in Palestine

BEFORE
1915 After crossing the Sinai Desert, Ottoman forces try to attack Egypt's strategic Suez Canal but are thwarted by British Empire troops.

1916 British forces defeat the Ottoman army at the Battle of Romani to strengthen their hold on the Sinai Peninsula.

AFTER
1918 The newly formed Zionist Commission for Palestine advocates Jewish immigration to the former Ottoman territory.

1920 The San Remo Conference assigns Britain to administer the League of Nations mandate in Palestine and Transjordan.

1921 Fighting between Arabs and Jews leaves more than 100 dead in Palestine's port city of Jaffa.

The invasion of Palestine carried out by the Egyptian Expeditionary Force (EEF) – comprising mainly Anzac and other British Empire troops – began in January 1917. It met firm resistance at Gaza in March and April, as the Ottoman army and its German advisers repelled British attacks. British commander Sir Archibald Murray was relieved of his post in the aftermath of these setbacks and replaced by Sir Edmund Allenby. Under new leadership, the EEF pushed further into Palestine, overwhelming Ottoman forces at Beersheba in late October and finally capturing Gaza in early November. This set the stage for an advance on Jerusalem.

Just a few days before Gaza surrendered, British foreign secretary Lord Balfour stated his government's support for a Jewish homeland in Palestine that would not "prejudice the civil and religious rights of existing non-Jewish communities". Realizing the sensitivity of the issue, Allenby hoped to avoid civil unrest between

On 11 December, after accepting Jerusalem's surrender, General Allenby enters the city on foot as a mark of respect for its religious significance.

religious groups, as well as the destruction of holy places during the impending attack on Jerusalem.

By the end of November, British forces had captured Jaffa on the coast and solidified their gains south of Jerusalem. Despite Ottoman counterattacks, the EEF almost surrounded the city, so the Ottoman troops withdrew in a bid to avoid a siege. The governor surrendered on 9 December without a shot being fired within the city walls. ∎

See also: Ottoman Turkey enters the war 84–85 ▪ The Arab Revolt 170–71 ▪ Battle of Megiddo 286–87 ▪ War-crimes trials 318–19

VICTORY AND DEFEAT

1918

AT

US President Woodrow Wilson presents his **Fourteen Points** to promote national sovereignty and world peace.

Faced by German military might, the **Bolshevik government signs** the **Brest-Litovsk peace treaty**.

A **long-range German siege gun shells Paris** for the first time. The gun has a maximum **range of 130 km (81 miles)**.

Austria launches an offensive **across the River Piave**. It is **repulsed by the Italian army**, reinforced by troops from France and Britain.

8 JAN 1918

3 MAR 1918

23 MAR 1918

15 JUN 1918

25 JAN 1918

21 MAR 1918

29 MAR 1918

26 JUN 1918

In Berlin, **Germany, 400,000 citizens** take to the streets to **protest about the lack of food** and to call for an end to the war.

The great German offensive on the Western Front, **Operation Michael**, begins. On the first day of fighting, **German forces advance nearly 16 km (10 miles)**.

The **Military Service Registry office in Quebec City**, Canada, is burned down and **all its records destroyed** as part of a protest against conscription.

Allied forces occupy Belleau Wood after 25 days of fierce fighting to counter the German Spring Offensive. **US Marines play a major role** in the battle.

By 1918, the world was war-weary. On the home front, food shortages were taking a toll on civilian life. In Britain, rationing was introduced for the first time, and the Allied naval blockade caused real hunger in Austria and Germany, where hundreds of thousands of citizens went on strike to protest against the privations and to call for an end to the war. In Austria, influenza also began to spread, and in Ireland and Canada forced conscription came under fire.

As the year began, German military commanders Paul von Hindenburg and Erich Ludendorff knew that, despite the apparent weaknesses of the Allied forces, their own military position was far from secure. Few American troops had so far arrived in Europe, but their growing numbers would eventually offset the German forces released from the Eastern Front after Russia's collapse at the end of 1917. The German high command decided to gamble on defeating the Allies outright with a massive spring offensive on the Western Front. Operation Michael, launched early on 21 March, was an initial success. By the end of the first day's fighting, many British troops were in retreat and continued to fall back. Yet, reinforced by French troops under General Ferdinand Foch, the Allies held the line.

Having failed to break the British Army with the Michael offensive, German forces delivered a second blow further north in Flanders along the River Lys on 9 April. They followed it with a new offensive against the French on 27 May – the Third Battle of the Aisne. German troops reached the Marne river, but it was the final push of a now-exhausted army.

Greater firing power

By early June 1918, German forces were just 56 km (35 miles) from the French capital, Paris. The city was easily within reach of a new German weapon, the Paris gun, which killed around 250 Parisians with its huge shells. On the battlefield, too, each side deployed increasingly powerful artillery to dislodge their opponents from deeper, ever more sophisticated trench systems. Tanks – although often unreliable – played an increasing role, as did ground-attack aircraft that dropped bombs and strafed troops with machine guns.

Another highly effective battle tactic was the infiltration of enemy lines with groups of close-combat

British war poets
Siegfried Sassoon and
Wilfred Owen **return to
active service in
France** after medical
treatment. Owen is killed
on 4 November.

**The US First Army
drives the German
army back** from the
Saint-Mihiel salient.

**General Ludendorff
is dismissed** as
Germany's supreme
commander. He is soon
**replaced by General
Wilhelm Groener**.

**Kaiser Wilhelm II
abdicates** and flees
Germany, taking refuge in
the neutral Netherlands.

13 JUL 1918   12–15 SEP 1918   26 OCT 1918   9 NOV 1918

8–12 AUG 1918   19–25 SEP 1918   3 NOV 1918   11 NOV 1918

The **Battle of Amiens**
includes an attack by more
than 550 British tanks.
General Ludendorff
calls the defeat, **"the
black day of the
German army"**.

Newly strengthened, the
Egyptian Expeditionary
Force **defeats two
Ottoman armies** at the
Battle of Megiddo
in Palestine.

Thousands of **German
sailors mutiny** at the
German naval base in
Kiel, seize the city the
following day, and set up
workers' councils to **defy
the government**.

The **Armistice** is
signed between
Germany and the Allies
in General Foch's
railway carriage in the
forest of Compiègne,
ending hostilities.

---

elite soldiers armed with the latest submachine guns. German *Sturmtruppen* (stormtroopers) perfected this approach.

Fighting back
Ultimately, the military backing of the US combined with better leadership among the Allies on the Western Front would turn the tide of war in the Allies' favour. Newly arrived US Marines, dubbed the "Devil Dogs", saw action in June at the Battle of Belleau Wood, where they were credited with halting the German advance.

The Allied fightback began in earnest with British success at the Battle of Amiens on 8 August, which greatly damaged German morale. Half of the 30,000 men that Germany lost that day surrendered. A series of well-coordinated Allied

attacks then steadily forced the German army back towards home, as fresh waves of American troops arrived to reinforce the Allies. By September, Allied troops were attacking Germany's Hindenburg Line, a series of formidable defence barriers stretching from the coast of Belgium to Verdun in France.

The Central Powers fall
As the war continued, the Ottoman, Bulgarian, and Austro-Hungarian armies grew weaker and more dependent on outside aid, which dwindled as Germany's position deteriorated and its troops were transferred to France and Belgium. On the Palestine front, Indian army reinforcements enabled the British to renew their offensive against Ottoman forces in September 1918 and finally achieve a total victory at

the Battle of Megiddo. Austria-Hungary, where Slav nationalism was tearing the empire apart, also began to waver. A reorganized Italian army, bolstered by Allied troops and equipment, defeated Austro-Hungarian forces in October. Germany's southern flank was now undefended by its one-time allies.

Germany's end soon followed. Mutinies broke out in the navy, and revolution spread through the nation; the government and high command collapsed. On 7 November, a German delegation crossed the front line to discuss an armistice with the Allies.

Signed in the early hours of 11 November, the Armistice took effect at 11am that day. The war was over, but the assignment of blame and the settlement of borders and reparations had still to be agreed. ∎

LONG LIVE THE MASS STRIKE!

THE HOME FRONT IN 1918

IN CONTEXT

FOCUS
The home front

BEFORE
1915 The US-run Commission for Relief in Belgium extends its food-aid programme to cover 2 million inhabitants in occupied northern France.

1916 Famine hits parts of the Ottoman Empire.

1917 Thousands of Germans die of malnutrition during the Turnip Winter.

AFTER
1919 Restrictions on food imports to Germany are lifted after the signing of the Treaty of Versailles.

1919–23 Food aid continues across Central and Eastern Europe through the privately funded American Relief Administration European Children's Fund (ARAECF).

By the end of 1917, both the Allies and the Central Powers had suffered appalling casualties. Every nation was broken by the conflict's financial cost and running out of men to send into battle. The morale of governments and soldiers was lower than at any point during the war. On the home front, citizens deprived of food and fuel began to see military defeats as national humiliations in a purposeless conflict, and they looked to their leaders with exhaustion and anger.

In Italy, units of the American Red Cross had been arriving since December 1917, distributing food to civilians. They set up kitchens

See also: The Easter Rising 160–61 ▪ Society under strain 184–87 ▪ Mutiny and revolution in Germany 288–89 ▪ Shattered by war 310–11

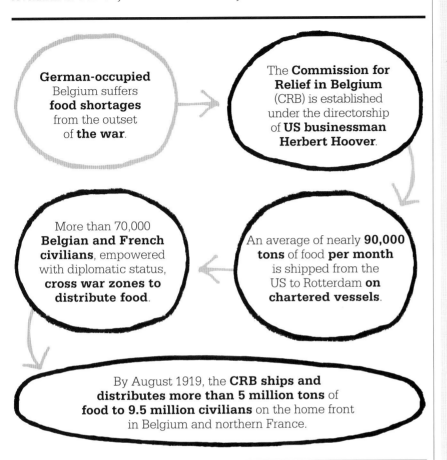

German-occupied Belgium suffers **food shortages** from the outset of **the war**.

The **Commission for Relief in Belgium** (CRB) is established under the directorship of **US businessman Herbert Hoover**.

More than 70,000 **Belgian and French civilians**, empowered with diplomatic status, **cross war zones to distribute food**.

An average of nearly **90,000 tons** of food **per month** is shipped from the US to Rotterdam **on chartered vessels**.

By August 1919, the **CRB ships and distributes more than 5 million tons** of **food to 9.5 million civilians** on the home front in Belgium and northern France.

in regions where the need was greatest, issuing around 30,000 rations each day.

European protests

In Britain, despite the first use of food rationing in January 1918, the country was faring better than most on the continent. Shops and pubs closed early to save on heat and light. Churches held services in the afternoons, and the revised Defence of the Realm Act (DORA) also specified that no gas or electric current should be used on stage at theatres or places of entertainment between 10:30pm and 1pm the following day. There were protests, but they were small.

The Central Powers suffered even greater food shortages, and earlier in the war, than the Allies. By 1918, the situation had reached crisis point. Following the halving of flour rations on 14 January, workers in Vienna, Austria, went on strike, demanding more food, better work conditions, and an end to the conflict. More than 40,000 workers joined in 15 demonstrations, and in the following days the strike spread from the capital to Lower Austria and Budapest, drawing in around 250,000 workers.

German people were quick to follow, since all but the richest were exhausted by work and hunger. On 25 January, 400,000 citizens took »

Food rationing

By the start of 1918, every European combatant nation was suffering food shortages. In Britain, rationing was introduced for the first time – for sugar in January, with meat, flour, and butter soon following. Ration books stipulated how much of these items each person could have. The French introduced bread rationing in Paris in January; people were allowed 300g (10.5oz) per day. In Italy, food rationing was severe, with even stricter limits than in other Allied nations.

In Germany, where grain had been rationed since 1915, crop yields fell to almost half their pre-war levels, affecting fodder supplies for animals. Livestock weights dropped, reducing meat and milk supplies. By July 1918, the consumption of meat was just 12 per cent of its pre-war level. However, the daily calorie intake had risen from summer 1917 – from 1,000 to 1,400 per day – as a result of a better harvest. Wealthier Germans ate better than industrial workers, because a third of all food was traded illicitly.

Women and children queue for sugar in Keighley, England, in 1917. That year, ration books were introduced in many countries.

to the streets of Berlin in a strike over lack of food and a call to end the war. The strike spread to major cities across the country, and clashes with the authorities led to injuries and deaths before it ended on 3 February.

Conscription crisis

While food shortages and hunger were the primary reason underlying social unrest, continued demands for more men for the front added to the growing anger. These were key factors leading to the Russian Revolution – and that country's withdrawal from the war – in late 1917. Then the success of the 1918 German Spring Offensive on the Western Front generated new demand for Allied soldiers.

In Britain, Prime Minister David Lloyd George drew up the Military Service Bill, extending conscription to men of 50 or younger, including men in Ireland. Anticipating that this would be controversial in Ireland, he appointed a new lord lieutenant of Ireland, Sir John French, to impose it. The Irish Parliamentary Party – previously sympathetic to Britain and the war – reacted to the bill with fury.

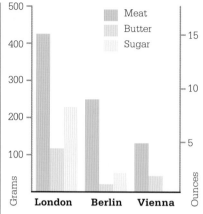

Food rationing varied according to both country and region. This chart compares the weekly per-person allowances in three European capitals.

Complaints of English military occupation and tyranny were no longer just separatist rhetoric. The Sinn Féin party drafted an anti-conscription pledge that was signed by hundreds of thousands of people, and the republican women's movement Cumann na mBan called for a day of protest. Plans were made for an insurrection, which was likely to be bloody.

On 23 April 1918, the threat of conscription in Ireland was ended – not by an uprising but because of a general strike. All work across all businesses was suspended, and, with the exception of a small part of Ulster, the country was paralysed. With Ireland at a standstill, the British backed down. Unrest continued, however. Public gatherings such as fairs and sports events were banned, for fear of republican meetings. Militant leaders were arrested over an alleged plot with Germany, which was no more than a rumour. The British were seen as cruel, unsympathetic overlords, a perception that led to the landslide victory of the radical Sinn Féin party in the general election of December 1918 and, ultimately, the declaration of Irish independence.

Canadian unrest

The conscription crisis in Ireland mirrored the Canadian experience from 1917, which affected Canadian attitudes towards Britain and bitterly divided Canada's French- and English-speaking populations. Prime Minister Robert Borden was a great supporter of the war, and in his New Year's Day message of 1916 he had promised the Allies a force of 500,000 men. With no volunteers in sight, a Military

A Hello Girl sits at the switchboard in a poster produced in 1918. More than 220 women travelled from the US to Europe to fill the role.

Hello Girls

On 8 November 1917, US Army officer General John Pershing sent a cable to his superiors to "request organization and dispatch to France [of] a force of women telephone operators all speaking French and English equally well". Pershing hoped to improve communications on the Western Front and wanted women to operate front-line switchboards. The women needed to act as translators between French- and English-speaking officers, so even bilingual women with no switchboard experience were offered training. Although they were civilian workers, the women were given uniforms and took an army oath.

Known as "Hello Girls", they began arriving in Europe in March 1918. Stationed across France and southern England, they handled switchboard duties around the clock.

At the end of the war, the women were refused honourable discharge papers. Despite a long-running campaign, it was not until 1977 that they were recognized as war veterans.

> The passing of the Conscription Bill ... must be regarded as a declaration of war on the Irish people.
> **Éamon de Valera**
> **Sinn Féin**

Service Act was announced that became law on 29 August 1917. It ruled that the government could, if necessary, call on men aged 20–45, which, by the end of the war, made more than 400,000 men liable for conscription.

Of the men who were liable for conscription, 93 per cent of the French Canadians of Quebec requested exemption. On 28 March 1918, federal officers in Quebec City arrested a man for not producing his exemption certificate and were assaulted by a crowd. The following day – Good Friday – the city's Military Service Registry office was burned and all records lost. By Saturday, troop reinforcements amounting to almost 2,000 men were called in. Rioters stormed shops for arms and threw snowballs at the soldiers. By the evening of 1 April, bricks and ice were used as missiles to attack a troop force that was nearly 2,500 strong, and shots were fired on both sides. Four civilians died in the violence before order was restored.

Famine and flu
By early summer 1918, the Central Powers' food supplies were failing. In Austria-Hungary, the weekly potato ration had fallen to 500 g (17.5 oz) per person, and with news from the front of between 69,000 and 118,000 men wounded, killed, or missing on the Piave river, tens of thousands of starving citizens rioted in Vienna's streets. Hungry protesters invaded the nearby potato fields to steal whatever they could.

The first wave of the Great Influenza had proved disastrous for all nations, with the number of dead increased by malnourishment and overcrowding on the front and in camps. In Austria-Hungary, deaths rose rapidly, reaching 18,500 by the end of the summer, and daily life in many towns ground to a halt when a lack of staff led to the cessation of transport and closure of public buildings.

American relief work
In the US, the home front was mobilized through the work of the US Food Administration (USFA), with women bolstered by the slogan "Food will win the war". Children were encouraged to eat their meals by being told to "think of the starving orphans of Europe", and women were exhorted to cut waste and eat less meat and wheat. Volunteers put care packages together with cigarettes, soap, safety pins, and socks for soldiers on the front; women and children knitted millions of pairs of socks.

The need for labourers in the northern states saw many Black Americans migrate from the south to take up jobs left vacant by men going to war. Women entered the workforce for the first time, many employed in factories. By the summer of 1918, women working to produce food, such as the Women's Land Army, had succeeded in improving conditions for agricultural workers, with labour contracts and guaranteed wages. Such advances finally put paid to objections to female suffrage, although this was not granted until the passing of the 19th Amendment in 1919.

By the autumn of 1918, all countries were experiencing degrees of economic and social unrest as the monetary and human cost of the war continued. For the German people on the home front, revolution was close. ∎

Three French women working the fields feature on an American poster of 1918. The USFA used such campaigns to encourage lower wheat consumption.

A WAR OF CRATERS AND POTHOLES

TRENCH WARFARE TRANSFORMED

IN CONTEXT

FOCUS
Trench warfare

BEFORE
1905 At the Battle of Mukden, in the Russo-Japanese War, mass firepower forces soldiers in the open to dig trenches to escape annihilation.

September 1914 Allied and German forces start to build deep trenches on the Western Front – a line that eventually stretches from Switzerland to the Belgian coast.

AFTER
1936–39 During the course of the Spanish Civil War, Nationalist and Republican forces build field fortifications, including trenches.

1950–53 Trench warfare becomes commonplace during the Korean War, especially in the later, static phase of the conflict.

The trench systems on the Western Front were in a constant state of development, becoming both deeper and more durable over the course of the war. This was particularly true of the German system, since the German army was on the defensive from 1915 to early 1918. It improved the living quarters of its front-line troops by excavating large underground caverns. Equipped with washing and sleeping facilities, these acted as artillery-proof barracks, enabling the trenches to be manned swiftly in case of attack.

The German army pioneered the use of reinforced concrete defences, too, which included the pillbox.

See also: Trenches take over 74–77 ▪ Artillery 228–29 ▪ The Nivelle Offensive 208–11 ▪ The Spring Offensive 260–67 ▪ The Battle of Amiens 274–77

A German deep-defence trench system

Supply lines

First support-line trench

Communication trench

Machine-gun nest

Sap (shallow, probing trench)

Wire obstacles

No-man's-land

Artillery battery

Underground bunker

Front-line trench

Barbed-wire entanglement defence line

Direction of enemy

Willy Rohr

Born in Metz, Alsace–Lorraine, in 1877, Willy Rohr attended the Prussian officer cadet's training school at Lichterfelde, in Berlin. Commissioned into an infantry regiment in 1896, Rohr rose to command a company in a Prussian Guards rifle battalion just before the outbreak of war in 1914.

After combat against the French on the River Aisne and in Champagne, Rohr was transferred to a company in the Vosges mountains of Alsace in 1915. During the fighting for the rocky spur of the Hartmannswillerkopf, he conceived the idea of using independent assault units – *Sturmtruppen* – to lead attacks. Throughout 1915 and 1916, Rohr trained German units in infiltration tactics, placing emphasis on the importance of grenades and flame-throwers.

Rohr's work brought him to the attention of Crown Prince Wilhelm and General Erich Ludendorff, who both encouraged him to spread his ideas throughout the army. He led his own assault battalion in numerous operations, before leaving the army in 1921. Rohr then worked in a bank until his death in 1930.

This was a small blockhouse – often hexagonal – with loopholes, or firing slits, that was virtually invulnerable to all but direct hits from heavy artillery. With vast stores of ammunition at their disposal, German troops deployed their MG 08 heavy machine guns inside the pillboxes, siting them to produce interlocking fields of fire. This would stop any unsupported infantry advance in its tracks.

Fortification lines

Barbed wire was a further defensive feature. Throughout 1914 and 1915, defences typically consisted of strands of barbed wire stretched between picket posts. However, by 1917, both sides on the Western Front were using huge rolls of concertina wire of increasing depth. On the Hindenburg Line system of fortifications, the Germans deployed razor wire up to 30 m (98 ft) deep – all but impenetrable to infantry.

For 1916 and much of 1917, the response to defensive advantages lay in increased artillery. The French army was well supplied with heavy guns and howitzers, which were far more effective than large numbers of smaller-calibre weapons. The British Army, by comparison, was slower to produce and deploy large-calibre artillery.

Creeping barrages

A long, heavy artillery barrage proved highly effective in smashing an opponent's front line, which could then be occupied by the infantry of the attacking army. The tactic of the "creeping barrage" became increasingly common, with the guns firing a protective curtain of exploding shells just in front of the advancing infantry, thereby preventing the opponent from defending forward positions. As the infantry moved forwards, so too did the artillery barrage.

The downside was that the artillery – along with other ancillary elements such as ammunition supply – could not advance through the churned-up battlefield. This meant that once the infantry had » advanced beyond the protective range of their guns, it became vulnerable. Consequently, most Allied offensives of 1916–17 slowed after about 3 km (2 miles).

Seeking a breakthrough

Other techniques were put forward to break the trench deadlock. British troops enjoyed some success with underground mining. They would dig shafts and galleries under no-man's-land to positions below the enemy front line, then pack them with vast amounts of explosives. Such methods were used at the Somme, but with limited effect. More successful was the blowing up of the mine under the Messines ridge in 1917, but even there the result was limited in scope.

Poison gas was first used on the Western Front by Germany at the Second Battle of Ypres in 1915. It did not win any battles, however, because the rapid and widespread acquisition of gas masks reduced its potentially fatal consequences.

Hopes of an Allied breakthrough were raised with the introduction of the tank by the British in 1916. Initially, these armoured monsters alarmed front-line German troops,

Machine after machine caught fire, and in a few seconds they were red glowing masses of metal.
Major Edward Spears
on a failed British tank attack, 1917

but new tactics and weapons, such as early anti-tank guns (artillery intended to destroy armoured vehicles), were introduced to slow their progress. Also, the mechanical unreliability of tanks minimized their usefulness on the battlefield.

More than defence

During the great battles of Verdun and the Somme, in 1916, the German army had launched instant and determined counterattacks against Allied incursions into their front line. This tactic helped hold the Allied attacks, but it was

extremely costly in casualties. During 1917, however, the Germans transformed their system into "defence in depth". The old linear-defence system – two or three continuous trench lines – was replaced by a front-line zone around 200–300 m (650–980 ft) deep that contained a series of interlocking strongpoints. Each strongpoint could deploy devastating firepower on any incoming attacker. The formidable Hindenburg Line, constructed in early 1917, utilized all the latest advances in German defensive tactics.

Despite its focus on defence, it was the German army that succeeded in breaking the trench deadlock. While Allied forces tended to concentrate on firepower, German strategists looked at developing new tactics. They tried out their ideas in the battles of the final three months of 1917, before unleashing the Spring Offensive against the Allies in March 1918.

New ways of shooting

A key element of the new German tactical approach was "predicted shooting". Previously, the operator of each artillery piece would fire

---

Ground-attack aircraft

From 1916 onwards, ground-attack aircraft were used on the Western Front – most of them existing aircraft given the new role of attacking opposing troops and vehicles with machine guns and bombs. These aircraft – made of wood and canvas – were, however, vulnerable to enemy small-arms fire, so special planes with steel panels around the engine and crew compartment were introduced. They included the experimental all-metal Junkers

J series and the Sopwith Salamander, the latter arriving too late to see war service.

Perhaps the best example was the German Halberstadt CL.II, a two-seat escort aircraft. Although it lacked any special armour, the CL.II was effective in a ground-attack role. The observer's machine gun was mounted on a wide and elevated gun ring, which enabled him to fire downwards at targets on the ground. The plane was also equipped with a tray to carry ten stick grenades, as well as small mortar bombs.

A German observer throws bombs from a Halberstadt CL.II. The CL.II was used at the Battle of Cambrai and during the 1918 Spring Offensive.

British soldiers of the 10th Battalion, Cameronians (Scottish Rifles), huddle in a sap awaiting orders. A sap was a shallow, crude trench extending into no-man's-land towards enemy lines.

"registering shells" at proposed targets to establish range, but this gave away both position and intention. With predicted shooting, gunners could calculate their target's position through accurate map plotting alone, allowing guns to be hidden and so maintain the element of surprise. A mass of guns could then fire a short but intense bombardment at a specific point on the enemy's front line.

Predicted shooting was developed independently by both sides, although it was the German army that would use it to particularly devastating effect in the 1918 Spring Offensive. Other advances introduced towards the end of 1917 included smoke shells, designed to obscure the infantry advance, and special fuses that detonated shells on immediate impact with any object. This made it much easier for explosives to cut through barbed wire.

Enter the stormtroopers

Throughout much of the war, tactics had been based on linear assaults by waves of infantry, which made troops vulnerable to well-sited machine guns. During the Verdun battles of 1916, the French army had begun to experiment with a new approach: the infiltration of enemy positions by small groups that could adapt their plans quickly to bypass the opponent's strongpoints and push to the next position.

The small-group idea was refined by the German army, which used it effectively during its counterattack at the Battle of Cambrai in November 1917. In a crucial strategic shift, conceived by Captain Willy Rohr, small units of well-trained troops were armed with light machine guns, flame-throwers, grenades, automatic pistols, and (in 1918) the new sub-machine gun. They also used light artillery guns that could be dragged across the broken terrain of the battlefield. These *Sturmtruppen* (stormtroopers), organized at company level and then at battalion level, became Germany's battlefield elite. The Allies never developed the skilful infiltration tactics of the German troops, but they came up with trench-warfare strategies that eventually broke the German army in the summer and autumn of 1918.

Combined arms

Part of the Allied success lay in the slow wearing down of Germany as a whole, but tactical innovations also played their part. During 1918, Allied strength was deployed in combined-arms operations that involved the coordinated use of all the military means available to the commanders of the Allied forces.

Infantry worked closely with tanks, which, while of limited overall use, proved adept at breaking into the enemy defences. The ground troops were supported by the artillery's creeping barrages, while scores of aircraft attacked the more exposed enemy positions with machine guns and bombs. Together, these disparate elements proved highly effective, so much so that the German army was forced to acknowledge it had been beaten on the battlefield. ∎

A line of British skirmishers advanced against the left of our trench. We were only just in time to stop them …
Lieutenant Kostlin
122nd Infantry Regiment, German army, on the Battle of the Somme

WE MUST SIGN AT ONCE. THE BEAST SPRINGS QUICKLY

GERMAN VICTORY IN EASTERN EUROPE (MARCH 1918)

IN CONTEXT

FOCUS
Russia defeated

BEFORE
1915 The Russian army evacuates Poland and parts of the Baltic States during the Great Retreat. Germany moves in and occupies them.

1917 The Russian Revolution sows chaos in Russia and fears of socialism among both the Allies and the Central Powers.

AFTER
1918–20 Forces from Allied nations fight on Russian soil in support of the White armies against the Soviet Red Army.

1945 At the end of World War II, the Russian armies reoccupy most of Eastern Europe, incorporating much of it into the USSR.

1991 After the break-up of the USSR, Russia's borders return very nearly to those in effect immediately after the Treaty of Brest-Litovsk.

O n 2 December 1917, after Russia and the Central Powers had signed a ceasefire agreement, a train from Petrograd pulled into the station at Brest-Litovsk (now Brest, in Belarus). It carried the Bolshevik armistice commission, led by fellow Russian revolutionaries Adolph Joffe and Lev Kamenev. They had come to meet the representatives of the Central Powers, including General Max

German officers greet Lev Kamenev (in the middle) and the Bolshevik delegation at the station of Brest-Litovsk, where treaty talks were held in the winter of 1917–18.

Hoffmann and Richard von Kühlmann for Germany, Count Ottokar Czernin for the Austro-Hungarian Empire, and Talaat Pasha for the Ottoman Empire.

Negotiating a peace treaty
A few days into the conference, Romania, Germany's other opponent on the Eastern Front, obtained a ceasefire from the Central Powers. With all fighting on the Eastern Front now halted, the negotiations at Brest-Litovsk shifted from discussions about armistice terms to demands for a permanent peace treaty – one that was unlikely to be accommodating towards Russia. To obtain a peace

See also: Crisis in Russia 24 ▪ The Battle of Tannenberg 78–81 ▪ Russia retreats 138–39 ▪ The Brusilov Offensive 166–69 ▪ The February Revolution 192–93 ▪ The Kerensky Offensive 224–25 ▪ The October Revolution 240–41

> The comrades must simply swallow what we have put before them.
> **General Max Hoffmann**

treaty on the most favourable territorial terms, the Bolshevik leaders had only one card to play: the threat of actively fomenting socialist revolution in every European empire.

The German negotiators in particular remained unswerving. The Baltic provinces, Poland, and Ukraine were to become satellite states of the German Empire. Trotsky countered, hoping for self-determination in those territories. However, on 18 January 1918, he was presented with a map, and

there was no mistaking the scale of territorial loss. He returned to Moscow to confer with Lenin and the Central Committee. The Bolsheviks vacillated for so long that the armistice expired, and by mid-February, Germany was back at war with Russia.

Russia defeated

The German army entered Minsk in Belarus on 20 February. It was closing in on Petrograd when Lenin persuaded the Central Committee of the Communist Party to accept peace on any terms – and they were particularly humiliating. Russia would lose a third of its pre-war population, half of its industrial land, a third of its arable land, and the majority of its coalfields. These resources all fell under German control. Russia signed the Treaty of Brest-Litovsk on 3 March.

After holding power for less than five months, the Bolshevik government had taken Russia out of World War I, thus fulfilling the promise made to the peasants

and workers who had elevated its leaders to supreme command. This move, however, alienated Britain, France, Italy, and the US, all of which refused to negotiate with the new regime.

The Treaty of Brest-Litovsk strengthened Imperial Germany, partly through colossal territorial concessions, when Bolshevik strategy had originally been to instigate socialist revolution there. Germany could now turn its full attention to the Western Front. ▪

Prince Leopold of Bavaria (seated, left) signs the Treaty of Brest-Litovsk. Russia had to make huge concessions, and some saw the Bolsheviks as traitors for agreeing to the terms.

Red Army troops salute as their banner is raised to celebrate the establishment of Soviet power in Tashkent, Uzbekistan, in 1917.

The Russian Civil War

In December 1917, the conflict on the Eastern Front was close to ending, but an undeclared war was just beginning – one that would probably be twice as bloody for Russia as World War I had been. Up to 10 million people, mostly civilians, died between 1917 and 1923, when the Red Army was challenged by competing White armies determined to destroy the Bolshevik menace.

Although 13 foreign nations, including Britain and the US, intervened on the side of the

Whites, the Red Army prevailed. This was partly because it was centred in the heart of Russia, while its antagonists invaded from around the periphery. By the end of the hostilities, the Red Army controlled such a vast area that it was standing on many of the old frontiers of the Russian tsarist empire.

Throughout the conflict, few prisoners were taken; instead, summary executions became the norm. In addition, the warring armies left paths of scorched earth and total destruction behind them.

AN UNIMAGINABLE AMOUNT OF GUNS

THE SPRING OFFENSIVE
(21 MARCH–18 JULY 1918)

IN CONTEXT

FOCUS
German offensive on the Western Front

BEFORE
February 1917 The German army begins withdrawing to the Hindenburg Line.

June 1917 The first 14,000 men of the American Expeditionary Forces (AEF) arrive in France.

February 1918 Anticipating the Treaty of Brest-Litovsk, General Ludendorff moves more than 40 divisions from the East to the Western Front.

AFTER
August 1918 The Allies launch the Battle of Amiens and the Hundred Days Offensive, which will result in victory over Germany.

October 1918 After two months of German retreats, Ludendorff resigns in disgrace and has to leave Germany in disguise.

The **German army** expects **fresh troops from the east**.

↓

General Erich Ludendorff seizes what might be the **last chance to launch** a **German offensive**.

↓

Stormtroopers' **infiltration tactics** bring **initial success**.

↓

But Germany's momentum cannot be sustained.

The final weeks of 1917 saw pressure mount on General Erich Ludendorff, the mastermind of the German high command. His forces were all but exhausted after three years of fighting. Allied forces were as well, but they could at least expect the assistance of larger numbers of US troops. The numbers of the American Expeditionary Forces (AEF) had been building slowly, but the pace was accelerating. While Russia's collapse in the east looked like it might free up German troops for the fight in France, these soldiers would not necessarily transform Germany's fortunes – they were tired and battle-weary. The war at sea had gone well for the Germans, but while their U-boat submarines remained a potent threat, it no longer seemed likely that they would be enough to win the conflict.

British commander Sir Douglas Haig was no more optimistic than Ludendorff. Just when he felt able to envisage a new offensive, he had seen five of his divisions transferred to the Italian front and had then been ordered to extend his line southwards to assist the French army. This turned a favourable position into a disadvantageous one. With a longer line to cover, Haig's forces were stretched too thinly to maintain anything more than a defensive posture – and a tenuous one at that.

Ludendorff became convinced that this was an opportunity – perhaps his last – to win the war. The British had spearheaded the Allied force, and now they were outnumbered on a lengthy front. With their seasoned troops worn out, and their new arrivals raw recruits, there was never going to be a better time to take on the Allies. The German army needed to deliver a devastating blow before the US Army could arrive in strength. So much depended

With a crash our barrage begins ... it must be from tens of thousands of gun barrels and mortars ... as if the world were coming to an end.
Lt Herbert Sulzbach
German 63rd Field Infantry

See also: The First Battle of the Marne 64–69 ▪ Germany's war machine 182–83 ▪ The Battle of Belleau Wood 268–69 ▪ The Second Battle of the Marne 270–73 ▪ The Battle of Amiens 274–77 ▪ Breaking the Hindenburg Line 290–93

on what Ludendorff loyally called the *Kaiserschlacht* ("Kaiser Fight") and historians, more prosaically, the German Spring Offensive.

Punching a hole

By his own admission, Ludendorff had no developed strategy. His armies would "punch a hole" in the British line, and then he would improvise. To ensure that first "punch" was forceful enough, he ordered several simultaneous attacks under the overall name of Operation Michael. The action opened on 21 March. "Michael I" saw General Otto von Below and his 17th Army advancing on Bapaume, and "Michael II" saw General Georg von der Marwitz heading southwest from Cambrai with his Second Army. Meanwhile, General Oskar von Hutier pushed westwards around Saint-Quentin with his 18th Army.

Ludendorff also kept some options in reserve. Operation Mars, around Arras, would assist the attack there if necessary, and Operation George could drive towards the River Lys region, which had major railway junctions and access to the Channel ports.

A knockout blow?

Launched at 4am by some 6,600 guns and more than 3,500 trench mortars, the opening bombardment surpassed even the inferno at Verdun in February 1916. More than 3.5 million shells were fired in the first five hours. These salvoes alternated with waves of gas and registration (aiming) fire before the German infantry advanced at 9:40am. They did so along a front stretching 110 km (68 miles) from Arras in the north to La Fère in the

south. Reconnaissance was carried out by 326 fighter planes, which also gave covering fire and fought the aircraft sent out by the British.

Led by General Hubert Gough, the British Fifth Army bore the brunt of the attack. It was well equipped, with almost as many planes as the opposing forces, and

more than 100 tanks. That there were as yet no German tanks might have been a mark of Germany's failing industrial capacity: despite the best efforts of the U-boats, the Allied blockade was taking its toll. Moreover, German bombardments apart, this was overwhelmingly an infantry attack. That appears to »

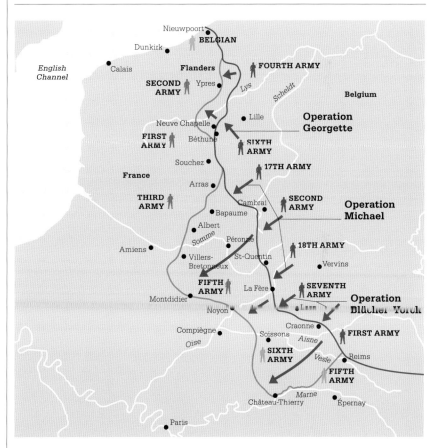

Operation Michael opened on 21 March with an artillery barrage and multipronged infantry offensive involving Germany's Second, 17th, and 18th armies. It made big territorial gains but came to a halt east of Amiens. On 7 April, the Second and Fourth armies launched the Operation Georgette offensive around Ypres. Operation Blücher–Yorck saw the First and Seventh armies push close to the Paris outskirts by 6 June.

Key:

- Belgian army
- British army
- French army
- German army
- → German offensives
- German front line, 21 March
- German front line, 6 June

have been a choice, though – many of the soldiers were stormtroopers, trained in infiltration tactics. They were highly mobile, using machine guns, mortars, flame-throwers, and *Stielhandgranate* (stick hand grenades) to spectacular effect.

Gough's troops were by now hardened to the grim realities of bombardment. They knew what it was to go "over the top" and run forwards into machine-gun fire. They had experienced the shock of being bombed from planes and attacked with poison gas. But the stormtroopers' close-quarters combat – dropping into trenches and fighting hand to hand – revealed a new, intimate, and utterly terrifying face of war.

The British line buckled before the attack, resistance wilting away. However, it did not collapse completely. Despite losing 17,000 killed or wounded men on the first day, Gough's troops conducted a courageous fighting retreat. The

Stormtroopers armed with stick hand grenades, rifles, and pistols attack Allied positions during the 1918 Spring Offensive. They were trained to infiltrate opposing trenches and generate panic.

German army had, though, broken through. Within the first three days, the attack had opened a gap of 80 km (50 miles) in the British front and forced the Fifth Army back some 64 km (40 miles), beyond the River Somme. By 26 March, the Germans had pushed forwards a further 32 km (20 miles) and forced Haig, with the remaining British armies, to fall back to Amiens. Meanwhile, a German breakthrough at Bapaume had introduced the possibility of the German troops driving a wedge between the British and their French allies further south.

Change of command

On 26 March, senior French and British politicians and army officers gathered in conference at Doullens, north of Amiens. French president Raymond Poincaré and Prime Minister Georges Clemenceau attended. A member of the British War Cabinet, Alfred Milner, represented Prime Minister David Lloyd George. Among the military commanders present were French generals Philippe Pétain and Ferdinand Foch; Haig led the British deputation. The meeting agreed that Foch should be placed in

command of Allied forces, not only on the Western Front but overall. Haig was known to be sceptical about Foch's abilities, and the appointment was almost certainly a slight by Lloyd George, who was sceptical about Haig. The British commander had to accept the decision. It mattered more to Haig that the conference had also resolved to send French reinforcements to bolster the British troops around Amiens.

Heading for Amiens

Encouraged by the progress his armies had made, Ludendorff set new objectives for them. The capture of Amiens, a relatively remote ambition until now, became a priority. A first outing for Britain's Whippet light tanks on 26 March sowed consternation among the German troops in the north, near Colincamps, 35 km (22 miles) northeast of Amiens, but their impact was strictly localized.

Further south, the British line gave way at Bray-sur-Somme, while French divisions around Roye were forced to retreat. German soldiers quickly occupied the town. Overnight, they reached

The Paris Gun

At the end of March 1918, the Germans were still 120 km (75 miles) from Paris, but their Kaiser Wilhelm Gun, or Paris Gun, had a range of 130 km (81 miles). Weighing nearly 230 tons and with a barrel length of 21 m (69 ft), it fired a 106 kg (234 lb) shell, which could reach an altitude of 42 km (26 miles). The range of the shell was such that the Earth's rotation affected its trajectory, and allowance for this had to be made when the gun was fired. Even so, the gun's accuracy was poor, and its explosive charge relatively small, although this scarcely mattered because its impact was largely psychological. The gun was so far from its Paris target that the people in the city had no way of knowing it had been fired. The shell fell without any warning.

The Krupp engineering company built the Paris Gun at its Essen works. Between March and August 1918, more than 320 shells bombarded Paris, killing around 250 people.

Albert, and the following day they were at Rosières-en-Santerre, only 30 km (20 miles) east of Amiens.

Operation Michael had made large territorial gains, but the Germans had not taken Amiens yet, and after its spectacular start, their advance risked losing momentum. With the Allies well dug in around Amiens, the German focus shifted again. On 28 March, Ludendorff gave the go-ahead for Operation Mars. The 17th Army pushed along both banks of the River Scarpe near Arras. The idea was to break the British forces there, prevent the Allies further south from securing the supplies they needed, and therefore ease pressure on the main Operation Michael attacks.

In the event, Operation Mars was unsuccessful. Huge as it was, its opening bombardment failed to suppress the British artillery, which then severely hindered the German infantry's advance. The offensive collapsed on its first day, calling into question all that Operation Michael had achieved.

By 5 April, Ludendorff was forced to acknowledge the failure of the operation when his troops were turned back at Villers-Bretonneux. They had come very close to taking this small but significant railway town east of Amiens. However, resolute resistance by British troops of the Third and Fifth armies – reinforced at the last moment by infantrymen of Australia's 15th Brigade – brought the German advance to a standstill.

Reassessing the situation

Even now, Ludendorff was not entirely out of options – although none looked like it might deal the

We reached the barbed wire, our objective … The wire was completely destroyed. There wasn't really any trench left, just craters and craters.
Private Paul Kretschmer
German 28th Pioneer Battalion

Allies the devastating blow that the German general had once imagined. It was an indication of his reduced strength that when Ludendorff now decided to execute Operation George, it had to be in a scaled-down form, as Operation Georgette. However, he could still field a formidable force: the 35 divisions – some 612,000 men – of his Sixth and Fourth armies, all trained in the stormtrooper tactics that had proved successful in the initial days of Operation Michael.

In the early morning of 7 April after a powerful bombardment, Ludendorff's forces pushed westwards across the valley of the River Lys. At the northern edge of their attacking line was what remained of the city of Ypres. (This engagement is often referred to as the Fourth Battle of Ypres.) As with earlier assaults in this area, the hope was to dislodge the British from Ypres and force them back to the Channel coast, leaving the French isolated from their Allies.

A British retreat to the coast was not inconceivable. Operation Michael might have failed, but the enemy was flagging. Rallying his exhausted troops on 11 April, »

German A7V tanks advance over rubble during Operation Michael. The relatively flat terrain of the region made tank-on-tank combat possible for the first time.

Haig had little to offer them by way of reassurance. They had to fight: they had their "backs to the wall", he told them. To the north of the British Army's line, its Belgian allies waited, in the difficult position of trying to defend an already conquered homeland; to the south were two depleted, disaffected Portuguese divisions.

Operation Georgette cut a swathe through the Allied lines, but, like Operation Michael, it ultimately failed. The Allied armies had no answer to the German stormtroopers, but again the attackers found themselves unable to follow through.

The first thrust of the German attack was in the south, against the Portuguese, whose resistance collapsed quickly and completely. The whole section crumpled as, immediately to the north, the British 40th Division fell back. Further north, though, the remaining British troops and the Belgians held firm. By the

time it had reached the River Lys, the German advance was losing impetus. With the Allied front-line forces defeated, the German stormtroopers now faced reserve troops who in theory could not compete with their battle skills. Greater Allied numbers, however, meant they were more than a match for the exhausted attackers.

Between 24 and 27 April, a second battle at Villers-Bretonneux witnessed the first time tanks had confronted each other, with 13 German A7Vs facing three British Mark IVs, backed up by a group of

lighter Whippets. However, the outcome was ultimately decided by hand-to-hand infantry combat. Australian and French-Moroccan troops braved a mustard-gas bombardment before seeing off Germany's Second Army after three days of ferocious fighting.

Germany advances again

A month went by before Ludendorff felt ready to resume his offensive. The immediate target of Operation Blücher–Yorck (27 May–6 June) was the French Sixth Army, commanded by General Denis

Portuguese soldiers rest before entering combat. They suffered heavy casualties in the German offensive of Operation Georgette.

Portuguese forces

Many British and French soldiers viewed their Portuguese allies with derision. It was claimed that they were lazy, unmotivated, and even cowardly. To some extent this was no more than northern European condescension towards a southern, "Latin" people – compounded by racial prejudice shown towards Black troops from Portugal's African colonies.

The reality was that Portugal was a reluctant combatant in World War I. A neutral country in 1914, Portugal had seen its

trade routes hampered by the U-boat campaign and found itself at odds with Germany along the borders of its colony Angola and German South-West Africa (modern-day Namibia). Despite this antagonism, it had been Germany that declared war on Portugal in 1916. Badly paid, poorly fed, and – by the late stages of the war – often leaderless due to the loss of so many officers, Portuguese troops saw little reason to risk their lives.

Auguste Duchêne. Supported by a section of the British IX Corps, the French troops were positioned along the Chemin des Dames ("The Ladies' Way"), on the high ground dividing the Aisne and Ailette river valleys. Although two previous battles had been fought over this ridge, which stood between the German armies and the approach to Paris, Ludendorff envisaged his main advance taking place in more level country to the north. The German general ordered an attack in strength, with 20 divisions of the First and Seventh armies. The sector had been quiet in recent months, so the French and British were taken by surprise.

A ruinous strategy

For Duchêne, who had helped recover the ridge from the Germans at the Second Battle of the Aisne the previous year, the Chemin des Dames was a hard-won prize. He was determined to defend it to the deaths of his French and British infantrymen. He had them massed together in a single defensive trench line, in defiance of Pétain's order to defend in depth. Consequently, the sudden German bombardment of 27 May took a dreadful toll, and the gas attack that followed killed many more. Over the next few days, in what became known as the Third Battle of the Aisne, the French sustained 98,000 casualties, the British, 29,000. The Germans lost a similar number but gained a tranche of territory, and they were 55 km (34 miles) nearer to Paris than they had been before.

Duchêne was dismissed, and the victorious Ludendorff tried to capitalize on the advantage he had won by unleashing Operation Gneisenau (8–11 June). This was

> So we had met our rivals at last! For the first time in history tank was encountering tank!
> **Frank Mitchell**
> **British tank commander**

initially successful, but France's General Charles Mangin handled his defensive operation much more capably than Duchêne had managed to do. The German forces became overstretched, which gave the French the chance to launch a successful counterattack.

One last push

The last throw of the dice for Ludendorff came on 15 July, when he tried to draw the Allies south and open up their front further with another diversionary thrust. The aim of this two-pronged attack was to envelop the city of Reims.

Ludendorff was optimistic. The Allies had yet to come up with an answer to the stormtrooper-style tactics he planned to use again for Operation Marneschutz–Reims. However, his army was exhausted, its numbers depleted, and its soldiers demoralized. German troops were increasingly angry at their poor rations – a consequence of the Allied blockade. The equally weary Allied troops could at least expect a decent amount of food and drink. In another ominous sign for Ludendorff, American troops were now starting to arrive in numbers on the Western Front. ∎

The Zeebrugge Raid

While the Allied blockade was biting hard in late 1917, trade was still reaching Germany, and U-boat submarines were still taking a toll on Allied shipping. In early 1918, the Royal Navy decided to mount a raid against Zeebrugge. A canal connected this Belgian port with Bruges, 12 km (7 miles) inland, which had an important U-boat base.

The plan was for the cruiser HMS *Vindictive* to approach behind a smokescreen and anchor by the sea wall shielding the harbour so that commandos could slip ashore and disable the gun batteries. Three old cruisers – the *Thetis*, *Intrepid*, and *Iphigenia* – would be sunk to block the canal entrance. On the night of 23 April, the raid went ahead, but it had to be abandoned when the wind blew away the smokescreen, exposing the attackers. More than 200 British men were killed and 365 wounded in the aborted raid.

The Zeebrugge block ships were sunk in the wrong place in the canal, and the German navy cleared them within days.

DO YOU WANT TO LIVE FOREVER?

THE BATTLE OF BELLEAU WOOD (1–26 JUNE 1918)

Following the withdrawal of Russia from the war in March 1918, Germany was able to move 33 divisions from the Eastern Front to the Western Front. The reinforcements allowed the German commanders to begin the first stage of their Spring Offensive – Operation Michael – pushing west and northwest towards Paris, Amiens, and the Channel ports.

On 27 May, Germany faced troops of the US Army when elements of the US First Division fought alongside French forces at Cantigny, 32 km (20 miles) southeast of Amiens. Philippe Pétain, French

We need support, but it is almost suicide to try to get it here as we are swept by machine-gun fire.
Clifton B. Cates
First lieutenant, US Marine Corps

commander-in-chief, asked for further American assistance. In response, General John J. Pershing, commander of the American Expeditionary Forces (AEF), sent the US Second and Third divisions. Further south, at Château-Thierry on the River Marne, the US Third Division fought alongside French colonial troops from Senegal on 31 May to successfully hold up the German advance.

Marines take the lead
Having been stopped at Château-Thierry, German soldiers advanced through Belleau Wood to the west. There, the US Second Division and a brigade of US Marines and their French colleagues fought off a large German attack with intense rifle fire.

When the French troops began falling back, they urged the Marines to do the same. However, the Americans fought on, repelling the German advance on 4 June. This bold stand marked a significant moment in the Marines' history.

A painful learning curve
After its failure to break the line, the German attack lost momentum, and the French and American troops launched a counterattack.

See also: The US and World War I 134–35 ▪ The US enters the war 194–95 ▪ Putting the US on a war footing 196–97 ▪ The Battle of Saint-Mihiel 278–79 ▪ The Meuse–Argonne Offensive 280–83

A gun crew from the US 23rd Infantry fires a 37 mm (1.5 in) infantry support gun at Belleau Wood. The gun, which required an aimer and a firer, could deliver up to 35 rounds per minute.

in hand-to-hand combat, the attackers succeeded in penetrating German defences at Belleau Wood.

The "Devil Dogs"

Battle raged on for 20 days, with attacks and counterattacks from both sides, until, by 26 June, the American troops were in possession of Belleau Wood. The victory marked a turning point in the war. The German forces had been made aware of the fighting spirit of their new enemy, especially the Marine Corps, whom they called the "Devil Dogs". The Marines' stand, in particular, was credited with halting the German advance towards Paris. With more than 1 million US Army troops in France by July and hundreds of thousands more arriving each month, any realistic possibility of Germany winning the war had effectively disappeared ▪

On 6 June, the US Marines and Britain's Third Infantry Brigade attacked Belleau Wood. The Marines' limited experience was soon evident, though, as they lacked the sophisticated infantry tactics British and French fighters had learned over four years of conflict, and their artillery and infantry were not closely coordinated. As American infantry advanced in waves, the fields were soon filled with the dead and wounded. The Marines suffered more than 1,000 casualties on the first day, but they refused to give in. Often engaging

James Harbord

Born in Bloomington, Illinois, in 1866, James Harbord built a reputation as one of the most influential US Army officers of the early 20th century. This is all the more remarkable considering his failure to get into the US Military Academy as a young man. Instead, he trained as a teacher before enlisting in the US Army in 1889, later being promoted through the ranks.

Harbord served as chief of staff of the AEF in 1917, building up large numbers of US Army troops on the Western Front. In spring 1918, he took command of the Fourth Marine Brigade, which fought with distinction at both Château-Thierry and Belleau Wood. Following his success at the latter, he was tasked with organizing AEF supply and troop movements, described as the largest business undertaking ever carried out by a single man. Harbord won widespread praise and the Distinguished Service Medal for his efficient organization. He left the army in 1922 to pursue a civilian career and died in New York in 1947.

THE STRONG AND BRAVE HEARTS OF FREE MEN BEAT IN YOUR BREAST

THE SECOND BATTLE OF THE MARNE (15–18 JULY 1918)

T he final German offensive on the Western Front, the Second Battle of the Marne, might have been another in a series of German victories in 1918. Instead, it was a German defeat, thanks to outstanding French leadership, fresh American troops, and a stubborn strategic blindness on the part of Erich Ludendorff, the German high command's chief strategist and operations planner.

Multiple offensives
Ludendorff's Spring Offensive had brought victory tantalizingly close, but each of its four operations had fallen short. All had been mounted to advance the ultimate objective,

See also: The First Battle of the Marne 64–69 ▪ The Gallipoli Campaign 122–29 ▪ The Spring Offensive 260–67 ▪ The Battle of Belleau Wood 268–69

With **the entry of the US into the war** imminent, Germany realizes it must make a **renewed push** for a quick victory.

⬇

Ludendorff breaks out of the **Soissons salient** and pretends his goal is Paris, **drawing Allied troops** from Flanders.

⬇

Foch preempts Ludendorff's strategy. Through bold counteroffensives, he changes the balance of power.

Ferdinand Foch

Born in Tarbes, France, in 1851, Ferdinand Foch had a conventional military career prior to World War I, one that alternated between field commands and military academies. He was a thinker, as well as a fighter, and he brought fresh ideas to the battlefield. He was excellent at coordinating men and plans, too, and in 1917 became chief of the French general staff. Foch also possessed diplomatic skills, invaluable in the Allied high command, with its clashing personalities from four nationalities.

In late March 1918, when the Spring Offensive and Germany victory were moving closer, Foch was made Allied Supreme Commander. After the success of the Second Battle of the Marne, for which he was made a Marshal of France, he planned the Grand Offensive, which ultimately won the war for the Allies. Within just six months, Foch had turned a perilous situation into a victorious one, and he is widely credited for formulating the strategy that led to Allied victory. He died in 1929 and was buried close to Napoleon I in Les Invalides, Paris.

an attack in Flanders, codenamed Operation Hagen, that would knock Britain out of the war and bring a peace treaty before American soldiers arrived en masse in Europe.

The first two operations of spring 1918 – Michael and Georgette – had been aimed directly at the British forces. France then shifted massive reserves north of the River Somme in support of the British, so a third offensive was little more than a diversionary attack on the French sector, designed to draw away those reserves while secretly building up German forces in Flanders. The offensive captured Soissons and threatened Paris, but the French reserves remained in place north of the Somme.

Salient problem

Ludendorff was now left with a huge salient – a front line bulging well into opposing territory close to the town of Soissons. This had to be supplied and defended against French troops and the rising

numbers of American forces fighting along its margins. The salient's single railway was not functioning, so the soldiers there would soon be starved of food and ammunition. The salient's southern face was on the River Marne, but the other two flanks were exposed, with no natural barriers to defend them.

With his pool of reinforcements running dry, discontent increasing in the ranks, the influenza epidemic taking its toll on his armies, and more US Army troops arriving every day, Ludendorff had no alternative but to launch a fifth offensive (a fourth one having collapsed) along the Marne. The attack had to be strong enough to divert the French reserves, even if Operation Hagen had to be postponed until August.

Foch's opportunities

The Allies had been studying the German salient. It stretched 40 km (25 miles) south from Soissons, just inside the salient's northwest face, to Château-Thierry on the south » bank of the Marne. It was a little wider than it was deep, enclosing a largely open, partially wooded countryside of farms and villages that the Allies knew well, having recently been pushed from it.

By early July, Supreme Allied Commander Ferdinand Foch began to draw up a plan. The rail and road junction of Soissons was within easy reach of a strike from the western face of the salient, as was the main road to Château-Thierry, just 13 km (8 miles) behind the front. By punching through near Soissons, the French would have an excellent chance to encircle and destroy the German divisions in the salient.

Foch did not find it easy to convince French commander-in-chief Philippe Pétain or American Expeditionary Forces (AEF) commander John J. Pershing to undertake the offensive, but he was helped by a lucky break. A trench raid had netted a number of German prisoners, and interrogations of those men had gleaned enough intelligence to adequately prepare for a forthcoming German onslaught. It was codenamed Operation Marneschutz–Reims, but the German planners also called it

Friedensturm, or "Peace Offensive", supposing it would be the final attack of the war. When it came, however, the Franco-American forces would be ready.

Ludendorff's strategy

The *Friedensturm* plan had several objectives. First, the offensive would capture Reims, the rail junction northeast of the salient, via a two-pronged attack, one prong driving down from north of the Aisne river, the other up from the south, bursting out of the salient. Then the offensive would make a strong feint at Paris, which would force the French reserves to cross the Somme and fight for the capital.

Officers of the 62nd Division of the British Army consult with French and Italian counterparts during the Battle of Tardenois, one phase of the Allied counteroffensive on the Marne.

Other divisions would smash through Champagne, overrunning Châlons-sur-Marne, Épernay, and the Argonne Forest, and neatly outflanking Verdun. That would attract every available Allied division, leaving the British line in the north vulnerable. Ludendorff planned to commit all 52 divisions he had in reserve to *Friedensturm*.

The German attack was due to start at 12:10am on 15 July, but French batteries preempted it on 14 July at 11:30pm, raining shells down on the massed assault columns. The subsequent three-hour German bombardment, including poison gas, pulverized the French first line. The oncoming attack waves were not surprised to encounter no resistance there – until they realized that the French had purposely left their posts and were massed 5 km (3 miles) to the rear. This tactic meant that the German attack from the northeast towards Champagne, along a front 32 km (20 miles) long, was repulsed the same day.

Aborted plans

The breakout from the salient was a closer-fought battle. Stormtroopers crossed the Marne on boats, rafts, and skeleton bridges, establishing a bridgehead on the south bank. Furious fighting erupted, and at one point the US Third Division was nearly surrounded, but it stood fast, its 38th Regiment winning the sobriquet "Rock of the Marne".

In the meantime, Foch had extinguished any panic in Paris and ensured that the French reserves remained north of the Somme.

Siamese involvement

One of the "associated nations" siding with the Allied powers also sent an expeditionary force to the French front in 1918, but its detachments arrived at the Marne just after the fighting there had ended. The Kingdom of Siam (now Thailand), which was opposed to unrestricted submarine warfare, had declared war on Germany in 1917. To its nationalist head of state King Vajiravudh, this was no empty gesture. He wanted the Siamese flag to fly over the battlefields of the "Great War", and expose his small army to modern combat.

On 30 July 1918, more than 1,200 Siamese officers and troops arrived in Marseille, although none was destined to fight at the front. However, a motor corps was in Châlons-sur-Marne by October, moving men and materials between the front and the rear. This also helped supply the US Army during the Meuse–Argonne Offensive. Later, the Siamese Expeditionary Force participated in the occupation of the German Rhineland.

Despite a 32-km (20-mile) expansion of the salient, the German high command cancelled the offensive when it was barely two days old. It had been a costly failure. Ludendorff began transferring men and heavy artillery out of the salient, sending them north for a knock-out blow against British forces in Flanders. Soon that plan was rescinded, too.

Allied counterattack

In the days before the German offensive was due to start, while Ludendorff moved his men north, Foch was putting his own plan into action on the Marne. All appeared quiet on the front west of Soissons. After nightfall, however, there was much activity, confusing the many American soldiers moving into the sector, because even their officers did not know what was happening.

Foch would strike both outer faces of the salient, the main blow delivered by General Charles Mangin's Tenth Army just south of Soissons, with the aim of cutting the road and rail line. Mangin's spearhead would be the US First and Second divisions, the most experienced of the 26 American

French 75 mm (3 in) field guns are trained on German positions in the Soissons salient in July 1918, just prior to the Second Battle of the Marne.

The history of the world was played out in three days.
Georg von Hertling
German chancellor

divisions that were then in France. The spearhead's leading edge, however, was the First Moroccan Division, including numbers of Senegalese troops. The Allied forces marshalling along the southern and eastern faces of the salient included two large French armies, the US 42nd, or "Rainbow", Division, and some Italian and British divisions.

On 17 July, the German *Friedensturm* was halted; but early the following morning, the Allied spearhead, having assembled under the cover of bordering forests, began sweeping towards the German positions. There was no preliminary bombardment, only a rolling barrage preceding the advance. Hundreds of French tanks took part in one of the largest armoured assaults of the war. Masses of Allied aircraft soon

appeared, bombing the defenders, who retreated. Foch had neatly reversed the German strategy – while keeping his own reserve north of the Somme, he now drew seven German divisions from the Hagen force into trying to stem his attack.

The beginning of the end

Fieldworks were rudimentary in this sector of the Western Front, so the Allies pushing into the salient fought in woodlands and wheat fields and around farms and villages, wherever machine guns could be sited quickly. Casualties were high on both sides – more than 300,000 men were killed, wounded, or captured during the operation – but the Allies' momentum proved unstoppable. Within 48 hours, the spearhead had reached the road and railway that were its principal objectives. Within a week, nearly half the salient had been cleared.

On 6 August, the front had nearly reached the Aisne river, not far from the original German position. Two days later came the British breakthrough at Amiens – the first of the Hundred Days victories that would bring the war to an end in November. "Foch's Counterstroke", as the battle was initially called, meant Operation Hagen would never be realized. ∎

WE STAND AT THE TURNING POINT OF THE WAR

THE BATTLE OF AMIENS (AUGUST 1918)

IN CONTEXT

FOCUS
Allied advances

BEFORE
March 1918 German General Erich Ludendorff launches his Spring Offensive.

April 1918 The Great Influenza arrives in Europe, ravaging the weary German army.

July 1918 After defeat at the Second Battle of the Marne, Ludendorff abandons plans for another Marne offensive.

AFTER
September 1918 Ludendorff orders his forces to withdraw to the Hindenburg Line.

October 1918 German chancellor Prince Maximilian von Baden writes to US president Woodrow Wilson, accepting his Fourteen Points.

November 1918 Germany's Kaiser Wilhelm II abdicates.

T he situation around the French city of Amiens had changed little since early April 1918, when Operation Michael – the first stage of Germany's Spring Offensive – had foundered there. The British were well dug in, and Field Marshal Sir Douglas Haig had been planning to make Amiens the centre of a counteroffensive led by General Sir Henry Rawlinson's Fourth Army. For a number of weeks, Allied reinforcements had been arriving in the utmost secrecy.

The forces at Rawlinson's disposal included more than 2,000 guns, 342 Mark IV and Mark V heavy tanks, and 72 lightweight

See also: The Somme 172–79 ▪ The Battle of Cambrai 237 ▪ The Spring Offensive 260–67 ▪ The Second Battle of the Marne 270–73

Whippets, in addition to 1,900 British and French aircraft. The German army was still there in some degree of strength. The 10 divisions of General Georg von der Marwitz's Second Army were encamped east of the city, but their numbers were much depleted and morale was low. Their position looked more vulnerable still in light of the French and American victory against General Erich Ludendorff's forces at the Second Battle of the Marne.

The fog of war

All the indications were that the German troops had no idea what action Haig had been preparing, as the British commander recorded in his diary on the night of 7 August. Even so, Marwitz must have known that it was only a matter of time before the Allies went on the attack at Amiens.

On 8 August, time ran out for Marwitz. A sudden barrage at 4:20am was the only warning the German troops received that battle was about to commence. This rolling barrage was followed by an advancing line of men. Not that Marwitz's troops could see them. The usual mists of morning had given way to a thick fog that reduced visibility to next to nothing. This was a problem for the attackers, too. They could scarcely see their comrades and could only hear the rumble of their tanks ahead.

Fortunately for the Allies, the German troops were scrambling to organize themselves, so the machine-gun fire that greeted them was sporadic; the foggy conditions ensured that it was inaccurate, too. The heavy tanks took the worst of it as they crushed the barbed wire beneath their tracks. Coming up behind, the British and Empire soldiers found themselves walking over a mat of tangled steel 15–20 cm (6–8 in) thick, an indication of just how much barbed wire there had been.

The French troops had waited about an hour before beginning their advance. With no tanks, they needed a longer bombardment – both to soften up the German positions and to shred the barbed wire in front of them. However, »

John Monash and the Australian Corps

Born in 1865 to Jewish parents in Melbourne, John Monash trained and worked as a civil engineer until the war broke out, although he had joined the Australian Army Reserve as a student in 1884. He rose fast through the ranks and in 1912 was given command of the 13th Infantry Brigade, which remained a reservist unit until the war.

Monash served at Gallipoli and Suez before being moved with his men to the Western Front and made a major general. He came into his own in actions against the German Spring Offensive of 1918, including the Second Battle of Villers-Bretonneux. In June, he was promoted to the rank of lieutenant general and given command of the Australian Corps – five divisions numbering more than 100,000 men. The victory at Amiens was the first in a string of successes for the Australian Corps during the Hundred Days Offensive.

Monash was knighted on the battlefield in 1918. He died in 1931 and received a state funeral in Australia.

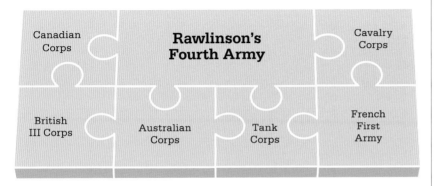

Field Marshal Haig's reinforcement plan doubled General Rawlinson's Fourth Army's divisions from seven to 14. It was a diverse combination of soldiers from Britain and its Dominions of Australia and Canada, backed up by the French First Army under the command of General Marie Eugène Debeney.

they had not wanted to deny their British allies the advantage of a surprise attack.

There were setbacks. In some places, the German soldiers reacted more speedily and resolutely than in others. Allied units struggled to break through. However, by 7:30am, the British had overcome the first line of defence in the German centre, opening up a gap through which the cavalry and Whippet tanks could seize positions at some distance behind the action at the front. ("We just motored straight through", Ralph Cooney of the Tank Corps would recall.) Further infantrymen followed in their wake. Above, the skies were crisscrossed by the planes of the RAF, which bombed and strafed enemy artillery and machine-gun nests. Such combined-arms coordination – of artillery, tanks, airpower, and infantry – had never been seen before and provided a glimpse of the future of land warfare.

Placing blame

The Allied infantry were braced for fierce resistance, but in many cases they found themselves pushing at an open door. In account after account, Allied veterans of Amiens recorded their astonishment at seeing so many German troops coming out of their trenches with their hands raised in surrender.

General Ludendorff took no responsibility for the condition of an army he had driven so hard since late March. Instead, he blamed the troops. Writing in his memoirs later, he recast this first of many mass surrenders as a symptom of the revolutionary socialism that would topple the German monarchy at the end of the war. He alleged that socialist agitators had undermined the discipline of the army and that crowds of deserters had jeered at comrades they saw advancing bravely into battle, denouncing them as "blacklegs". They were only "prolonging the war", the agitators claimed.

The **Allied blockade** paralyses the **German economy**, producing **widespread hardship**.

The **flu epidemic** takes a **disproportionate toll** on an **ill-nourished German population**.

↓

↓

The **Allied effort** is **reinvigorated** by the **arrival of fresh troops** and **new equipment** from the US.

Germany is **exhausted**.

↓

↓

The conditions are ideal for Allied advances.

Whippet tanks

Conceived initially as a support for the infantry, Whippet tanks trundled forwards, strafing the enemy front line and crushing barbed wire as the foot soldiers followed behind. The tanks' success in that role had suggested further possibilities for armoured vehicles that could move more swiftly. Such machines might, for example, be able to make lightning attacks on enemy lines through the gaps that the heavier tanks had opened up.

There was a degree of wishful thinking in calling the Medium Mark A the "Whippet" – its top speed was a sedate 13 kph (8 mph). However, this was twice as fast as the heavier Mark II or Mark IV tanks. As a result, the Whippet was a genuine step forwards and promised to transform the infant art of tank warfare.

The Medium Mark A Whippet, designed by British engineer William Tritton, was powered by two double-decker bus engines.

It would have been surprising if some of the disillusionment felt by the German population as a whole, after years of hardship and frustration, had not found its way into the armed forces. The soldiers at the front had been expected to sacrifice their lives and suffer desperate privations for a country that had failed to find a way even to feed them properly. However, it is doubtful that this mutinous spirit prevailed at the Battle of Amiens. Ludendorff certainly did not provide anything in the way of evidence for his claims, content to rely on comforting hearsay from like-minded friends.

The battle is decided

As many as 12,000 German troops were taken prisoner on the first day of the battle alone. To their captors, they seemed beaten, bedraggled, and in many cases physically reduced, especially by comparison with the tough soldiers they had encountered at the Somme in 1916. ("The scrapings of the barrel", as one Allied soldier described them.) Bursting into one dugout, ready to kill, Lieutenant Edgar Rule of the Australian army was disconcerted

> August 8 was the Black Day of the German army. It put the decline of our fighting powers beyond all doubt.
> **General Erich Ludendorff**

to find a group of frightened boys he felt could not have been more than 14 or 15 years old – "With a boot to help them along, they ran with their hands above their heads back to our lines."

The failure of the German army to mount a determined fightback undoubtedly decided the battle. The British Fourth Army pushed forwards more than 13 km (8 miles) that first day.

New arrivals

The Fourth Army encountered some difficulties, however. The speed of the Allied advance overstretched the column, creating communication problems between the advance guard and the rear. Certainly, the advance slowed abruptly. The German units that had managed to ride out the storm on the first day now had time to regroup, and the element of surprise was gone. The next day's fighting was ferocious, and the Allied forces secured an advance of only 5 km (3 miles). This brought them onto the unforgiving terrain

Captured German soldiers march along a road near Amiens. Handling such large numbers of prisoners became a major logistic challenge.

of the old Somme battlefield, further slowing their advance. The Allied army arrived there just in time to meet a fresh influx of German reinforcements – eight divisions, comprising around 100,000 men.

The Allied attackers faced other problems. As at Cambrai, in 1917, the Mark IV and Whippet tanks ceased to be a boon and started to become a liability. They were in constant need of maintenance and sometimes broke down completely.

Haig could see that it was time to withdraw. Like Ludendorff's offensive five months before, Haig's operation had stalled after a promising start. However, the British field marshal had the luxury of choice. Time was on his side, allowing his forces to grow in strength while Ludendorff's troops were fading. Haig now had a range of attacking options to try out elsewhere on the front. ∎

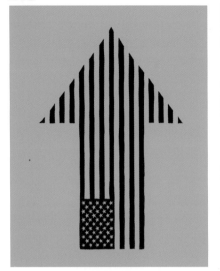

THE GREATEST ARMY EVER UNDER THE AMERICAN FLAG
THE BATTLE OF SAINT-MIHIEL (12–16 SEPTEMBER 1918)

IN CONTEXT

FOCUS
American forces

BEFORE
April 1918 General Pershing plans for a huge US army, properly trained and organized before entering combat.

May 1918 US Army troops go into action on the Western Front alongside the French.

August 1918 The First US Army is created, fulfilling Pershing's dream of an independent American army.

AFTER
September 1918 After Saint-Mihiel, US Army troops and equipment are moved 97 km (60 miles) in just ten days to take part in the Meuse–Argonne Offensive.

November 1918 The US Army continues fighting until the Armistice, by which time it is close to taking Sedan, near the France–Belgium border.

Some 300,000 American recruits arrived in France every month during the summer of 1918. Known as "doughboys", they learned combat skills in training camps or as fighting units under French or British command. By the middle of September, more than 1.5 million US Army troops were available to fight on the Western Front as part of the new US First Army. Their commander, General John J. Pershing, agreed with the overall commander of Allied forces,

American troops parade down Fifth Avenue, New York, before departing for France in September 1917. The number of army recruits accelerated in 1918.

Ferdinand Foch, that the American troops would attack the Saint-Mihiel salient, a triangular bulge in the front line 48 km (30 miles) wide between Verdun and Nancy, which the German army had occupied since 1914. The German withdrawal to the Hindenburg Line had left the bulge only lightly defended, so it was a relatively soft target.

Battle begins
On 12 September 1918, Pershing launched the war's first offensive by an independent American force. He used more than half a million US infantry, supported by Allied artillery, and 267 tanks, mostly crewed by Americans and led by Lieutenant Colonel George Patton.

See also: Germany's war machine 182–83 ▪ The US enters the war 194–95 ▪ The Battle of Belleau Wood 268–69 ▪ The Meuse–Argonne Offensive 280–83

The five-day offensive at Saint-Mihiel saw the recently organized US First Army and four French divisions under US command attack and capture positions that the Germans had held for nearly four years.

Key:

 French division

 US division  US corps

—— Allied front line, 12 September

—— Allied front line, 16 September

John J. Pershing

Born in Laclede, Missouri, in 1860, John Pershing graduated from the US Military Academy in 1886. He fought the Spanish army in Cuba, served in the Philippines, then led the campaign to capture Mexican revolutionary Pancho Villa. Pershing was appointed a major general before the US joined World War I and had established a reputation for being a strict disciplinarian.

Selected by President Wilson to command American troops in Europe, Pershing was known for his administrative capabilities and ability to put plans into action. He was convinced that the German army could only be beaten by superior numbers and suggested recruiting at least 1 million men. Pershing refused to allow his recruits to join existing Allied forces, fearing that they would suffer unacceptable losses. Instead, he insisted on the creation of an independent American force: the First US Army.

Pershing's nickname – "Black Jack" – was said to come from his admiration of the Black American cavalry he commanded early in his career. He died in 1948.

The US Army Air Service provided air support from 1,400 aircraft, whose operations were commanded by Colonel Billy Mitchell.

Facing the offensive, German commander Erich Ludendorff was short of men. Once he realized that American soldiers were amassing in huge numbers, he started to withdraw from the salient to a defensive line at the rear. Falling back, and with no artillery in place, the defenders were caught off-guard.

Light opposition

The battle started with a four-hour artillery bombardment, followed by an infantry and tank advance behind a creeping barrage. The troops crossed massed barbed wire under heavy machine-gun fire, while avoiding mortar bombs left by German fighters as booby traps. While some German soldiers fought back, many surrendered quickly.

By the end of the first day, the American advance was a day ahead of schedule. The following day, lead units of the First US Army met up with Allied troops advancing from the west. By 16 September, the salient was under American control, and the battle was called off. As many

as 16,000 German soldiers were captured, with at least another 7,500 killed or injured. American casualties were around 7,000 – far fewer than the expected 50,000.

Logistical failings

In the excitement of a first American victory, the logistical problems that beset the offensive were overlooked. These included massive traffic congestion behind the lines and severe supply failings, which left many troops short of food and water. Nevertheless, the Saint-Mihiel offensive was a triumph for Pershing and the US. ∎

… the United States physically enter[ed] the war, so god-like, so magnificent, so splendidly unimpaired …
Vera Brittain
British nurse, *Testament of Youth*, 1933

WHOLESALE MURDER

THE MEUSE–ARGONNE OFFENSIVE (26 SEPTEMBER–11 NOVEMBER 1918)

IN CONTEXT

FOCUS
American soldiers in battle

BEFORE
1775–83 During the American Revolutionary War, American forces win some victories but depend heavily on the French army and navy.

May–September 1918 The AEF shows its mettle at Belleau Wood, Château-Thierry, the Second Battle of the Marne, and the closing of the Saint-Mihiel salient.

AFTER
1937 The Meuse–Argonne Memorial commemorating the sacrifice of American troops is unveiled at Montfaucon-d'Argonne, near Verdun.

1944 In World War II, General Patton returns to France with the US Third Army to liberate Montfaucon-d'Argonne from the German army again.

The Meuse–Argonne Offensive was the largest operation of the American Expeditionary Forces (AEF) in World War I. More than 1 million soldiers were involved. The fact that so many had even reached France, at a time of unrestricted submarine warfare, was itself a miracle in overseas transport. The operation was also the deadliest military campaign in US history, thanks largely to the limited training and inexperience of the troops. Nevertheless, the AEF did manage to break through the Hindenburg Line and advance to its strategic objective – taking the town of Scdan, on the River Meuse.

See also: The Battle of Verdun 152–59 ▪ The US enters the war 194–95 ▪ The Battle of Belleau Wood 268–69 ▪ The Second Battle of the Marne 270–73 ▪ The Battle of Amiens 274–77 ▪ The Battle of Saint-Mihiel 278–79

About 15,000 officers and men of the 92nd Infantry served with the AEF on the Western Front; several won military honours.

Buffalo Soldiers

On the left flank of the Meuse–Argonne AEF formation, the Black American troops of the 92nd Division wore US Army uniforms but donned blue French helmets and wielded French weapons. Their own helmets were emblazoned with a bison, which led to them being called the "Buffalo Soldiers". Although the troops fought under US command, the racist policies of the army prevented them from serving in combat with white American soldiers – on the grounds that the latter might harass them or refuse to fight alongside them. Such prejudice was shared at every level in the US Army.

The other Black American unit to see service on the Western Front, the 93rd Infantry (or "Blue Helmets"), fought under French command and included the 369th Infantry, the Harlem Hellfighters.

When given the opportunity, Black American soldiers fought with distinction: 75 were later awarded Distinguished Service Crosses, and 527 received Croix de Guerre medals from France.

On 3 September 1918, after the British breakthrough at Amiens, the Allied commanders-in-chief agreed on a strategy to end the war. They believed one final coordinated offensive, from the Channel coast in the north to the River Meuse in the south, aimed at breaking the Hindenburg Line, would wipe out the German army.

US Army put to the test

For AEF commander General John Pershing, it was an opportunity to prove the skill of American soldiers when led by their own countrymen, rather than just shoring up the Allied line wherever fresh divisions were needed. The AEF would now fight as a unit on its own sector of the front, a 48-km (30-mile) stretch between the Argonne Forest in the west and the River Meuse.

Although narrow, the sector was critically important. The AEF's objective Sedan, backed by the forested Ardennes massif, was only 56 km (35 miles) north of the front. A four-tracked railway ran through Sedan, following the arc of the Western Front. It was the German army's lifeline, transporting supplies and reinforcements from one sector to another. At no other point on the Western Front was that railway so close to the fighting. If it were cut, the German army would be forced to fall back to the River Rhine.

The terrain between the AEF's starting point and Sedan, however, was formidably rugged. Like the Ardennes massif, beyond the Meuse, the north–south ridge of the Argonne Forest was cut by gorges and ravines. The countryside between the forest and the river was relatively open but studded with small hills and peaks. The terrain had seen intense fighting earlier in the war and was now heavily fortified, bristling with thousands of machine-gun nests, artillery emplacements, and pillboxes, all protected by large areas of barbed wire. The three primary German defensive lines, anchored on the Hindenburg Line, were here jumbled together rather than clearly delineated.

The AEF would have to punch its way through with a series of strong frontal attacks. It was hoped that such assaults would create »

Troops of the AEF prepare for the assault on the Argonne Forest. Progress was slow through the labyrinth of ravines, tangled vegetation, and lines of German defences.

saliens in the German line – providing opportunities for flanking movements. It would be bloody work, and Pershing was still extricating his veteran units from the successful Saint-Mihiel salient campaign when the combined Allied offensive launch date of 26 September was upon him.

The first phase

By the night of 25 September, the three corps of the US First Army were in place. However, only five of the nine divisions had seen combat, and only three had served with their own divisional artillery. Nevertheless, late that night, the French troops opened a preliminary bombardment with hundreds of phosgene and mustard-gas shells, catching the front-line German defenders by surprise, killing or disabling thousands of them. That was followed by the Americans' own two-hour bombardment from 2,700 guns – and at 5:30am on 26 September the US infantry advanced, following a creeping barrage and covered by dense fog.

The infantry easily overran the first line of stunned German survivors. Except for the left wing,

> The ground shook to the explosions. It was the supreme power of the artillery, absolute devastation.
>
> **Anonymous eyewitness**
> **on the barrage of 1 November**

which penetrated only 1.6 km (1 mile) into the forest, the American divisions advanced nearly 16 km (10 miles) that day. On 27 September, they assaulted and captured the ruined village of Montfaucon -d'Argonne – one of their principal goals – sitting atop high ground, and took 23,000 prisoners. Then German resistance stiffened, and the US advance crawled to a halt.

On the 29th, three days into his offensive, Pershing ordered the First Army to stand on the defensive. His advance into the tangled enemy trenches had outrun his artillery

support, which was hampered by the lack of roads. In addition, congestion in the rear had stalled the delivery of ammunition, tents, and overcoats, now vital in the cold, wet conditions. Furthermore, seven German divisions of reinforcements had been hurried to this sector. The fighting along the front was heavy and continuous, casualties were mounting, and one entire division (the 35th) had suffered so many losses that it had to be replaced. The lack of training in small-unit coordination was apparent.

French commander Ferdinand Foch was disappointed, and his British counterpart Douglas Haig was openly contemptuous. Their own units were steamrolling ahead, and the German high command was urging its government to tender a peace offer to the Allies.

The second phase

Pershing, meanwhile, had been furiously reorganizing. Engineers were rebuilding the roads despite rain and German shelling, so that men and ammunition could move to the front, and wounded men could be taken to field hospitals. On 4 October, the US First Army

A soldier releases carrier pigeons on the Western Front. The birds' speed and homing instinct made them useful message carriers.

The war pigeon

World War I was one of the last major conflicts in which carrier pigeons were still widely used. For thousands of years, warriors had recognized the carrier, or homing, pigeon's remarkable ability to zone in on its roost site from many miles away, even if that location was a portable one travelling with an army. Pigeons made natural messengers for troops on the move.

When American officer Charles Whittlesey needed to dispatch an important message to army

headquarters, he entrusted it to carrier pigeon Cher Ami, which flew through a hail of gunfire and lost most of one leg before arriving at divisional HQ 40 km (25 miles) away.

Cher Ami's heroism became renowned. The French awarded him a Croix de Guerre medal with an oak leaf cluster. General Pershing personally attended his departure by boat to the US. Even after the bird died of his wounds in 1919, he remained in the public eye – as a mounted specimen in the Smithsonian Institution in Washington, DC.

American infantry soldiers mount an attack against German lines through the Argonne Forest – in a sketch by French artist Lucien Jonas. The dense woodland was a more rugged challenge than much of the Western Front.

again went on the attack. Its tactical objectives were to clear the German artillery now firing from the Argonne Forest and the heights beyond the Meuse. That continuous shelling could not be withstood any longer.

The drive to outflank German positions in the Argonne Forest was particularly noteworthy. It is linked with the fate of the "Lost Battalion", 554 men who a few days earlier had crept so far forward in the forest that they had been cut off and surrounded. For four days, they huddled in a large ravine while German artillery and machine-gun fire rained down on them. Their dead lay unburied and their wounded untended. They had no food, no ammunition, and little water. The men were even mistakenly shelled by their own side, and their commander, Major Charles Whittlesey, sent his last carrier pigeon, Cher Ami, winging through German fire with a message saying, "Our artillery is dropping a barrage directly on us. For heaven's sake stop it."

The flank attack in the Argonne forced the Germans to break off the siege, and on 7 October Whittlesey and 193 others walked out. A further 202 were carried out on stretchers; the remaining 159 were dead.

By 9 October, the German formations were pulling north, abandoning the Argonne Forest. Across the Meuse, Pershing's divisions had also been successful, clearing the heights of much artillery and capturing 3,000 prisoners. In the centre, facing

north, his divisions had breached the Hindenburg Line in several places. By mid-October, however, the American momentum had once more slackened. Continuous fighting along a 78-km (49-mile) front had been punishing for both armies.

The final phase

On the night of 29 October, a new AEF faced its German counterpart on the ridges and plains east of the Meuse. The command structure had been reorganized; the roads had undergone repairs; and in the rear, depots, repair shops, and field hospitals were all in order. Fresh troops with winter coats were now in place.

After a superbly coordinated two-day artillery bombardment, the AEF mounted its final assault on the morning of 1 November. Before sunset, the broken Hindenburg Line lay far to the rear. Open country stretched all the way to Sedan. By 7 November, US soldiers were on the hills overlooking the town. There was no longer a need to cut the railway. The combined Allied offensive had been spectacularly successful, and Germany was collapsing due to civil unrest on the home front.

When the Armistice came on 11 November, the AEF continued fighting until the bells tolled the 11th hour. Pershing had cleared his sector and achieved his objectives, but it had come at a frightful cost. The 47 days of continuous fighting had left the AEF with some 117,000 casualties, more than 26,000 of whom had been killed ∎

WE MUST SAVE ITALY

THE END OF THE WAR IN ITALY (LATE 1918)

The disastrous defeat at Caporetto in autumn 1917, in the 12th Battle of Isonzo, sent Italy into a spiral of self-doubt and fear. The fighting had also taken a heavy toll on the Austro-Hungarians, as war exhaustion and economic problems started to set in. German reinforcements had given them an edge, but that had been eroded by fresh French and British support for the Italian troops. However, both Germany and the Allies could spare no further forces; nor did the Italians or Austro-Hungarians feel strong enough to take the conflict forward themselves. As a result, the Italian front stayed comparatively quiet.

Preparing for action
As 1918 wore on, however, Italian soldiers started taking comfort from the fact that Caporetto had not finished them. Indeed, the resolute stand they made in November 1917 along the Piave river, and victory at the First Battle of Monte Grappa, had given them something they could build on. Also, Russia's

> After **defeat at Caporetto**, the Italian forces make a **stand along the Piave river**.

> Despite **their Isonzo river victories**, the Austro-Hungarian armies are **exhausted and low on food**.

> **Italian troops successfully stop an ambitious Austro-Hungarian offensive in June 1918.**

> **Italy goes on** to win the **Battle of Vittorio Veneto** – and to become **a victor** in the war.

See also: The situation in Europe 18–19 ▪ Austro-Hungarian failures 82 ▪ Italy enters the war 120–21 ▪ The Brusilov Offensive 166–69 ▪ The final battles of the Isonzo 212–13 ▪ A lasting peace? 312–17 ▪ The rise of fascism 322–23

Gabriele d'Annunzio (left) and Captain Natale Palli prepare to take off for their propaganda air raid over Vienna in 1918.

Gabriele d'Annunzio and the Flight over Vienna

Many writers were caught in the call-up for World War I. While most reflected ruefully upon the conflict's tragedies, Italian poet Gabriele d'Annunzio embraced the war enthusiastically, serving with his country's elite Arditi ("Daring Ones") and in the Italian aviation corps as a fighter pilot.

D'Annunzio's belligerence did not seem out of place in the country where, in 1909, poet Filippo Tommaso Marinetti had launched his *Manifesto of Futurism*. This written declaration had called on Italy to renew itself in a spree of mechanization, cultural rejuvenation, speed, and destructive violence.

In August 1918, d'Annunzio led an air squadron on a round trip to Vienna of more than 1,000 km (620 miles). Once over the Austrian capital, the planes dropped 50,000 leaflets printed on green, white, and red paper, calling on the Viennese to acknowledge that the fight was over and to recognize the victory of the Allies.

collapse had not boosted the Central Powers as much as expected, and on the Western Front, the German Spring Offensive was fading.

Threefold offensive
In June 1918, Austria-Hungary launched a summer offensive, beginning with a threefold attack on northern Italy. One action sought to advance from the north through the Alps into Lombardy, the others tried to envelop the Veneto region from the north, via Trentino, and the east across the Piave river plain.

Determined defenders repulsed the Alpine attack, while the Second Battle of the Piave River (15–23 June) ended disastrously for the invaders. Italian general Armando Diaz was far more flexible in his strategic thinking than his predecessor, General Luigi Cadorna, and he devolved much responsibility to his senior officers. Having received intelligence of the offensive in the hours before it happened, Diaz had his artillery bombard the Austro-Hungarian troops as they staged a massive frontal attack. Many ran from the battle, fearing that the Italian troops were about to advance. Once they did advance, the Austro-Hungarian army was soundly defeated.

Italy pushes back
As summer ended and the situation on the Western Front began to resolve, more Allied soldiers could be deployed on the Italian front. On 24 October (the anniversary of Caporetto), Italian troops, with British, French, and American support, pushed across the Piave plain towards Vittorio Veneto. Five days later, the Allies surged forward, defeated the Austro-Hungarian forces, and took the town.

Fighting continued, but fortune was flowing only one way. On 31 October, Charles I, the Austro-Hungarian emperor, handed over his imperial navy – including all its bases – to the newly formed State of Slovenes, Croats, and Serbs. Meanwhile, the Allies kept pushing eastwards until, on 3 November, they took Trieste. An armistice signed at Villa Giusti, Padua, came into force the next day. ▪

Armed with machine guns on a rocky spur on the Monte Grappa massif, Italian soldiers hold the higher ground during the Battle of Vittorio Veneto.

A MAGNIFICENT VICTORY IN THE EAST

THE BATTLE OF MEGIDDO (19–25 SEPTEMBER 1918)

By the late summer of
1918, British commander
General Sir Edmund Allenby
had beefed up his Egyptian
Expeditionary Force (EEF). He
had reinforcements from several
British Empire territories, including
Australia, New Zealand, India,
South Africa, and the West Indies,
as well as French, Armenian,
Jewish, and Arab detachments.

Meanwhile, the Ottoman troops
and their German allies were
regrouping in northern Palestine
behind a defensive line from the
Mediterranean to the River Jordan.
Additionally, they appointed new
commanders, including German
general Otto Liman von Sanders
and Turkish general Mustafa Kemal,
who had both earlier distinguished
themselves during the Gallipoli
Campaign (1915–16).

Brilliant strategy
Allenby and Australian general Sir
Henry Chauvel devised a strategy
to confront the Turkish fighters that
revolved around mobile warfare
tactics they had learned in the Boer
War (1899–1902). The plan included
infantry advances with close
artillery support, cavalry, and
armoured vehicles, targeted
air strikes, and deception – to
trick the opponent into believing
the main strike would come in the
east rather than the west.

The Allied generals employed
ingenious military ruses. Troops
dispatched to the Jordan Valley
were ordered to advance by daylight,
return to their previous positions
under nightfall, and then repeat
their daytime advance the following
day to suggest that the EEF was
amassing forces for an eastern
attack. They took the deception
further by constructing fake camps,
stirring up dust clouds to simulate
troop movements, and staging feint

Such a complete victory
[had] seldom been known
in all the history of war.
**Major General
Edward Chaytor**
New Zealand army officer and EEF
troop commander, Megiddo

See also: Ottoman Turkey enters the war 84–85 ▪ The war in Mesopotamia 131 ▪ The Arab Revolt 170–71 ▪ Jerusalem falls 245 ▪ War-crimes trials 318–19

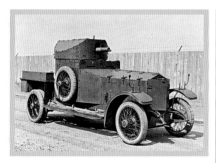

Although poorly suited to muddy Western Front battlefields, armoured Rolls-Royces were used effectively in speedy, targeted strikes in Palestine.

attacks against Ottoman positions in the Transjordan. British soldier-diplomat T.E. Lawrence played his part with large purchases of sheep and barley from Transjordan tribes, as if these supplies were needed to feed the thousands of troops and cavalry horses gathering in the area. In the west, where the main attack was planned, Allenby secretly moved troops and equipment into position under cover of darkness, hiding them in the daytime beneath trees and inside camouflaged tents.

Quick breakthrough

The week-long battle started at daybreak on 19 September with a massive artillery strike on Ottoman positions on the Plain of Sharon in the west, followed by a creeping barrage to support an infantry charge that quickly overwhelmed the entrenched troops. Charging through a huge hole in the Ottoman army lines, British cavalry quickly took Megiddo, Nazareth, and Jenin. Other EEF units positioned in the Judean Hills confronted Ottoman forces around the city of Nablus commanded by Mustafa Kemal and ventured across the River Jordan to attack Amman.

Although the mop-up would take another five days, the initial Blitzkrieg-like British assault had shattered two Ottoman armies, captured thousands of prisoners, and sent remnants of the combined Ottoman-German force retreating in disarray into Syria. Little of the combat actually took place in Megiddo, but Allenby chose that name for the overarching offensive to mirror the ancient Megiddo, where an Egyptian army crushed the Canaanites in the 15th century BCE. ▪

Guarded by EEF cavalry, German officers lead Ottoman and German prisoners of war who were captured shortly before the Battle of Megiddo.

The Ottoman armistice

Less than a month after its crushing defeat at Megiddo, the Ottoman Empire sued for peace. Anchored off Mudros on the Greek island of Lemnos, the British battleship HMS *Agamemnon* served as the venue for peace talks between Admiral Sir Somerset Arthur Gough-Calthorpe of the Royal Navy and Rauf Bey, the Ottoman minister of marine affairs. The British government had decided that other allies, including France and the US, should be excluded from the meeting so that it could negotiate quickly and on terms most favourable to Britain.

After three days of talks, the Armistice of Mudros was signed on 30 October. In addition to ending hostilities between the Ottomans and the Allies, the agreement called for free passage of Allied warships through the Dardanelles and Bosphorus, a complete demobilization of the Ottoman army and removal of whatever forces remained in the Middle East, and the repatriation of all prisoners of war. World War I was over, at least in the Middle East.

THE OLD AND ROTTEN, THE MONARCHY, HAS COLLAPSED

MUTINY AND REVOLUTION IN GERMANY (LATE 1918–EARLY 1919)

IN CONTEXT

FOCUS
The German home front

BEFORE
August 1914 Britain imposes a naval blockade of Germany at the outbreak of war.

November 1916 The Turnip Winter begins, and food shortages become a way of life.

October 1917 The Russian Revolution inspires Germany's political left.

January 1918 As many as 400,000 workers go out on strike in Berlin.

AFTER
1924–29 A thriving cultural and artistic scene develops in Germany during the golden years of the Weimar Republic.

1929 The Wall Street Crash has deep repercussions for the German economy, resulting in wide unemployment and renewed political instability.

The naval blockade and bad news from the front leave **German people demoralized**.

An elite appears to be **unaffected** by the **hardship and suffering**.

Left-wing claims that the war is **fought by workers** for the benefit of their masters prove persuasive.

Attacks on activists by the government and its right-wing supporters **stoke the furnace**.

Dissatisfaction on the German home front leads to revolution.

Austerity was old news in Germany by the autumn of 1918. Food rationing had been in force since early in the war, and it had become more punitive over time. The drafting of miners into the armed forces had hit coal supplies, which had disrupted industrial production and many aspects of domestic life – from street lighting to public transport.

All but the most wealthy had been affected. Middle-class families were reduced to poverty, while the already poor confronted extreme want. Hunger, malnutrition, and disease were rife. The suffering was underscored by evidence that a small elite was spared these deprivations. Sheltered from the general gloom, this privileged set reacted to it with often ostentatious displays of affluence.

Reform or revolution?
Radical rhetoric found a ready ear in Germany. The Russian Revolution of 1917 had shown what might be achieved by a determined people, although different groups interpreted its message in different ways. For moderate reformers, such as social democrat Friedrich Ebert, it provided a precedent for the

See also: The rise of Germany 20–23 ▪ The war at sea begins 88–93 ▪ Society under strain 184–87 ▪ The February Revolution 192–93 ▪ The October Revolution 240–41 ▪ The Second Battle of the Marne 270–73 ▪ The Battle of Amiens 274–77

> The Revolution is on the verge of winning. We cannot crush it but perhaps we can strangle it.
> **Maximilian von Baden**
> (early 1919)

abdication of Kaiser Wilhelm II and the pursuit of a negotiated settlement for the war. But some on the political left – including the Spartacus League, a Marxist revolutionary group – saw it as the cue for overthrowing the entire capitalist system in favour of rule by soviets, or workers' councils.

For a few weeks, from 3 October 1918, Germany was a constitutional monarchy. The kaiser appointed Prince Maximilian von Baden as chancellor. An aristocratic insider, Baden agreed to work with the Reichstag (parliament), but conditions continued to worsen. On 27 October, when the Admiralty ordered preparations for a climactic confrontation with the Royal Navy in the southern North Sea, sailors at sea off Wilhelmshaven, the navy's main base, refused to serve. While this revolt was soon put down, a mass mutiny at the Baltic base of Kiel on 3 November proved harder to suppress. Sailors and stokers called for a list of concessions – from better work conditions, to the release of political prisoners. Fundamentally, they were demanding "peace and bread", a cry taken up by protesters across Germany as the country spiralled into chaos.

A tale of two republics

On 9 November, Kaiser Wilhelm II abdicated and fled Germany. Social Democrat politician Philipp Scheidemann proclaimed Germany a republic. This announcement was intended to preempt that of Spartacist leader Karl Liebknecht, who went ahead anyway, declaring a revolutionary workers' state, the Free Socialist Republic of Germany, just hours later.

Weeks of turmoil followed as politicians argued over their various visions for post-war Germany. On the eve of elections in January 1919, a Spartacist uprising was crushed, and leaders Liebknecht and Rosa Luxemburg were murdered by the GKSD, a paramilitary unit working to suppress the communists. Violent unrest continued until February 1919, when a National Assembly met in the city of Weimar and agreed a new republican constitution. ▪

A sailor from Kiel holds a red flag as he celebrates the declaration of the Free Socialist Republic of Germany in Berlin in November 1918.

The November abdications

Kaiser Wilhelm II's Second Reich came to an end with the reminder that the Germany over which he had reigned had in fact been a federation. When he abdicated – fleeing to the neutral Netherlands, where he went into exile – he renounced two titles: German Emperor and King of Prussia.

Wilhelm's demise also removed the authority that had held up a host of lesser rulers – a disparate group of kings and dukes, along with the odd "imperial prince", totalling 19 in all. However uncertain the outlook for the new Germany might have been, it was clear that it was not going to have a place for such antiquated notions. Few went willingly. Indeed, King Ludwig III of Bavaria refused to "abdicate". Instead, he simply released his officials and troops from their oaths of loyalty to him, thereby effectively bringing down the curtain on his family's centuries of rule.

THEY STORMED THE BATTLEMENTS OF DEATH

BREAKING THE HINDENBURG LINE (SEPTEMBER–OCTOBER 1918)

IN CONTEXT

FOCUS
Breakthrough tactics

BEFORE
1 July 1916 Lacking sufficient firepower, the Allies try but fail to break the German defence lines during the first day of the Battle of the Somme.

24 October–19 November 1917 Austro-Hungarian and German forces breach the Italian front line at Caporetto, in the 12th Battle of the Isonzo.

8–11 August 1918 British, Australian, Canadian, and French troops rupture the German front line during the Battle of Amiens.

AFTER
May–June 1940 German troops use Blitzkrieg – "lightning attack" – tactics to invade Belgium, the Netherlands, Luxembourg, and France in World War II.

In the winter of 1916–17, after realizing that the Allies could not be beaten in an offensive war, the German commanders adopted a defensive strategy and retreated behind the newly built Hindenburg Line. Known in German as *Siegfriedstellung*, or Siegfried Position, after a dragon slayer in Germanic mythology, this defensive line stretched for 145 km (90 miles) between Arras and Laffaux, in northern France.

Foch's offensive strategy

After their success at the Battle of Amiens in August 1918, the Allies wasted little time in regrouping, determined to maintain the

See also: Germany's war machine 182–83 ▪ The Second Battle of the Marne 270–73 ▪ The Battle of Amiens 274–77 ▪ The Meuse–Argonne Offensive 280–83 ▪ Mutiny and revolution in Germany 288–89 ▪ The Armistice 294–99

momentum of their advance eastwards. In the three days from 21 August, Allied troops defeated German forces at the Battle of Albert, which was followed on 2 September by the breaching of the Drocourt-Quéant Line, part of the northernmost stretch of the Hindenburg Line. But these were just preliminaries to the multipronged offensive that would climax in late September.

Marshal Ferdinand Foch, the Allied supreme commander, adopted a policy of repeated yet separate offensives along different sections of the front. To some extent, this was to depart from the strategy in 1917, when attacks had become bogged down fighting over the same ground – as had happened during the Third Battle of Ypres. It was also designed to keep the German commanders guessing as to where the hammer would next strike, and give them no time to recuperate after it had fallen.

Foch and British commander Field Marshal Sir Douglas Haig were determined to press forwards

 A perfect modern battle plan is like nothing so much as a score for an orchestral composition.
Lieutenant General Sir John Monash

aggressively and bring the war to a successful conclusion by the close of 1918.

Combined attacks

Foch's series of offensives began on 26 September, with a combined attack by the French army and the American Expeditionary Forces (AEF) in the Meuse–Argonne region. On 27 September, the British First and Third armies attacked the northern section of the Hindenburg

Line around the Canal du Nord. Their objective was to secure the vital German communications and supply centre of Cambrai.

Spearheaded by the Canadian Corps, the attack caught the Germans by surprise. Progress was rapid and, after securing the main Canal du Nord position, the Canadian Corps, supported by British units, captured the high ground of Bourlon Woods. The scope of the attack moved northwards, on 28 September, to Flanders and the long-awaited breakout from Ypres by Belgian, French, and British forces.

Meanwhile, on 29 September, the British Fourth Army, supported by American and Australian forces, opened its assault on the strongest part of the Hindenburg Line, the Saint-Quentin Canal. General Sir Henry Rawlinson, commander of the Fourth Army, had wanted the battle-hardened Australian Corps to spearhead the attack on the canal. However, the Australian commander, Lieutenant General Sir John Monash, believed his »

Sir Henry Rawlinson

Born in Dorset, England, in 1864, Henry Rawlinson attended Eton College and the Royal Military Academy at Sandhurst before being commissioned into the British Army in India in 1884. He served in Burma and Sudan, as well as in the Second Boer War in South Africa. After returning to Britain in 1903, he was placed in charge of the Army Staff College in Camberley, Surrey, where he was pivotal in bringing the training of the British Army up to a more professional standard.

With the onset of war, Rawlinson commanded the Fourth Division of the British Expeditionary Force (BEF) before leading the Fourth Army for the Battle of the Somme in July 1916. The opening day of the battle was a disaster, for which he was partly to blame, although he redeemed himself later in the offensive.

Rawlinson achieved fame for his command of the Fourth Army during the Battle of Amiens, and for breaching the Hindenburg Line. In 1920, he was appointed to lead the Indian Army, but died suddenly in Delhi in 1925.

troops had undergone undue battle stress during the previous weeks and told Rawlinson his concerns about the forthcoming attack. Rawlinson, who had the US Army II Corps at his disposal, adjusted the strategy so that the Americans took the lead. According to the plan, once the American corps had broken into the Hindenburg Line, the Australian divisions would "leapfrog" over them and exploit the breakthrough.

American inexperience

The two divisions in the US II Corps (27th and 30th divisions) had roughly double the troop numbers of the British Army divisions and were packed with soldiers enthusiastic for action. Much was expected of them, but a problem lay in the Americans' inexperience, especially in matters of organization. A group of 200 experienced Australian officers and NCOs was assigned to II Corps to help rectify these shortcomings, but this fix fell apart under the stress of combat.

The steep-sided Saint-Quentin Canal was a formidable obstacle and formed an integral part of the

> Over we went, slipping and sliding down the canal bank to the cold water below.
> **Corporal George Parker**
> Sherwood Foresters, on the attack on the Saint-Quentin Canal

German defences on this section of the Hindenburg Line. The canal, however, went through a tunnel, roughly 5.5 km (3.4 miles) long, beneath the village of Bellicourt. It was on this flat, open ground that the main Allied attack was to be delivered, with the US 27th Division deployed on the left (to the north) and the US 30th Division on the right (to the south). The Germans were well aware of the vulnerability of this section of their defensive line and had increased its depth, which included an outpost line. According to Allied

plans, this outpost line needed to be in Allied hands before the start of the battle on 29 September.

Australian forces had previously captured the outpost line facing the US 30th Division, but the US 27th Division could not secure its part of the line. This meant that its forces were too far back to be protected by the artillery's creeping barrage when the main advance started. Although a suggestion was made to modify the barrage, both American and Australian commanders vetoed the idea because of concerns over friendly fire incidents.

Modified plan

Due to the failure to secure the outpost line, Rawlinson changed the battle plan to include an attack by the British IX Corps directly to the south of the American advance and over the challenging cutting formed by the Saint-Quentin Canal. Monash thought such an attack would fail, but the commander of IX Corps, Lieutenant General Sir Walter Braithwaite, had persuaded Rawlinson of its viability. The attack, to be led by the 46th Division, was ordered to proceed.

Triumphant soldiers of the 46th Division are addressed by Brigadier General Campbell on Riqueval Bridge after taking the Saint-Quentin Canal.

Crossing the canal

The greatest victory in the attack on the Saint-Quentin Canal was spearheaded by the British 46th (North Midland) Division. With the German troops forced back into their dugouts by artillery bombardment, the division's infantry was able to scramble down the sides of the canal. Aided by equipment that had been tested in a rehearsal on the Somme the previous day – floating piers and rafts made from petrol tins or cork slabs, and 3,000 life jackets taken from cross-Channel steamers – they crossed the water. Using scaling ladders to clamber to the top of the brick wall lining the other side, they overwhelmed the surprised German defences.

The soldiers then fought their way through four villages and across the lines of trenches to the far side of the Hindenburg Line, advancing 5 km (3 miles) and taking 4,200 prisoners and 70 guns, with the loss of just 800 casualties. The audacity of the assault was praised by General Monash, who declared it an "astonishing success" that had greatly aided the Allied advance.

The Hindenburg Line was a German defensive line on the Western Front. It came under attack several times in 1917 before finally being broken the following year.

Key:

```
----    Hindenburg Line
_____   Allied front line,
        18 July 1918
_____   Allied front line,
        2 September 1918
_____   Allied front line,
        11 November 1918
```

The battle opened with a hurricane bombardment – more than 1,000 field guns and just under 600 heavy guns and howitzers fired nearly a million shells over a 24-hour period. It was the greatest British artillery bombardment of the war. Approximately 150 British tanks were assigned to support the American advance, which the British commanders believed would be a simple exercise in occupying ground. However, this was not the case on the Allied left. The US 27th Division became entangled in the outpost line and completely failed to achieve its objectives; the 107th Infantry Regiment suffered the highest casualties of any US Army regiment in a single day during the war. The supporting Australian troops became caught up in the confused American ranks still fighting for the outpost line. Progress was minimal.

Breaching the line

On the right of the attack, the US 30th Division did much better than its colleagues on the left, although it faced sweeping gunfire on its left flank as a result of the 27th Division's failure to press forward. With the direct support of Australian troops, the 30th Division broke into the now-shattered Hindenburg Line, capturing the key village of Bellicourt and linking up with British troops on their right, who had carried out a daring crossing of the Saint-Quentin Canal.

Senior British and Australian commanders were critical of the Americans' performance, although they later noted that the troops had fought under difficult conditions. The Hindenburg Line had been breached, and over the next few days the Allies pushed forward to capture the village of Beaurevoir. The Beaurevoir Line – the last section of the Hindenburg Line – fell on 6 October, leaving open country ahead of the Allied forces.

More than 5,000 German soldiers were captured at the Battle of Saint-Quentin Canal. They were taken to a clearing depot in Abbeville, France

Elsewhere on the front, the Allied advances generally went to plan. After the success on the Canal du Nord, Allied forces pressed on to Cambrai. On 8 October, in a combined attack using artillery, tanks, infantry, and aircraft, the three German defensive lines were breached with little difficulty, allowing the Canadians to march through the city.

Peace is in sight

The collapse of German forces along the Hindenburg Line was enough to convince the German high command that their field army had been defeated and that peace terms must be sought. Throughout October, while diplomatic negotiations continued, the German army fell back towards its homeland, fighting rearguard actions to slow the Allied advance. Some German units continued to resist with fierce determination until the signing of the Armistice on 11 November, but others began to surrender. The war was finally coming to a close. ∎

THERE WAS NO CHEERING, NO SINGING

THE ARMISTICE (11 NOVEMBER 1918)

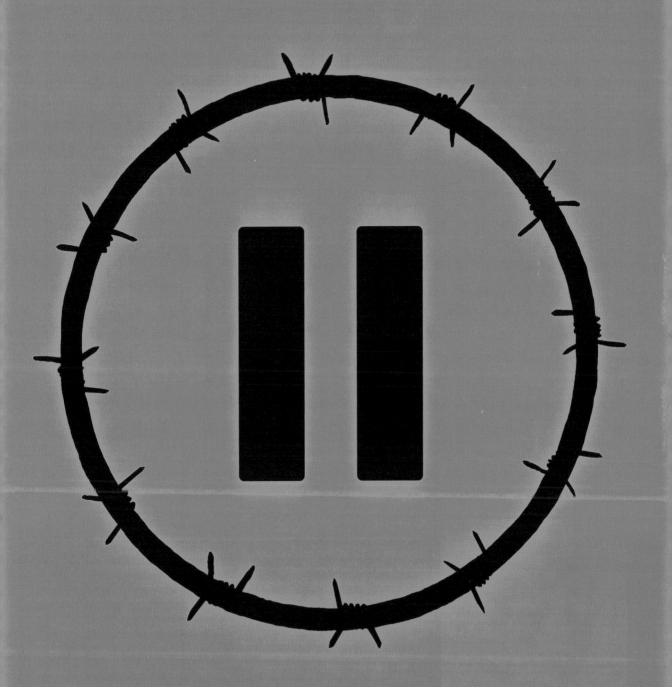

IN CONTEXT

FOCUS
Cessation of hostilities

BEFORE
8 January 1918 Woodrow Wilson makes his "Fourteen Points" speech to US Congress.

29 September 1918 Bulgaria and the Allies sign the Armistice of Salonika.

30 October 1918 The Armistice of Mudros ends the involvement of the Ottoman Empire in the war.

3 November 1918 Austria-Hungary and the Allies sign the Armistice of Villa Giusti near Padua, Italy.

AFTER
February 1919 The new German Constitutional National Assembly sits for the first time, in Weimar.

June 1919 The Treaty of Versailles is signed in Paris.

Germany's fortunes had been in steep decline since the summer of 1918. After the Allied victories at the Second Battle of the Marne and Amiens, the German army gave up ground (and prisoners) on a daily basis. Following the initial success of the multipronged Allied attacks on 26 September, the German high command concluded that the war was lost. On 29 September, First Quartermaster General Erich Ludendorff confessed to Kaiser Wilhelm II that he could not be sure of holding on to the front line for even a few hours more. The kaiser, he insisted, was going to have to sue for a ceasefire.

In early October, the kaiser ordered his new chancellor, Prince Maximilian von Baden, to send US president Woodrow Wilson a communication enquiring about the prospects for a peace accord. Germany, Maximilian said, was open to the idea of an agreement based on the president's Fourteen Points – principles for peace that he outlined in January 1918. Wilson's reply emphasized the need for Germany not only to return the territories it had taken but also to show a commitment to democracy. This included, he implied, the removal of Kaiser Wilhelm, whose warmongering had brought the world to its present plight. Wilson's response had been hardened by the sinking of the mail boat RMS *Leinster*, with great loss of life, on 10 October.

Second thoughts

At first, the German high command saw no alternative to accepting Wilson's demand, humiliating though it was. As the days passed,

Erich Ludendorff (left) directed Germany's military strategy from 1916. Shortly before the war's end, the kaiser (right) asked him to resign.

Matthias Erzberger

Born in 1875 in Buttenhausen (now part of Münsingen), Germany, Matthias Erzberger started his career as a teacher, at the same time studying law and economics. He joined the Catholic Centre Party and in 1903 was elected to the Reichstag.

Erzberger initially supported the war, but as time went on he began to have grave doubts. He was disillusioned by the Armenian Genocide – carried out by the Ottoman Empire, Germany's ally – and was one of very few German politicians to condemn it publicly. By 1917, he was questioning the point of a conflict that seemed to have reached a bloody stalemate. In October 1918, Erzberger was appointed to the government without a specified portfolio; a month later, he was sent to head the peace delegation in France.

Erzberger was vice chancellor of Germany from July to October 1919, but he endured hostility from the political right. He was assassinated on 26 August 1921 in the Black Forest, Baden.

See also: War is declared 42–43 ▪ The invasion of Belgium 50–51 ▪ The war at sea begins 88–93 ▪ The Armenian Genocide 132–33 ▪ The US enters the war 194–95 ▪ Mutiny and revolution in Germany 288–89 ▪ A lasting peace? 312–17

however, and with the immediate crisis averted, Germany's top generals began to recover some of their military spirit.

Although it was a shock that the Allies had breached the Hindenburg Line, they continued to pay a high price for their gains. Germany had been beaten but not destroyed. Field Marshal Paul von Hindenburg still wanted the fighting to stop – an armistice was absolutely necessary for his forces, he conceded – but only as a way of buying time to rest and regroup. By 1919, he argued, his soldiers would be fit to fight again – and to win. He was not convinced that Germany should sacrifice Wilhelm II, who was a key symbol of the country's imperial destiny.

The kaiser and Ludendorff
Ludendorff was in agreement with Hindenburg. In his optimism, he saw an advantage in his country's beleaguered situation. He believed that if Germany's troops could start out on the defensive, so much the better. Its forces had only been defeated, he now reasoned, because the war had been fought on foreign ground. If his soldiers had been fighting to protect their homes and their families, had their fatherland been threatened, no power on earth could have hoped to prevail against them. The entire nation would have come together as one to fight for every piece of sacred German soil.

On 17 October, Ludendorff told Maximilian to break off peace negotiations altogether. The war might yet be won if the kaiser would just hold his nerve. Wilhelm was no longer listening – it was clear that the stress of recent months had taken its toll on his general health and that he had become erratic in his judgement. In frustration, Ludendorff resigned on 26 October. His replacement, General Wilhelm Groener, was more of a realist than either Ludendorff or Hindenburg. Despite his loyalty, he had no doubt that the sacrifice of the kaiser would be a small price to pay for a much-needed peace. The challenges Germany faced now extended far beyond the war. The country itself was descending into chaos, with mass strikes and riots.

Accepting reality
Regardless of all of the German prevarications, the Allies were far too wary to agree to a settlement that would leave their enemy with »

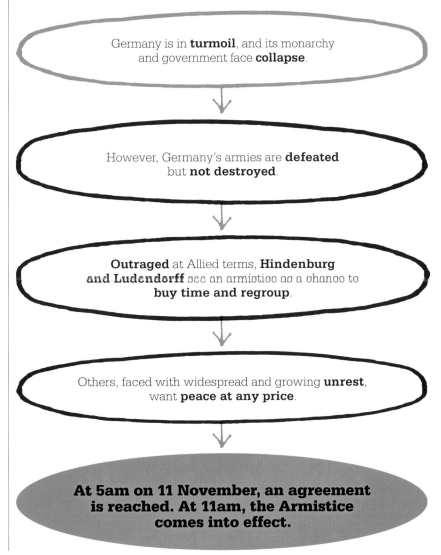

Germany is in **turmoil**, and its monarchy and government face **collapse**.

However, Germany's armies are **defeated** but **not destroyed**.

Outraged at Allied terms, **Hindenburg and Ludendorff** see an armistice as a chance to **buy time and regroup**.

Others, faced with widespread and growing **unrest**, want **peace at any price**.

At 5am on 11 November, an agreement is reached. At 11am, the Armistice comes into effect.

The Compiègne Wagon

The railway carriage in which the Armistice of Compiègne was signed had been built in 1914 as an ordinary dining car. In October 1918, it was commandeered by the French government and converted into the mobile headquarters of Ferdinand Foch, who had been promoted to the rank of marshal two months earlier. The location of the peace negotiations in France, rather than on neutral ground, underlined the point that any agreement was to be made on the Allies' terms.

The German negotiators protested at the harshness of the terms – and the humiliation rankled for many years afterwards. In June 1940, having vanquished France, Germany's Nazi leader Adolf Hitler forced the French to sign a second armistice in the same carriage, on the same spot. The wagon was then taken to Germany, where it was paraded as a trophy of war.

The Allied delegation, including Ferdinand Foch (second from the right), is pictured outside the train after the signing of the Armistice.

any remaining capacity for waging war. If there had been any doubt that the removal of the kaiser was a strict condition of their coming to terms, this was eliminated in subsequent communications. On 6 November, conceding to the inevitable, Maximilian sent his recently appointed minister Matthias Erzberger to the forest of Compiègne, France. Here, a private train used by Supreme Allied Commander Marshal Ferdinand Foch was parked on a remote siding, far from the eyes of the press or public, ready to receive the negotiating parties.

German resignations

In Berlin, the political crisis was escalating. On 9 November, Kaiser Wilhelm II stepped down. The same day, Maximilian also relinquished office, making way for Friedrich Ebert, the leader of the Social Democratic Party (SPD), to take over as chancellor. A conservative by his party's standards, Ebert had supported the war insofar as he had called for the SPD to curb its criticisms and back the kaiser in the national interest. Even

now, although he saw Wilhelm's abdication as a necessary gesture, he believed that the monarchy as an institution might be retained. To most of the military elite, such views represented a dangerous radicalism, but Maximilian recognized that change was needed. The appointment of a more right-wing chancellor would have provoked the political left within Germany and caused alarm in the capitals of the Allied nations.

The talks in Compiègne were under way, but by this time there was little to discuss. The Allies gave the defeated Germans a list of conditions they expected to be met.

Armistice terms

Foch had greeted Erzberger's delegation and remained at hand while discussions took place, but for the most part he left the negotiators alone. Only when agreement had been reached, at 5am Central European Time (CET) on Monday, 11 November, did Foch return to add his signature.

The agreement had 34 clauses. Essentially, though, it called for a complete cessation of hostilities

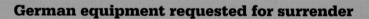

German equipment requested for surrender

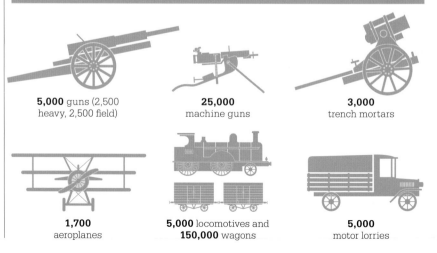

5,000 guns (2,500 heavy, 2,500 field)

25,000 machine guns

3,000 trench mortars

1,700 aeroplanes

5,000 locomotives and **150,000** wagons

5,000 motor lorries

The Krupp steelworks in the Ruhr area was central to German armaments manufacture during the war. After the Armistice, surrendered arms were taken to Krupps for destruction.

by both sides. As the price for this, Germany had to commit to the removal of its forces from all territories it had taken, and to the return of those territories. It also had to accept Allied forces across a large area of its western edge, to create a protective cordon for France and Belgium. These Allied forces were to be maintained at Germany's expense.

In the east, Germany had to withdraw from Romania and retreat to the borders with the Ottoman and Austro-Hungarian empires that had existed prior to August 1914. The Treaty of Brest-Litovsk, between Soviet Russia and the Central Powers, was to be undone, and Germany was to respect the autonomy of Russia. In spite of this condition, the Allies gave tacit support to the German-backed West Russian Volunteer Army, which they perceived as valuable opposition to the communists in the Russian Civil War.

In addition to looted assets, the Germans were to surrender huge amounts of arms, ammunition, and equipment, and to guarantee no further destruction to the territories being evacuated. All minefields were to be identified. Most modern warships and all submarines were to be surrendered. All Allied prisoners of war were to be freed, while German prisoners remained captive. The blockade of Germany was to remain in place until a definitive peace treaty was signed.

A terrible time lag
The Armistice came into force six hours after agreement was reached, at 11am CET – the 11th hour of the 11th day of the 11th month. In those six hours, the war at the front continued. While many of the commanders on both sides were happy to let their soldiers stand down as the news of the Armistice gradually spread, some were determined to fight to the bitter end. Allied officers were under pressure from their superiors to keep up an attacking posture, to leave the Germans in no doubt of the determination on their side.

It is thought that almost 3,000 lives were lost in this six-hour shadow war. The last official death was that of Private Henry Gunther, a 23-year-old from Baltimore, Maryland, US, who took it upon himself to charge a German machine-gun nest. Its occupants shot him at 10:59am.

The celebrations start
For the most part, the mood after 11am on 11 November was relaxed, albeit muted – given a lack of certainty about what was actually happening and the sheer exhaustion, both physical and mental, that most soldiers felt. However, exultant French villagers in the war zone celebrated joyously. Back home in Allied towns and cities, crowds formed in the streets as the word began to filter through. In Paris at 11am CET, a peace gunshot was fired from Fort Mont-Valérien; British prime minister David Lloyd George made an announcement at 10:20am GMT; and Americans awoke to news of the Armistice. As the day progressed and information spread – and as the implications of the war's end gradually sank in – incredulity and excitement gave way to unbridled revelry. ∎

… we were surrounded by a seething crowd of people simply delirious with joy.
Major Thomas Westmacott
Headquarters, 24th Division

DEATH IS NOT AN ADVENTURE

WAR POETRY AND LITERATURE

IN CONTEXT

FOCUS
Interpreting the war

BEFORE
1854 British poet Alfred, Lord Tennyson "The Charge of the Light Brigade" celebrates the heroism of a brigade of cavalry during the Crimean War.

1865 American poet Walt Whitman publishes *Drum-Taps*, a collection of poems based on his experiences tending wounded soldiers during the American Civil War.

AFTER
1922 The fractured narrative of T.S. Eliot's *The Waste Land* reflects the shattered nature of the post-war world.

2018 On the centenary of the Armistice, an installation at the Tower of London includes a choral setting of American poet and war nurse Mary Borden's "Sonnets to a Soldier".

Between 1914 and 1918, an unprecedented outpouring of verse occurred as thousands of combatants on both sides turned to poetry to express their experience of the conflict. Poets had long written about war, but not usually as serving soldiers. By contrast, in World War I, many poets served and died in the trenches. The terms "war poet" and "war poetry" came into use initially to describe their writings.

Just as this war was unlike any other, so too was its literature. At the start, poets reflected the general sense of patriotism and enthusiasm for battle and a belief in the heroism of death. However,

> What passing-bells for these who die as cattle?
> – Only the monstrous anger of the guns.
> Only the stuttering rifles' rapid rattle …
> **Wilfred Owen**
> **"Anthem for Doomed Youth", 1917**

the brutal nature of the war – its mechanized killing, the experience of huddling terrified in rat-infested trenches, and seeing comrades slaughtered – shattered illusions. Poets responded by addressing this reality using powerful and poignant imagery. In doing so, they had a profound impact on the way in which the war has been interpreted, as did the large number of novels and memoirs that were published by combatants in the years following the war.

Self-sacrifice to disillusion
In the first years of the war, British poets such as Rupert Brooke and Julian Grenfell reflected the heroic view. Brooke, an established and widely admired poet, enlisted in August 1914 and died the following year of blood poisoning. In poems such as "The Soldier", he idealized war and sacrifice. Other poets who expressed a romantic view of combat and the heroism of death were Canadian army surgeon John McCrae, who wrote "In Flanders Fields", and young American poet Alan Seeger, who joined the French Foreign Legion in 1914 and was killed in 1916.

By 1916, a number of young British poets were making their mark. Most were junior officers, though some served in the ranks. They included Wilfred Owen, Isaac Rosenberg, Charles Sorley, and Edward Thomas – all of whom were killed – and Siegfried Sassoon. »

The relentless destruction of people and property, such as at Ypres – for no gain – caused many to express their feelings of despair through poetry and other creative writing.

Siegfried Sassoon

Born in 1886 near Tunbridge Wells, in Kent, England, Siegfried Sassoon studied at Cambridge University. In August 1914, he volunteered in the Sussex Yeomanry and the following year was commissioned with the Royal Welch Fusiliers. A brave and often reckless officer, he gained the nickname "Mad Jack" and was awarded the Military Cross.

In 1917, Sassoon was wounded and sent back to Britain. By now disillusioned with the war, he handed back his Military Cross and refused to return to the front. Friend and fellow poet Robert Graves arranged for him to be diagnosed with shell shock in order to avoid court martial. He was sent to Craiglockhart War Hospital, in Scotland, where he met and befriended Wilfred Owen, before returning to active service. After the war, Sassoon wrote poetry and *Memoirs of an Infantry Officer* (1930). He died in 1967 and is widely known for his compassionate and angry war poetry.

Edmund Blunden, and David Jones. Shocked by the carnage on the battlefield and the ineptitude of those in charge, they sought to challenge jingoistic and romantic attitudes to war and portray its horror as truthfully as possible. Sorley died at the Battle of Loos in 1915; among the papers in his kitbag was a sonnet scribbled in pencil, "When You See Millions of the Mouthless Dead". With a disturbing but lyrical description of a broken body, it became one of the most influential poems of the war.

The poets tackled every type of experience – from Rosenberg's description of a soldier's attempts to rid himself of lice, to Sassoon's of men weighed down with kit going into battle over the top of a trench, and Owen's horror at watching a comrade die in a gas attack. The mud was evoked in all its misery by American poet Mary Borden, in "At the Somme: The Song of the Mud". Borden ran a nursing station for French soldiers and wrote poems (not published until 2015) that chronicled the exhaustion and hopelessness of treating the men's horrific wounds, as did British writer Vera Brittain.

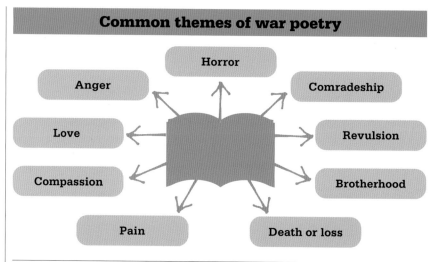

Common themes of war poetry

- Horror
- Anger
- Comradeship
- Love
- Revulsion
- Compassion
- Brotherhood
- Pain
- Death or loss

Sassoon's attacks on military leaders in poems such as "The General" became increasingly angry and satirical, while Owen, in "Dulce et Decorum Est", opposed the idea that it is glorious to die for your country. Owen's poem was a direct rebuke to those back home, such as Jesse Pope, for their continued jingoism. Pope wrote popular poems glorifying military combat and urging men to enlist, but in the end it was the work of poets such as Rosenberg, Owen, and Sassoon that would come to define the World War I experience.

In France, people looked forward to war, as reflected in the work of Charles Péguy. In 1913, he praised those who died in a just war; in September 1914, he was killed on the eve of the First Battle of the Marne. Two years later, French poet Guillaume Apollinaire, who served in the army and was injured in 1916, included several poems about the madness of war in his *Calligrammes: Poems of Peace and War 1913–1916*, published in 1918, the year he died.

German and Italian poets
Like their British and French counterparts, German poets also initially welcomed war. During the build-up, Ernst Stadler was one of those who saw it as a means of cleansing German society, but within two months of arriving in Flanders he wrote of the violence and pointless death he had seen. He was killed in October 1914. Socialist Ernst Toller wrote of looking forward to doing his bit, but by 1917 he was a pacifist. August Stramm, who was killed in Russia in 1915, wrote impressionistic poems that reflected the chaos he saw around him. Young Italian modernist poet Giuseppe Ungaretti,

Gerrit Engelke

Born in Hanover, Germany, in 1890, Gerrit Engelke saw his parents and sister emigrate to the US by the time he was 20, leaving him in Germany. While he was working as a commercial decorator, he started writing poetry, taking machinery and industry as his subjects. His first poems were published in 1912. When the war started, Engelke was living in Denmark, but he returned to Germany to start military training.

From February 1915, Engelke served on the Western Front and was awarded the Iron Cross for bravery. Wounded in 1917, he became engaged while on sick leave. He returned to the front but was wounded again and taken prisoner in October 1918. Engelke died in a British field hospital near Cambrai two days later. His war poetry – such as "An den Tod" ("To Death") – reflects his despair at the war and the needless waste of life.

The all-Black 369th Infantry regiment parades in New York City before being posted to the Western Front. Racism is a theme of much Black American World War I poetry.

who served in the trenches in northern Italy, was another who enlisted with enthusiasm but in his first collection of poems – published in 1917 – expressed horror at what he had witnessed.

Black voices

More than 4 million non-white soldiers were recruited into the European armies, and many Black Americans served in the US Army. They produced their own body of poetry, which has only recently been acknowledged. For Black American soldiers, the awfulness of war was compounded by racism, a reality expressed by poets such as Joseph Seamon Cotter Sr, who captured the experiences of those he saw going off to die in his poem "Sonnet to Negro Soldiers". This recognizes that for Black soldiers, the enemy was not Germany but racial injustice, and hopes that in death the "thorn of prejudice" will be cast down. But the war did not end prejudice. In 1919, Jamaican American poet Claude McKay

wrote "If We Must Die", noting that despite the end of war, Black Americans had returned home to face more battles, this time against white America.

Anti-war narratives

French novelist Henri Barbusse's *Le Feu* (*Under Fire*) appeared in 1916. Based on his experiences on the Western Front, it offers a savage portrayal of the war. He presented it in serial form to escape the censors. German novelist Erich Maria Remarque's poignant *All Quiet on the Western Front*, which was published in 1929, was one of the most influential war novels. It describes the daily life and fates of a platoon of young German soldiers and sold 2.5 million copies within 18 months. Other German anti-war novelists included Gerrit Engelke and Ludwig Renn. French novelists Gabriel Chevallier and Jean Giono also drew on their experiences on the Western Front.

Some writers dealt with the ways in which war changed soldiers. One of the first British war novels was Rebecca West's *Return of the Soldier* (1918), about an officer suffering from shell shock. American writer Ernest Hemingway's short story "Soldier's Home" features a

protagonist who cannot talk to his family about his war experiences. Hemingway was injured in 1918 while serving as an ambulance driver in Italy. His novel *A Farewell to Arms*, set against war on the Isonzo front, influenced American public opinion with its criticism of those who glorify war.

A large number of British memoirs was published in the 1920s, including Edmund Blunden's *Undertones of War* and Robert Graves's *Goodbye to All That*. Vera Brittain's autobiography, *Testament of Youth*, which appeared in 1933, describes her war-time experiences as a nurse in France and the loss of her brother, fiancé, and friends. In Britain, playwrights also tackled the subject. In 1925, gay author Joseph Randall Ackerley's *Prisoners of War* was performed on the London stage. Based on his time as a prisoner of war, the play tells of an officer's unrequited attraction to another male officer.

Together, the work of the war poets and the mass of anti-war literature that appeared from the 1920s helped shape the anti-war movement that emerged between the two world wars. ∎

… Their blind eyes see not your tears flow.
Nor honour. It is easy to be dead.
Charles Sorley
"When You See Millions of the Mouthless Dead"

A WAR TO END ALL W

1919–23 AND BEYOND

ARS?

In Berlin, more than **10,000 German veterans demand** higher pensions and greater honour for the **nation's 2.7 million disabled soldiers**.

In Italy, Benito **Mussolini forms the Blackshirts**, a paramilitary wing of his Italian Fasces of Combat party, **renamed the Fascist Party** in 1921.

The **League of Nations** is inaugurated. Two months later the **US Senate** will vote **against the US joining** the organization.

The neutral Netherlands **rejects Allied demands to extradite Kaiser Wilhelm II** to be tried for war crimes. The next year, **minimal trials** are held in Leipzig.

22 DEC 1918   **23 MAR 1919**   **10 JAN 1920**   **23 JAN 1920**

18 JAN 1919   **10 SEPT 1919**   **17 JAN 1920**   **27–28 MAR 1920**

The **Paris Peace Conference** opens in **Versailles**, France. Its purpose is to **prevent further wars** through international mediation.

The **Treaty of Saint-Germain-en-Laye confirms the independence** of Czechoslovakia, Poland, Hungary, and the Kingdom of the Serbs, Croats, and Slovenes (future Yugoslavia).

France's wartime leader, Georges Clemenceau, loses the French presidential election, **resigns his premiership**, and gives up all political activities.

Anton Denikin's defeated **White Russian forces** are evacuated from the Black Sea port of Novorossiysk. Thousands left behind are **killed by Bolshevik troops**.

World War I was among the great transformative wars in history. For the first time, mass armies fought each other with weapons that reflected the technological advances of the Industrial Revolution. Increasingly powerful artillery and sophisticated machines were an underlying cause of the war's huge casualty lists. While accurate figures for the lives lost in many individual nations are difficult to find, an overall total for military deaths can be reasonably estimated at more than nine million. Many more millions were wounded and disabled, their injuries both physical and mental – a grim and enduring legacy of the conflict.

Civilian deaths, predominantly caused by disease and starvation, were also extensive. In a further miserable twist, the war contributed to the outbreak of influenza that spread around the world in 1918 and 1919, killing up to 50 million people.

Peace terms

The immeasurable cost of the war in terms of lives and resources led the victorious Allies to impose severe terms on the defeated Central Powers. At the Paris Peace Conference in Versailles, German policy was identified as the prime cause of the war; a clause inserted into the treaty stated that Germany was to be held "responsible". Faced by overwhelming Allied military superiority – and the continuing economic blockade – the German deputation reluctantly signed the treaty on 28 June 1919.

Alsace–Lorraine (taken by Germany in 1871) was returned to France; the newly formed state of Poland was given a land "corridor" to the Baltic through Prussia; and Germany's armed forces were significantly reduced. These terms left a lingering sense of resentment throughout Germany during the 1920s and beyond. The prosecution of alleged war crimes at trials held in Leipzig in 1921 – though limited by extradition problems – further fuelled bitterness towards the Allies.

A more positive consequence of the Versailles treaty was the formation of the League of Nations in 1920. It was the first-ever global intergovernmental organization, and its role was to maintain world peace, encouraging disarmament and settling international disputes. While it did useful work, the League had no permanent armed force, and its voice was weakened by the refusal of the US to join it.

The **Treaty of Sèvres** abolishes the Ottoman Empire and **forces Turkey to yield land and economic rights** to Britain, Italy, Greece, and Armenia.

Field-Marshal **Sir Douglas Haig co-founds the British Legion**, bringing together four national **organizations of ex-servicemen**.

The **US signs separate peace treaties** with Germany and Austria, officially **ending its role in the war**.

Mussolini's **Blackshirts** converge on Rome, confirming the **fascist take-over**. Mussolini is **appointed prime minister** three days later.

10 AUG 1920   15 MAY 1921   24–29 AUG 1921   28 OCT 1922

18 MAR 1921   29 JUL 1921   9 SEP 1922   8–9 NOV 1923

Poland and **Bolshevik Russia** sign a **peace treaty** in Riga, Latvia, bringing the **Russo-Polish conflict to a close**.

Adolf Hitler is made **party chairman** and **absolute leader** of the far-right **National Socialist German Workers' Party (Nazi Party)** in Germany.

Turkish forces capture Smyrna, ending the long-standing **Greek presence in Asia Minor**.

Hitler storms a Munich beer house in **an attempted coup** and is **briefly imprisoned**.

In the 1930s, its position would be further undermined as Japan, Germany, and Italy left to pursue their own aggressive policies.

After the main Paris conference, further treaties were agreed. The old Austro-Hungarian Empire was dismantled, bringing into existence the new states of Czechoslovakia, Poland, and, under Serbian rule, the Kingdom of the Serbs, Croats, and Slovenes (later Yugoslavia). Hungary lost territory to the three new states and, like Austria, became a single sovereign state.

A new USSR and Turkey

After the world war and its own early revolutions, Russia remained in turmoil as civil war broke out between communist Red and anti-Communist White forces. While the White armies received some military support from the Allies, they were too fragmented to overcome the better focused Red forces led by Vladimir Lenin and Leon Trotsky. In December 1922, Russia became the Union of Soviet Socialist Republics (USSR).

In the Middle East, the Turkish Ottoman empire disintegrated. The Turkish heartland of Anatolia became the new Republic of Turkey, while its largely Arab-populated empire was divided up into mandated lands under the control of Britain and France. Turkey objected to the terms of the peace settlement and conducted military operations against the Allied powers, especially Greece. In 1922, Turkey launched a major offensive to take Greek-held land around its border area. The territory won included the city of Smyrna, which

Greece had occupied in 1919 with the blessing of the Allies. After the conflict, Turkey expelled more than a million Greek Christians from its newly won land, and Greece expelled up to 400,000 Muslims.

Fascism on the rise

The far-right doctrine of fascism emerged from the ashes of World War I and achieved its first success in Italy. Led by Benito Mussolini, the Italian Fascist Party gained effective political power in 1922.

Over the next decade, fascism became increasingly influential in Europe, led by Adolf Hitler in Germany and Francisco Franco in Spain. Like Mussolini, they believed that war was an essential political tool to achieve their goals – a belief that would help pave the way for the next great world war. ∎

IT SEEMS TO BE A PLAGUE

THE GREAT INFLUENZA (1918–19)

IN CONTEXT

FOCUS
Contagious diseases

BEFORE
1892 German scientist Richard Pfeiffer mistakenly believes he has isolated the agent responsible for influenza.

1899 A global pandemic of cholera begins in India. It lasts throughout World War I.

1917 Trench fever, a disease spread by lice, is responsible for over a fifth of all casualties attending clearing stations.

AFTER
1945 The US Army sponsors the development of a flu vaccine at the University of Michigan.

1976 An American soldier dies of swine flu, leading to a large vaccination programme.

2020 The World Health Organization declares a global emergency over the spread of Covid-19.

A flu-like **disease** appears in **Europe and the US**.

By summer 1918, **2 million US troops** arrive in France. **Cramped conditions** in ships, hospitals, and cities **spread the virus**.

There is **little understanding** of **viruses** and how they **spread**.

Hugely **increased travel** during and after the war helps **spread the disease**.

Influenza is incorrectly believed to be **spread by a bacterium** rather than a virus, so **no vaccine is created**.

The Great Influenza kills somewhere between 50 million and 100 million people worldwide.

In spring 1918, doctors noticed the first occurrences of a severe flu, at both a US Army camp in Kansas and an Allied field hospital in northern France. Soon afterwards, the flu caused its first deaths. The disease spread rapidly in military camps that could house up to 55,000 personnel. As US troops sailed across the Atlantic Ocean in overcrowded transports and wounded soldiers left the front lines to receive treatment, they took the virus with them. No one knows whether the flu originated in the US or Europe,

See also: Society under strain 184–87 ▪ Treating the wounded 218–21 ▪ The home front in 1918 250–53 ▪ Shattered by war 310–11

> No other disease, no war, no natural disaster, no famine comes close to the great pandemic.
> **Albert Marrin**
> **American historian (1936–)**

but it certainly spread east across the Western Front into Germany and Poland. While media in the combatant nations played down the pandemic, in neutral Spain the press reported that King Alfonso XIII was sick with the mystery illness. From that point on, it was unfairly dubbed the "Spanish flu".

The deadly wave

Over the summer, the outbreak appeared to abate, only to emerge in a more lethal form on both sides of the Atlantic in the early autumn. One of the oddities of this new strain of the virus, which remains unexplained, is that it particularly struck down healthy people between 20 and 40 years of age, as well as the very young and very old. Victims' lungs filled with fluid, sometimes within hours of infection, and they effectively drowned from lack of air.

Cities such as London, England, and Philadelphia, Pennsylvania, in the US, were overwhelmed with thousands of cases. At the time, almost nothing was known about viruses, and a bacterium was believed to be responsible. It soon became clear that close contact between people helped transmit the disease and that it was most likely to be spread by droplets. Many people began to wear cloth masks of varying degrees of effectiveness over their noses and mouths, and some areas enforced forms of social distancing. However, with no public health systems to speak of, there were few coordinated measures to quarantine the sick, just as there was no vaccine to protect the healthy.

The third wave

On 11 November 1918, civilians around the world poured into the streets in jubilant mood to celebrate Armistice Day – thereby giving the virus a chance to spread. That winter, the third wave of the virus was less deadly but spread more widely, partly because hundreds of thousands of soldiers sailed home from Europe. The flu reached as far as Australia and the Pacific Islands. In India, 5 per cent of the country's population died – some 16.7 million people.

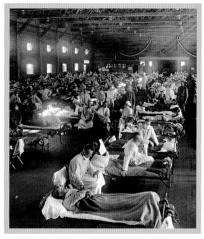

A hospital ward at US Army camp Fort Riley, in Kansas, is overrun with men suffering from the Great Influenza. This is where the first few cases of the disease appeared in spring 1918.

Over the course of 1919, the Great Influenza, which experts now know was a strain of swine flu, H1N1, disappeared as the virus mutated into less lethal forms. In just two years, the flu had killed between 50 million and 100 million people and infected almost one-third of the world's population. ▪

Infectious diseases

Although the Great Influenza pandemic was by far the single most fatal outbreak during World War I, a range of other infectious diseases also affected both combatants and civilians. In overcrowded army camps and trenches, poor sanitation, inadequate nutrition, and a lack of clean water provided the ideal conditions for disease to spread. Away from the front, food shortages left civilians weakened and susceptible to common diseases such as measles, chickenpox, and mumps, as well as other, more serious conditions, such as tuberculosis, meningitis, and pneumonia. Nearly 50 per cent of all those who caught bacterial pneumonia died as a result.

In the trenches, vaccines helped to reduce the effects of typhoid fever and tetanus, but typhus transmitted by lice killed between 2 million and 3 million people on the Eastern Front. Lice were also responsible for trench fever among troops, with symptoms such as fever, dizziness, and headache.

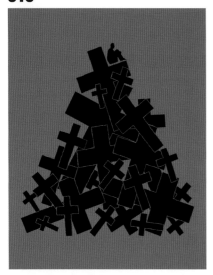

SURVIVORS PERCHED ON A MOUNTAIN OF CORPSES

SHATTERED BY WAR

IN CONTEXT

FOCUS
Impact on humanity

BEFORE
1870–71 Nearly 80–90 per cent of soldiers badly wounded in the Franco-Prussian War die from their injuries, leaving few disabled veterans to fund.

1914 Germany produces hundreds of barrel organs in anticipation of future disabled veterans needing them to beg for alms.

AFTER
1919–30s Globally, war-related pensions cost 8–18 per cent of government expenditure.

1921 Sir Douglas Haig co-founds the British Legion, which is established to support veterans and commemorate the war.

1930s The decline in birth rate during and after World War I affects the numbers of men available for conscription on the eve of World War II.

In the months that followed the Armistice of 11 November 1918, the world hoped for a return to peaceful normality. However, the cessation of the conflict, in which 11 million soldiers had died, required the dismantling of the whole war apparatus.

Demobilization was a priority, since servicemen expected a swift return to their home countries from the ravaged lands of the front. Repatriation was a huge logistical undertaking. The state took charge for Allied soldiers, with priority based on a soldier's age, length of service, and number of times he had been wounded in battle. The broken governments of the Central Powers, however, provided little help. Their men often made their own way home, with 1 million German soldiers alone reaching their fatherland on foot.

Soldiers travelled from crowded camps and trenches on similarly packed transport, some bringing

American soldiers wave from their packed troop ship as they approach the docks at Hoboken, New Jersey, US, after serving on the front line in France.

See also: The home front in 1918 250–53 ▪ The Great Influenza 308–09 ▪ Post-war conflicts 320–21 ▪ The rise of fascism 322–23 ▪ Remembering the war 324–27

a third wave of the Great Influenza home with them. By the summer of 1919, the pandemic had claimed the lives of at least 50 million people worldwide.

The servicemen leaving the front were joined by the displaced. Unrest following the Russian Revolution led to migrants heading to Europe and, in some cases, the US and Canada. At the same time, newly drawn European borders resulted in people being ejected from their homes when their nationality, religion, or ethnicity did not comply with new state rules. In the two years after the Armistice, almost 10 million people were deported or expelled, and more fled voluntarily.

Changing societies

Home nations absorbed millions of returning men into societies that remained short of food and were mourning the dead. The huge numbers of men lost to the war led to a dramatic fall in birth rates and a disproportionate number of adolescents, elderly

> None of us had had any money for many weeks. We were hoping to get a decent meal, and they had nothing to offer us.
> **Edgar Woolley**
> **British soldier, on returning to Britain, January 1919**

A British soldier stands with his wife and children outside makeshift accommodation following his return from the front line.

people, and women in affected populations. There was also a large number of widows and orphans, so three generations suffered loss. In Britain, more than half of the bereaved women did not remarry. In all combatant nations, young women now greatly outnumbered the eligible bachelors, reducing their prospect of marriage.

Rationing remained in place in Britain until 1921, and wartime disruption to food supplies continued globally. The German population, which had suffered a higher civilian death rate in the autumn of 1918 than any other warring nation, had to recover from severe malnourishment.

By the end of 1919, men had taken back their jobs or found new employment where they could. Women returned – sometimes reluctantly – to the home. People longed for the normality of their traditional family life, and some found it. For most, however, the old plans for their future had been shattered by the war, and it was not yet clear what paths their lives would take in the post-war society. ▪

The war wounded

Around 8 million people worldwide were permanently injured in the war. Some were disfigured or blinded or had lung problems from poison gas; many were amputees. A quarter had shell shock. Reintegration into society depended on the disability, state support, family situation, and public attitudes.

In December 1918, more than 10,000 German veterans marched to Berlin's ministry of war office to demand better pensions and greater honour for the country's 2.7 million disabled soldiers. Some had already taken to the streets to beg. From a disorganized beginning, the German rehabilitation system soon became the world's most advanced, with institutions run by Church and state that guaranteed treatment and retraining for veterans.

In Britain, the government provided pensions linked to the level of disability, but for most it was not enough to live on. There was no state retraining and care fell to families or charities.

Soldiers are fitted with prosthetic legs at London's Roehampton House hospital, which specialized in the care of amputees.

WE HAVE COME HERE AS FRIENDS

A LASTING PEACE? (1919)

IN CONTEXT

FOCUS
Peace talks

BEFORE
1915 The International Congress of Women in The Hague, Netherlands, leads to the founding of the Women's International League for Peace and Freedom.

March 1918 The new Bolshevik government in Russia negotiates a separate peace with the Central Powers.

October 1918 Germany appeals for a peace based on US President Woodrow Wilson's Fourteen Points.

AFTER
November 1920 The first meeting of the League of Nations Assembly opens in Geneva, Switzerland.

1933 After joining the League of Nations in 1926, Germany withdraws as a member.

For US president Woodrow Wilson, the war was not a clash of national interests but a conflict of ideals. He distrusted the war aims of both the Allies and the Central Powers, and saw the US as the world's moral leader. On 30 May 1919, speaking at the Suresnes American Cemetery outside Paris, Wilson argued for governments to embrace a new order "in which the only questions will be, 'Is it right?', 'Is it just?', 'Is it in the interests of mankind?'"

European officials demanded vindication and accountability for the immense human and material losses their countries had endured during World War I. In contrast, Wilson took a large world view of democracy, self-determination, and free trade. For him, the centrepiece was the creation of an international organization to ensure peace through collective security, in which law, diplomacy, commerce, and public opinion would deter aggressors.

Many in Europe applauded Wilson's vision, but some others, including the president's conservative critics in the US, perceived collective security

> God gave us the Ten Commandments, and we broke them. Wilson gave us the Fourteen Points – we shall see.
> **Georges Clemenceau**

as an infringement on national sovereignty. The potential conflict between war and national interest could not be denied. If world opinion failed to deter an aggressor motivated by fear, pride, or ambition, then it remained hard to establish who would stop the invader.

A victor's peace

In January 1919, President Wilson travelled to Paris to negotiate in person with the heads of the Allied powers, gathered in the Palace of Versailles. Representatives of Russia and the defeated states

---

Georges Clemenceau

Born in the Vendée, in southwest France, in 1841 and trained as a physician, Georges Clemenceau was a politician, statesman, and journalist. After Germany's victory in the Franco-Prussian War (1870–71), he was elected to the National Assembly, where he voted against the humiliating cession of most of Alsace and parts of Lorraine. Out of politics in the 1890s, he gained his nickname "the Tiger" for his crusading journalism. At that time, he vigorously defended the innocence of Jewish officer Alfred Dreyfus, convicted in 1894 of selling secrets to Germany. As premier from 1906 to 1909, Clemenceau stengthened the Entente Cordiale with Britain. Re-elected in November 1917, when France was exhausted and dispirited after years of conflict, he exhorted the nation and the army to victory.

Despite Clemenceau's impressive record of leading his country, many blamed him for not extracting more for France from the Treaty of Versailles. After failing in a bid to become president, he resigned as premier in 1920, dying in 1929.

See also: The US and World War I 134–35 ▪ The US enters the war 194–95 ▪ Putting the US on a war footing 196–97
▪ German victory in Eastern Europe 258–59 ▪ The end of the war in Italy 284–85 ▪ Breaking the Hindenburg Line 290–93

Representatives of the Allies – including Sir Douglas Haig, sitting back in his chair – meet at Versailles to work out the terms of the treaty.

his long-cherished idea for a collective security structure to promote peace and prevent war.

The US president, however, met stiff resistance from the European leaders, who forcefully defended their national interests. Clemenceau demanded the break-up of Germany and the transfer of territory west of the Rhine to France. These requests were unsuccessful, but the French premier did secure the return of Alsace–Lorraine, the demilitarization of the Rhineland, and a limit on the number of German armed forces. The British and French negotiators insisted that Germany pay reparations, and Wilson agreed in principle, with potentially huge payments to be determined.

A raft of treaties
Throughout 1919 and 1920, the defeated Central Powers signed a series of peace agreements that »

were not present, and most of the key decisions were worked out by the "Big Four": Wilson himself, British prime minister David Lloyd George, French premier Georges Clemenceau, and Italian prime minister Vittorio Orlando.

The Big Four were negotiating a victor's peace – one enforced by, and in the interests of, the winning side. Of necessity, it centred on the disposal of German power. In secret sessions, Wilson also worked to convince the others to accept the

Fourteen Points he had articulated in January 1918. Not only did he come with facts prepared by the Inquiry – a study group of American diplomats, lawyers, and historians set up in 1917 – but he also had international public support. Wilson could credibly assert the importance of the US to Europe, as demonstrated by American contributions to the military victory. He was determined to include in the final treaties the creation of the League of Nations,

---

The devastating **loss of life and property** in the war makes the victors determined to **punish Germany and its allies**.

European leaders force Wilson to **compromise on his demands** to gain their acceptance of the **League of Nations**.

After the peace talks end, the fragile structure of the League of Nations fails to prevent another world war.

US president Woodrow Wilson calls for **"peace without victory"** and **reform** of the **old politics of power**.

Wilson believes the inclusion of the **League of Nations** in the **peace settlement** will prevent future aggression and **help secure peace**.

formally terminated World War I. The central document – concluded on 28 June in the Hall of Mirrors – was the Treaty of Versailles with Germany. It included a "war guilt clause" (Article 231) that named Germany as the sole aggressor and made it responsible "for causing all the loss and damage" suffered by the Allied nations and their citizens.

Redrawing the map

On 10 September, Austria signed the Treaty of Saint-Germain-en-Laye, confirming the break-up of its once formidable navy and also recognizing the independence of Czechoslovakia, Hungary, the Kingdom of Serbs, Croats, and Slovenes (future Yugoslavia), and Poland. With the Treaty of Neuilly of 27 November, Bulgaria ceded land to Greece and the Kingdom of Serbs, Croats, and Slovenes. Following the Treaty of Trianon of 4 June 1920, Hungary gave up more than half of its territory to other nations. The Treaty of Sèvres (10 August) forced the Ottoman Empire to yield land and economic rights to France, Britain, Italy, Greece, and Armenia.

All of these treaties included a charter of the League of Nations. Several of the specific Fourteen Points appeared in the treaties, too: Belgium was restored, Poland's independence was recognized, subject peoples in the Austro-Hungarian Empire won self-determination, and American troops withdrew from Russia.

A flawed outcome

Wilson had accomplished much, but the peace was confusing and critically flawed. Germany was given no choice in the terms, and Article 231 burdened subsequent German leaders with a reparations bill their country would struggle to meet. The drawing of new national boundaries in Eastern Europe had mixed results, and self-determination often proved to be an impossible ideal.

The break-up of Austria-Hungary left Eastern and Central Europe in economic and political chaos and created a power vacuum between Germany and Russia. Consigning purely German areas, such as the Sudetenland, to the new Slavic nations hardly served the principle of self-determination or the cause of peace. In addition, the Bolshevik revolution had alienated Britain and France from Russia, making cooperative efforts to control tensions in Eastern Europe unlikely.

Post-war redistribution of the colonies of the defeated nations also fell victim to big-power politics. Wilson had envisaged a mandate system to prepare colonial areas for independence under temporary tutelage by advanced nations. In reality, the victorious Allies ended up appropriating the territories of the losers for themselves. Despite Wilson's rhetoric about self-determination, appeals by subject peoples in places such as French Indochina received no hearing at Versailles.

Japan had entered the war on the side of the Allies in 1914 and quickly seized German territorial concessions in China's Shandong province. With backing from Britain and France, Japan gained confirmation of this transfer in the Treaty of Versailles. China, which had joined the Allied war effort in 1917 with a view to preventing this very development, withdrew from the peace conference and became the only participating nation not to sign the treaty.

How to achieve peace

Aware that he had compromised many of his principles in the Paris negotiations, Wilson remained convinced that the League of Nations would ultimately correct biases and inequities without

European boundaries before and after the war

Before the war, Central and Eastern Europe were dominated by three empires. Afterwards, Austria-Hungary was broken up, Germany lost its empire, and Russia – soon to be the USSR – relinquished much territory.

Vittorio Orlando

Born in Sicily in 1860, Vittorio Orlando was one of Italy's leading legal scholars and a supporter of liberal reforms. He was elected to the Chamber of Deputies in 1897, and between 1903 and 1909 headed the ministries of education and justice. From June 1916, he served as interior minister and then as prime minister following Italy's military disaster at Caporetto in October 1917.

Since Italy had lost almost 2 million lives in the war, Orlando rightfully took his place among the Big Four at Versailles, but the other leaders overshadowed him.

He did not speak English, had a divided delegation, and was often away in Rome on government business. He left the Paris Peace Conference following the decision not to award the disputed Adriatic port of Fiume (Rijeka) to Italy. Orlando took pride in not signing the treaty, but having failed to serve Italy's territorial interests, he resigned as prime minister in June 1919, though he stayed in government until the rise of Mussolini.

After World War II, Orlando became a senator – a role he held until his death in 1952.

committing nations to the use of force to preserve peace. He believed that collective security would operate through the power of world opinion. This principle was expressed in Article X of the covenant of the League of Nations and was included in all of the treaties. It committed members of the League to respect the territorial integrity and political independence of all of its members against external aggression. The question was how to achieve this goal. The European leaders knew that without any commitment of force it was idealistic; however, they accepted Wilson's language in the hope of keeping the traditionally isolationist US constructively engaged with post-war Europe.

Senate opposition

Wilson had succeeded in getting the leaders of the exhausted European states to sign up to his dream of peace, but he faced opposition at home. Senator Henry Cabot Lodge, a long-time Republican opponent of the Democratic president, expressed 14 reservations about the League and especially Article X.

Partly motivated by political calculations about who would get credit with American voters or the form the peace took, Lodge also had genuine concerns about protecting US sovereignty in the League. While Wilson adamantly opposed attaching any conditions to entry of the US into the League, Lodge argued that Article X would subvert its sovereignty by pledging the country's commitment to a future war declared by an international organization. The

> This age ... rejects the standards of national selfishness that once governed the counsel of nations and demands that they shall give way to a new order of things.
> **Woodrow Wilson**

senator understood that the US had an interest in the security of Britain, in particular, and he was willing to accept League membership providing the US was not required to commit its forces to the defence of other nations without the consent of Congress.

Wilson's campaign fails

President Wilson insisted that Article X was a moral, not legal, obligation and would accept no modifications. He embarked on a cross-country speaking tour to mobilize the public behind his view. This came to an abrupt end when he suffered a massive stroke in October 1919, but the lines had already been drawn. In November, the Senate voted against ratifying the treaty as it stood, then against ratification with reservations. Ironically, most senators supported some form of participation by the US in the settlement, but a final vote in March 1920 with reworded reservations failed by seven votes to gain the two-thirds required for ratification. In 1921, the US signed separate peace treaties with Germany and Austria, officially ending its role in the war. ∎

A SCANDALOUS FAILURE OF JUSTICE
WAR-CRIMES TRIALS (1921)

Those who framed the 1919 Treaty of Versailles were keen to underline Germany's responsibility for the war. Germany had not just lost – it had been in the wrong. The treaty ordered that a special tribunal should be set up to try Kaiser Wilhelm II "for a supreme offence against international morality and the sanctity of treaties". In addition, Germany was to recognize the right of the Allies to try all those accused of having committed "acts in violation of the laws and customs of war".

Bulgaria and the Ottoman Empire were also ordered to produce their criminals for trial.

Extradition resisted
The quest to hold Germany's leaders accountable for war crimes was dealt a decisive blow in January 1920, when the neutral Netherlands, which had granted the kaiser asylum, formally rejected Allied demands to extradite him. Initially undeterred, the Allies proceeded to present the government of the Weimar Republic with a list of people who they considered war

---

The **Allies demand** that **war criminals** be extradited to **face trial**.

→

Defeated Imperial Germany has **no choice** but to **agree**.

↓

The Allies produce a **list of 900 defendants** they want prosecuted, but **Germany drags its feet**.

←

The **Dutch government's refusal** to extradite the kaiser **undermines Allied plans** to try German leaders.

↓

Germany negotiates a dramatic reduction of the number of indictments.

See also: The invasion of Belgium 50–51 ▪ The sinking of the *Lusitania* 106–07 ▪ Concentration camps 108–09 ▪ The Armenian Genocide 132–33 ▪ The end of the Serbian campaign 140–43 ▪ The U-boats on the attack 200–05

> ... the German Supreme Court is making of a few privates and minor officers scapegoats for the army and the nation.
> **The New York Times**
> **3 June 1921**

criminals. Their names included the leading statesmen, generals, and admirals of Imperial Germany.

It soon became clear that the failure to bring Wilhelm II to trial seriously compromised the plans to try other former German leaders before Allied judges. The focus then shifted to lower-ranking former officers who were directly involved in "acts in violation of the laws and customs of war", such as submarine commanders known to have sunk passenger liners or hospital ships, or army officers involved in the killing of civilians or mistreatment of prisoners of war.

The Allied demand for the extradition of war criminals, like the demand for reparations, was extremely unpopular with the vast majority of German citizens, and the Weimar Republic refused to comply. Bulgaria and the Ottoman Empire followed suit, and all three countries proposed instead to try their own citizens before their own courts. Ultimately, the Allies agreed, and the indictments against German citizens were negotiated. Of these, only 11 defendants ever stood trial. Some of the most serious German crimes – such as the massacre of 6,500 civilians in Belgium in 1914 – were never prosecuted.

A shameful charade

The trials, held in Leipzig in 1921, proved controversial. Although deeply resented by the German public as an exercise in "victor's justice", the proceedings appeared farcical to Allied observers. Just four defendants were convicted, none of whom received more than four years' imprisonment.

The trials had a lasting impact. In convicting two U-boat lieutenants, German judges rejected the idea that they had simply been "following orders", thus setting a precedent for future war-crimes proceedings. The unsatisfactory outcome also informed the way the Allies approached prosecution of war crimes at the end of World War II. ▪

A group of British witnesses, who had been prisoners of the Germans during the war, leaves the Supreme Court building after a hearing of the 1921 Leipzig trials.

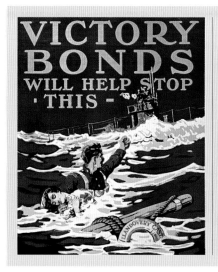

HMHS *Llandovery Castle*

On 27 June 1918, the Canadian hospital ship HMHS *Llandovery Castle* was off the southern coast of Ireland when it was struck by a torpedo and started to sink. The torpedo had come from the U-boat *U-86*, captained by Helmut Brümmer-Patzig. Attacking a hospital ship was an atrocity in itself, but Patzig had compounded

Propaganda posters used dramatic imagery from the sinking of HMHS *Llandovery Castle* to sell Victory (or war) bonds.

his crime by ploughing through life rafts and machine-gunning survivors. By the time he had finished, 234 people – doctors, nurses, army medics, soldiers, and sailors – had been killed. There were only 24 survivors.

At war's end, Patzig fled to independent Danzig, leaving his *Oberleutnants* Ludwig Dithmar and John Boldt to be tried in 1921. They pleaded that they had only been obeying orders. Both were found guilty but had their convictions overturned.

ONLY THE DEAD HAVE SEEN THE END OF THE WAR

POST-WAR CONFLICTS (1919–22)

IN CONTEXT

FOCUS
Wars and revolutions

BEFORE
1899 The February Manifesto limits the autonomy of Finland as a Grand Duchy of the Russian Empire.

April 1916 Irish nationalists launch a revolt against British rule in what becomes known as the Easter Rising.

March 1918 British troops arrive in Murmansk, Russia. French, Japanese, and American forces soon follow.

AFTER
January 1924 The first full constitution of the USSR comes into effect.

March 1924 King George II of Greece is overthrown, marking the birth of the Greek Republic.

1949 The Irish Free State officially becomes the Republic of Ireland.

The chaos at the end of world war in 1918 provided the opportunity for the revival of old local conflicts. It also saw the rise of new flashpoints.

In Ireland, the Sinn Féin republican party's election victory in December 1918 triggered the Irish War of Independence. When the British government conceded all but Ireland's northernmost six counties as a "Free State" in 1921, the conflict turned into civil war. Free Staters, who accepted the concession, feeling that the loss of Northern Ireland was a price worth

The Third Tipperary Brigade was responsible for the first act of the Irish War of Independence when it ambushed a convoy carrying explosives in the village of Soloheadbeg in January 1919.

paying, fought a bitter war with Republicans, who did not. In 1923, "pro-treaty" forces prevailed.

Russia after the Revolution

In early 1918, the Allies had hoped to work with Russia's Bolsehvik revolutionaries to stop Germany's eastwards expansion. This was thwarted, though, when the Soviet government signed the Treaty of Brest-Litovsk with Germany in March and withdrew from the war.

Russia was now cast instead into a civil war against anti-communist forces, known as the Whites, who were backed by Western powers, including Britain and France. By the end of 1920, however, the Soviet Red Army had defeated the White forces.

The Russian Revolution also had deep repercussions for countries that were previously part of the Tsarist empire. With Soviet support, workers' movements had sprung up in Finland, Latvia, Lithuania, and Estonia, as well as in Belarus, Ukraine, Moldavia, and the Caucasus. The Soviets would fight several wars on behalf of their communist supporters in those countries against what they saw as reactionary interests. Some

See also: The situation in Europe 18–19 ▪ The Balkans 25 ▪ The Ottoman Empire in decline 26–27 ▪ Ottoman Turkey enters the war 84–85 ▪ The Easter Rising 160–61 ▪ The Arab Revolt 170–71 ▪ Greece and the Macedonian Front 226–27

Bolshevism is a disease which is peculiar to Russia. It will never grow deep roots in any countries which are not entirely Russian.
Józef Piłsudski
Polish chief of state, 1918–22

Young Red Army soldiers march through Moscow after being recruited for the Polish-Soviet War, which broke out in 1919, following Poland's invasion of Ukraine in November 1918.

they won – followed by Soviet annexation – others they lost, producing independent states.

In April 1919, Russia went to war against the recently established Second Polish Republic, which had invaded Ukraine with the support of local anti-Soviet fighters. Russia counterattacked and almost conquered Poland, but its forces were turned back at Warsaw. The Peace of Riga (1921) divided Belarus and Ukraine between Poland and Soviet Russia.

The Greco-Turkish conflict

Scrambling to secure support at the start of the war, the Allies had made many, often conflicting, commitments, including what seemed to be the promise of Eastern Thrace to both Greece and Ottoman Turkey, the two countries that straddled the region. On 15 May 1919, with the blessing of the Allies, Greek troops occupied the western Turkish city of Smyrna. Much of the local population was of Greek origin (just as much of that of western Thrace and Macedonia was Turkish), and they welcomed the intervention. Turkey did not, and a Greco-Turkish war broke out in August 1922, ending with Turkish victory in the Battle of Dumlupinar (26–30 August). By October, Turkey had recaptured Smyrna and won the war.

A population exchange was agreed between the nations. Up to 400,000 Muslims were expelled from Greece and some 1.2 million Greek Christians were expelled from what was now definitively Turkish territory. ▪

The rise of Egyptian nationalism

At the Paris Peace Conference in 1919, there was an unwelcome presence for Britain – Egyptian nationalist Saad Zaghloul. He had led a campaign of civil disobedience, demanding independence for Egypt and Sudan from the Ottoman Empire. Britain was reluctant to see independence granted as its stewardship of the Suez Canal created an interest in Egypt that overrode the wishes of the people. The canal was vital to world trade, and particularly important for Britain given its possessions in India.

Britain sent Saad Zaghloul into exile in Malta, inflaming the situation in his homeland. A cause first embraced only by intellectuals and students was now also taken up by workers and peasants. The heavy-handed response of British soldiers to the unrest only exacerbated the Egyptians' anger. In February 1922, Britain granted Egypt a limited amount of autonomy, delivering the revolutionaries a partial victory.

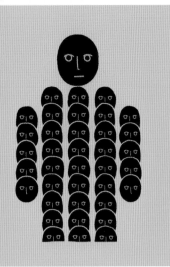

THE STATE IS ABSOLUTE

THE RISE OF FASCISM (1921–23)

IN CONTEXT

FOCUS
Extreme nationalism

BEFORE
1909 Italian poet Filippo Tommaso Marinetti publishes the *Manifesto of Futurism*, an influence on the development of fascist ideology.

1914 Benito Mussolini founds the Fasces of Revolutionary Action, a movement promoting Italy's entry into the war.

AFTER
1929–39 Global mass unemployment during the Great Depression helps fuel the popularity of fascism.

1933 Adolf Hitler is appointed chancellor of Germany. He begins laying the groundwork for a fascist dictatorship.

1936–39 The Spanish Civil War takes place. Victory for the Nationalists marks the start of General Francisco Franco's authoritarian regime.

After the end of World War I, millions of people turned to fascism, an emerging political ideology that promised order, protection, and prosperity. This, however, came at the expense of minority groups and competing political views.

Fascism took its name from the fasces, a bundle of rods tied around an axe, and a symbol of authority in ancient Rome. The movement found wide support, especially in Europe, where the ideology had started to coalesce in the late 19th century.

Fascism did not come to power through normal means. It arrived there by marching on Rome *armata manu*, with a real insurrectional act.
Benito Mussolini
from a speech given in 1924

Many thinkers were outraged at the apparent decadence of an industrialized, individualistic, and increasingly democratic Europe, and they called for a more ordered society. In the chaos of post-war Europe, with communism a rising influence, fascists began to focus their ideas more clearly.

An Italian breeding ground
Fascism found fertile territory in Italy, where there was widespread disillusionment with the cost of the war. The country's main fascist party was the Fasci Italiani di Combattimento (Italian Fasces of Combat), founded in March 1919 and renamed the National Fascist Party in 1921. It was led by political agitator and former journalist Benito Mussolini, who sought to appeal to fellow army veterans – men who went on to form the spine of his militia, the Blackshirts.

Another prominent figure was Gabriele d'Annunzio, a poet who had risen to fame for the Flight over Vienna in August 1918, a mission to drop propaganda leaflets. Angered that the disputed territory of Fiume might not be assigned to Italy despite its significant Italian population, d'Annunzio seized the

See also: Public opinion 44–45 ▪ The end of the war in Italy 284–85 ▪ Mutiny and revolution in Germany 288–89
▪ The Armistice 294–99 ▪ Shattered by war 310–11 ▪ A lasting peace? 312–17 ▪ Post-war conflicts 320–21

Populism feeds into **hyper-nationalist views** and sees the **formation of paramilitary groups**.

Patriarchy is emphasized, promoting modernity and romanticizing **violence as a positive force**.

Conspiracy theorists concoct elaborate plots to explain their **government's shortcomings**.

Racists and xenophobes blame **minority groups** for society's ills. In Europe, this is often **antisemitic** in nature.

Promoting extreme nationalism, a sole leader seizes power. Police and military rule replaces democratic governance.

city in September 1919 and made himself *Duce* ("leader"). He only surrendered in December 1920, following an attack by the Italian military and five days of fighting.

Inspired by d'Annunzio's action, in October 1922 Mussolini ordered his Blackshirts to march on Rome and seize strategic points. King Victor Emmanuel III, fearing a breakdown in order, appointed Mussolini prime minister, creating the world's first fascist government.

Fascism in Germany

Mussolini's ideas soon found many admirers, particularly in Germany, where there was widespread political turmoil following the country's defeat in World War I and its acceptance of the Treaty of Versailles, the terms of which were perceived as excessively harsh. Hundreds of thousands of veterans, seeking to recapture the camaraderie of the front line, joined *Freikorps* – independent militias that fought against communist groups. Their members were often sympathetic to fascist ideas, such as those spread by Adolf Hitler, the *Führer* ("leader") of the Nazis, then a small party based in Bavaria.

In 1923, seeking to emulate Mussolini and take advantage of an economic crisis caused by hyperinflation, Hitler tried to seize power in a coup. The Munich Putsch – which had the support of the wartime military leader Erich Ludendorff – swiftly collapsed, and Hitler was imprisoned. However, it placed Hitler and the Nazis in the national consciousness. Later, during the Great Depression, the Nazis and other fascist groups would take advantage of economic upheaval to rise to power. ▪

Adolf Hitler

The architect of the most destructive fascist dictatorship, Adolf Hitler was born in Branau am Inn, Austria, in 1889. He grew to hate multinational Austria and became a German nationalist.

When World War I broke out, Hitler was living in Munich. He volunteered for the Bavarian Army, where he served in the infantry and became lance corporal. He fought in a number of battles, including Ypres, the Somme, and Passchendaele, was wounded several times,

and awarded the Iron Cross Second Class in 1914 and First Class in 1918. When he heard of Germany's defeat, Hitler was convalescing after a gas attack. The Armistice and subsequent Treaty of Versailles instilled in him a sense of injustice and thirst for revenge that he never lost.

After the war, Hitler remained in the military as an intelligence agent monitoring nationalist groups. After being discharged in 1920, he would go on to join – and lead – one of them: the German Workers' Party, which later developed into the Nazi Party.

IN FLANDERS FIELDS THE POPPIES BLOW

REMEMBERING THE WAR

IN CONTEXT

FOCUS
Memorialization

BEFORE
1836 In Paris, the Arc de Triomphe, commissioned after Napoleon I's victory at Austerlitz in 1805, is unveiled.

1843 Nelson's Column, in London, commemorates the British admiral's victory at the 1805 Battle of Trafalgar.

AFTER
1946 The ruins of the French village of Oradour-sur-Glane, site of a 1944 Nazi massacre, become a national memorial.

1982 The Vietnam Veterans Memorial is inaugurated in Washington, DC, in the US.

1988 At Choeung Ek, in Cambodia, human skulls are the centrepiece of a memorial to the victims of the Khmer Rouge regime.

O nce the guns had stopped in Belgium and northern France in November 1918, carpets of bright red poppies began to spread over the heavily cratered and blasted landscape. They had seeded easily in ground blown open by bursting shells.

Poppies inspired John McCrae, a Canadian military surgeon who had been tending the wounded at the Second Battle of Ypres, to write "In Flanders Fields" – on 3 May 1915, the day after his friend Alexis Helmer was killed. The poem – which ends with the lines, "We shall not sleep, though poppies grow/In Flanders fields" – was published in the British magazine *Punch* and

See also: Public opinion 44–45 ▪ Replacing the fallen 198–99 ▪ The home front in 1918 250–53 ▪ The Armistice 294–99 ▪ A lasting peace? 312–17

Wild red poppies grow around the Trench of Death, or *Dodengang*, in Diksmuide, Belgium. This preserved section of World War I military trenches is now a memorial site.

immediately captured the public mood. It was copied, reprinted, and widely passed from hand to hand.

The poppy as a symbol

McCrae died in early 1918. By then, the poppy had become a symbol of the bloodshed on the Western Front. Following the war, it was a Frenchwoman, Anna Guérin, who made it a symbol of remembrance. Inspired by McCrae's poem, she persuaded the American-Franco Children's League to take the poppy as its emblem; she also originated the idea of holding fundraising Poppy Days, when paper poppies were handed out in return for donations. In 1921, "the Poppy Lady from France", as Guérin became known, travelled to Canada and Britain proposing an Inter-Allied Poppy Day.

The British Legion, a veterans' association co-founded by Field Marshal Sir Douglas Haig in 1921, took to the idea, and a Poppy Day was declared for the third anniversary of the Armistice,

11 November 1921. Poppy Days were also held in Australia, New Zealand, and Canada; and Britain and its empire – and later Commonwealth – countries would go on to hold poppy days each year.

Honour and remembrance

Remembrance was a pressing issue as the war drew to a close and in the years that followed. Rather than looking to celebrate their victory, people in Allied nations wondered how best to honour the dead and injured, and how to create "spaces" where those who had lost loved ones could grieve. In the past, memorials had been raised to great generals and admirals, while wealthy families might remember a son lost in battle with a monument in a church. Most "ordinary" soldiers were not memorialized in stone, bronze, or national ceremonies. The aftermath of the war, however, saw mass memorials erected, on which, for the first time, the names of the dead were listed in alphabetical order rather than by military rank. »

Is it a break of faith with you, Peter, if I can now see only madness in the war?
Käthe Kollwitz
German artist,
diary entry, 11 October 1916

A mother's grief

On 22 October 1914, soon after the start of the war, German sculptor and printmaker Käthe Kollwitz's son Peter died in Belgium. Aged 18, he had volunteered for the German army. "There is in our lives a wound which will never heal", the devastated Kollwitz told a friend, speaking for herself and her husband Karl. "Nor should it", she added. A socialist and pacifist, Kollwitz pondered how she might create a fitting memorial, eventually conceiving the idea of a sculpture of herself and her husband, kneeling in grief before their son's grave. She started work on the sculpture after the war, and it was installed in Roggeveld cemetery in Belgium in 1932. Tragically, Kollwitz would later also lose a grandson during World War II.

Since 1993, a replica of Kollwitz's *Mother with Her Dead Son* has been the centrepiece of the Central Memorial of the Federal Republic of Germany for the Victims of War and Dictatorship, in Berlin.

Käthe Kollwitz's *Mother with Her Dead Son* was inspired by traditional *Pietà* depictions of the Virgin Mary with the dead Christ.

Throughout the war, the act of memorialization had to respond to new levels of suffering, but also patriotism. Initially, in London's East End, people created street shrines to celebrate local soldiers. After the German victory at Tannenberg, in 1914, a huge wooden statue of General Paul von Hindenburg was erected in Berlin's Tiergarten. People could buy nails to hammer into it, with all money raised going to the war effort. Inevitably, though, the mood changed. Soon, shrines began to appear in homes, where a corner of a room might be set aside for mementos of a dead son or husband. In Berlin, the number of people buying nails to hammer into the Hindenburg statue began to decrease, as people began to grow weary of the war.

Public occasions

When the Treaty of Versailles brought the war to an official end in June 1919, Allied leaders considered how to celebrate the occasion. French prime minister Georges Clemenceau arranged a victory parade in Paris on 14 July, while British prime minister David Lloyd George called for a similar parade in London on 19 July. The centrepiece of the London event was a cenotaph (from the Greek for "empty tomb"), designed by British architect Edwin Lutyens and made from wood, plaster, and canvas. Its pared-back dignity appealed to people, and they queued in their thousands to lay wreaths around it. Urged on by popular demand, the government voted to have it rebuilt in stone as a permanent structure.

November 1919 marked the first anniversary of the Armistice. In Washington, DC, US president Woodrow Wilson recalled the ways in which his nation had brought material and moral aid "to the assistance of our associates in Europe". And in Britain, King George V instituted the tradition of a two-minute silence at 11am in order to concentrate everyone's thoughts "in remembrance of the glorious dead". Without any sense in Germany of lives having

> Many of them carried wreaths, and there were few who had not brought some simple token to place by the Cenotaph.
>
> **Anonymous observer**
> **London, November 1920**

been lost in the name of victory, national monuments came much later. It was not until 1935 that the Tannenberg Memorial (finished in 1927) was declared a Reich memorial by Adolf Hitler.

The unknown warrior

What made bereavement especially hard for many was the lack of a body, since many fallen soldiers were never found or identified. This problem was partly addressed in 1920, when Armistice Day saw burials of the "unknown soldier" in London and Paris. For the British, the idea arose in 1916, when an army chaplain in France, the Reverend David Railton, saw a solitary grave marked with the words "An unknown British soldier". It struck Railton that men whose remains had never been found could be honoured by bringing home the body of an unidentified soldier to bury at Westminster Abbey, in London. He suggested the idea to the abbey's dean, who proposed it to the prime minister and king.

Members of the Allied armies march through the Arc de Triomphe and down the Champs-Elysées in Paris on 14 July 1919, in celebration of the recently signed Treaty of Versailles.

On 7 November 1920, several British bodies were exhumed from various battlefields in Belgium and France. They were taken to a chapel in Saint-Pol-sur-Ternoise, in northern France, where a senior British officer selected one. The chosen coffin travelled to the English port of Dover by warship, then to London by train. On 11 November, it was taken on a gun carriage to Westminster Abbey, where a funeral service was held. Some 1.25 million people filed past the tomb in the week that followed. In France, a body was similarly chosen and buried under the Arc de Triomphe. In November 1921, an unidentified American was buried at the Tomb of the Unknown Soldier in Arlington National Cemetery, Virginia. Germany also buried an unknown soldier, but not until 1931.

War graves and memorials

Beyond the anonymous dead, millions of bodies were identified and buried. For most British soldiers this meant being interred on foreign soil, since the British government had decided not to repatriate the dead. Article 225 of the Treaty of Versailles stipulated that the Allied and German governments had to

The white headstones at Tyne Cot Cemetery, just outside Ypres, Belgium, are intensely moving, not least for their sheer number – almost 12,000 Commonwealth soldiers are buried here.

respect and maintain the graves of those soldiers and sailors buried on their respective territories, regardless of nationality. Most countries created commissions for overseeing their war cemeteries. The French already had Le Souvenir Français, founded in 1887. In Britain, former civil servant Fabian Ware was the driving force behind the Imperial (later Commonwealth) War Graves Commission. The German War Graves Commission began as a private charity in 1919,

and in 1923 US president Warren Harding authorized the American Battle Monuments Commission.

Battlefield memorials were also created, including Ypres' Menin Gate Memorial to the Missing by Britain's Sir Reginald Blomfield, and Thiepval's Memorial to the Missing of the Somme by Lutyens. Canada erected a memorial at Vimy Ridge, and France the Trench of Bayonets near Verdun. In Italy, the Redipuglia memorial honours the huge losses on the Isonzo front. In Gallipoli, the Helles Memorial stands in tribute to the fallen of Australia, New Zealand, and Britain.

Remembrance sculptures

Villages, towns, churches, clubs, and workplaces also erected memorials, such as the *Floating Angel*, which hung in the cathedral of Güstrow, Germany. Sculptor Ernst Barlach modelled the face on that of his friend Käthe Kollwitz. Condemned by the Nazis as "degenerate", the sculpture was removed in 1937 and later melted down. Luckily, a copy survived and was hung in a Cologne church after World War II. Another copy has hung in Güstrow since 1953. ∎

Turning to spiritualism

Made desperate by grief, some bereaved families turned to spiritualism as a means, they believed, of contacting the dead. Involving séances presided over by mediums supposedly in tune with the spirit world, spiritualism had been popular in the US, Britain, and France since the mid-19th century.

One enthusiast was British physicist Sir Oliver Lodge, who was a researcher in the field of electromagnetic radiation. When his son Raymond died,

in 1915, Lodge and his family found solace through British medium Gladys Leonard, who claimed to have made contact with Raymond. In 1916, Lodge published a book about their experiences, *Raymond or Life and Death*. His friend Sir Arthur Conan Doyle, author of the Sherlock Holmes stories, was another spiritualist believer who also lost a son in the war.

After the war, spiritualism declined in popularity. This was due in part to a campaign to debunk it by American illusionist Harry Houdini.

Ribbons of little crosses each touching each across a cemetery, set in a wilderness of annuals … One thinks for the moment no other monument is needed.
Edwin Lutyens
from a letter to his wife, July 1917

INDEX

QUOTE ATTRIBUTIONS

ACKNOWLEDGMENTS

Dorling Kindersley would like to thank Arshti Narang, Medha Ghosh, Shaarang Bhanot, and Tanya Varkey P for design assistance; Vanessa Hamilton for additional illustrations; Mrinmoy Mazumdar for DTP assistance; Ciara Law, Gwion Wyn Jones, and Jess Unwin for editorial assistance; Assistant Picture Research Administrators Manpreet Kaur and Samrajkumar S.; Senior Jackets Designer Suhita Dharamjit; Kathryn Hill for proofreading; and Helen Peters for indexing.

PICTURE CREDITS

The publisher would like to thank the following for their kind permission to reproduce their photographs:

(Key: a-above; b-below/bottom; c-centre; f-far; l-left; r-right; t-top)
19 Alamy Stock Photo: Shawshots (cla); World History Archive (br). **21 Alamy Stock Photo:** Historical Images Archive (cla). **23 Alamy Stock Photo:** GL Archive (bl); Niday Picture Library (tr). **24 Alamy Stock Photo:** Chronicle (crb). **26 Alamy Stock Photo:** GRANGER - Historical Picture Archive (c). **27 Alamy Stock Photo:** Chronicle (bl, cra). **28 Alamy Stock Photo:** Chronicle (bc). **29 Alamy Stock Photo:** Zuri Swimmer (cla). **30 Alamy Stock Photo:** Archive PL (bc). **32 Alamy Stock Photo:** The Granger Collection (br). **33 Alamy Stock Photo:** Pictorial Press Ltd (tr). **www.britannica.com:** Norman Friedman (ca). **36 Alamy Stock Photo:** Chris Hellier (tr). **37 Alamy Stock Photo:** GRANGER - Historical Picture Archive (tr). **38 Alamy Stock Photo:** Sueddeutsche Zeitung Photo / Scherl (b). **40 Alamy Stock Photo:** Niday Picture Library (bc). **41 Alamy Stock Photo:** Sddeutsche Zeitung Photo / Scherl (cla). **42 Alamy Stock Photo:** GRANGER - Historical Picture Archive (br). **43 Alamy Stock Photo:** The Picture Art Collection (tr). **Dreamstime.com:** Pavel Eltsov (cla). **44 Alamy Stock Photo:** De Luan (bc). **45 Alamy Stock Photo:** Maurice Savage (cla). **51 Alamy Stock Photo:** D and S Photography Archives (bl). **Getty Images:** Hulton Archive / Print Collector (tr). **53 Alamy Stock Photo:** Chronicle (cla); Iconographic Archive (br). **54 Alamy Stock Photo:** Interfoto / History (tr); Prisma by Dukas Presseagentur GmbH / Schultz Reinhard (bl). **55 Alamy Stock Photo:** Photo 12 (bl). **56 Alamy Stock Photo:** World History Archive (br). **57 Alamy Stock Photo:** Glasshouse Images / JT Vintage (tr). **58 Getty Images:** Hulton Archive / Print Collector. **59 Alamy Stock Photo:** Shawshots (bc). **Getty Images:** UniversalImagesGroup (tr). **61 Alamy Stock Photo:** Lebrecht Music & Arts (br); World History Archive (cla). **62 Alamy Stock Photo:** Chronicle (bl). **63 Alamy Stock Photo:** Hilary Morgan (tr). **67 Alamy Stock Photo:** Prisma by Dukas Presseagentur GmbH / Schultz Reinhard (cra); The Picture Art Collection (bl). **69 Alamy Stock Photo:** Pump Park Vintage Photography (br); World History Archive (tl). **70 Getty Images:** Archive Photos / Paul Thompson / FPG / Stringer (br). **71 Alamy Stock Photo:** Sueddeutsche Zeitung Photo (cla). **73 Alamy Stock Photo:** Mirrorpix / Trinity Mirror (br). **Getty Images:** Universal Images Group / Universal History Archive (cla). **75 akg-images:** Jean-Pierre Verney (br). **Getty Images:** Popperfoto / Paul Popper (cla). **77 Alamy Stock Photo:** Chronicle (tl). **79 Getty Images:** Hulton Archive / Galerie Bilderwelt (tr). **80 Alamy Stock Photo:** Interfoto / History (tr). **Getty Images:** Archive Photos / Paul Thompson / FPG / Stringer (bl). **81 Getty Images:** Hulton Archive / Print Collector (tr). **83 Alamy Stock Photo:** Hilary Morgan (cr). **85 Alamy Stock Photo:** De Luan (br). **Bridgeman Images:** Picture Alliance / DPA (cla). **87 Alamy Stock Photo:** GRANGER - Historical Picture Archive (cla). **Getty Images:** Popperfoto (br). **90 Alamy Stock Photo:** GL Archive. **91 Bridgeman Images:** Gert Maehler. **92 Alamy Stock Photo:** Chronicle (bl); Historical Images Archive (tl). **94 Alamy Stock Photo:** FLHC MDB6 (cr). **95 Alamy Stock Photo:** The Print Collector (cb). **97 Alamy Stock Photo:** agefotostock / Historical Views (cla); Sddeutsche Zeitung Photo / Scherl (br). **98 Shutterstock.com:** Everett Collection (bl). **99 Alamy Stock Photo:** akg-images. **104 Alamy Stock Photo:** Art Media / Heritage Images / The Print Collector (c). **105 Niall Ferguson:** (ca). **Shutterstock.com:** Urbanbuzz (br). **106 Library of Congress, Washington, D.C.:** LC-DIG-ppmsca-55686/ Irishmen - avenge the Lusitania. Join an Irish regiment to-day/W.E.T. ; John Shuley & Co., Dublin. Great Britain Ireland, 1915. [Dublin: Central Council for the Organisation of Recruiting in Ireland] Photograph. https://www.loc.gov/item/2003668198/. (bc). **108 Alamy Stock Photo:** Chronicle (br). **109 akg-images:** Heritage-Images / The Print Collector (br). **112 Getty Images:** Hulton Archive / Stringer (tr). **113 Alamy Stock Photo:** GRANGER - Historical Picture Archive (bl). **114 Bridgeman Images:** NPL - DeA Picture Library (bl). **115 Alamy Stock Photo:** Chronicle (tl); De Luan (br). **117 Getty Images:** Corbis Historical / Museum of Flight Foundation (tl). **118 Alamy Stock Photo:** The Print Collector (tr). **Getty Images:** Popperfoto (bl). **119 Alamy Stock Photo:** Lordprice Collection (tr); Science History Images / Photo Researchers (bl). **121 Alamy Stock Photo:** Chronicle (tr); D and S Photography Archives (bc). **124 Alamy Stock Photo:** Science History Images / Photo Researchers (tr). **125 Alamy Stock Photo:** CBW (br). **126 Alamy Stock Photo:** CPA Media Pte Ltd / Pictures From History (tl); GRANGER - Historical Picture Archive (bc). **128 Alamy Stock Photo:** CBW (br). **129 Alamy Stock Photo:** Lordprice Collection (tr). **130 Alamy Stock Photo:** Album (crb). **132 Alamy Stock Photo:** Dom Slike (cr). **133 Alamy Stock Photo:** Science History Images (cra). **135 Alamy Stock Photo:** IanDagnall Computing (cla). **Library of Congress, Washington, D.C.:** LC-DIG-hec-02572 / Harris & Ewing, photographer (br). **136 Alamy Stock Photo:** Science History Images / Photo Researchers (br). **137 Wikipedia:** Korteenea (ca). **139 Alamy Stock Photo:** Yogi Black (tr); Chronicle (bl). **141 Alamy Stock Photo:** Gainew Gallery (cla). **Shutterstock.com:** Everett Collection (br). **142 akg-images:** (br). **Alamy Stock Photo:** Chronicle (tl). **143 Alamy Stock Photo:** The Print Collector (tl). **145 Alamy Stock Photo:** World History Archive (bl). **From the collections of the Gurkha Museum, Winchester:** (tr). **151 Alamy Stock Photo:** Classic Image (bl); Everett Collection (ca). **154 Alamy Stock Photo:** Antiqua Print Gallery (tr); GRANGER - Historical Picture Archive / Granger, NYC (bl). **156 Alamy Stock Photo:** Chronicle (tc). **157 Getty Images:** Hulton Archive. **158 Alamy Stock Photo:** Scherl / Sddeutsche Zeitung Photo (cra). **159 Getty Images:** Roger Viollet (bl). **161 Alamy Stock Photo:** Zuri Swimmer (tl). **163 Alamy Stock Photo:** IanDagnall Computing (tr). **164 Alamy Stock Photo:** akg-images (bl); M&N (tr). **165 Getty Images:** ullstein bild Dtl. **167 Alamy Stock Photo:** Fine Art Images / Heritage Images (tl). **169 Getty Images:** Hulton Archive / Print Collector (tl). **171 Alamy Stock Photo:** Fremantle (tl); IanDagnall Computing (br). **175 Alamy Stock Photo:** Signal Photos (tr). **Getty Images:** Mirrorpix (bl). **176 Alamy Stock Photo:** CBW (bl). **Getty Images:** Photo 12 (tr). **178 Getty Images:** Universal History Archive (tc). **179 Alamy Stock Photo:** CBW (bl). **Getty Images:** Imperial War Museums (tl). **181 Alamy Stock Photo:** Scherl / Sddeutsche Zeitung Photo (bl); World History Archive (tr). **183 Alamy Stock Photo:** IanDagnall Computing (br); Scherl / Sddeutsche Zeitung Photo (cla). **185 Getty Images:** Corbis Historical / Hulton Deutsch (br). **186 Getty Images:** Hulton Archive / Topical Press Agency (tr). **192 Alamy Stock Photo:** CBW (bl). **193 Alamy Stock Photo:** Album (cla); IanDagnall Computing (tr). **195 Alamy Stock Photo:** stock imagery (bl). **Library of Congress, Washington, D.C.:** LC-DIG-acd-2a06155/ Berryman, Clifford Kennedy, Artist. Hand carving up a map of the Southwestern United States. United States, 1917. March 4. Photograph. https://www.loc.gov/item/2016678747/. (cra). **197 Alamy Stock Photo:** Glasshouse Images / Circa Images (bc); Science History Images / Photo Researchers (cla). **198 Getty Images:** Daily Mirror / Mirrorpix (br). **199 Getty Images:** Hulton Archive / Topical Press Agency / Stringer (br). **202 Alamy Stock Photo:** Sueddeutsche Zeitung Photo (bl). **203 Getty Images:** Popperfoto (cla). **205 Alamy Stock Photo:** M&N (tl). **Getty Images:** Archive Photos / Interim Archives (br). **207 Alamy Stock Photo:** Everett Collection Historical (bl). **Getty Images:** Universal Images Group Editorial / Universal History Archive (tl). **209 Getty Images:** Hulton Archive / General Photographic Agency (br). **210 Getty Images:** Universal Images Group Editorial / Windmill Books (bl). **211 Alamy Stock Photo:** Archive Pics (bl). **213 Alamy Stock Photo:** Everett Collection Historical (cla, br). **215 Getty Images:** Hulton Archive / Print Collector. **217 Getty Images:** Hulton Archive / Galerie Bilderwelt. **219 Alamy Stock Photo:** INTERFOTO / Personalities (tr). **Getty Images:** Circa Images / GHI / Universal History Archive / Universal Images Group (tl). **220 Getty Images:** Imperial War Museums / Lt. Ernest Brooks (bl). **221 Getty Images:** Archive Photos / Hulton Archive / FPG / Staff. **222 Getty Images:** Corbis Historical (br). **223 Alamy Stock Photo:** CBW (tc); Prisma by Dukas Presseagentur GmbH / TPX (br). **225 Alamy Stock Photo:** Chronicle (br). **Imperial War Museum:** German official photographer (Photographer) (cla). **227 Alamy Stock Photo:** BMH Photographic (br). **229 Alamy Stock Photo:** Classic Image (cra); De Luan (bl). **232 Alamy Stock Photo:** Photo12 Collection (bl). **233 Alamy Stock Photo:** Chronicle (bl); Mirrorpix / Trinity Mirror (cra). **235 Alamy Stock Photo:** Historical Images Archive (tl). **237 Alamy Stock Photo:** Historical Images Archive (cr). **238 Alamy Stock Photo:** Aviation History Collection (bc). **239 Alamy Stock Photo:** Science History Images / Photo Researchers (bl). **Getty Images:** Hulton Archive / Culture Club (tr). **241 Alamy Stock Photo:** Fine Art Images / Heritage Images (bl). **243 Alamy Stock Photo:** Sueddeutsche Zeitung Photo (br). **Imperial War Museum:** (cla). **245 Getty Images:** Hulton Archive / Heritage Images (cr). **251 Alamy Stock Photo:** KGPA Ltd (crb). **252 Getty Images:** David Pollack (bl). **253 Alamy Stock Photo:** Venimages (br). **255 Alamy Stock Photo:** History and Art Collection (tr). **256 Alamy Stock Photo:** PF-(sdasm3) (crb). **257 Imperial War Museum:** Brooke, John Warwick (Lieutenant) (tr). **258 Getty Images:** Universal Images Group / Universal History Archive (br). **259 Getty Images:** Gamma-Keystone / Keystone-France (cr); Universal Images Group / Universal History Archive (bl). **264 Alamy Stock Photo:** Science History Images / Photo Researchers (b). **265 Alamy Stock Photo:** Chronicle (tr). **266 Alamy Stock Photo:** PF-(wararchive) (clb); Shotshop GmbH / Historic Collection (tr). **267 Alamy Stock Photo:** Chronicle (crb). **269 Alamy Stock Photo:** Everett Collection Historical (cla); FAY 2018 (br). **271 Alamy Stock Photo:** World History Archive (tr). **272 Imperial War Museum:** Aitken, Thomas Keith (Second Lieutenant) (Photographer) (tc). **273 Getty Images:** FPG (b). **275 Alamy Stock Photo:** Pictorial Press Ltd (tr). **276 Alamy Stock Photo:** The Protected Art Archive (bl). **277 Alamy Stock Photo:** De Luan (tr). **278 Getty Images:** DE AGOSTINI PICTURE LIBRARY (br). **279 Alamy Stock Photo:** Stocktrek Images, Inc. / Vernon Lewis Gallery (tr). **281 Getty Images:** Education Images (tl); Print Collector (br). **282 Getty Images:** Apic. **283 Alamy Stock Photo:** Science History Images / Photo Researchers (tr). **285 Alamy Stock Photo:** Universal Images Group North America Llc / Marka / Jarach (br). **Getty Images:** Roger Viollet (cla). **287 Getty Images:** Universal Images Group (b). **Imperial War Museum:** (cla). **289 Alamy Stock Photo:** dpa picture alliance (cra). **291 Alamy Stock Photo:** SOTK2011 (bl). **292 Getty Images:** Hulton Deutsch (bl). **293 Alamy Stock Photo:** Science History Images / Photo Researchers (br). **296 Alamy Stock Photo:** INTERFOTO (bl). **Getty Images:** Corbis Historical / Historical (cr). **298 Getty Images:** Universal Images Group Editorial / Photo 12 (bl). **299 Getty Images:** Bettmann (tl). **301 Alamy Stock Photo:** GL Archive (bl). **Getty Images:** Bettmann (cra). **303 Getty Images:** Bettmann (tl). **309 Alamy Stock Photo:** GL Archive (tr). **310 Getty Images:** Archive Photos / Interim Archives (br). **311 Getty Images:** Hulton Archive / Brooke / Stringer (tc); Universal Images Group / Arterra (br). **314 Alamy Stock Photo:** Photo 12 (bl). **315 Alamy Stock Photo:** PA Images (cla). **317 Alamy Stock Photo:** Historic Collection (tl). **319 Alamy Stock Photo:** Sddeutsche Zeitung Photo / Scherl (cr). **Getty Images:** Hulton Archive / Heritage Images (bl). **320 Alamy Stock Photo:** History and Art Collection (cb). **321 Alamy Stock Photo:** Sueddeutsche Zeitung Photo (cla). **323 Getty Images:** Popperfoto (br). **325 Alamy Stock Photo:** Eden Breitz (br); Dennis K. Johnson (tl). **326 Getty Images:** Universal Images Group / Photo 12 (bl). **327 Shutterstock.com:** Willequet Manuel (tc)

BIG IDEAS SIMPLY EXPLAINED